P9-CUK-088

Voices of the Religious Left

A Contemporary Sourcebook

D'YOUVILLE COLLEGE
LIBRARY

Voices of the Religious Left

A Contemporary Sourcebook

EDITED BY

Rebecca T. Alpert

TEMPLE UNIVERSITY PRESS

PHILADELPHIA

To Christie Balka

who teaches me daily about love and justice

Temple University Press, Philadelphia 19122
Copyright © 2000 by Temple University
All rights reserved
Published 2000
Printed in the United States of America

ⓧ The paper used in this publication meets the requirements of the American
National Standard for Information Sciences—Permanence of Paper for Printed
Library Materials, ANSI Z39.48-1984

Library of Congress Cataloging-in-Publication Data
Voices of the religious left : a contemporary sourcebook / edited by Rebecca T.
  Alpert.
      p.   cm.
    Includes bibliographical references.
    ISBN 1-56639-756-1 (cl. : alk. paper). — ISBN 1-56639-757-x (paperback : alk.
paper)
    1. United States—Religion.   2. Religion and sociology—United States.
  3. Liberalism (Religion)—United States.   I. Alpert, Rebecca T. (Rebecca
  Trachtenberg), 1950–
  BL2525.V65   2000
  291.1′7′0973—dc21   99-37972
                                                                         CIP

BL 2525
.V65
2000

Contents

DEC 8 2000

Focusing on the Issues

ALTHOUGH SUFFERING IS LIMITLESS, I VOW TO END IT
(The Boddhisatva Vow)

THE EARTH IS THE LORD'S   (Psalm 24:1)

AM I MY BROTHER'S KEEPER?   (Genesis 4:9)

PROCLAIM LIBERTY THROUGHOUT THE LAND   (Leviticus 25:10)

THERE IS NEITHER MALE NOR FEMALE FOR YOU ARE ALL ONE
(Galatians 3:28)

Building Bridges: Know One Another

Acknowledgments

A while back Doris Braendel of Temple University Press invited me to lunch. Her goal was to ask me a simple question she had been thinking about for some time: What happened to the religious left during these past two decades while the religious right has grown? From that question came this edited volume. The vision and inspiration for it belong to Doris, as does the responsibility for keeping this process on track and helping me discover the answer to her question. For all this, I am deeply grateful to her.

I am also much in debt to the thirty-six authors whose works appear here. Some are friends, some are strangers. Their commitment to writing about the issues that confront us today is the reason this work exists. Their words, and those of many others that could not be included here, made me know for certain that there is indeed a passionate and committed religious left alive in this country. It is my privilege to be able to share their thoughts with you.

Without the diligent, meticulous, patient, and cheerful technical support of Susan Levasseur and Yvonne Ramsey this volume could not have come into being. I am most grateful for all their assistance.

Several people read this manuscript in its various forms. My thanks to Paul Lyons, David Gracie, Lori Ginzberg, and Christie Balka for their thoughtful and helpful comments.

My work has been supported by the religious group to which I belong, Mishkan Shalom, and its rabbi Brian Walt who models those values to which this volume speaks. I also find sustenance among my colleagues in the Religion Department of Temple University, many of whom are also engaged in living and understanding the connection between religious traditions and social justice.

For the past four years I have had the privilege to co-direct the Women's Studies Program at Temple with Sonia Sanchez. When I become discouraged about the possibility of bringing justice to this society, or speaking truth to power, I need only think about how Sonia lives her life to remember that it can be done. For that, and many other lessons, I am profoundly in her debt.

Lynn and Avi Alpert are the joys of my life. I hope this book will contribute in some small way to making the world they inherit into a more just and peaceful place.

Introduction

When I was growing up in the 1960s, no one questioned the possibility that religion could be an important force in bringing about progressive social change. Pope John XXIII brought a new openness to Roman Catholicism. The Reverend Martin Luther King, Jr., was the leading force behind the deeply spiritual civil rights movement. Malcolm X's message was mediated through the teachings of Islam. Rabbis Abraham Joshua Heschel and Maurice Eisendrath led Jews in "praying with their feet," marching in the American South and to end the war in Vietnam. Daniel Berrigan and Reverend William Sloane Coffin also led the struggles to end the war. My young adulthood was saturated with images of religious leaders (albeit almost exclusively male) standing up for what they believed was right. What they believed in was peace, justice, and human freedom: an end to war, hunger, poverty, and the American version of apartheid. And their beliefs were spoken in a religious voice of protest. From these men I learned to believe that one important role of religion was to invoke religious authority to challenge social norms that did not conform to the highest moral standards of the ancient teachings of Judaism, Christianity, and Islam.[1]

Today the most powerful voices of protest come from a different place on the religious spectrum. Organizations like the Christian Coalition, the Family Research Council, and the Promise Keepers are seen as the "true" voice of religion in contemporary life. They focus not on the economic and political inequalities in contemporary American culture, but on the need for public demonstrations of Christianity, supporting social regulation of family and personal life and fighting against the social and cultural changes of a generation ago that were inspired by the movements for the rights of women and sexual minorities. The religious right is so dominant in our public culture today that the voices of protest on the other side of the spectrum—those voices that support the freedom and dignity of all individuals to choose the kind of family they wish to belong to, and that are also vitally concerned about global and domestic issues of peace, justice, and racial equality—all but seem to have disappeared from the public consciousness.

Despite the fact that we hear little about what I shall call the religious left, it has been an active force in the United States these last two decades of the twentieth century since the start of the Reagan revolution. Of course, there is no one entity called "the religious left." I am using this terminology to describe many different groups that advocate a range of issues with common themes of peace, justice, and support for the disenfranchised and speak from a religious perspective. The religious left is composed today of groups and individuals with progressive political values that are undergirded by their religious beliefs in justice, freedom, and peace. But these groups and individuals do not agree about all of the issues that comprise a progressive political agenda. And they do not share a unified set of religious beliefs, either within or among the religions and denominations to which they belong. While some parts of the religious left focus on economic issues, others are more concerned with social issues. For some the emphasis is domestic, for others the emphasis is global.

The ideas represented in this volume come from all over the religious spectrum, including groups and individuals from most religions present in the United States today. As Diana Eck points out in her essay in this volume, our awareness of the variety of those groups has changed greatly over the last two decades. Any study of the religious left must include the voices of Muslims, Buddhists, and Native Americans, as well as Protestants, Catholics, and Jews. It is also striking that those on the religious left come from different perspectives within each religion. Those who are religious conservatives and liberals in spiritual practice or theology may share political values. For this reason, the religious left is multifaceted rather than cohesive. The absence of theological or political consensus contributes to the inability of the religious left to have a unified voice or a stronger public presence today.

This book is a collection of the writings and teachings of the religious left from the last twenty years. Its goal is to bear witness to the vital role of protest and struggle for change in which religious communities have been engaged. What is included here represents but a fraction of the writings and organized activities on behalf of progressive issues that the religious left has undertaken these past two decades.

If There Is a Religious Left, Why Don't We Hear about It?

Why do we hear so little about the religious left? One answer to that question has to do with the idea that America is involved in a "culture war." This thesis suggests that there is a battle in this country between a religious right and a secular left. The effect of such an argument is to obscure the roles of both the secular right and the religious left.

Scholars who propound the "culture wars" thesis, such as James Davison Hunter, suggest that battle lines have been drawn in our culture simply between left and right, conservatives and liberals. They don't see any difference between the voices of the religious left and those of the secular mainstream. According to this argument liberal and left religious ideologies merely support a secular agenda of peace, justice, and human freedom rather than defining an agenda on their own terms.

Hunter's conservative "culture war" analysis of American society promotes the idea that there are two dominant and polarized perspectives in American public life today: orthodoxy, which represents traditional values of God and family, and progressivism, which focuses on individual rights and freedom.[2] In this analysis, the orthodox are the bearers of religious values, while progressives are identified with "secular humanists" whose values derive from the Enlightenment ideals of individual freedom rather than from religious sources. This analysis depicts those who are religious liberals as accommodating completely to the values of secular society.

In this scenario the religious left (and the secular right) disappear off the landscape, so that the battle for American culture is described as between religion and secularism, rather than two competing religious (or secular) visions. Hunter and his followers assume that religion only functions as a conservative force against modern values and that those religious people with progressive politics are simply using religious language to espouse what they really believe in—the values of secularism.

We live today (and for the past century at least) in a society that is predominantly secular in its orientation.[3] No religious group in contemporary society can avoid some kind of interaction with secularism. Whether the group chooses to accommodate, critique, or separate, it must make that decision in the context of the reality that secularism (the idea that the world centers in human rather than divine endeavors) is the dominant "religion" of the modern era. To deal with this change, most religious groups have used a variety of strategies that combine criticism of secular values with agreement on some of those values as well. Scholars who come from the perspective of the culture wars often assume that the religious right has opposed modernity, while the religious left has survived by accommodating to secular perspectives. The religious right is described as standing outside secular culture and critiquing it. But both the religious right and left have opposed and made accommodation to dimensions of secularism. Seeing the right as outside the secular framework ignores the crucial connections between the religious right and the secular values of patriarchy and capitalism, for example.

Early modernists expected religion (especially the religions they defined as non-accommodationist, that is, fundamentalist) to die away as secular perspectives took hold in the late nineteenth century. Students of religion have been quite surprised by the religious revivals that have taken place around the globe during the last few decades of what is now being called the postmodern era. And although both conservative and liberal strands of religion have been pronounced moribund at various points, all types of religious life are flourishing, despite the fact that the dominant perspective in the United States is largely secular. Religions have adjusted well to being minority voices in society.[4]

Culture war theorists make the assumption that being religious means being politically conservative. The religious right has indeed benefited from this cultural connection and the resurgence of political conservatism. The right has the financial and social resources to get its message heard. The religious right has used these financial resources to mobilize opinion. The religious right has focused energy on battles to limit reproductive rights and the rights of sexual minorities, putting themselves in the role of prophets who are opposing changes that seem acceptable to society. The religious right has also supported economic policies that have widened economic inequality.

The religious right's status as an insurgent movement has also played a role in the postmodern era. As such, the right has both an ideological focus and a strategic plan that the left has lacked. The right has responded to the gains made by women, sexual minorities, and people of color by scapegoating those groups for the growing economic problems faced by the United States in an era of globalization, and with efforts to roll back affirmative action programs that contributed to those gains. The right has also redefined sensitivity to issues raised by these groups as "political correctness," a term signifying that change has gone far enough, and indicating an unwillingness to allow these groups to make further demands for inclusion and rights.

Robert Wuthnow, a leading scholar of American religion and proponent of the culture wars perspective, gives more credence to the existence of a religious left. He argues that the religious left has been subsumed under a restructured American religion, consisting of two groups: liberal and orthodox. In contrast to Hunter, Robert Wuthnow describes the culture war as he understands it to have played out within the major religions in the United States. Wuthnow suggests that there has been a reorganization of American religious groups, connecting different religious denominations and religions across the political spectrum.[5] Similar to the culture war argument, this argument suggests that there are two distinct groups in religious life today based on political perspectives. Doctrinal differences have fallen away, leaving all religious conservatives on one side and all religious liberals on the other. In this analysis, mainline Protestants and liberal Jews, Muslims, and Buddhists have more in common with one another than with the orthodox of their own religions. This part of the culture wars thesis has some validity when looking at political stances of the religious left. It explains the connections across denominations that religious people have made in issue-oriented groups that have become more prevalent in the last two decades. The Religious Coalition for Reproductive Rights, religious groups that worked to change U.S. policy in Central America or opposed the arms race in the 1980s, or groups today that support gay rights or are working to rebuild our cities are more often than not interdenominational. A sample from my mail yesterday gives credence to this perspective. It included an invitation to an event for the Sabbath of Domestic Peace Interfaith Worship Service, a newsletter from the Religious Organizing Chapter of Pennsylvania Abolitionists United Against the Death Penalty, and one from the National Forum for Worker Justice.

Doctrinal differences have become less significant in the current era of acceptance of pluralism and interfaith relationships. What a thesis about cooperation fails to take into account is that these connections are based on agreement about single issues, not on an entire agenda. Many groups that could not work together on some issues find themselves united on others. While Catholics and Unitarians could not agree about abortion, they have formed coalitions to fight against welfare reform. While there has been significant cooperation across denominational and religious lines in regard to individual issues, there has not been a breakdown of those denominational lines to form one unified, multi-issue religious left.

The existence of these groups united by individual issues illustrates the extent to which denominationalism is still a strong factor. There have been fewer instances of denominational realignment based on issues than there were in this country's past. The fact that denominations still retain strong identities is a good indication that while cross-religious and cross-denominational cooperation may occur today, there is a greater commitment to pluralism rather than a real realignment in religious structures.

The simple division of left and right articulated in the culture war thesis breaks down because many groups and individuals that can be defined as religiously conservative or liberal may hold political views that are not consistent with their religious practices. Studies suggest that religious affiliation may not so simply predict positions on issues of personal freedom or social and economic justice.[6] This division does not account for the strong position Catholic bishops have taken in favor of distributive justice or against nuclear war, for Protestant evangelicals who have been involved in the sanctuary movement or who support affirmative action, or for Catholics who demand the ordination of women or who founded Dignity (an association of gay and lesbian Catholics). It also cannot explain those belonging to mainline Protestant denominations who oppose the ordination of gay clergy and support the recent dismantling of the welfare system, Reform Jews who oppose lifting restrictions on immigration or do not support gay marriage, black Muslims who support the death penalty, or Hispanic Protestants who oppose Puerto Rican independence.

The culture war theory gives us some understanding of why the religious left has been less prominent in the past two decades. But it fails to explain that people's religious values may persuade them to have political views that don't necessarily correlate directly with their religious behavior. It also does not account for religious motivation in regard to progressive views, erroneously attributing that motivation to an acceptance of secular values.

The culture war theory leaves no room for those who are liberal on economic and political issues but conservative on social issues, or for those who are conservative on economic and political issues but liberal on social issues. And it also does not provide a complex view of the relationship between people's political attitudes and religious behavior or affiliation.[7] In fact, this complexity on the religious left also contributes to its current fragmentation.

The Complex Character of the Religious Left

The culture war thesis suggests that the religious left believes predominantly in secular, not religious, values. It is true that many on the religious left believe that the ancient authoritative texts of their traditions are not the only source of wisdom, and that they are willing to gain insight from the contemporary world as well. They believe that scripture must be interpreted in each generation in light of new social realities. Many on the religious left have been influenced by the social movements of the 1960s and 1970s (primarily black nationalism, women's liberation, and gay rights, but also including the rights of the disabled and other ethnic and racial groups) and see good in the movements' ideas and perspectives. This influence of various social movements is the primary factor contributing to a lack of unity among the religious left.

While the religious left finds resources in ancient scripture to support its work for peace, justice, and human freedom, many of its proponents also are aware that not all insights come from ancient tradition. The religious left perspective leaves room for insights from contemporary ideas and traditions outside the denominations to which individuals belong. Many of these insights come from other religions, and many are also derived from secular ideologies.

Scholars have attributed the continued vitality of religion to the failure of modernity to provide the progress it had promised and to the related failure of meaning.[8] But it also may be attributed to the effective methods that religious groups have used in translating secular insights into religious language. In the postmodern era, many philosophies compete to provide humans with meaning and values, and religious systems still provide some of the most effective mechanisms for meeting these human needs.

The religious left provides a possible framework for meaning in a secular society. As part of that search for meaning, the religious left has consciously tried to incorporate certain secular insights in the creation of new religious expressions. By its willingness to respond to black, feminist, and gay critiques and to create theological versions of those critiques, the religious left has transformed itself.[9]

The civil rights and antiwar movements of the 1960s had great religious leadership and clear support from the liberal religious establishment. But the social movements that were born out of that time—the movement for women's liberation, the gay and lesbian rights movement, and the black power movement—had little or no religious leadership and a strong critique by the religious establishment.[10] One of the main contributions of the religious left was to respond to the arguments of these groups and find ways to address their concerns, for these movements were not only a critique of society but of American religious groups as well. Through serious consideration of the demands of feminists, people of color, and gays and lesbians, and by inclusion of the perspectives of those who have felt excluded and marginalized by the religious mainstream, some on the religious left made a commitment to model those values that they espoused for the rest of the world. It is important to note here that these struggles were not only about identity, but also about ideology. The black church has remained fairly conservative on matters of gender and sexuality. There are many women who are active members of right-wing religious groups who call themselves anti-feminist. And there are homosexuals who do not challenge their church's understanding that they are sinners, and continue to hide or seek to change their sexuality. It is the ideas (for example, women religious leaders, African roots, or gay marriage) of these groups rather than simply their identities that the religious left has incorporated.

The religious left has expended much energy in recent years struggling to find adequate theological responses to issues of gender hierarchy, segregation, and the absence of a role for sexual minorities in religious traditions, and to create internal changes to welcome these differences. This effort has included acknowledging the racism in churches as well as in their formation of missions, coming to terms with African and Native roots and religious traditions that have been ignored or denied, working to end segregation in churches, and responding to the challenge of blacks who have turned away from Christianity to embrace African religions. Churches, synagogues, and mosques have had to ask questions about sexism: to rethink the roles of women in leadership and hierarchy, look at the gender of the language that is used in prayer, consider the values in relationship to family and work that religious leaders espouse, and question the willingness to ignore issues like domestic violence. Religious groups have had to look at homophobia: to question why gays and lesbians have felt unwelcome in churches and to figure out how to welcome them, to confront why clergy have felt compelled to hide their sexual orientation, and to face gays' and lesbians' desire for respect regarding their families of choice and interest in religious ceremonies that honor those commitments. The willingness of religious groups to deal with these questions has significantly changed the face of American religion today, as the section titled "There is neither male nor female for you are all one. . . ." suggests. It is important to note that this effort on the part of mainstream churches, synagogues, and mosques is more a positive reaction to the demands of these groups than it is a capitulation to secular values.

Most of this work has been done in groups traditionally labeled theologically liberal, but change has also taken place in more theologically traditional strongholds like the Roman Catholic and evangelical churches, in mosques, and in conservative and orthodox synagogues.[11] This reality suggests that it is a great oversimplification to assume that theologically liberal religious denominations are the only places where a left political perspective can grow in religious soil and that left perspectives can only exist where there is accommodation to secularism. This book includes contributions from sources across the religious spectrum to illustrate that tendency. Those expecting to read only the thoughts of Unitarian Universalists, the Society of Friends, and Reform Judaism will find few such articles here. Although these groups have made major contributions to the issues and struggles of the religious left, I have chosen to include very little of their writings in order to emphasize the complexity of the religious left.

The willingness to admit that not all wisdom is derived from scripture, but that scripture must sometimes be challenged by contemporary ideas, is an important dimension of the religious left. This strength has made it possible to incorporate insights of the new social movements, and to grow from them.

The emphasis on these social issues has also been responsible for the fragmentation of the religious left, however. While many on the religious left have been transformed by the movements for social liberation, others have seen these efforts as a distraction from the important issues of economic justice: poverty, prison reform, the environment, and human rights. This split has been a great challenge to those working on the religious left. While liberal Jews and urban blacks can create coalitions about improving public schools, the fact that gay members of Jewish congregations might not be welcome proves to be a point of friction.

Even with these frictions, what we observe is a religious left that works well on single issues across denominational lines. But contrary to what the culture war thesis suggests, there is no multi-issue, broad-based, cross-denominational religious or secular left. This lack of a unified presentation, combined with the complexity of religious and political perspectives and a constant need on the part of the religious left to react to the religious right rather than develop its own agenda, has obscured the religious left from public prominence and muted its voice. Most of the writings of the religious left are published in journals whose readers are already supportive of the positions taken. This book is meant to bring those writings to a wider audience.

What Unites the Religious Left?

Despite the absence of unity, there are certain attributes that identify a religious left perspective in the United States today. First, its values are derived from the authoritative texts of religious traditions (the Hebrew Torah, the Christian Bible, the Muslim Qur'an, the teachings of the Buddha, Native American lore), which are believed to contain wisdom about the way human society should be constructed. At the same time, those on the religious left challenge literal interpretations of those texts, and are also willing to disagree with some of the teachings found within them. Thus, the religious left is distinguished from the secular left in that the religious left derives its ideas and organizational structures from religion.

The other factor that unites the religious left is a shared belief with activists of the 1960s and with their counterparts on the religious right today that religion has a public role—a moral obligation to speak out in the public arena in order to influence public policy. Those on the religious left believe that this is one of the most important contributions religious groups can make to the debate over issues and values in society. They do not assume that the doctrine of separation of church and state precludes actively witnessing for values that have a religious basis.

The Importance of Scripture

There are as many definitions of religion as there are people who claim to be religious. One criterion that defines a religious perspective is a connection to an authoritative body of written or oral tradition that makes a truth-claim about ultimate values. From that body of text, religious people gain a sense of what they ought to do in order to live in the world. The authoritative texts of every religious tradition contain prescriptions for attaining a virtuous life. While all religious people derive meaning from scripture, those on the religious left are focused on the parts of scriptural tradition that suggest the ways in which human beings are morally obligated to create a world in which all of God's creatures may live in harmony and peace. In other religious perspectives, the authority of those texts is absolute and the scripture of the group is the only source of wisdom. In contrast, while those on the religious left define the scriptures they read and interpret as sacred, they also believe that there are many possible interpretations of those scriptures. In addition, although each scriptural tradition speaks in a different language, a religious left perspective assumes that all religions teach ultimate truths in different languages. So the Christian learns ultimate messages from gospel, the Jew from the Torah, the Muslim from the Qur'an, the Buddhist from the teachings of the Buddha, but each can also learn from the others. There is also an understanding that the individual has the right to choose his or her religious path.

The story of Cain and Abel from the book of Genesis teaches those on the religious left the lesson of social responsibility in a global world. The answer to the question "Am I my brother's keeper?" (Genesis 4:8) is a resounding yes. From that story, Christians, Jews, and Muslims on the religious left in the United States derive their obligation to connect across national lines to speak out about injustice around the globe.

The admonition in Psalms 24:1 that "the Earth is the Lord's" reminds the religious left of the obligation to care for the earth and empowers its vision of humanity's obligations to preserve the world's resources and to protect nature and other species from the harm that humans have caused them.

The Buddhist idea that individuals are obligated to mitigate suffering (Boddhisatva vow) involves the religious left in an examination of the economic inequities in our society and a reexamination of poverty and how society cares for those who lack resources, whether financial or spiritual, to care for themselves adequately.

The demand to "proclaim liberty throughout the land" (Leviticus 25:10) in the Torah makes the religious left ask questions about the rights of prisoners, the treatment of indigenous people, and the need for freedom of speech.

The claim in the Christian scripture that we are neither "male nor female" before God (Galatians 3:28) suggests to the religious left that society must pay attention to gender and sexual inequity and reevaluate the gender roles in our religious cultures.

The Qur'an states that "we . . . have made you nations and tribes that you may know one another" (Surah 49:13), demanding that we make the effort to reach out to others who are different and to build coalitions across religious and racial lines.

One of the important contemporary developments in keeping with this use of scripture to support radical religious notions has been the development of liberation theology in the context of Latin American revolutionary movements.[12] The use of the Exodus narrative as a paradigm for the movement from slavery to freedom has had great influence on the thinking of many on the religious left. The biblical story of the small band of Israelites who were enslaved and were able to go out from slavery to freedom serves as a model for contemporary movements of liberation. It has given many on the religious left a language and narrative through which to interpret oppression in contemporary society. Liberation theology assumes that God cares about the poor and oppressed; to do God's work is to work for the liberation of the poor and those who have not had the opportunity to speak for themselves, and to satisfy basic human needs. Liberation theology is a model for how those on the religious left have understood their connection with authoritative text that commands them to work for peace and justice.

Despite the power of these images, we must keep in mind Robert Allan Warrior's problems with the liberation theology from a Native American perspective, which he describes in "Canaanites, Cowboys, and Indians" included in this volume. Warrior reminds us that those who were liberated from Egypt conquered the lands of Canaan, and that taking others' land is a model that Europeans emulated too well in their conquest of the Americas.

Warrior's objections are in keeping with the way many on the religious left think about scriptural tradition. Although there is much to learn from ancient texts, those texts were written in a context bound by time and geography. Therefore, those on the religious left are willing to be critical of scripture when the values and stories found there do not conform to contemporary ideals of peace, justice, and human dignity.

Of course, people in contemporary society who espouse the values described above need not be religious. What defines the religious left is that its members derive these values not from the teachings of the Enlightenment, but from the mandate they perceive through the authority of their religious traditions. This distinction is often overlooked by secular scholars and those on the religious right who assume religious leftists deny scriptural authority. This mistaken impression is probably related to the extent to which the values of the religious right are associated with a literal interpretation of scripture, and to the right's willingness to say in public that "the Bible says. . . ." This authority derived from literal interpretation of scripture has often eclipsed equally passionate commitments to scriptural authority on the left. The religious right is more comfortable with both an absolute espousal of scriptural values and a concomitant commitment to a literal interpretation of certain scriptural texts.

Furthermore, the religious right has been associated with the demand that scripture (and in particular the scripture of the Protestant faith) be read and taught in public schools. This was of course illustrated by the fundamentalist position in the debate about the teaching of evolution made famous by the Scopes trial in 1925, and the negative response of the religious right to the banning of prayer in public schools in 1963. Fighting to teach the biblical view of creation and requiring prayer in the public schools links the Bible and the religious right in the public mind. Such connections are not so readily made concerning the religious left, yet the connections are there. All the articles in this volume attest to that connection, deriving their arguments from scriptural sources.

While the religious left emphasizes texts that speak about God's kingdom of justice and peace and human dignity and freedom, the right focuses on texts that establish God's dominion over the earth, and the divine imperative that sanctifies certain kinds of familial and sexual relationships. Needless to say, both perspectives are present in scripture. When Africans were enslaved in the American South, some preachers used Jewish and Christian scripture to support slavery while others used it to denounce slavery. Some claim that the Qur'an provides a context for equal rights for women (as Laila Al-Marayati suggests in "The Worth of a Woman") while others say it does not. Clearly, scripture has been put to different uses at different times. There is an ancient saying in the Mishnah, a Jewish text compiled in 200 C.E., that suggests in reference to Torah that we "turn it and turn it, for all is in it." In the opinion of the religious left, it is unproblematic that texts considered sacred include perspectives that are contradictory. It is our obligation as human beings to decide which among those passages are timeless and which applied to a society radically different from our own and are no longer relevant today. This willingness to set sacred text in context and to make choices about which parts of ancient texts are indeed still relevant are attributes of the religious left that set its relationship to scripture apart from the religious right. While this is a major difference between the perspectives of the religious right and left, both groups share the tendency to focus on those verses or passages that speak to the perspective they support.

Bringing Together Politics and Religion

Separation of church and state is a central value in the United States. For many this has meant not simply that there should be no one established church, as a plain reading of the First Amendment would imply, but that religious values should have no role in public conversations. Although studies have shown that most Americans consider themselves religious, most have little interest in mixing religion and politics.[13] While they readily admit that religious values influence their thinking about issues as individuals, they reject the notion that political viewpoints should be determined based on religious values. For many people, religion is related predominantly to their notion of the spiritual and their individual relationships with God. Religion is what comforts them and gives them strength to meet life's difficulties. As a group experience, religious affiliation (whether liberal or conservative) creates bonds of community with other people who share a common perspective. Today's society puts great emphasis on spiritual concerns, and most people get involved in religious groups to deal with spiritual matters. Only a small percentage see a correlation between their religious practice and affiliation and concerns for the common good; an awareness that the meaning of life for which religious people are searching may be found in creating a world in which people experience justice, peace, and freedom.

The decline of mainline Protestant denominations in the 1970s has been attributed in part to their leaders focusing too much on political issues.[14] Research often suggests that most Americans prefer a "live and let live" attitude towards others, thus rejecting both the "fanaticism" of the religious right and the "do gooder" attitudes of the religious left.[15] This attitude explains why both the religious left and right are defined as outside the mainstream of American political thought, which accepts religion as something people do in private and protects their freedom to do so.

Yet both the religious right and the religious left believe that religious values cannot be left out of the conversation about public issues. Both groups see themselves as inheritors of the tradition of the biblical prophets who publicly decried injustice and were rejected by society.[16] It is their belief that their religious viewpoints compel them to speak out about what they see in society that needs to change—that religion is functioning effectively when it is a disruptive force in society, compelling people to engage in moral reasoning to create a good society.

Given the common understanding of separation of church and state, religious thinkers can offer their perspectives but must not expect that religious opinions will rule simply because they are "true."[17] Nor should religious politics attempt to make its beliefs into law against the will of the majority. As long as religious thinkers are prepared to publicly debate their ideas on the issues, they can make an important contribution. Ironically, in the political arena it is precisely the prophetic outsider stance that gives authority to those who speak from a religious perspective. The religious perspective must be that of a persuasive outsider rather than an authoritarian insider. As long as religious politics plays by the rules of American society, providing a critical perspective in determining policy rather than seeking direct influence in government, it has enormous persuasive power. The "religious critic"[18] has an important role to play in public debate in American society over complex moral issues.

Those who take on the role of religious critic have every right in American society to voice opinions and make every effort, using persuasive strategies, to change people's minds about public policies. They cannot assume that their ideas should be accepted because they have religious authority, but because they are persuasive moral arguments. For their opinions to be taken seriously, religious critics must argue based on values and principles that can be incorporated into the public, secular debate. Authority cannot be based on quotations from scripture alone. Religious ideas must be explained in language that is accessible to common reasoning and understanding.

Religious critics may speak, but they must also be open to public challenge and judgement.[19] In contemporary debates about issues in American culture, the religious critic can adopt a role of public intellectual, using the language, stories, and teachings of a particular religious tradition to contribute a perspective based on religious values. The articles in this volume do precisely that. When Andrew Linzey argues for a theological basis for animal rights, he uses scriptural quotation to support his position, but he also translates those quotations into a moral argument that is accessible to all readers, no matter what their beliefs.

When religious groups do mobilize they tend to have strong persuasive powers. This may be attributed to several factors. While Americans do not want religions to coerce, they see themselves as religious people and are open to arguments made from religious perspectives. Religion has a great deal of legitimacy and force of authority behind its opinions—clergy easily gain respect because of their ascribed authority.

Religious movements also have power because they have human resources to work for their goals. Clergy can mobilize parishioners in any number of political activities, from letter writing campaigns to acts of public protest.[20] Grassroots religious activists as well as religious lobbies have had an important impact in determining public policies.[21] While such power has been utilized most frequently in the past two decades by the religious right, the religious left has also mobilized human resources to gain political strength and feels obligated to continue doing so.

Principles of Selection

In putting this volume together, I surveyed hundreds of articles in dozens of publications. This volume could have included many more articles on many more subjects. I selected the ones you will read here for a variety of reasons. The vast majority of authors are from the United States, and all of the publications from which these articles are derived were published here, because the focus of the volume is on what happened to the religious left in this country during the past two decades since the start of the Reagan revolution. I wanted to create a portrait of the religious left in the United States that underscores its breadth and depth—both in terms of who is writing, and what they are writing about. Inclusivity was a primary goal: presented here are the perspectives of many different religions, and many different adherents of those religions as defined by race, class, sexual orientation, geographic location, and gender. The authors are academics and activists, clergy and laity. But I also chose these articles because they are written by people who are deeply engaged with their religious traditions and who care about what the ancient teachings of those traditions have to say about justice, peace, and human freedom. Some write in a general way about these issues, while others tackle specific problems and situations. All these authors write with the passion of the ancient prophets who firmly believed that our efforts can make this world a better place for all who inhabit it.

Conclusions

Although the religious left is not unified, it has been far from silent. Groups have formed across denominational and political differences to speak out on various issues from a progressive perspective. And individual denominations have done much work to make visible issues that the religious left supports. The following collection witnesses these efforts. The articles are testimony to the vitality of religious perspectives on issues of peace, justice, and human freedom over the past two decades. They share in common a respect for the authority of religious texts that bear witness to values, a willingness to respond to the arguments of contemporary social movements for change in religious structures, a passion for bringing a religious dimension to public discussions of social concerns, and a remarkable variety of religious perspectives in terms of both the religions they represent and the religious viewpoints within those religions.

These articles represent the power of the written word as a vehicle for advocacy and social change. It is often said that actions speak louder than words. But words motivate action. It is my hope that the readers of these essays will themselves feel compelled to think more about the importance of taking a stand on issues from religious perspectives, and to act on something that compels them.

Words are also a valuable witness. This volume documents a very small percentage of the writings of the religious left over the past few decades, found mostly in journals such as those represented here. Although it is clear that what is compiled here does not describe one movement, bringing these works together makes visible a phenomenon of which many people remain unaware: that there is much going on in the progressive world of religion and politics. After reading these essays, you will surely conclude that there is a religious left of which we can speak, and that it is a prophetic voice that demands a hearing from society.

Notes

1. There is of course a long history of public expression of progressive religion in the United States. From the abolitionist movement to the social gospel to the peace and civil rights movements of the 1960s, social activism has been expressed in religious form. While studies abound about each of these movements, about the general connections between religion and politics in the United States, and about the religious right today, there are no histories of progressive religious politics. Robert Craig's *Religion and Radical Politics: An Alternative Christian Tradition in the United States* (Philadelphia: Temple University Press, 1992) describes some of these movements, but does not claim to be comprehensive.

2. See James Davison Hunter, *Culture Wars: The Struggle to Define America* (New York: Basic Books, 1991).

3. Secularization theory suggests that during the period of modernity, and particularly in the last century, the hegemony of religion has been eclipsed by secular values. Events of the last few decades of religious resurgence, and in particular fundamentalist and nationalist religious resurgence, has compelled a rethinking of this thesis. See Mary Douglas and Steven Tipton, eds., *Spiritual Life in a Secular Age* (Boston: Beacon Press, 1983); Phillip Hammond, ed., *The Sacred in a Secular Age* (Berkeley and Los Angeles: University of California Press, 1985); Bruce Lawrence, *Defenders of God: The Fundamentalist Revolt against the Modern Age* (San Francisco: Harper and Row, 1989); and José Casanova, *Public Religions in the Modern World* (Chicago: University of Chicago Press, 1994).

4. Although most Protestant scholars look at the United States as a secular culture, scholars and participants of the other religious traditions present in this country are clear that America was built on Protestant values and mores that are still central to the way life here is conducted. See Stephen Feldman, *Please Don't Wish Me a Merry Christmas: A Critical History of the Separation of Church and State* (New York: NYU Press, 1997).

5. See Robert Wuthnow, *The Restructuring of American Religion: Society and Faith since World War II* (Princeton, N.J.: Princeton University Press, 1988).

6. See Stephen Hart, *What Does the Lord Require? How American Christians Think about Economic Justice* (New Brunswick, N.J.: Rutgers University Press, 1996).

7. See Fred Kniss, "Culture Wars (?): Re-mapping the Battleground" in Rhys Williams, ed., *Culture Wars in American Politics: Critical Reviews of a Popular Myth* (New York: Aldine de Gruyter, 1997), 290.

8. See Kenneth Wald, *Religion and Politics in the United States* (Washington, D.C.: CQ Press, 1997) 3rd ed., 16–19.

9. For an analysis of this process, see Gary Parrien, *The Soul in Society: The Making and Renewal of Social Christianity* (Minneapolis: Fortress Press, 1995); Elizabeth Bounds, *Coming Together/Coming Apart: Religion, Community and Modernity* (New York: Routledge Press, 1997).

10. Some examples of the challenges to mainstream religion by gays and lesbians, people of color, and white feminists include: Katie Cannon, *Black Womanist Ethics* (Atlanta: Scholar's Press, 1988); Mary Daly, *Gyn/Ecology: The Metaethics of Radical Feminism* (Boston: Beacon Press, 1978); Beverly Harrison, *Making Connections: Essays in Feminist Social Ethics*, edited by C. Robb (Boston: Beacon, 1985); Ada-María Isasi-Díaz, *En la lucha: In the Struggle: A Hispanic Women's Liberation Theology* (Minnesota: Fortress Press, 1993); Susan Thistlethwaite and Mary Potter Engel, eds., *Lift Every Voice: Constructing Christian Theologies from the Underside*, revised and expanded ed. (Maryknoll, N.Y.: Orbis Books, 1998); Judith Plaskow, *Standing Again at Sinai* (San Francisco: Harper and Row, 1990); James Cone, *Malcolm and Martin and America: A Dream or A Nightmare?* (Maryknoll, N.Y.: Orbis Books, 1991); Vincent Harding, *There Is A River: The Black Struggle for Freedom in America* (San Diego: Harvest Books, 1981); Cornel West, *Prophesy Deliverance! An Afro-American Revolutionary Christianity* (Philadelphia: Westminster Press, 1982); Richard Cleaver, *Know My Name: A Gay Liberation Theology* (Louisville, Ky.: Westminster Press, 1995); Michael Stemmler and J. M. Clark, *Constructing Gay Theology: Proceedings of the Gay Men's Issues in Religion Consultation of the American Academy of Religion* (Las Colinas, Tex.: Monument Press, 1991); Carter Heyward and Ellen Davis, *Speaking of Christ: A Lesbian Feminist Voice* (New York: Pilgrim Press, 1989).

11. Studies by Nancy Taton Ammerman of evangelicals (see Ammerman and Wade Clark Roof, eds., *Work, Family, and Religion in Contemporary Society* [New York: Routledge, 1995]) and by Lynn Davidman of Orthodox Jewish women (*Tradition in a Rootless World: Women Turn to Orthodox Judaism* [Berkeley: University of California Press, 1991]) support the idea that feminism, even if rejected in name by these groups, has had a great impact on the behavior and beliefs of traditional women.

12. Some of the more significant works on liberation theology include: Phillip Berryman, *The Religious Roots of Rebellion: Christians in Central America* (Maryknoll, N.Y.: Orbis Books, 1984); "Latin American Liberation Theology" in *Theology in the Americas*, Sergio Torres and John Eagleson, eds. (Maryknoll, N.Y.: Orbis Books, 1976); Gustavo Gutierrez, *A Theology of Liberation*, translated by Sister Caridad Inda and John Eagleson (Maryknoll, N.Y.: Orbis Books, 1973); Jon Sobrino, *Christology at the Crossroads: A Latin American Approach*, translated by John Drury (Maryknoll, N.Y.: Orbis Books, 1984); Michael Walzer, *Exodus and Revolution* (New York: Basic Books, 1985).

13. Wald, 124.

14. See Dean M. Kelley, *Why Conservative Churches Are Growing: A Study in Sociology of Religion* (New York: Harper and Row, 1972).

15. See Alan Wolfe, *One Nation After All: What the White Middle-Class Americans Really Think*

About: God, Country, Family, Racism, Welfare, Immigration, Homosexuality, Work, the Right, the Left, and Each Other (New York: Viking Penguin, 1998); Rhys Williams, ed., *Culture Wars in American Politics: Critical Reviews of a Popular Myth* (New York: Aldine de Gruyter, 1997). Both works, based on sociological research, suggest that the culture war thesis is greatly exaggerated, and that most Americans are simply not that exorcised over the agenda of the religious right.

16. Although his politics support the religious right, Richard Neuhaus's ideas about the "naked public square" support both the left and the right in their goal to bring religious conversation and values to public notice. *The Naked Public Square: Religion and Democracy in America* (Grand Rapids, Mich.: Wm. B. Eerdmans Publishing Co., 1984).

17. See Phillip Hammond, *With Liberty For All: Freedom of Religion in the United States* (Louisville: Westminster John Knox Press, 1998).

18. A thesis articulated by William Dean in *The Religious Critic in American Culture* (Binghamton, N.Y.: SUNY Press, 1994).

19. Casanova, 57.

20. See Christian Smith, "Introduction" in *Disruptive Religion: The Force of Faith in Social Movement Activism* (New York: Routledge, 1997), 9–23; Ted G. Jelen, *The Political World of the Clergy* (Westport, Conn.: Praeger Publishers, 1993).

21. For the most recent discussion of religious lobbies, see Daniel J. B. Hoffrenning, *In Washington, But Not of It: The Prophetic Politics of Religious Lobbyists* (Philadelphia: Temple University Press, 1995).

Making Progressive
Religious Theology:
Warrant for Progressive
Religious Thought
and Action

This part sets up the themes that will be discussed throughout this volume: the connection to
ancient sources of wisdom that undergird the thinking of the religious left, the vision of unity
that is required for change, a strong concern for the poor, and an awareness of the needs of the
religious left to respond to the critiques of white women and people of color in their demands
for justice.

That vision of hope, pluralism, and inclusion is followed through by the authors in this
section. Jim Wallis, the leading spokesperson for progressive politics among the Christian
evangelical movements, describes his vision for a new common ground that comes from the
prophetic biblical perspective. Womanist theologian Delores Williams brings insight from the
theology of black feminism. Catholic theologians Richard McCormick and Richard McBrien
challenge the Roman Catholic church to allow dissent in the public arena.

Liberation theologian Gustavo Gutierrez writes about the relationship between God and the
poor, emphasizing the importance of grassroots efforts for social change. Robert Allan Warrior

writes from the perspective of Native American peoples with a caution about the limits of the story of the Israelite exodus.

Feminist theologian Rita Nakashima Brock writes about the importance of making new images for God that correspond to the realities of women's lives. Black theologian Vincent Harding looks to Martin Luther King, Jr., Malcolm X, and Rabbi Abraham Joshua Heschel as teachers from the past who provide models for coalition building for the future.

Taken together, these essays set the blueprint for the combination of theological perspectives that exist today on the religious left. They emphasize a connection to prophetic tradition both ancient and contemporary; a series of cautions about inclusion of perspectives that have been underrepresented; a willingness to dissent from the right, the mainstream, and also from one another; and a vision of cooperation for the future.

Jim Wallis

1 Renewing the Heart of Faith: A Prophetic Convergence of the People of God

Reading the signs of the times becomes even more crucial in a period of transition—exactly where we find ourselves now. On so many fronts, the old assumptions and structures that have long governed are dying, while the new are still begging to be born. The moment calls for fresh visions and dreams that hold the promise of change.

This is especially apparent in the churches. Out of their institutional and spiritual crisis, a new theological convergence is occurring, with new ecumenical relationships being forged. The result is an emerging ground upon which diverse people from previously divided communities are finding a place to stand. Their standing and walking together opens up the possibility of significant and hopeful new configurations for the church's future and its contribution to the wider society.

The Crisis of Religious Institutions

Ironically, the institutions of established religion are in internal crisis just as the real issues of society are being revealed as essentially religious. I speak here of what I most know—the Christian churches—but those from other faith traditions tell a similar story. Virtually all the vertical structures of American Christianity are in great distress.

Mainline American Protestantism is in serious decline. Decreasing membership and budget cutbacks have caused denominational bureaucracies and seminary ad-

Originally published in *Sojourners* (February 1993), 22:10–15. Reprinted with Permission from *Sojourners*, 2401 15th Street NW, Washington, DC 20009; (202) 328-8842/(800) 714-7474.

ministrations to pull back into survival mode. Risk taking and faith ventures are out; cautious management is in.

There are pastors, teachers, denominational officials, and countless local church members who struggle valiantly for an authentic Christian faith. But they constantly face fearful bureaucracies, sterile curriculums, culturally captive congregations, confused theology, and empty spirituality.

American Catholicism is also in deep conflict. A rigid and repressive hierarchy, emanating from Rome is in direct confrontation with a grassroots hunger for change felt throughout the church. Some of the most creative impulses in American religious life today are found in the Catholic Church. Leading the way are communities of religious women, a strong number of progressive bishops and priests, and, of course, ordinary parish members who draw upon faith for personal and community survival. But the patriarchal hierarchies fear and do not understand the populist impulses that would reshape the church.

The evangelical movement in America has been taken over by its fundamentalist right wing. The Religious Right's extreme nationalist and theocratic agenda bears little resemblance to the gospel. The culture war they have declared on everyone who disagrees with them is alarming to many Americans and genuinely embarrassing to more moderate evangelicals. Many people long for evangelical integrity to re-assert itself.

Perhaps the greatest irony of U.S. church history is that a church created by racial marginalization has arguably made the most distinctive and significant American contribution to world Christianity. The black churches provided a sanctuary for an oppressed people, created our most vibrant spirituality, became the base for the most important social movement in American history, and have served as a conscience to the nation. Yet America's black churches are also facing a dilemma. The failure to reach the alienated young of the nation's cities has created a crisis of confidence and leadership. After a shooting incident during a black church service in Boston, one African-American street pastor remarked, "If the church doesn't go out into the streets, the streets will come into the church." Newer racial and ethnic churches are struggling to force cultural and spiritual identity in a framework of white ecclesiastical control. And a small number of American Indian congregations wrestle with their denominations for respect for native traditions and spirituality.

A Quiet Coming Together

In the midst of this institutional church crisis, a number of new and ecumenical connections are being made between kindred spirits from all the traditional constituencies. A new sense of community is not based on the old vertical structures, but in horizontal relationships and networks.

After years of very limited results from formal ecumenical dialogues, a vital ecumenism is emerging between people who have found one another while putting faith into action. A new Christian community has begun to emerge in urban ministry centers, homeless shelters, and soup kitchens; in street protests and jail cells; in racial and ecological battlegrounds; in prayer and Bible study groups; and in diverse experiments in community and spiritual renewal.

Our historical crisis, in all its varied manifestations, is bringing us together. Indeed, a *kairos* moment is creating a new faith-based community of response. Though most apparent around works of mercy and prophetic actions, activism is only its most public expression. Much biblical reflection, prayerful searching, theological conversation, and community building are going on. This shared activity and discernment holds promise for both transcending the old categories that have divided us for so long, and revitalizing the faith traditions from which we have come.

The New Theological Convergence

There is, of course, no fixed creed or dogma that controls this emerging ecumenical community. But there are characteristics, concerns, and points of convergence that describe a new theological common ground.

It will be biblical without being fundamentalist. The practice of action and reflection with a biblical focus is now widespread. A new generation of biblical teachers and practitioners defies the old doctrinal categorizations of conservative and liberal that still dominate most of our theological schools. Now the primary concern is to discover the meaning of the Word of God in our present moment—to allow it to change our lives and our history.

It will be spiritual without being withdrawn from the world. There is a growing intuition, even outside the religious community, that our most important political and cultural problems have a spiritual core. A new politics and a new spirituality will go hand and hand; one is not really possible without the other. A consciousness of the spiritual resources required to sustain persons and communities in the struggle for social transformation is also growing. More and more people find themselves drinking at the wells of each other's spiritual traditions, and engaging in a deep and common quest to root their lives in God.

This theological convergence will be rooted in action, without losing its reflective power. We've learned both that faith without works is dead and that overwork can lead to idolatry and a loss of faith. Faith becomes alive in action; subsequent reflection on the action further clarifies faith's meaning. The life of faith is the inward and outward journey, contemplation and action.

It will be evangelical without being sectarian or self-righteous. By evangelical, I mean a centeredness on Jesus and his radical proclamation of the reign of God. The gospel values of the Sermon on the Mount are finding fresh meaning and application.

To be faithful to the way of Jesus does not require disrespecting other believers and non-believers. There are church-based activists who believe Christian obedience welcomes mutual collaboration in a pluralistic society, and who oppose any effort to translate the precepts of certain religious constituencies into theocratic control. At the same time, they insist that focusing on the enormous implications of discipleship is absolutely essential, even at those "politically correct" seminaries where the name of Jesus has all but disappeared.

It will be catholic, but not just Roman. That is to say, the diversity and integrity of the whole church will be greatly respected, as will the importance of interfaith dialogue that recognizes the particularities of each tradition. Indeed, the new theological convergence lives at the crossroads of the whole church, and of the world's concerns. The exploration of the churches' many spiritual treasures and traditions is one of its richest characteristics and greatest contributions. Perhaps the best image of this new ecumenical community is that of a deep, flowing river, fed by many streams.

It will be political without being ideological. Predictable and partisan politics are anathema to authentic prophetic witness. For much too long, evangelicals have been the Republican Party at prayer, liberals have been easily confused with the left wing of the Democratic Party, and even grassroots religious peace and justice activists have not always distinguished themselves from the politics of other secular and solidarity movements. That may be one of the most important things that is changing. A truly religious, moral, and ethical perspective has much to contribute to shaping a new kind of politics, and we must make the nature of that contribution increasingly clear.

It will bring a theological dimension to political discussions and social problems. By revealing the essential theological character of racism, sexism, poverty, environmental destruction, violence, abortion, sexuality, and family, the religious community could help deepen the public dialogue and response. In creating diversity, practicing equality, demonstrating justice, re-connecting with the Earth, helping to resolve conflicts, seeking a consistent ethic of life, and nurturing covenantal relationships, faith communities could make a decisive contribution and provide leadership by example. Faith communities must strive to be and do what they envision for the larger society.

This common ground will be rooted in the sufferings and hopes of poor and marginalized people. At the heart of Christian faith is incarnation—God becoming flesh among the poor and the outcast. Indeed, the cry, of the poor has helped to bring us all together.

We have been converted to a more radical faith through relationship with the children of God who are oppressed by the social crisis that defines the modern world. The reality of the poor must continue to shape the new visions and dreams that we hope to help birth. In fact, the possibility of a new partnership of the middle-class and the poor, born of faith and for the sake of justice, has the potential to transform the political landscape.

Those who stand on this new ground will try to live out a faith that is both personal and social, based in community and ecumenical in spirit, deeply rooted and open to change. This faith will actively engage the world and yet seek not to conform to it. It will hold forth alternative visions of racial, economic, gender, and environmental justice, and insist on the essential connection between spiritual and social transformation, between politics and spirituality.

The new ground has yet to be named. But it draws evangelicals with a compassionate heart and a social conscience. It brings together mainline Protestants who desire spiritual revival and justice. It invites Catholics who seek a spirituality for social change. It includes African-American, Latino, Asian and American Indian faith communities that will help shape a more pluralistic and just society. No seminary represents this new theological center, but one can find evidence of it at almost every one. No national church embodies it, but the new ground is emerging in virtually every denomination and constituency.

At this point, naming the common theological ground is less important than naming ourselves as standing on it. It is a network, not an institution, a movement in many places, not a new denomination, an extended community for the sake of the church's renewal, not a substitute for it.

Covenantal Relationships

While this progressive religious network is getting connected in many local communities, some people and groups have yet to find each other. The future tries in crossing ecumenical, racial, and regional lines to knit ourselves together. Catholic peace activists need to connect with black churches in common causes. Evangelicals need to pray with mainline Protestants about how to minister to the inner city. Local churches need to come together for community organizing projects. Weary activists need to find quiet refreshment in monastic communities. White Christians need to listen to black preachers and Protestant ministers need spiritual direction from Catholic sisters. For too long, we have been churches behind walls; now the walls are coming down.

We need to recognize, respect, and build on our great ecclesiastical diversity. We are local parishes and congregations, intentional communities and house churches, Bible study and prayer groups, houses of hospitality and monastic communities, projects for justice and ministries for spiritual renewal. This new ground provides a foundation that supports many different structures; our tree has many branches. That is a real strength and a protection from narrow thinking.

But we do need to find each other and build up our networks for support and action. That is the biggest task ahead of us. At the heart of our networks will be covenantal relationships established across constituency lines—relationships that have binding authority in our lives. Political convenience, mutual use, or institutional self-interest won't bring us together; new friendships based on a real spiritual companionship will. The courage to enter into such covenantal relationships and remain faithful to them will be an essential quality of leadership in the days ahead.

An Alternative to the Religious Right

Conservatives have tapped into a genuine energy for a new discussion about basic moral values in the public debate. But that longing is much wider than the narrow interpretations of moral values offered by the evangelical right wing. Their extremism suggests that the only alternatives are to be totally secular or a religious bigot. Fortunately, those are not the only choices. A moral vacuum is waiting to be filled.

We seek a prophetic biblical perspective that is progressive rather than repressive; inclusive and respectful of pluralism instead of exclusive and sectarian. It will speak the language of both social justice and personal responsibility. In economics, it will take us beyond the "bottom line" of profit and the stagnation of bureaucracy to an economic ethic rooted in the religious requirements of community.

On the environment, this biblical perspective transcends old notions of exploitation, stewardship, and protection and proposes a theology of relationship. In foreign relations, it puts human rights over national self-interest and seeks alternatives to war as a solution. It sees racism and sexism as spiritual as well as social sins, and calls for repentance. And it will insist on the vital connection between politics and morality. It will be open to broad collaboration and could provide a social reservoir of prophetic imagination.

Examples of prophetic religion abound. Bread for the World has become an effective Christian citizens movement against hunger. Pax Christi is a growing national and international Catholic peace and justice network. Witness For Peace is an interfaith initiative seeking reconciliation in war-torn Central America and elsewhere. Evangelicals for Social Action links evangelism and justice. SCUPE, a network of seminarians, pastors, and church workers, now convenes the largest "urban congress" in the nation.

Street ministers, deployed from black churches such as the Azusa Christian Community in Dorchester, Massachusetts, daily confront the challenge of reaching alienated inner-city youth. *Tikkun,* a progressive Jewish magazine, plays a similar role in its own religious community as our *Sojourners* magazine and network plays in the Christian community—a connection point and catalyst for a new movement. In cities and rural areas across the country, the number of faith-based ventures and coalitions to heal and rebuild local communities is beyond counting.

A Place to Stand—A Mission to Carry Out

The new theological convergence offers the possibility of free, safe, creative, and holy space—both healing and prophetic. From that space, new visions could surely come. From all the corners of the churches' life, a new and ecumenical community could boldly proclaim the reign of God in this world. That is our purpose. To demonstrate the power of the gospel in the midst of a great social crisis is our vocation. Our goal is to lift up alternative spiritual and social possibilities at this crucial juncture of history; and our task is to demonstrate concretely what those alternatives might be.

The Spirit calls us and provides the gifts and power to respond. We act, not just for the sake of the church, but for the sake of the world. In a time shrouded with death, we seek to bring the light of hope and healing. Faithful acts, great and small, can bring forth evidence of justice, peace, truth, goodness, dignity, grace, and love. We are those who are "looking for the day of God and trying to hasten it" (2 Peter 3:11–12). We are finding a new place to stand together.

Delores S. Williams

2   Womanist Theology: Black Women's Voices

DAUGHTER: Mama, why are we brown, pink, and yellow, and our cousins are white, beige, and black?

MOTHER: Well, you know the colored race is just like a flower garden, with every color flower represented.

DAUGHTER: Mama, I'm walking to Canada and I'm taking you and a bunch of slaves with me.

MOTHER: It wouldn't be the first time.

In these two conversational exchanges, Pulitzer Prize-winning novelist Alice Walker begins to show us what she means by the concept "womanist." The concept is presented in Walker's *In Search of Our Mother's Gardens,* and many women in church and society have appropriated it as a way of affirming themselves as *black* while simultaneously owning their connection with the Afro-American community, male and female. The concept of womanist allows women to claim their roots in black history, religion, and culture.

What then is a womanist? Her origins are in the black folk expression "You acting womanish," meaning, according to Walker, "wanting to know more and in greater depth than is good for one . . . outrageous, audacious, courageous and willful behavior." A womanist is also "responsible, in charge, serious." She can walk to Canada and take others with her. She loves, she is committed, she is a universalist by temperament.

Her universality includes loving men and women, sexually or nonsexually. She loves music, dance, the spirit, food and roundness, struggle, and she loves herself. "Regardless."

Originally published in *Christianity and Crisis* 47 (March 2, 1988), 66–70. Reprinted with permission of *Christianity and Crisis.*

Walker insists that a womanist is also "committed to survival and wholeness of entire people, male and female." She is no separatist, "except for health." A womanist is a black feminist or feminist of color. Or as Walker says, "Womanist is to feminist as purple is to lavender."

Womanist theology, a vision in its infancy, is emerging among Afro-American Christian women. Ultimately many sources—biblical, theological, ecclesiastical, social, anthropological, economic, and material from other religious traditions—will inform the development of this theology. As a contribution to this process, I demonstrate how Walker's concept of womanist provides some significant clues for the work of womanist theologians. I will then focus on method and God-content in womanist theology. This contribution belongs to work of prolegomena—prefatory remarks, introductory observations intended to be suggestive and not conclusive.

Codes and Contents

In her definition, Walker provides significant clues for the development of womanist theology. Her concept contains what black feminist scholar bell hooks in *From Margin to Center* identifies as cultural codes. These are: words, beliefs, and behavioral patterns of a people that must be deciphered before meaningful communication can happen cross-culturally. Walker's codes are female-centered and they point beyond themselves to conditions, events, meanings, and values that have crystallized in the Afro-American community *around women's activity* and formed traditions.

A paramount example is mother-daughter advice. Black mothers have passed on wisdom for survival—in the white world, in the black community, and with men—for as long as anyone can remember. Female slave narratives, folk tales, and some contemporary black poetry and prose reflect this tradition. Some of it is collected in "Old Sister's Advice to her Daughters," in *The Book of Negro Folklore* edited by Langston Hughes and Arna Bontemps (Dodd Mead, 1958).

Walker's allusion to skin color points to an historic tradition of tension between black women over the matter of some black men's preference for light-skinned women. Her reference to black women's love of food and roundness points to customs of female care in the black community (including the church) associated with hospitality and nurture.

These cultural codes and their corresponding traditions are valuable resources for indicating and validating the kind of data upon which womanist theologians can reflect as they bring black women's social, religious, and cultural experience into the discourse of theology, ethics, biblical and religious studies. Female slave narratives, imaginative literature by black women, autobiographies, the work by black women in academic disciplines, and the testimonies by church women will be authoritative sources for womanist theologians.

Walker situates her understanding of a womanist in the context of nonbourgeois black folk culture. The literature of this culture has traditionally reflected more egalitarian relations between men and women, much less rigidity in male-female roles, and more respect for female intelligence and ingenuity than is found in bourgeois culture.

The black folk are poor. Less individualistic than those who are better off, they have, for generations, practiced various forms of economic sharing. For example, immediately after Emancipation mutual aid societies pooled the resources of black folk to help pay for funerals and other daily expenses. *The Book of Negro Folklore* describes the practice of rent parties which flourished during the Depression. The black folk stressed togetherness and a closer connection with nature. They respect knowledge gained through lived experience monitored by elders who differ profoundly in social class and world view from the teachers and education encountered in American academic institutions. Walker's choice of context suggests that womanist theology can establish lines of continuity in the black community with nonbourgeois traditions less sexist than the black power and black nationalist traditions.

In this folk context, some of the black female-centered cultural codes in Walker's definition (e.g., "Mama, I'm walking to Canada and I'm taking you and a bunch of slaves with me") point to folk heroines like Harriet Tubman, whose liberation activity earned her the name "Moses" of her people. This allusion to Tubman directs womanist memory to a liberation tradition in black history in which women took the lead, acting as catalysts for the community's revolutionary action and for change. Retrieving this often hidden or diminished female tradition of catalytic action is an important task for womanist theologians and ethicists. Their research may well reveal that female models of authority have been absolutely essential for every struggle in the black community and for building and maintaining the community's institutions.

Freedom Fighters

The womanist theologian must search for the actions, opinions, experience and faith of women whose names sometimes slip into the male-centered rendering of black history, but whose actual stories remain remote. This search can lead to such little-known freedom fighters as Milla Granson and her courageous work on a Mississippi plantation. Her liberation method broadens our knowledge of the variety of strategies black people have used to obtain freedom. According to scholar Sylvia Dannett, in *Profiles in Negro Womanhood*:

> Milla Granson, a slave, conducted a midnight school for several years. She had been taught to read and write by her former master in Kentucky . . . and in her little school hundreds of slaves benefited from her learning. . . . After laboring all day for their master, the slaves would creep stealthily to Milla's "schoolroom" (a little cabin in a back alley). . . . The doors and windows . . . had to be kept tightly sealed to avoid discovery. Each class was composed of twelve pupils and when Milla had brought them up to the extent of her

ability, she "graduated" them and took in a dozen more. Through this means she gradu-ated hundreds of slaves. Many of whom she taught to write a legible hand [forged] their own passes and set out for Canada.

Women like Tubman and Granson used subtle and silent strategies to liberate them-selves and large numbers of black people. By uncovering as much as possible about such female liberation, the womanist begins to understand the relation of black his-tory to the contemporary folk expression: "If Rosa Parks had not sat down, Martin King would not have stood up."

While she celebrates and emphasizes black women's culture and way of being in the world, Walker simultaneously affirms black women's historic connection with men through love and through a shared struggle for survival and for productive quality of life (e.g., "wholeness"). This suggests that two of the principal concerns of womanist theology should be survival and community building and maintenance. The goal of this community building is, of course, to establish a positive quality of life—economic, spiritual, educational—for black women, men, and children. Wal-ker's understanding of a womanist as "not a separatist" ("except for health"), how-ever, reminds the Christian womanist theologian that her concern for community building and maintenance must ultimately extend to the entire Christian community and beyond that to the larger human community.

Yet womanist consciousness is also informed by women's determination to love themselves. "Regardless." This translates into an admonition to black women to avoid the self-destruction of bearing a disproportionately large burden in the work of community building and maintenance. Walker suggests that women can avoid this trap by connecting with women's communities concerned about women's rights and well-being. Her identification of a womanist as also a feminist joins black women with their feminist heritage extending back into the nineteenth century in the work of black feminists like Sojourner Truth, Frances W. Harper, and Mary Church-Terrell.

In making the feminist-womanist connection, however, Walker proceeds with great caution. While affirming an organic relationship between womanists and feminists, she also declares a deep shade of difference between them ("Womanist is to feminist as purple to lavender"). This gives womanist scholars the freedom to explore the particularities of black women's history and culture without being guided by what white feminists have already identified as women's issues.

But womanist consciousness directs black women away from the negative divi-sions prohibiting community building among women. The womanist loves other women sexually and nonsexually. Therefore, respect for sexual preferences is one of the marks of community. According to Walker, homophobia has no place. Nor does "Colorism" (i.e., "Yella" and half-white black people valued more in the black world than black-skinned people), which often separates black women from each other. Rather, Walker's womanist claim is that variety is the substance of universality. Color, like birth and death, is common to all people. Like the navel, it is a badge of humanity connecting people with people. Two other distinctions are prohibited in Walker's womanist thinking. Class hierarchy does not dwell among women, who " . . . love struggle, love the Folks . . . are committed to the survival and wholeness of an entire people." Nor do women compete for male attention when they " . . . appreciate and prefer female culture . . . value . . . women's emotional flexibility . . . and women's strength."

The intimations about community provided by Walker's definition suggest no genuine community building is possible when men are excluded (except when women's health is at stake). Neither can it occur when women's self-love, culture, and love for each other are not affirmed and are not considered vital for the community's self-understanding. And it is thwarted if black women are expected to bear "the lion's share" of the work and to sacrifice their well-being for the group. Yet, for the womanist, mothering and nurturing are vitally important. Walker's womanist reality begins with mothers relating to their children and is characterized by black women (not necessarily bearers of children) nurturing great numbers of black people in the liberation struggle (e.g., Harriet Tubman). Womanist emphasis upon the value of mothering and nurturing is consistent with the testimony of many black women. The poet Carolyn Rogers speaks of her mother as the bridge that brought her over. Walker dedicates her novel *The Third Life of Grange Copeland* to her mother " . . . who made a way out of no way." As a child in the black church, I heard women (and men) give thanks to God for their mothers " . . . who stayed behind and pulled the wagon over the long haul."

It seems, then, that the clues about community from Walker's definition of a womanist suggest that the mothering and nurturing dimension of Afro-American history can provide resources for shaping criteria to measure the quality of justice in the community. These criteria could be used to assure female-male equity in the presentation of the community's models of authority. They could also gauge the community's division of labor with regard to the survival tasks necessary for building and maintaining community.

Womanist Theology and Method

Womanist theology is already beginning to define the categories and methods needed to develop along lines consistent with the sources of that theology. Christian womanist theological methodology needs to be informed by at least four elements: (1) a multidialogical intent, (2) a liturgical intent, (3) a didactic intent, and (4) a commitment both to reason *and* to the validity of female imagery and metaphorical language in the construction of theological statements.

A multidialogical intent will allow Christian womanist theologians to advocate and participate in dialogue and action with *many* diverse social, political, and religious communities concerned about human survival and productive quality of life for the oppressed. The genocide of cultures and peoples (which has often been instigated and accomplished by Western white Christian groups or governments) and the nuclear threat of omnicide mandates womanist participation in such dialogue/action. But in this dialogue/action the womanist also should keep her speech and action focused upon the slow genocide of poor black women, children, and men by exploitative systems denying them productive jobs, education, health care, and living space. Multidialogical activity may, like, a jazz symphony, communicate some of its most important messages in what the harmony-driven conventional ear hears as discord, as disruption of the harmony in both the black American and white American social, political, and religious status quo.

If womanist theological method is informed by a liturgical intent, then womanist theology will be relevant to (and will reflect) the thought, worship, and action of the black church. But a liturgical intent will also allow womanist theology to challenge the thought/worship/action of the black church with the discordant and prophetic messages emerging from womanist participation in multidialogics. This means that womanist theology will consciously impact *critically* upon the foundations of liturgy, challenging the church to use justice principles to select the sources that will shape the content of liturgy. The question must be asked: "How does this source portray blackness/darkness, women and economic justice for nonruling-class people?" A negative portrayal will demand omission of the source or its radical reformation by the black church. The Bible, a major source in black church liturgy, must also be subjected to the scrutiny of justice principles.

A didactic intent in womanist theological method assigns a teaching function to theology. Womanist theology should teach Christians new insights about moral life based on ethics supporting justice for women, survival, and a productive quality of life for poor women, children and men. This means that the womanist theologian must give authoritative status to black folk wisdom (e.g., Brer Rabbit literature) and to black women's moral wisdom (expressed in their literature) when she responds to the question, "How ought the Christian to live in the world?" Certainly tensions may exist between the moral teachings derived from these sources and the moral teachings about obedience, love, and humility that have usually buttressed presuppositions about living the Christian life. Nevertheless, womanist theology, in its didactic intent, must teach the church the different ways God reveals prophetic word and action for Christian living.

These intents, informing theological method, can yield a theological language whose foundation depends as much upon its imagistic content as upon reason. The language can be rich in female imagery, metaphor, and story. For the black church, this kind of theological language may be quite useful, since the language of the black religious experience abounds in images and metaphors. Clifton Johnson's collection of black conversion experiences, *God Struck Me Dead,* illustrates this point.

The appropriateness of womanist theological language will ultimately reside in its ability to bring black women's history, culture, and religious experience into the interpretive circle of Christian theology and into the liturgical life of the church. Womanist theological language must, in this sense, be an instrument for social and theological change in church and society.

Who Do You Say God Is?

Regardless of one's hopes about intentionality and womanist theological method, questions must be raised about the God-content of the theology. Walker's mention of the black womanist's love of the spirit is a true reflection of the great respect Afro-American women have always shown for the presence and work of the spirit. In the black church, women (and men) often judge the effectiveness of the worship service not on the scholarly content of the sermon nor on the ritual nor on orderly process. Rather, worship has been effective if "the spirit was high," i.e., if the spirit was actively and obviously present in a balanced blend of prayer, of cadenced word (the sermon), and of syncopated music ministering to the pain of the people.

The importance of this emphasis upon the spirit is that it allows Christian womanist theologians, in their use of the Bible, to identify and reflect upon those biblical stories in which poor oppressed women had a special encounter with divine emissaries of God, like the spirit. In the Hebrew Testament, Hagar's story is most illustrative and relevant to Afro-American women's experience of bondage, of African heritage, of encounter with God/emissary in the midst of fierce survival struggles. Kate Cannon among a number of black female preachers and ethicists urges black Christian women to regard themselves as Hagar's sisters.

In relation to the Christian or New Testament, the Christian womanist theologian can refocus the salvation story so that it emphasizes the beginning of revelation with the spirit mounting Mary, a woman of the poor: (" . . . the Holy Spirit shall come upon thee, and the power of the Highest shall overshadow thee. . . ." Luke 1:35). Such an interpretation of revelation has roots in the 19th century black abolitionist and feminist Sojourner Truth. Posing an important question and response, she refuted a white preacher's claim that women could not be equal to men because Christ was not a woman. Truth asked, "Whar did your Christ come from? . . . From God and a woman! Man had nothin' to do wid Him!" This suggests that womanist theology could eventually speak of God in a well-developed theology of the spirit. The sources for this theology are many. Harriet Tubman often "went into the spirit" before her liberation missions and claimed her strength for liberation activity came from this way of meeting God. Womanist theology has grounds for shaping a theology of the spirit informed by black women's political action.

Christian womanist responses to the question "who do you say God is?" will be influenced by these many sources. Walker's way of connecting womanists with the spirit is only one clue. The integrity of black woman's faith, their love of Jesus, their commitment to life, love, family, and politics will also yield vital clues. And other theological voices (black liberation, feminist, Islamic, Asian, Hispanic, African, Jewish, and Western white male traditional) will provide insights relevant for the construction of the God-content of womanist theology.

Each womanist theologian will add her own special accent to the understandings of God emerging from womanist theology. But if one needs a final image to describe women coming together to shape the enterprise, Bess B. Johnson in *God's Fierce*

Whimsy offers an appropriate one. Describing the difference between the play of male and female children in the black community where she developed, Johnson says:

> the boys in the neighborhood had this game with rope . . . tug-o'-war . . . till finally some side would jerk the rope away from the others, who'd fall down. . . . Girls . . . weren't allowed to play with them in this tug-o'-war; so we figured out how to make our own rope—out of . . . little dandelions. You jest keep adding one to another, and you can go on and on. . . . Anybody, even the boys, could join us. . . . The whole purpose of our game was to create this dandelion chain—that was it. And we'd keep going, creating till our mamas called us home.

Like Johnson's dandelion chain, womanist theological vision will grow as black women come together and connect piece with piece. Between the process of creating and the sense of calling, womanist theology will one day present itself in full array, reflecting the divine spirit that connects us all.

Richard A. McCormick, S.J.,
and Richard P. McBrien

3   Theology as a Public Responsibility

In an address to the National Federation of Priests' Councils on April 30, 1991 (*Origins*, 5/23/91), Bishop Kenneth E. Untener of Saginaw, Mich., discussed three characteristics of the true prophet. One was freedom, the freedom to speak the hard message for the right reasons and the freedom not to speak it for the wrong reasons or at the wrong time. Bishop Untener then noted: "I believe that there is a lack of this freedom among bishops today," not on all issues, but certainly on issues within the church. In his words: "But on issues within the church, I am embarrassed. We have seemed fearful to speak on church issues that are right before our eyes, but which are unmentionable. We are like a dysfunctional family, unwilling to talk openly about things that are on everyone's mind even when we are together at an N.C.C.B. [National Conference of Catholic Bishops] meeting" (p. 38).

Being "unwilling to talk openly" is not an innate episcopal reluctance. It is a response to, and reflection of, an atmosphere of coercion resulting from a policy of intimidation. Its impact goes far beyond episcopal silence on certain issues. When applied to theology, this policy seeks the privatization of theological reflection. Because we regard this as a noxious development and inconsistent with the very notion of theology, we want to (1) describe this development and (2) underline the public nature of the discipline of theology. We hope that this will encourage others to fulfill courageously the public dimensions of their theological responsibility.

By "privatization" of theology we mean the removal of its critical and creative functions from public scrutiny and their confinement to a narrow few in the church (the hierarchical magisterium and theologians). It is as if the rest of the believers had no interest and stake in theological inquiry. Privatization has the practical effect of excluding from theological deliberation the very people whose faith and lives are being discussed and whose reflection and input are utterly essential if the magisterial process of the church is to avoid the accusation of presumptuousness and magic.

Originally published in *America* (September 28, 1991), 165:184–189, 203–206. Reprinted with the permission of Richard A. McCormick and Richard P. McBrien and America Press, Inc., 106 West 56th Street, New York, NY 10019.

Vatican II rejected the privatization of theology in any number of places, but perhaps nowhere more clearly than in the Pastoral Constitution on the Church in the Modern World (No. 62). After stating its hope that lay people would be well formed in the sacred sciences, the council continued: "In order that such persons may fulfill their proper function, let it be recognized that all of the faithful, clerical and lay, possess a lawful freedom of inquiry and of thought, and the freedom to express their minds humbly and courageously about those matters in which they enjoy competence." The council pointedly did not say that clergy and lay people should speak up only if they agreed with magisterial statements. They are to speak because presumably the church can and must learn from them. There is no talk here about taking one's problems quietly to magisterial authorities, about writing only in professional journals, about not speaking to the media, about suffering in silence. Such caveats flow from a rather remarkably different ecclesiology.

The open and unthreatened perspectives we find in the council contrast quite notably with those in the June 26, 1990, document of the Congregation for the Doctrine of the Faith (C.D.F.) entitled, "Instruction on the Ecclesial Vocation of the Theologian" (*Origins*, 7/5/90). We believe that document to be a veritable charter for the privatization of theology and all that it involves.

The C.D.F. Instruction, signed by Cardinal Joseph Ratzinger, Prefect of the Congregation for the Doctrine of the Faith, and Archbishop Alberto Bovone, secretary of the Congregation for the Doctrine of the Faith, distinguishes between dissent and the personal difficulties a theologian might have with a particular teaching. The document describes dissent as "attitudes of general opposition to church teaching which even come to expression in organized groups." Or again, it is said to be "public opposition to the magisterium of the church." It is further depicted as an attitude toward noninfallible teachings that sees them as having "no obligatory character about them, leaving the individual completely at liberty to adhere to them or not. The theologian would accordingly be totally free to raise doubts or reject the noninfallible teaching of the magisterium, particularly in the case of specific moral norms" (pp. 123–25). In brief, dissent involves disrespect for, and even rejection of, the authoritative magisterium.

This idiosyncratic description of dissent leaves us with two unrealistic alternatives. Either there is no dissent in the church according to the document's description (for we know of no theologians who believe they are totally free to reject noninfallible teachings) or any dissent is unacceptable because it inevitably involves disrespect. We view this as idiosyncratic because most people understand dissent as disagreement with a particular teaching, not overall rejection of the teacher or of teaching authority as such.

That leads to what the document refers to as the "personal difficulties" of a theologian with a particular teaching. We shall cite the document fully here because it is at the heart of our accusation of privatization. The case concerns "non-irreformable magisterial teaching." The document states: "If despite a loyal effort on the theologian's part the difficulties persist, the theologian has the duty to make known to the magisterial authorities the problems raised by the teaching in itself, in the arguments proposed to justify it or even in the manner in which it is presented. He [sic] should do this in an evangelical spirit and with a profound desire to resolve the difficulties. His objections could then contribute to real progress and provide a stimulus to the magisterium to propose the teaching of the church in greater depth and with a clearer presentation of the argument.

"In cases like these, the theologian should avoid turning to the 'mass media' but have recourse to the responsible authority, for it is not by seeking to exert the pressure of public opinion that one contributes to the clarification of doctrinal issues and renders service to the truth.

"It can also happen that at the conclusion of a serious study, undertaken with the desire to heed the magisterium's teaching without hesitation, the theologian's difficulty remains because the arguments to the contrary seem more persuasive to him. Faced with a proposition to which he feels he cannot give his intellectual assent, the theologian nevertheless has the duty to remain open to a deeper examination of the question.

"For a loyal spirit, animated by love for the church, such a situation can certainly prove a difficult trial. It can be a call to suffer for the truth, in silence and prayer but with the certainty that if the truth really is at stake it will ultimately prevail" (p. 123).

These interesting paragraphs give rise to a host of tantalizing questions. For instance, what confidence would an individual theologian have that his "recourse to the responsible authority" would do any good if even public statements by whole groups of theologians (e.g., the so-called Cologne Statement) are ignored? Does not the hierarchical magisterium also have a "duty to remain open to a deeper examination of the question," especially when it knows that large numbers of theologians worldwide disagree with certain of its teachings? What are theologians to do when their theological representations are met with intransigence? Or when genuinely debatable issues are prematurely closed or said to be no longer a matter of free theological debate? Is every statement to the mass media an attempt "to exert the pressure of public opinion"? Why can it not be viewed as an attempt to inform the public or air one's own view "humbly and courageously," as Vatican II worded it? It is our belief that the Holy See is not concerned about theologians using the media, but their using the media to voice disagreement. In this sense the Holy See is not opposed to publicity, but only to bad publicity. But it cannot defend such inconsistency. If Rome wants support for its good statements from its theologians in the media, it must expect a similar honesty when its deliverances are less than compelling.

But our concern with such questions is peripheral. The single feature in the C.D.F. document that we wish to underline is that when the theologian finds her/himself unable to assent—we would call this dissent—that person is to (1) represent the dissent to magisterial authorities; (2) not state it to the media, and (3) indeed, remain silent. Some commentators have stated that the Ratzinger document does not mean to exclude publication in scholarly journals. Perhaps that is so, but we find no basis for that reading in the Instruction. The Instruction regards a dissenting opinion as a "call to suffer for the truth, *in silence. . . .*" (our emphasis). At one point Cardinal

Ratzinger refers to "*untimely* public expression" of an opinion divergent from that of the magisterium (our emphasis). But the C.D.F.'s statements and actions, for example in the Curran case (*America*, 9/8–15/90), indicate that *any* public expression of dissent is regarded as untimely. In sum, the C.D.F. removes any disagreement with authoritative noninfallible teaching from the public realm. We call that the privatization of theology.

This privatization of theology has its roots in a very definite ecclesiology, one we believe was abandoned by Vatican II. The key element in this ecclesiology is the pyramidal structure of the church and, as a result, the heavily obediential character given to the teaching-learning process of the church. It is basically an authority problem. Bishop Raymond A. Lucker, Bishop of New Ulm, Minn., words our point as follows: "For those in power in Rome, the church is not 'the people of God' that Vatican II talked about. It is an imperial monarchy that must maintain absolute control" (*The New Yorker*, 7/22/91, p. 52). The teaching-learning process of the church is viewed within the dominance of the superior-subject relationship. For this reason Bishop Lucker accurately notes that "in such a system, those in charge can exercise raw power, because their judgment is automatically correct and they need not worry about the consequences. They have to be right; that is the highest aim, good, object. And conversely, error has no rights. So if you are deemed to be in error, Rome feels that it has the duty to punish you."

The glaring symbol of all this is the Instruction's unqualified assertion that "the pastoral task of the magisterium is one of vigilance" (No. 20, p. 122). Once that foot is forward, it becomes clear why open discussion amounts to "confusion of the faithful" and why confusion at any level is seen as an unmitigated disaster. It also becomes clear why unity is confused with uniformity on all matters. It becomes clear why consultation is limited, why authorship is secret, why disagreement is not tolerated—in brief, why theology *must be* privatized. If vigilance is the self-description of the pastoral task of the magisterium, then theologians are above all those who are watched, scrutinized and eventually controlled.

The working out of this ecclesiology is inexorable and predictable. Only a privatized theology is a safe theology, and only an atmosphere of coercion will keep theology safely privatized. Thus it is that bishops are "unwilling to talk openly." Thus it is that theologians avoid subjects where disagreement is not tolerated, or seek employment in non-Catholic institutions where disagreement is no occupational threat. Thus it is that seminarians are directed to "safe" seminaries where teaching and scholarship are second-rate at best.

But coercion can be extremely harmful. Avery Dulles, S.J., once noted (*Church*, Fall 1986) that the effort to stamp out dissent "inhibits good theology from performing its critical task, and is detrimental to the atmosphere of freedom in the church." Just how detrimental was made clear by Archbishop Rembert G. Weakland, O.S.B., Archbishop of Milwaukee, Wisc., in a column he wrote for his archdiocesan newspaper in 1986. He noted that the suppressions associated with the Modernist crisis "resulted in a total lack of theological creativity in the U.S.A. for half a century."

We see the following effects of a coercive ecclesial atmosphere that attempts to privatize theology:

The Weakening of the Episcopal Magisterium.

Here we should recall the theological force of episcopal agreement described in Vatican II's Constitution on the Church, No. 25. If the bishops around the world are united with the pope in their teaching, then that teaching can achieve a greater level of stability and certainty, and indeed can achieve infallible status if the teaching is a proper object of infallibility and is presented as something to be held definitively. But the unity must be genuine and clear.

In a coercive atmosphere both the genuineness and clarity are put in serious doubt. First, the genuineness. Here we should recall one of the arguments made during the deliberations of the so-called Papal Birth Control Commission. It was contended that the church could not modify its teaching on birth regulation because that teaching had been proposed unanimously as certain by the bishops around the world with the pope over a long period of time. To this point Cardinal Leo Josef Suenens, former Archbishop of Malines-Brussels, replied: "We have heard arguments based on 'what the bishops all taught for decades.' Well, the bishops did defend the classical position. But it was one imposed on them by authority. The bishops didn't study the pros and cons. They received directives, they bowed to them and they tried to explain them to their congregations" (see Robert Blair Kaiser, *The Politics of Sex and Religion,* Leaven, 1981, p. 170). In a coercive atmosphere people will repeat things because they are told to and are threatened with punishment if they say anything else. Episcopal unity is revealed as enforced, not genuine.

As for clarity, the more likely scenario in a coercive atmosphere is that the bishops (some at least) will say nothing if they disagree. In such circumstances, to read episcopal silence as unanimity is self-deceptive.

When the genuineness and clarity of episcopal agreement have been cast into grave doubt by a coercive atmosphere, the episcopal magisterium itself has been undermined. The meaning of consensus has been eviscerated. The bishops should be the first ones to protest this diminishment of their magisterium and the atmosphere that grounds it.

The Weakening of the Papal Magisterium.

This follows from the first point. If bishops are not speaking their true sentiments, then clearly the pope is not able to draw on the wisdom and reflection of the bishops in the exercise of his ordinary magisterium. When this happens, the presumption of truth in papal teaching is weakened, or even destroyed, because such a presumption assumes that the ordinary sources of human understanding have been consulted, as the late Karl Rahner so repeatedly argued. That is why what is called the "enforcement of doctrine" is literally counterproductive. It weakens the very vehicle (papal magisterium) that proposes to be the agent of strength and certainty.

The Marginalization of Theologians.

Coercive measures will almost certainly have the effect of quieting theologians, at least on certain issues. This feature erodes both the episcopal and papal magisterium by silencing yet another source of understanding and growth. If reputable theologians are marginalized, the magisterium is proportionately weakened. And it is no response to exclude from the "reputable" category those with whom one disagrees. That begs the question.

The Demoralization of Priests.

When juridical coercion too easily dominates the church's teaching-learning process, priests (and other ministers) become demoralized because they are expected to be the official spokespersons for positions they cannot always and in every detail support. Thus they become torn between their official loyalties and their better judgments and compassion, and become victims of a kind of occupational schizophrenia. This was explicitly observed in a 1988 document issued by the N.C.C.B.'s Committee on Priestly Life and Ministry (*Origins*, 1/12/89). The document, entitled "Reflections on the Morale of Priests," noted that differing perceived ecclesiologies lead to demoralization. Specifically, it called attention to the fact that "some priests feel that at times they are passing on to parishioners, who clearly disagree, pastoral decisions which they sense their bishops do not fully endorse and which they themselves personally question. 'Caught in the middle' is an apt description" (p. 501).

The Reduction of the Laity.

Coercive insistence on official formulations tells the laity in no uncertain terms that their experience and reflection make little difference—this in spite of Vatican II's contrary invitation to the laity to express themselves "humbly and courageously." If such humble expression counts for nothing, we experience yet another wound to the authority of the ordinary magisterium.

The Compromise of Future Ministry.

When a rigid orthodoxy is imposed on seminarians in the name of unity and order, the very ability of these future priests to minister to post-Vatican II Catholics is seriously jeopardized. We have seen this happen. Many thousands of Catholics have studied and struggled to assimilate the council's perspectives. They do not understand and will not accept a new paternalism in pedagogy. This means frustration and crisis for the minister trained to practice such a pedagogy.

The Loss of the Catholic Leaven.

Coercive insistence that the term "official teaching" is simply synonymous with "right," "certain," "sound" and "unchangeable" (an identification powerfully supported by the suppression of any public dissent) will lead to the public perception that the role of Catholic scholars is an intellectual form of public relations. That means the serious loss of theological credibility in precisely those areas of modern development (e.g., science and technology) where the church should desire to exercise a formative influence. The present pontiff wants both to unite the church and to shape the world, both utterly laudable apostolic objectives. The means to the former could doom the latter.

In summary, the exclusion of public theological questioning and critique will deprive the People of God of the fruits of open and honest reflection on the practical implications of their faith. They have a right to this, as we shall develop below. For this reason we agree with a recent statement of the distinguished theologian and homilist Walter J. Burghardt, S.J. Speaking of controversial issues and preaching he noted: "On such issues, in a short span of time, I dare not speak in dogmatic fashion, as if I alone am the trumpet of the Lord. But if I dare not dogmatize, I may still raise the issues, lay them out, even say where I stand and why. Not to impose my convictions as gospel, but as a spur to personal and communal reflection" (Woodstock Report, June, 1991). If this is true of the homilist, it is, we believe, *a fortiori* true of the theologian.

This brings us to our second major point, the public nature of theology. Theology is public in nature, first because *faith* is public in nature; second, because it is done always in the service of the *church,* which is the whole People of God; third, because it serves the *pastoral* needs of the church, and fourth, because theologians are true *teachers.*

Theology is public in nature, first, because *faith* is public in nature. St. Anselm of Canterbury's definition of theology is "faith seeking understanding." If theology is private, then so, too, is faith.

But such a conclusion would be absurd on its face. Faith has always been understood as a gift of God to be shared with others. God communicated and made a covenant in Christ with a people, a community. This self-communication and covenant are public in character. Therefore, deepening Christian faith by critical reflection upon it is an inherently public undertaking. Consequently, this faith is to be proclaimed, witnessed to and even died for. " 'This word is near you, in your mouth and in your heart' (that is, the word of faith that we preach), for if you confess with your mouth that Jesus is Lord and believe in your heart that God raised Him from the dead, you will be saved" (Rom. 10:8–9).

Thus, it is impossible (because radically illogical) for a faith inherently public to be critically reflected upon and articulated only in private. To be sure, those who argue for the private nature of theology are not consistent. When a particular theologian's conclusions are consonant with, or supportive of official teachings, no objection is raised against making those conclusions public. Theology is public in nature, second, because it is done always in the service of the *church.* But, as Vatican II reminded us, the church is the whole People of God, not just the hierarchy. This is to say that theology is not done primarily, much less exclusively, in the service of the hierarchy, but primarily for the sake of the whole community of faith and, beyond that, for the wider human community.

The proposal, even by implication, that the theologian is only a behind-the-scenes adviser to the hierarchy (the pope, the other bishops and the curia) serving always and only under their mandate and at their pleasure, is to suggest that the other members of the church (the vast majority) have no direct personal or communal interest in the process by which their own faith is examined and explained, nor in the practical outcomes of those deliberations.

Such a proposal, even if only implicit, suggests that those outside the hierarchy have no capacity—intellectual, moral or spiritual—to grasp the theological process or its outcomes. Accordingly, the attempt to privatize theology and the faith that theology seeks to understand insults the intelligence, good will and powers of spiritual discernment of educated lay persons, religious and clergy, and deprives them of what is theirs by baptismal right: an understanding of their faith commensurate with their intellectual, psychological, moral and spiritual development.

Even the Revised Code of Canon Law, following the lead of Vatican II, acknowledges this as a right. The Christian faithful "have become sharers in Christ's priestly, prophetic and royal office [and] are called to exercise the mission which God has entrusted to the church to fulfill in the world, in accord with the condition proper to each one" (Canon 204, No. 1).

As such, they have "the right to a Christian education by which they will be properly instructed so as to develop the maturity of a human person and at the same time come to know and live the mystery of salvation" (Canon 217). More specifically, "Lay persons are bound by the obligation and possess the right to acquire a knowledge of Christian doctrine adapted to their capacity and condition so that they can live in accord with that doctrine, announce it, defend it when necessary, and be enabled to assume their role in exercising the apostolate" (Canon 229, No. 1). They also "possess the right to acquire that deeper knowledge of the sacred sciences" (No. 2).

Theology is public in nature, third, because it serves the *pastoral* needs of the church. Religious educators, catechists and preachers of the word depend upon theology because they have the ministerial responsibility of "echoing" (the literal meaning of catechesis), handing on and proclaiming the faith—a responsibility that is simply impossible to fulfill without theology. Indeed, faith itself cannot be apprehended except theologically. To be self-conscious of one's faith is already to be engaged in a theological interpretation of it, no matter how rudimentary, inchoate or unscientific that interpretation may be.

The question, therefore, is not *whether* the faith will be echoed, handed on and proclaimed theologically, but rather *what kind of* theology will be employed in the process. As suggested above, the privatization of theology is not really the privatization of all theology, but only of the theology done by scientifically competent theologians who will inevitably disagree from time to time with one aspect or another of certain official teachings. There is no attempt to privatize the "safe" theology of many bishops, of many members of the curia and of "approved" theologians. But the public—both inside and outside the church—is less and less interested in that "safe" theology because it seems to them incapable of illuminating and strengthening their faith or of drawing out its implications in an increasingly complex world. It is widely met with apathy.

Unfortunately, the Vatican's view of today's laity seems to be captured in the odious term "simple faithful." In a well-publicized paper given at St. Michael's College, Toronto, on April 15, 1986, Cardinal Ratzinger put it straightforwardly: "The church's main job is the care of the faith of the simple. A truly reverential awe should arise from this which becomes an internal rule of thumb for every theologian" ("The Church and the Theologian," *Origins,* 5/8/86, p. 769). Moreover, Cardinal Ratzinger has made this the governing rule for ecclesiastical authorities as well. Their primary responsibility is to protect the simple faithful against theologians who criticize in any way whatever an official teaching of the church. "The care of the faith of the 'little ones,'" he insisted, "must always be more important than the fear of some conflict with the powerful" (p. 770).

Theology is public in nature, fourth, because theologians are true *teachers*. As Avery Dulles, S.J., has persuasively argued, the term "magisterium" itself applies to theologians as well as to bishops, and this has been the case since the Middle Ages (see *A Church to Believe In*).

Father Dulles has characterized as "reductionist" the view that collapses theology into the hierarchical magisterium. "On the ground that the ecclesiastical magisterium has a higher access to the truth (*charisma veritatis*), it is argued that the pope and bishops, by virtue of their grace of office, can do better everything that the theologian as such can do. The idea that the theologian might also have a grace of office seems not to be considered." That idea is conspicuously absent from the Vatican's "Instruction on the Ecclesial Vocation of the Theologian."

Our argument is that the theologian's grace of office necessarily involves him/her in public discourse and indeed the kind of discourse that cannot exclude some tension and disagreement. The theologian engages in this public discourse at a variety of levels and through a variety of means: the media, the academy, publications and conferences.

First, in the electronic and print media. If theology has no place in the media, then a critically examined faith has no place in the media. And if that is the case, then society itself is effectively closed off from a critically examined faith. The result is that religion, and Christianity in particular, will remain for society a naive belief at best, a dangerous superstition at worst. Nevertheless, the Vatican Instruction looks upon the media only in negative terms, as the place to which dissident theologians repair in order to "exert the pressure of public opinion" on the formulation of doctrine (No. 30).

Other groups take a broader and more positive view of the media. For instance, one does not hear the American Medical Association complaining when almost every month on network television news a tentative scientific finding in the latest issue of *The New England Journal of Medicine* is broadcast to millions of viewers. Professionals know that if their journals are not cited or if society takes no interest in their research, they are simply irrelevant. Therefore, they see the media as extensions of their work, not as its enemies.

More to the point, if theologians are not engaged with the media, they lose an extraordinary opportunity for education and at the same time a vacuum is created. Religious issues *are* of profound interest to the wider public. But if competent theologians are not available (or willing) to discuss them, others will be sought out for comment and interpretation in their stead. Vacuums have a way of attracting amateurs. The real concern of the church should not be to restrict or stifle such public reflection, but to educate the public to both its need and its limits.

The theologian engages in public discourse, second, in academic settings, especially the university. Several aspects of this engagement highlight the public character of theology. Universities and colleges, even those which are private, are public institutions in the sense that they are subject to law and open to public scrutiny. Next, while there are a few theologians who engage only in research (the so-called "ivory tower" scholar), almost all professionally active theologians have teaching positions, a public function. Furthermore, all active theologians, in turn, are members of professional organizations, e.g., the Catholic Theological Society of America and the American Academy of Religion, whose meetings and publications are also public in nature. The theologian engages in public discourse, third, through his or her own scholarly writings in professional journals, collections, monographs, encyclopedias and journals like *America* and *Commonweal.* It is important to note that even scholarly journals, such as *Theological Studies,* are public in nature. Anyone can subscribe to them; anyone can go to a library and read them. It is utterly naive, therefore, to think that the general public can be insulated from theological controversy if theologians confine their "speculations" to professional journals, just as naive as to think that the general public can be insulated from medical controversy by medical scientists' confining *their* writing to *The New England Journal of Medicine.*

The theologian engages in public discourse, fourth, through lectures and addresses given at national, regional and local conferences of religious educators and other pastoral ministers. Theologians do not invite themselves to these meetings. They are asked to speak because religious educators, catechists and other pastoral ministers perceive the need for up-to-date, academically and pastorally credible theological interpretation and recognize, at the same time, the limited usefulness of approved theology, which is little more than a "party line."

Because faith is a public possession and theology is a public reflection, the real and abiding challenge to the church today is first-class education at all levels. Public theological discourse, whether through the media, academic institutions, publications or conferences, is an essential vehicle of this education. Theology has a responsibility to the church, the intellectual and professional communities and society at large to provide a critical explanation and interpretation of the faith and to clarify its personal and social (economic, cultural and political) implications in an increasingly complex world. The attempt to privatize theology is a flight from this responsibility.

Gustavo Gutierrez

4 Reflections from a Latin American Theologian

The following excerpt is taken from Irruption of the Third World, *a compilation of papers from a conference of the Ecumenical Association of Third World Theologians (EATWOT) held during August, 1981, in New Delhi, India. The conference was the second of two such gatherings, the first having been held at Dar es Salaam, Tanzania, in 1976.*
—The Editors [of *Sojourners*]

In the years between the EATWOT conferences in Dar es Salaam (1976) and New Delhi (1981) something unusual occurred in the churches of the Third World. Christians who had shouldered ecclesial responsibility and the task of theologizing in those countries, and among the black and Hispanic minorities in the United States, began to get together to share their diverse reflections on their common faith in the God of Jesus Christ. In the past they had customarily met as students in the major theology departments of Europe and North America, or had occasionally been invited to meet in those surroundings. Now they were meeting on their own initiative in the setting of poor countries.

The first country to host these meetings was Tanzania, a small country inhabited by a poor, very poor, population. Its people bears the marks of a harsh past involving colonial rule and racial contempt. But Tanzanians have also shown much courage and creativity in undertaking a thoroughgoing process of liberation. Exploring their roots in their native African tradition, they have set out on their own to construct a just and humane order. This accounts for the disproportionate moral authority exercised by that small nation and its president, Julius Nyerere, in the concert of nations. The achievements of the Tanzanian people enable us to perceive and concretely experience the significance of the poor in history.

After continental meetings in Africa, Latin America, and Asia, a tricontinental meeting was held in New Delhi. There in India we encountered a country whose

This article was translated by John Drury. Originally published in *Sojourners* (February 1983), 12:26–29. Reprinted with permission from *Sojourners*, 2401 15th Street NW, Washington, DC 20009; (202) 328-8842/ (800) 714-7474.

vastness is both geographical and historical in nature. We were deeply impressed by the poverty of its people, and the thin bodies of New Delhi are still before our eyes. But we were also deeply impressed by its rich cultural and religious heritage. Held in the midst of a small minority of native Christians, our meeting of theologians became aware of its own insignificance. The people of India, poor and profoundly religious, brought us back forcefully to the center of our faith: the mystery of God.

Thus Tanzania and India were not just different geographical locales and different cultural landscapes. They were real theological lessons. The peoples of those countries were living witnesses of God and the poor. For us those experiences represent the starting point for a theology that seeks to combine diverse efforts into a process of reflection carried out from the underside of history. As was the case in the Bible, God and the poor are its great themes.

Some may well see all this as an obsession, feeling that it is time to move on to new questions. But the fact is that poverty, the result of unjust national and international structures, is our historical territory. It is there that our peoples affirm their faith and hope in God. If our theology is not framed in the context of the salvific dialogue between God and the poor, then it ceases to be the word of God in history about the gift of faith.

When we began in Dar es Salaam, we said in the final statement, "We are prepared for a radical break in epistemology which makes commitment the first act of theology and engages in critical reflection on the praxis of the reality of the Third World." The point was spelled out a bit further on in the same statement: "Our conviction is that the theologian should have a fuller understanding of living in the Holy Spirit, for this also means being committed to a lifestyle of solidarity with the poor and the oppressed and involvement in action with them." The New Delhi document picks up the same perspective:

> The starting point for Third World theologies is the struggle of the poor and oppressed against all forms of injustice and domination. The committed involvement of Christians in this struggle provides a new locus for theological reflection. Their participation is faith in action and the manifestation of Christian commitment, which constitute the first act of theology.

To say that commitment is the first act of Christian living is to say that the reflection of faith on it must be deeply rooted in the Christian community. It is the assembly of the Lord's disciples as such that is responsible for the proclamation of the gospel message in words and deeds. One is a theologian insofar as one is linked to the life and commitments of a Christian community. Only within such a community does one have a theological function to carry out; that function is an ecclesial task.

This view necessarily makes for a more fluid boundary between those we usually call theologians and those we regard as committed Christians with some sort of ecclesial responsibility. In the broadest and most basic sense, every Christian is a theologian. The first and primary initiator of discourse on the faith is the Christian community located within nations and peoples who are struggling to assert their dignity as human beings and children of God, and to build a just society. And that is our situation, of course.

It is here that we are confronted with various questions, if our theological reflections are supposed to be based on the concretely experienced life of the poor in our world. Can we convene only those who are professionals in the theological world: professors, authors, and so forth? Or should we also invite other Christians involved with other functions within the Christian community? And there is another uncomfortable question raised by the Dar es Salaam statement about a "radical break." If we take that seriously, must we not restrict the kind of theologian we invite to these meetings? And if we do, what effect will that have on strictly theological work?

I do not think we have fully faced up to those questions or answered them yet, which is not surprising. But there the questions stand in any case, forcing us out of our old certainties and opening up new pathways that we must travel one step at a time.

Let me give one example. Our new way of conceiving the work of theologizing has prompted us to hold joint meetings between those whose focus and specialty is theology and those whose work is basically on the grassroots level. Continental meetings, in particular, have tended to be joint meetings of that sort. All of us have gained a wider, overall vision and found our reflection enriched by such joint meetings. But it cannot be denied that they have also given rise to certain tensions.

It is our deep and irreversible conviction that we must avoid an academic theology dissociated from grassroots work, where the "first act" of theology is taken. The point is important and bears stressing. Such a dissociation is ruled out, not just because we want to elaborate a committed theology, but even more importantly because we want to develop a discourse on faith that will respond to the real questions raised by the contemporary world and the Christian community living in it. In short, we rule out such a dissociation because we want a truly serious and scientific theology. By the same token, however, we must acknowledge that the work of theologizing, if it is to be rigorous in its elaboration and universal in scope, calls for a painstaking knowledge of Scripture and careful correlation with both the Christian tradition and contemporary theology. But proper handling of those theological fonts and all the requirements entailed in the process are not always fully appreciated from the standpoint of grassroots urgencies.

These differences in emphasis have sometimes led to sharp debates at our meetings, and the resulting tensions have not been completely resolved. The point I want to stress here, however, is that such confrontations are basically sound and healthy. They are to be found not only in and between groups but also inside every Christian individual who wants to be committed and at the same time wants to reflect on the faith. In short, this tension is to be found in all those persons we call theologians. In the last analysis it is a very beneficial and enriching thing, stemming from our new way of viewing theology rather than from minor or transient issues. In our conception there is really no place for the old circle of theologians as a separate, clearly defined and delimited group within the Christian community.

When we say that commitment to the struggles of the poor for decent and just living conditions is an indispensable precondition for a sound, intelligent under-

standing of the faith, we are not simply raising a question of theological methodology. We are talking about a specific way of understanding what it means to be a
Christian. We are framing method (Greek *hodos,* "way" or "path") within the broader
context of the Christian life. And in the Acts of the Apostles we find that the Christian
life is actually described as "the way" initiated by Jesus (Acts 9:2, 18:25, 19:9). The
Christian way is prior to the theological way.

The first and most basic thing in this process is charity or love, the only thing that
will endure (1 Corinthians 13). The discourse of theology, which in the last analysis
is always reflection on God, comes from and moves toward the love of God. That love
implies contemplation and practice: we worship God and we put his will into practice by accepting the gift of his kingdom. Only then is it time to bring up discourse
about God. To put it in our by now familiar terms: contemplation and practice together constitute the first act; theologizing is the second act. First comes the mystical
life and practice; only then can we have any authentic, respectful reflection about
God. The mystery of God comes to live in contemplation and in practice (i.e., in solidarity with the poor). Only then, in the second stage, can that way of life give rise to
a reasoning process, a discourse.

Contemplation and practice make up the moment of silence before God. Theology
(Greek *logoa,* "reason," "word") is a reasoned talking about God. But to this contemplative aspect of silence we must add the dimension of committed solidarity with the
poor and their efforts to end centuries of oppression. We know that from the witness
of the poor in our nations, of which Tanzania and its people are one example. Both
dimensions of the first act are to be found in the concrete experience of the poor, and
they are mutually related.

Silence, then, is one of the preconditions for any talk about God. And distinguish-
ing between these two moments is not simply a question of methodology, as I noted
above; it involves a particular style of life. It is a particular way of living our faith in
the Lord, of living according to the Spirit. It is a question of spirituality in the strict
sense of the word. Our epistemological break in the work of theologizing, as proclaimed in Dar es Salaam, also entails a break in the way we live as Christians and
theologians. We must not forget that exigency if we wish to be faithful to the Lord
and our peoples.

This way of viewing our theological approach only serves to emphasize the point I
made earlier: the close tie between the process of discoursing on the faith on the one
hand, and the life of the churches on the other. It becomes clear that our experiences
over the past five years entailed more than meetings between theologians, they were
confrontations between theologies. They were efforts to link the life and death, the
hopes and struggles, of this world's poor to salvation in Jesus Christ. And the primary
agents of such efforts are the poor themselves and the communities in which they
share their faith in a liberating God. Such a theology imposes an obligation on those
Christians who engage in the specific field of theology. It demands that theologians
have deep, ongoing involvement in the evangelizing work of their churches and in
the struggles of their peoples. Only then can they be both bearers and articulators of
the faith-understanding arising from the underside of history.

In the final document of the Dar es Salaam conference we said:

> The theologies from Europe and North America are dominant today in our churches and represent one form of cultural domination. They must be understood to have arisen out of situations related to those countries, and therefore must not be uncritically adopted without our raising the question of their relevance in the context of our countries.

Despite all that has been written about this matter in recent years, the phenomenon is still new. For the first time in centuries a new type of theological reflection is arising outside the major European centers of theological work and their North American extensions. The fact still evokes surprise, if not skepticism, hostility, or paternalistic condescension. These varied reactions are not confined to theological circles in Europe or North America. They can also be found in churches of the Third World and churches ministering to minorities in the United States. In all of them some segments still follow and respond to the dominant theologies, for a variety of reasons.

Given that situation, we can readily understand why our advocacy of a new approach to theological reflection might spark controversy. Such controversy is inevitable and necessary in certain circumstances; but it is not the fundamental thing, and it is not without its own ambiguities. The really crucial thing is to realize and appreciate the fact that there are different perspectives associated with different historical situations and different interlocutors.

I have offered my own characterization of the difference in approach between our theology and that of the affluent countries. In the churches living in affluent countries, theology more attentive to contemporary problems tends to regard the modern mind and spirit as its chief interlocutor. It addresses itself to the modern person, who is an unbeliever in many instances, and to the liberal ideology espoused historically by the middle class. By contrast, theology deriving from the poor majorities of the human race seeks to answer the questions raised by those "without history," by the "nonpersons" who are oppressed and marginalized specifically by the interlocutor of the dominant theologies. So the issue is not simply one of theological niceties. We are talking about two theological perspectives that respond to different needs and questioners.

When theologies take shape as reflection on the faith insofar as it is lived out in solidarity with the lives and struggles of the poor, they are not being driven by any terrible itch for originality in their field. They are simply trying to be loyal to the Lord of history, to lend their support to the proclamation of the gospel and the liberation efforts of their peoples.

Theologizing is both a right and a duty for any people that is both poor and Christian. To evade that task is to create a vacuum that will quickly be filled by reflections centered around other categories, interests, and goals. Such was the case in the past, and it remains the case today. To evade the task would be to betray the experiences and aspirations of the poor and oppressed.

A theology stemming from the poor and their breakthrough into church life and world history is necessarily framed in terms of the dialectic between life and death.

It is from there that it seeks to talk about God, the ultimate ground of the meaning that the poor have for any and every Christian.

Solidarity with the human struggle against poverty and for a more just and humane social order presupposes an option for life. One thing, at least, is becoming increasingly clear to our peoples: poverty means death. We see the untimely and unjust death of the vast majority of humanity produced by a socio-economic system that is international in scope. That majority is made up of the poor people in Third World countries and the oppressed minorities in affluent nations. We see death occasioned by starvation, illness, and the repressive measures of those who find their privileged position threatened by every effort at liberation on the part of the oppressed. To physical death is added cultural death. The ruling sectors seek to destroy everything that will give unity and strength to the deprived sectors, so that the latter may more readily fall prey to the machinery of oppression.

All this is implied in our talk about poverty and the destruction of persons, nations, cultures, and traditions. When the poor seek to liberate themselves from those death-dealing conditions, which some are euphemistically calling "living conditions," they are expressing their will to live. Contrary to what is sometimes thought, the challenge facing us is not simply that of a "social situation." It is not something wholly extraneous to the basic demands of the gospel message. Instead we face a situation that runs directly contrary to the kingdom of life proclaimed by our Lord.

In the mystery of Jesus there is revealed to us a dialectic between death and life. That same dialectic pervades our historical situation, surprising us by its current relevance and its demands. Our discourse of faith arises out of our involvement with the reality of the poor—their premature death and their struggles for liberation. Such a discourse, such a theology, cannot help but be an affirmation of life. To be more specific, it cannot help but be a paschal theology dealing with the passage from death to life.

The conditions surrounding the life and death of the poor bring us back to the essence of the biblical message: paschal faith in the life-giving victory of the risen one over death. In a real sense we cannot depart from that central theme if we want to forge what our Asian brothers call a relevant theology. Because of our focus on this essential message of the gospel, our theology may be very unsophisticated and indeed elementary. This only makes for closer ties between theologians and nontheologians in the Christian community.

Proclamation of Christ's resurrection is the heart of the gospel message because it fully and forcefully reveals the kingdom to be a kingdom of life. That message calls us together as church, as a community of witnesses to the fact that death is not history's last word. As the perplexed disciples stood before the empty tomb, they were asked: "Why search among the dead for one who lives?" (Luke 24:5). To be witnesses to the resurrection means to give life, and bearing witness to life takes on special importance from the standpoint of Third World poverty.

Such witness compels us to find a way to talk about God. We need a language rooted in the unjust poverty that surrounds the vast majorities, but also nurtured by the faith and hope of a people struggling for its liberation. We need a language that is both contemplative and prophetic: contemplative because it ponders a God who is love; prophetic because it talks about a liberator God who rejects the situation of injustice in which the poor live, and also the structural causes of that situation. As was the case in the book of Job, both idioms arise in Third World countries out of the suffering and hope of innocent victims.

How are we to talk about God in terms of such a state of affairs? Here we come to what may well impress and exasperate the ruling classes most. It is the fact that the poor see their struggle for liberation as a way of "cleaving to God," to echo a phrase from Deuteronomy in which the fundamental dilemma of a believing life is brought vividly before us:

> Today I offer you the choice of life and good, or death and evil . . . I offer you the choice of life or death, blessing or curse. Choose life and then you and your descendants will live; love the Lord your God, obey him and hold fast to him. (Deuteronomy 30: 15, 19–20)

The fight for liberation is an option for life and a rejection of untimely and unjust death. What is more, the poor and exploited see this fight as an exigency of their faith in God the liberator.

A new prophetic and mystical language about God is arising in these lands filled with exploitation and hope. We are learning anew how to say God. We are seeing the first stages of a process of reflection that seeks to give expression to the life of faith and hope being lived by the oppressed everywhere. It is the language of those in whose faces, noted the Puebla conference, "We ought to recognize the suffering features of Christ the Lord, who questions and challenges us."

This new language reminds us that the ultimate reason behind our option for the poor and our solidarity with their struggles is the God in whom we believe. There may well be other reasons for this privileged commitment. For the follower of Christ, however, this solidarity is ultimately rooted in our faith in the God of life. Above and beyond all the efforts, limitations, and achievements of our theologizing from the standpoint of the poor, we find that something fundamental is at stake: our very faith in God.

Ours is an effort to speak from the standpoint of the poor and their silence. If those who have the role of theological articulation mean to do that, then they must share in that silence of contemplation and practice; they must participate in the sufferings of the innocent poor. Otherwise our theology will merit the same reproach that Job hurled at his pompous friends:

> I have heard such things often before, you who make trouble, all of you, with every breath, saying, "Will this windbag never have done? What makes him so stubborn in argument?" If you and I were to change places, I could talk like you; how I could harangue you and wag my head at you! But no, I would speak words of encouragement, and then my condolences would flow in streams. (Job 16:2–5)

Robert Allan Warrior

5   Canaanites, Cowboys, and Indians: Deliverance, Conquest, and Liberation Theology Today

A Native American theology of Liberation has a nice ring to it. Politically active Christians in the U.S. have been bandying about the idea of such a theology for several years now, encouraging Indians to develop it. There are theologies of liberation for African Americans, Hispanic Americans, women, Asian Americans, even Jews. Why not Native Americans? Christians recognize that American injustice on this continent began nearly 500 years ago with the oppression of its indigenous people and that justice for American Indians is a fundamental part of broader social struggle. The churches' complicity in much of the violence perpetrated on Indians makes this realization even clearer. So, there a lot of well-intentioned Christians looking for some way to include Native Americans in their political action.

For Native Americans involved in political struggle, the participation of church people is often an attractive proposition. Churches have financial, political, and institutional resources that many Indian activists would dearly love to have at their disposal. Since American Indians have a relatively small population base and few financial resources, assistance from churches can be of great help in gaining the attention of the public, the media, and the government.

It sounds like the perfect marriage—Christians with the desire to include Native Americans in their struggle for justice and Indian activists in need of resources and support from non-Indians. Well, speaking as the product of a marriage between an Indian and a white, I can tell you that it is not as easy as it sounds. The inclusion of Native Americans in Christian political praxis is difficult—even dangerous. Christians have a different way of viewing the relationship between politics and religion.

Originally published in *Christianity and Crisis* (September 11, 1989), 261–264. Reprinted with the permission of *Christianity and Crisis*.

These differences have gone all but unnoticed in the history of church involvement in American Indian affairs. Liberals and conservatives alike have too often surveyed the conditions of Native Americans and decided to come to the rescue, always using *their* methods, *their* ideas, and *their* programs. The idea that Indians might know best how to address their own problems is seemingly lost on these well-meaning folks.

Still, the time does seem ripe: to find a new way for Indians and Christians (and Native American Christians) to be partners in the struggle against injustice and economic and racial oppression. This is a new era for both the church and for Native Americans. Christians are breaking away from their liberal moorings and looking for more effective means of social and political engagement. Indians, in this era of "self-determination," have verified for themselves and the government that they are the people best able to address Indian problems as long as they are given the necessary resources and if they can hold the U.S. government accountable to the policy. But an enormous stumbling block immediately presents itself. Most of the liberation theologies that have emerged in the last 20 years are preoccupied with the Exodus story, using it as the fundamental model for liberation. I believe that the story of the Exodus is an inappropriate way for Native Americans to think about liberation.

No doubt, the story is one that has inspired people in many contexts to struggle against injustice. Israel, in the Exile, then Diaspora, would remember the story and be reminded of God's faithfulness. African Americans, given Bibles to read by their masters and mistresses, would begin at the beginning of the book and find in the pages of Pentateuch a god who was obviously on their side, even if that god was the god of their oppressors. People in Latin American base communities read the story and have been inspired to struggle against injustice. The Exodus, with its picture of a god who takes the side of the oppressed and powerless, has been a beacon of hope for many.

God the Conqueror

Yet the liberationist picture of Yahweh is not complete. A delivered people is not a free people, nor is it a nation. People who have survived the nightmare of subjugation dream of escape. Once the victims have been delivered, they seek a new dream, a new goal, usually a place of safety away from the oppressors, a place that can be defended against future subjugation. Israel's new dream became the land of Canaan. And Yahweh was still with them: Yahweh promised to go before the people and give them Canaan, with its flowing milk and honey. The land, Yahweh decided, belonged to these former slaves from Egypt and Yahweh planned on giving it to them—using the same power used against the enslaving Egyptians to defeat the indigenous inhabitants of Canaan. Yahweh the deliverer became Yahweh the conqueror.

The obvious characters in the story for Native Americans to identify with are the Canaanites, the people who already lived in the promised land. As a member of the Osage Nation of American Indians who stands in solidarity with other tribal people around the world, I read the Exodus stories with Canaanite eyes. And it is the Canaanite side of the story that has been overlooked, by those seeking to articulate theologies of liberation. Especially ignored are those parts of the story that describe Yahweh's command to mercilessly annihilate the indigenous population.

To be sure, most scholars, of a variety of political and theological stripes, agree that the actual events of Israel's early history are much different than what was commanded in the narrative. The Canaanites were not systematically annihilated, nor were they completely driven from the land. In fact, they made up, to a large extent, the people of the new nation of Israel. Perhaps it was a process of gradual immigration of people from many places and religions who came together to form a new nation. Or maybe, as Norman Gottwald and others have argued, the peasants of Canaan revolted against their feudal masters, a revolt instigated and aided by a vanguard of escaped slaves from Egypt who believed in the liberating god, Yahweh. Whatever happened, scholars agree that the people of Canaan had a lot to do with it.

Nonetheless, scholarly agreement should not allow us to breathe a sigh of relief. For historical knowledge does not change the status of the indigenes in the *narrative* and the theology that grows out of it. The research of Old Testament scholars, however much it provides answer to the historical question—the contribution of the indigenous people of Canaan to the formation and emergence of Israel as a nation—does not resolve the narrative problem. People who read the narratives read them as they are, not as scholars and experts would *like* them to be read and interpreted. History is no longer with us. The narrative remains.

Though the Exodus and Conquest stories are familiar to most readers, I want to highlight some sections that are commonly ignored. The covenant begins when Yahweh comes to Abram saying, "Know of a surety that your descendants will be sojourners in a land that is not theirs, and they will be slaves there, and they will be oppressed for four hundred years; but I will bring judgment on the nation they serve and they shall come out" (Gen. 15:13, 14). Then, Yahweh adds: "To your descendants I give this land, the land of the Kenites, the Kenizzites, the Kadmonites, the Hittites, the Perizzites, the Rephaim, the Amorites, the Canaanites, and the Jebusites" (15:18–21). The next important moment is the commissioning of Moses. Yahweh says to him, "I promise I will bring you out of the affliction of Egypt, to the land of the Canaanites, the Hittites, the Amorites, Perizzites, the Hivites, and the Jebusites, a land flowing with milk and honey" (Exodus 3:17). The covenant, in other words, has two parts: deliverance and conquest.

After the people have escaped and are headed to the promised land, the covenant is made more complicated, but it still has two parts. If the delivered people remain faithful to Yahweh, they will be blessed in the land Yahweh will conquer for them (Exodus 20–23 and Deuteronomy 7–9). The god who delivered Israel from slavery will lead the people into the land and keep them there as long as they live up to the terms of the covenant. "You shall not wrong a stranger or oppress him [sic], for you were strangers in the land of Egypt. You shall not afflict any widow or orphan. If you do afflict them, and they cry out to me, I will surely hear their cry; and my wrath will burn, and I will kill you with the sword, and your wives shall become widows and your children fatherless" (Exodus 22:21).

Whose Narrative?

Israel's reward for keeping Yahweh's commandments—for building a society where the evils done to them have no place—is the continuation of life in the land. But one of the most important of Yahweh's commands is the prohibition on social relations with Canaanites or participation in their religion. "I will deliver the inhabitants of the land into your hand, and you shall drive the them out before you. You shall make no covenant with them or with their gods. They shall not dwell in your land, lest they make you sin against me; for if you serve their gods it will surely be a snare to you" (Exodus 23:31b–33).

In fact, the indigenes are to be destroyed. "When the Lord your God brings you into the land which you are entering to take possession of it, and clears away many nations before you, the Hittites, the Girgashites, the Amorites, the Canaanites, the Perizzites, the Hivites, and the Jebusites, seven nations greater and mightier than yourselves, and when the Lord your God gives them over to you and you defeat them; then you must utterly destroy them; you shall make no covenant with them, and show no mercy to them" (Deut. 7:1–2). These words are spoken to the people of Israel as they are preparing to go into Canaan. The promises made to Abraham and Moses are ready to be fulfilled. All that remains is for the people to enter into the land and dispossess those who already live there.

Joshua gives an account of the conquest. After ten chapters of stories about Israel's successes and failures to obey Yahweh's commands, the writer states, "So Joshua defeated the whole land, the hill country and the Negeb and the lowland and the slopes, and all their kings, he left none remaining, but utterly destroyed all that breathed, as the Lord God of Israel commanded." In Judges, the writer disagrees with this account of what happened, but the Canaanites are held in no higher esteem. The angel of the Lord says, "I will not drive out [the indigenous people] before you; but they shall become adversaries to you, and their gods shall be a snare to you."

Thus, the narrative tells us that the Canaanites have status only as the people Yahweh removes from the land in order to bring the chosen people in. They are not to be trusted, nor are they to be allowed to enter into social relationships with the people of Israel. They are wicked, and their religion is to be avoided at all costs. The laws put forth regarding strangers and sojourners may have stopped the people of Yahweh from wanton oppression, but presumably only after the land was safely in the hands of Israel. The covenant of Yahweh depends on this.

The Exodus narrative is where discussion about Christian involvement in Native American activism must begin. It is these stories of deliverance and conquest that are ready to be picked up and believed by anyone wondering what to do about the people who already live in their promised land. They provide an example of what can happen when powerless people come to power. Historical scholarship may tell a different story; but even if the annihilation did not take place, the narratives tell what happened to those indigenous people who put their hope and faith in ideas and gods that were foreign to their culture. The Canaanites trusted in the god of outsiders and their story of oppression and exploitation was lost. Interreligious praxis became betrayal and the surviving narrative tells us nothing about it.

Confronting the conquest stories as a narrative rather than a historical problem is especially important given the tenor of contemporary theology and criticism. After 200 years of preoccupation with historical questions, scholars and theologians across a broad spectrum of political and ideological positions have recognized the function of narrative in the development of religious communities. Along with the work of U.S. scholars like Brevard Childs, Stanley Hauerwas, and George Lindbeck, the radical liberation theologies of Latin America are based on empowering believing communities to read scriptural narratives for themselves and make their reading central to theology and political action. The danger is that these communities will read the narratives, not the history, behind them.

And, of course, the text itself will never be altered by interpretations of it, though its reception may be. It is part of the canon for both Jews and Christians. It is part of the heritage and thus the consciousness of people in the United States. Whatever dangers we identify in the text and the god represented there will remain as long as the text remains. These dangers only grow as the emphasis upon catechetical (Lindbeck), narrative (Hauerwas), canonical (Childs), and Bible-centered Christian base communities (Gutierrez) grows. The peasants of Solentiname bring a wisdom and experience previously unknown to Christian theology, but I do not see what mechanism guarantees that they—or any other people who seek to be shaped and molded by reading the text—will differentiate between the liberating god and the god of conquest.

Is There a Spirit?

What is to be done? First, the Canaanites should be at the center of Christian theological reflection and political action. They are the last remaining ignored voice in the text, except perhaps for the land itself. The conquest stories, with all their violence and injustice, must be taken seriously by those who believe in the god of the Old Testament. Commentaries and critical works rarely mention these texts. When they do, they express little concern for the status of the indigenes and their rights as human beings and as nations. The same blindness is evident in theologies that use the Exodus motif as their basis for political action. The leading into the land becomes just one more redemptive moment rather than a violation of innocent peoples' rights to land and self-determination.

Keeping the Canaanites at the center makes it more likely that those who read the Bible will read all of it, not just the part that inspires and justifies them. And should anyone be surprised by the brutality, the terror of these texts? It was, after all, a Jewish victim of the Holocaust, Walter Benjamin, who said, "There is no document of civilization which is not at the same time a document of barbarism." People whose theology involves the Bible need to take this insight seriously. It is those who know these texts who must speak the truth about what they contain. It is to those who believe in these texts that the barbarism belongs. It is those who act on the basis of these texts who must take responsibility for the terror and violence they can and have engendered.

Second, we need to be more aware of the way ideas such as those in the conquest narratives have made their way into Americans' consciousness and ideology. And only when we understand this process can those of us who have suffered from it know how to fight back. Many Puritan preachers were fond of referring to Native Americans as Amelkites and Canaanites—in other words people who, if they would not be converted, were worthy of annihilation. By examining such instances in theological and political writings, in sermons, and elsewhere, we can understand how America's self-image as a "chosen people" has provided a rhetoric to mystify domination.

Finally, we need to decide if we want to accept the model of leadership and social change presented by the entire Exodus story. Is it appropriate to the needs of indigenous people seeking justice and deliverance? If indeed the Canaanites were integral to Israel's early history, the Exodus narratives reflect a situation in which indigenous people put their hope in a god from outside, were liberated from their oppressors, and then saw their story of oppression revised out of the new nation's history of salvation. They were assimilated into another people's identity and the history of their ancestors came to be regarded as suspect and a danger to the safety of Israel. In short, they were betrayed.

Do Native Americans and other indigenous people dare trust the same god in their struggle for justice? I am not asking an easy question and I in no way mean that people who are both Native Americans and Christian cannot work toward justice in the context of their faith in Jesus Christ. Such people have a lot of theological reflection to do, however, to avoid the dangers I have pointed to in the conquest narratives. Christians, whether Native American or not, if they are to be involved, must learn how to participate in the struggle without making their story the whole story. Otherwise the sins of the past will be visited upon us again.

No matter what we do, the conquest narratives remain. As long as people believe in the Yahweh of deliverance, the world will not be safe from Yahweh the conqueror. But perhaps, if they are true to their struggle, people will be able to achieve what Yahweh's chosen people in the past have not: a society of people delivered from oppression who are not so afraid of becoming victims again that they become oppressors themselves, a society where the original inhabitants can become something other than subjects to be converted to a better way of life or adversaries who provide cannon fodder for a nation's militaristic pride.

With what voice will we, the Canaanites of the world, say, "Let my people go and leave my people alone?" And, with what ears will followers of alien gods who have wooed us (Christians, Jews, Marxists, capitalists), listen to us? The indigenous people of this hemisphere have endured a subjugation now 100 years longer than the sojourn of Israel in Egypt. Is there a god, a spirit who will hear us and stand with us in the Amazon, Osage country, and Wounded Knee? Is there a god, a spirit, able to move among the pain and anger of Nablus, Gaza, and Soweto? Perhaps. But we, the wretched of the earth, may be well-advised this time not to listen to outsiders with their promises of liberation and deliverance. We will perhaps do better to look elsewhere for our vision of justice, peace, and political sanity—a vision through which we escape not only our oppressors, but out oppression as well. Maybe, for once, we will just have to listen to ourselves, leaving the gods of this continent's real strangers to do battle among themselves.

Rita Nakashima Brock

6 Re-imagining God: Reflections on Mirrors, Motheroot, and Memory

Barbara de'Souza worked for almost eight years among poor communities in Sao Paolo, Brazil, and developed a two-year course in health education for women. The area she served had only one public health clinic for more than 80,000 people. Barbara provided basic health care information and instructions for doing community health work. Women gathered each week to learn anatomy from the head down, learning about the illnesses of various systems and their causes and about the politics of health care in Brazil.

To help them learn, she had her classes create a life-sized doll and put the correct anatomical features on her, and she had them draw posters to illustrate biological processes. A peak moment during the course was reached after about a year of instruction when they studied the reproductive system. The women lost their inhibitions with each other and developed a group spirit.

In the act of learning how their bodies worked, the women came to what Barbara describes as a spiritual awakening. Barbara says,

> It is at this [mid]point that they can feel the power and beauty of their [reproductive] system as women. . . . Then the image of God includes their image, that of creation, creating a new being, and God is also feminine! Now remember, this is not a theology course but a health course! Yet it became obvious to me, after years of experience, that women cannot discuss their bodies, learn the beauty of them, without theology entering, without a questioning of the patriarchal system—not only of the church, but of all society! And with this comes the questioning of the lack of control they have, in this system, over their own bodies; the questioning of who is responsible for their feelings of guilt and shame when it comes to knowing and enjoying these bodies.[1]

Originally published in *Church and Society* (May/June 1994), 20–30. Reprinted with permission of the author.

One woman's story stands out from the others, and I tell it with Barbara's permission. Dona Julietta was from an abusive marriage, could not handle money, was unable to do anything outside of her home without her husband's permission, and believed she was stupid, slow, and unable to learn. In order to come to the meetings, she told her husband she was attending a prayer meeting at church. And she had to bring her seven-year-old daughter along. As the weeks proceeded, it became evident that she was slowly able to learn. Although she could barely read, she was good at spatial relationships and made well-organized posters. She was also a lively member of the group, supporting and cheering others on as they struggled to learn new material.

At the time the peak of the course arrived, Julietta's husband said to her that he was tired of her going to prayer meeting every Wednesday. He beat her and forbade her to go by locking her in the bedroom. When she did not come and there was no word, the group discussed what to do. Because her husband was rude and abusive, they decided not to go to her house. The next Wednesday when Julietta's husband saw her whispering to her daughter, he suspected something, so he repeated that she could not go. Her daughter, to be helpful, said, "But Papa, they don't really pray at the meeting; they look at a big naked doll and talk about it." Furious, he beat Julietta and locked her in her room again.

But Julietta had had a taste of feeling loved and important, so she climbed out through the window and arrived in her beaten state. She told the group that as a child she had been passed from one member of her family to another, because her mother had died in childbirth. No one cared for her because she was plump and shy. She felt ugly and useless. She hated mirrors all her life because she looked ugly and stupid to herself. But she told the group, "Now when I look in a mirror, I see someone I love!"

The whole group cried and began to tell stories of their own years of oppression. They ended that meeting by praying together for strength to continue toward the time when they could love themselves as made in God's image, the image in the mirror.

What re-imagining of God would allow us to look in a mirror and say that we see, in our embodied, whole selves, someone we love? How can divine images affirm the complex, ambiguous, often difficult lives of women all over the world who swim in the riptides of oppressive, exploitative systems?

How can we come to understand our daily, earthbound, ordinary acts of care; our emotionally charged, demanding relationships; our solitary, reflective moments; our work for our societies, for our churches, for each other, and for our life on the earth; and our very physical selves as images of sacred power, of God with us and in us in our very flesh?

Nancy Mairs, an American Catholic feminist who struggles to live with multiple sclerosis, opens her spiritual autobiography *Ordinary Time* by declaring that

> God is here. And here, and here, and here. Not an immutable entity detached from time, but a continual calling and coming into being. Not transcendence, that orgy of self-alienation beloved of the fathers, but immanence: God working out Godself in every-thing . . . the holy as verb.[2]

Mairs invites us to plunge ever deeper into our very flesh, our existence as matter—the same root word as mother, *mater,* the growing trunk of a tree. To explore our earthbound lives, we must look, as Mairs says, "where we are needed." The life-giving power of women is this seeing of sacred power in ordinary needful acts, in daily care, persistent presence, and embodied living.

. . .

And what images will open our own eyes, so long clouded by patriarchal ideas and images? What enables us to touch, to smell, and to see here the presence of God, the motheroot? What will help us to see in the mirror an image of God, an image to love?

Three theological principles guide the journey into re-imagining God that follows.

First, incarnation compels us to look within ordinary, earthbound existence for clues to divine presence, within the humble lives of those, in Adrienne Rich's words, "who age after age, perversely, with no extraordinary power, reconstitute the world."[3] Looking for incarnation as verb is to look for the activity, not the individual, in which love is manifest. For the Spirit of God in our midst moves fluidly, finding homes for her presence as hearts open, looking elsewhere when hearts close. The revelation of incarnate spirit comes from the margins of life, from the heart of life-giving power, from motheroot.

The second principle is emmanuel, images of God who is with us in the ambiguous realities of our lives—not in the idealized realm of one-dimensional heroes or sanitized saviors, but in the messy middle of life as lived each day. We need images of lives that touch deeply into our own pain and struggle, a touching which, at its most powerful, points to God with us, Emmanuel.

The third principle is *ecclesia,* from *ek,* out, and *kalein,* to call. *Ecclesia* means to call out, to summon together into an assembly. It is grounded in the Christian confession that God is love and we are to love one another. We must look for images that bind us to each other more strongly in communities—*ecclesia*—struggling for justice, for wholeness within ourselves, with each other, and with the earth, for passionate, committed living. We must look to images that help us resist disconnection, alienation, denial, and apathy. For we need each other beyond all speaking and more deeply than we know, at the core of our deepest motheroot, in our very body-selves, as *ecclesia.*

And so I offer images for these three principles, incarnation, emmanuel, and *ecclesia.*

Incarnation

For incarnation I begin with an old story.

> Jesus . . . went away to the district of Tyre and Sidon. Just then a Canaanite woman from that region came out and started shouting, "Have mercy on me, Lord, Son of David, my daughter is tormented by a demon." But he did not answer her at all. And his disciples

came and urged him, "Send her away, for she keeps shouting after us." He answered, "I was sent only to the lost sheep of the house of Israel." But she came and knelt before him, saying, "Lord, help me." He answered, "It is not fair to take the children's food and throw it to the dogs." She said, "Yes, Lord, yet even the dogs eat the crumbs that fall from their masters' table." Then Jesus answered her, " Woman, great is your faith! Let it be done for you as you wish." And her daughter was healed instantly. (Matt. 15:21–28)

This is the story of a woman with no extraordinary power. The disciples find her persistence obnoxious. And even Jesus is rude to her. She, however, will not be deterred. She has courage and audacity in the face of their rejection—what my friend Rebecca Parker calls mother-bear energy, fiercely protecting her child. She gives Jesus a smart retort, and wins the argument.

She gets Jesus to concede because she shifts the focus of the debate away from her own status as outsider and toward Jesus' responsibility for his power. Jesus refuses her because she is outside his people, "It is not fair to take the children's food and throw it to the dogs." She replies, "yet even the dogs eat the crumbs that fall from their masters' table." In other words, "Although I am a Gentile, true justice will nourish me as well as it nourishes any Jew, because it is time." She turns the tables on Jesus.

The transformative power of love comes from the marginal and from those abused by the powers of domination and injustice who demand responsibility from the powerful. When Jesus is oppressed by the principalities and powers of the world, he reveals the incarnate power of God, as he does through much of his life and at his death. But when Jesus has structural power over another—marginalizes her—divine power confronts Jesus from those margins. In other words, she is the incarnation of God to Jesus. Jesus acknowledges this revelation when it happens with the words, "Woman, great is your faith! Let it be done for you as you wish." And this is how the transformative power of God is revealed, the power of motheroot.

In being concerned with the status of victims, we are prevented from facing squarely the misuse of power, which is always wrong, regardless of the status of the victim. Churches that would be in solidarity with women must learn this lesson. Women must be included equally in all decision-making capacities and leadership roles of the church, not because women can do things like men or better than men, but because the marginalization and disenfranchisement of any group by another within the church is a corrupt abuse of power. True justice is not partial. It excludes no one.

To take responsibility for power and to find incarnation, we must understand the ambiguous realities of human existence. To exist at all is to have some power to hurt others. Even a fetus has power to affect the life of its mother. Infant children do things that drive parents to distraction. No living thing is totally without power. We must not be confused, living in the messy middle of things. Those who have power must understand their power and take responsibility where they can for preventing harm to others.

In the web of complex relationships in which we live, each of us finds ourselves in both positions. Sometimes we hurt; sometimes we cause hurt. It is up to us to be alert to our own uses of power so that we are able to resist abuse and to resist abusing, to resist oppression and to resist oppressing others. Remember, incarnation is an activity—God as verb—not a state of being. When we take responsibility, we can use our power to love, to nurture, to enable freedom and willfulness in others, thereby incarnating the love of God. In taking responsibility we can say that the incarnation of God is here, working where she is needed, where we are needed.

The activity of incarnation is loving, what Audre Lorde has called erotic power. The Canaanite woman loves her daughter against all odds. Hers is neither a sweet, sentimental love that is quiet and passive, nor an objective love that is selfless and detached, but a fierce love that stands against the powers that thwart her passion for healing and wholeness. This power of God reaches out from the margins as mother-oot. She does not allow her need for approval or respectability to interfere with her need to keep her daughter alive.

The Canaanite woman's daughter is possessed of a terrible demon. What does it mean to be possessed of a demon? It means we have lost ourselves. Our psyches have split themselves off from our flesh, from our bodily home, and they wander lonely and afraid. We no longer possess conscious control of our own behavior and have lost our capacity for incarnation. Our psyches have become subject to powers too painful to resist. In children, such demons are named emotional abuse, molestation, rape, and physical violence. Possession is the sign of soul murder happening in a child. The Canaanite woman is fighting for the soul of her daughter, for the return of her daughter's incarnation to her. We are fighting for the soul of the church too long possessed by patriarchy.

Millions of the world's women have lived out love's fierce commitments at great risk to themselves, perversely persisting against all odds. Erotic power, God incarnate, enters into life through the work of ordinary women, through our struggles and vulnerabilities. That power is born in our passion for physical and spiritual healing and wholeness. It is found in our protective embracing of relationships against powers of control and violence and destruction. Our passions feed motheroot. Without it no society can survive.

Emmanuel

The second image of God I propose, emmanuel, is contained in a story the ethicist Sarah Ruddick tells of a mother named Julie, whose first child was born colicky and difficult. For four months the baby slept no more than one hour at a time and for six more months slept only two hours. Like many mothers in male-dominated industrial societies, Julie spent hours alone with her baby. Her husband, a struggling student, was often away, studying and working. Day and night Julie helplessly paced the floor as her beloved baby gasped for air. Sleep deprivation drove her mad. One night alone, in her dreams, Julie heard the baby screaming, only to awaken to the reality of that awful sound. In her own words, Julie says,

> I stumble toward your room and switch on the low lamp so the light will not startle you. You . . . wail and call. Trembling, I walk to your bed and check your diaper. I try to speak, to soothe, to give voice to my presence but my throat constricts in silent screaming and I find I cannot touch your tangled blankets. I force myself to turn and walk away, leaning against the doorjamb. My knees buckle beneath me and I find myself huddled on the floor. "Please do not cry. Oh child I love, please do not cry. Tonight you can breathe, so let me breathe."
>
> And I realize my chest is locked and I am gasping for breath. I picture myself walking toward you, lifting your tininess in both my hands and flinging you at the window. Mixed with my choking I can almost hear the glass as it would smash and I see your body, your perfect body, swirl through the air and land three stories below on the pavement.[4]

Sick from her vision, Julie vomits, changes her baby's diaper, and barricades the nursery door against herself. Later that night she wraps her daughter in blankets, carries her down the stairs, and rides the bus all night long thinking her child would be safe with her if they were not alone.

In a society that neither values nor supports her commitment to her child's well-being, Julie struggles to keep her child alive. Despite having reached her own breaking point, she summons the energy to protect her child's life and preserve their bond, even when the enemy is her own exhaustion. Her daughter grows into a fine young woman.

Julie did all she could to keep her child alive and safe; what she did was enough. In the midst of despair closing in on her, her love for her baby was shield enough. The blankets and her arms are a mother's compassionate embrace, the embrace of God with us, emmanuel. And she is one of millions of mothers in places like Mogadishu, Managua, Manila, Moscow, and Minneapolis who struggle against hunger and malnutrition, AIDS, abandonment, domestic violence, political repression, racism, and war. These mothers struggle body and soul to protect and nurture life. Sometimes they sell their very own flesh to keep themselves and their children alive. Sometimes they fail and grieve the losses. Nonetheless, millions of women perversely persist against a myriad of destructive principalities and powers. This God emmanuel rides the bus with us all night long and is with us in our suffering and struggle in the messy middle of our lives.

Such acts of loving care are lived out also by those who are not biological mothers. I am not a biological mother, but I care about the fate of our world and its people, especially its children. Anyone who has struggled to reduce suffering in our world has probably at some point felt that raw edge of exhaustion and hopelessness. Our experiences of tragedy and evil may drive us to the brink of despair. If we care at all, we will feel pain, over and over. Hostility to children and to women in the world is rising, as is evident in the escalation of child prostitution and the growing sex industries around the world. Values such as loving care and interdependence in industrial and post-industrial societies are in grave danger as multinational capitalism continues to spread like an epidemic. And an increasing number of women struggle in the Two-Thirds World under a myriad of dire circumstances.

It is miraculous that so many of us still make commitments to care for each other and our children—and honor them. And such commitments must be made by everyone, including men. Saving our difficult world from its own destruction requires our fiercest, most committed loving from women and men.

The passion of such love is governed by a commitment that perseveres persistently through every feeling we experience. This commitment is emmanuel indeed, the pain and joy of motheroot.

Ecclesia

I suggest one more image of God, drawn from the story of my own life. Almost exactly a decade ago, I learned that I had a Puerto Rican birth father. I had grown up believing my stepfather, who brought my mother and me from Japan when I was six, was my birth father, my only father who had died in 1976. When my Japanese mother passed away ten years ago, she left behind my adoption papers. They contained no information about my lost father. Through a series of coincidences, accidents, and searching, I discovered his name and an old address in Dorado Beach, Puerto Rico. I went there to find what I could, not knowing if he knew anything about me or why such a secret had been kept from me for so long.

I found ten aunts and uncles and many cousins who had hoped that I would be found someday. My father, who had left Korea when I was six months old, was living in New York. My mother had cut all contact with him, which is why I did not know of him. I met him later. In that visit to Puerto Rico, I found grandparents, including a grandfather who prayed every night before he slept that he would see his first grandchild before he died.

My grandmother did not pray; she was sure this child she loved only from a few faded baby pictures would someday be found. She was so sure I would come that she had pasted those pictures to her dresser mirror, where she peered expectantly at them for thirty-three years. And my Abuela Maria was right. I arrived unexpectedly one winter looking for a family I wasn't sure existed. It never occurred to me they would be waiting for me with open arms. I was amazed to learn that a grandmother, whom I did not know and who knew me only from faded photographs, cared passionately that I would be well and that I would return. My grandmother's commitment to loving me did not rest on my knowing her but on her memory of me. Abuela Maria loved me although she was unknown to me.

To be loved even when we do not know we are being loved is the power of *ecclesia* in our lives: to be called out by those who care. And this *ecclesia* of motheroot comes through flesh, through the legacy of bodies of our people who enfold us in a vast circle of kinship and care. Belonging to generations of a people creates a huge sea of memory that nurtures hope and love. This sea surrounds us with people who did not know us and whom we may never know. The imaginations and promises of generations of grandmothers and grandfathers have called us out and remain in the memory of our legacies. God here, and here, and here, *ecclesia*.

To be a citizen of the world without generations of memory to anchor us to herstory and to the earth is to float without patterns, without dreams, without meaning— without *ecclesia*. Without a people and their legacies, we live without those who made miracles and kept their promises, without those who held fast against the winds of pain. For each of us there have been thousands of people, over many centuries and across many miles, who have loved us without knowing us, hearts unsung, unseen. Their hopes and dreams for the future, and their hard grittiness that clings to life against all odds, keep life going as they hold fast to the bonds of love and care. And through our hopes and dreams, through our holding to life against all odds, we too pass on this legacy of loving those who will never know us.

Because I was adopted by my stepfather, I have been given an additional legacy. It binds me to many other adoptees who struggle to understand the legacies, the *ecclesia*, brought to us by the suffering of our biological parents. Without people to belong to, whether through birth or adoption, without those people whose hopes are like faded photographs on a dresser mirror peered at expectantly, the world is a cold, lonely, and hopeless place.

But *ecclesia* is not easy. While the world without *ecclesia* may be lonely, the legacy of our peoples includes the ghosts of those who murdered souls, the demons, as well as those who loved us, the angels. To have a people means to inherit an ambiguous historical legacy, an enfleshed reality passed body to body, incarnate spirit to incarnate spirit, heart to heart, truth and pain grounded in earthly life. For all its ambiguities and tragedies, this affirmation of *ecclesia* is why my life is tied to the church. Church that is defined in the broadest sense possible includes the wild women, the marginalized, and the heretics, as well as the patriarchs. In the church I have a legacy of the lives of ordinary women. To live with integrity within that highly ambiguous legacy, we must listen to the angels and the demons.

Without a people we have no healing presence in our lives, no incarnate spiritual legacy. We have no solidarity in our suffering, no emmanuel. And we have no context of meaning within which to shape a life, no *ecclesia*. As we struggle with incarnation, emmanuel, *ecclesia*, we must continue to peer into the mirror and say, "I see someone I love."

In case you were wondering, Dona Julietta continued to attend the health course. She sometimes came late and teary-eyed, but she came. She also summoned the courage to give a Blood Pressure Awareness Day lecture in church, educating everyone about how to control high blood pressure, which affects about 50 percent of the Brazilian population. She took more than a hundred blood pressures. Someone in the congregation told her husband of her work in such glowing terms that he asked her to read his blood pressure, his mother's, and two friends'. She finished the whole two-year course.

· · ·

Notes

1. Quoted from a private 1993 letter to the author. Used with permission.

2. Nancy Mairs, *Ordinary Time: Cycles in Marriage, Faith, and Renewal* (Boston: Beacon Press, 1993), pp. 11–13.

3. Adrienne Rich, *Natural Resources: The Dream of a Common Language* (New York: W. W. Norton and Co. Inc., 1978).

4. Sarah Ruddick, *Maternal Thinking: Toward a Politics of Peace* (Boston: Beacon Press, 1988), p. 67.

Vincent Harding

7   Martin Luther King and the Future of America

Every time I think about the possibilities of this nation of ours in the twenty-first century, I recognize that we are really citizens of a developing country. No matter how that term has been used in the past, that is who we are now. The United States of America is a work in progress—a shadow on the wall of a multiracial, compassionate democracy that does not yet exist, a project that requires the perseverance of lifetime workers. So I see us coming here this evening to think about, talk about, struggle about, shout about, sing about, where we might take our country as citizens of this land—how we might help each other awaken from the great moral and political sleep that has deepened among us in the 1990s and recognize again the continuing democratic urgency of Langston Hughes's call: "we the people must redeem our land and make America again." As we go forward in this moment and in the many moments before us, we will surely discover what our foreparents have already discovered in many, many places: we do not have the luxury of any kind of distanced research into the twenty-first century. The only research that will help to make the new century a human experience for this nation is a deeply engaged research, in which we offer ourselves as participants in and exemplars of what it is that we seek. And tonight, I ask you to meet in this place with two of the great citizen-teacher-workers of our century, seeking their wisdom and inspiration for this current stage of the ongoing, never-ending American project of creating a more perfect union. That, you see, is what we Americans have in common. We have been called upon, all of us, to create a more perfect union.

Considering such a national vocation, I'd like you to reflect on two people who have spoken deeply, importantly to me; the first is Rabbi Abraham Joshua Heschel, who escaped the moral and physical catastrophe of the Holocaust to bring his wis-

Originally published in *Cross Currents* (Fall 1996), 303–312. Reprinted with the permission of *Cross Currents*.

dom, courage, and commitment to our struggles for righteousness in this land. And I bring him, first, because Rabbi Heschel often chose to stand and march and sometimes risk his life with my brother friend, Martin Luther King, Jr. Just ten days before King was assassinated, Heschel stood with him to introduce his friend to a group of rabbis from the northeast section of this country. And it was necessary to bring Martin to the rabbis because the brother rabbis, like so many other religious and political people, were not sure, in 1968, that they liked the Martin King who was coming North as much as they had liked the King of Montgomery, Birmingham, Selma, and St. Augustine. Prophets on our doorsteps are always harder to deal with than prophets far away. So Heschel, who knew something about the world of prophets and who shared King's deep commitment to the necessity of fundamental change in this society, brought to his co-religionists a word about King that breaks through to our own time and to our own struggles for twenty-first century America. "Martin Luther King, Jr. is a voice, a vision, and a way," he said. Then continuing, Heschel declared, "I call upon every Jew to hearken to his voice, to share his vision, to follow in his way. The whole future of America will depend on the impact and influence of Dr. King."

This seems to me to be a clear word to those of us who are trying to find a way to recreate for the next century the great tradition that King and Heschel and Hughes represented, the tradition that is really for those of us who refuse to simply wait for the future. The words are for those of us who are committed to join in the creation process, those of us who want to help shape the future, those of us who want to help create the twenty-first century, rather than simply to wait around to see what the end will be. And I think something in us tells us that Heschel is right, that King—for all the ambiguity that we feel about him at many times—is indeed a voice, a vision, and a way, that he is somehow deeply related to the future of America, just as he was deeply related to its past. But what is also clear to me is the fact that all of us, being who we are, want to approach King in a manner that makes his voice, his vision, and his way as easy as possible for us to manage.

In that context, I remember the powerful poem by the young man who was only in his twenties when Martin was assassinated, Carl Wendell Hines. Long after the long-searching bullet had finally located King, Hines wrote,

> Now that he is safely dead
> Let us praise him
>   build monuments to his glory
>   sing hosannas to his name.
>   Dead men make
> such convenient heroes: They
>   cannot rise
>   to challenge the images
>   we would fashion from their lives.
>   And besides,
> it is easier to build monuments
>   than to make a better world.

We must let Hines speak to us as we try to overcome the fear and cynicism that says there is no such thing as a better world. For King is related to all who are called upon to help create the twenty-first century. Still, Hines is right: we insist on approaching King in a way that makes him easy to handle; we want King to fit our agendas.

One indication of this is our tremendous fixation on the Martin Luther King of the March on Washington, of "I Have a Dream"—magnificent, beautiful oratory, but not quite to the point for the twenty-first century. Something in us wants that triumphant, sun-drenched hero to stay right there, so that we can almost worship, not only him, but those words that he spoke. So often the act of worshiping becomes a process of denying life itself. The hard work of creating the twenty-first century demands something else from us—and from King. Those of us who want to create a twenty-first century marked by justice and compassion in this nation need a hero who is not always triumphant—who also works in the shadow times of fear, tragedy, betrayal, and death. They are all too much of our life; we need somebody who knows the way we walk, not a plaster-of-Paris somebody on top of a pedestal. If we are going into the twenty-first century, we need somebody who insists on going right on through the storm, through the night, doing the work that has to be done. We need to take a new look at King—at the King who presses us beyond the March on Washington.

Perhaps if we follow King carefully enough, we will realize that the official statement of the March on Washington in 1963 said, "This is a march for jobs and freedom." Not for little children to hold each other's hands, wonderful though that may be, but for their mothers and fathers to be able to work. If we keep going with King, we can more adequately take on the issues of our coming century. For instance, we may understand how King went out from the sunlight of the Mall to retrace his steps back to Birmingham, Alabama. There, just three weeks later, he was forced to deal with the fact that white terrorist bombers had destroyed a church—and the lives of four children.

If we keep going with King, we go into some very tough places. But anybody who is not ready for tough places, isn't ready for the twenty-first century in America. So I want to wonder out loud: what was on his mind when he went back to the Sixteenth Street Baptist Church and knew that that church had not been chosen accidentally; it had been bombed because it was the headquarters of the campaign that he and Shuttleworth had led in Birmingham, and those children were his offspring. How do you deal with that? I would like us to move with King in such a way that we take on the difficult questions that a woman or a man has to deal with when trying to give leadership in transforming a society that usually does not want to be transformed.

If we follow King closely enough, we might even get to the fall of 1963 and read again what Coretta King had to say about that day in November when they sat before their television screen in that house on Sunset Street in Atlanta, and she and Martin watched the somber and elegant processions that followed the assassination of President John F. Kennedy. As they watched, Martin turned to Coretta—turning just enough for her to be able to watch what was on his face, and in his mind—and said to her, "Cori, this is what's going to happen to me also. I keep telling you, this is a sick society." I'd like to stay with that King—the one who didn't make it to forty, the one who had this profound sense, deepening all the time, that the sickness of the country would get to him—but nevertheless kept on going.

Last January, I was at a middle school in Denver. I was talking to the youngsters about the King who kept going in spite of the dangers. Afterward, one young man about thirteen came walking up to me and said, "Now, listen here, Dr. Harding, if King knew that he was gonna get knocked off, how come he didn't just chill out for awhile?" I looked at him and started to think about the wonderful conversation we were going to have, but right in the midst of it a girl about the same age, who was right next to us, said, "Oh, come on now, Dr. King couldn't chill out. He had work to do!" If only we would listen to children and let them take on the hard issues.

Indeed, if we want to stay with King, we must also face those issues. In the summer of 1964 we would follow King as he gets the word that three young freedom workers in Mississippi were missing, probably dead. What King does then is remarkable. After all, he had almost nothing to do with the organizing of Mississippi Summer, but when he heard that three boys were missing and probably dead, he immediately got up and went there. No program, no solution, no search squad—he simply knew he had to be there, that's all. Sometimes, that's all you can know, and all you need to know to be human.

But of course, to follow King is to find the glory times as well. Like December 1964: we see him at the Nobel award ceremony in Oslo, bursting with pride, but also now growing into a deeper sense of what his ministry of peace-making and justice-making is all about, knowing more than he had ever known before that it could not be confined to this country, that he is responsible for so much more.

One of my favorite times with King is in Selma, Alabama. The people gathered there included some wonderfully crazy and bodacious adventurers from SNCC (the Student Nonviolent Coordinating Committee), who were the shock troops of the nonviolent revolution of this country. They had started plowing the ground in that place and had invited, of all people, Malcolm X to come down and spend some time with them in February 1965. It is simply fascinating what Malcolm wanted to do when he came to Selma in 1965. No great big speech burning white folks and black Christians and all kinds of other folks that he could burn so well, and often justifiably. No, Malcolm came to Selma and said, "I want to talk to Dr. King." But Martin, as was his unfortunate habit, was in jail. And they wouldn't let Malcolm break in. Instead, he went to talk with Coretta. And he said, "Mrs. King, will you tell Dr. King that I had planned to visit with him in jail? I won't get a chance now because I've got to leave. [But], I want Dr. King to know that I didn't come to Selma to make his job difficult. I really did come thinking that I could make it easier." When Martin got out of jail and Coretta told him about this, he was exultant: "Hey, that Malcolm is a beautiful brother. He really is."

As the poet put it, Malcolm "became much more than there was time for him to be"—and two weeks later, he was gone. I would like us to follow fast enough, far enough, deep enough, past the sunshine of the Mall and consider what it meant for King and Malcolm to be possibly complementary forces in the same struggle. What it meant to them, what it meant to black people, what it meant to this country, and what it meant to the people who thought they owned this country, to have these two men coming closer together. The only way that they could come together was for them to break loose from their older base communities and take great new risks. I think that's twenty-first century style, and that's why I'd like us to follow that kind of pathway.

Everybody who has seen *Eyes on the Prize*—and if you haven't seen it you should not consider yourself an educated American citizen—remembers those wonderful scenes of the Selma to Montgomery march, that great pilgrimage, that great dance through Alabama. And everybody remembers, too, that there is no pilgrimage, there is no dance, there is no facing the powers of injustice without there also being more martyrs. King had to deal with that. I keep seeing him in those post-Mall days constantly being reminded of the cost of personal and social transformation, and I think it is necessary that we face those costs and ask ourselves, "Now what do we do? Do we chill out and look for safety and security? Or do we accept the fact that we have work to do?"

I want us to remember what it meant for Martin Luther King to return to Montgomery after the march from Selma. A ten-year cycle had been completed: 1955, the beginning of the public ministry as it were; 1965, time maybe for him to retire on his laurels. And possibly to get a university professorship, which he always thought about in some back part of his mind. At the end of that fifty miles of marching through danger, at the end of those five days on the road, at the end of these ten years of his career, he gets to Montgomery, and can you imagine this? Martin King does not say, "Now I am ready to hang it up, and now we can rest." He says, "You rest, but rest for just a minute because we have got to keep going. Now we have got to face the Northern cities. Now, we have got to face the tremendous exploitation of poor people in the urban centers of our nation." He's saying this in the spring of 1965 to all of us who thought that the movement was not concerned about these things: "We've got to take on those terrible schools, terrible inside and dilapidated outside. We've got to figure out why people have to walk around our cities without jobs when they want to work. We can't stop, we've got to keep going." In other words, after ten years, King simply catches his breath for a minute and goes on into even more dangerous territory.

I would like us to be there when Lyndon Baines Johnson signs the act that does so much to transform the political system of this country, an act purchased in blood, developed by poor, so-called powerless people. Unless you see King there, unless you see the marvelous rejoicing of that day in August, you can't imagine what he must have been feeling when the next moment Watts breaks out in flames. The folks in Los Angeles are saying, "Thanks very much, we really appreciate that Voting Rights act, but that doesn't cut it for us. We've got other plans, we've got other stuff that must be dealt with." And they said it in fire. And as you might expect, Martin King hears about Watts, sees it on television, and again, he has no plan, has no program, has nothing concrete that he can offer—but he decides he's got to go to the fire, partly because of the fire burning in his own bones. He's got to go to the young people, partly because they are his people.

And when he gets to Watts, some of the folks don't have the slightest idea who he is, and they start throwing rocks at him and Bayard Rustin. But afterward, they sit and talk and Martin looks around at the burning buildings and asks, "What are you hoping to accomplish here?" And they say, "We won." And he said, "What? You won? What did you win? Look at this." And they said, "We made everybody pay attention to us." I want us to go with Martin past the Mall, to the moment when he comes to a new understanding of what it means to pay attention to the cries of the rejected ones, because there's going to be a lot of attention needed in the twenty-first century. More than just arm's-length public policy programs—real attention.

From my perspective, one reason we have to follow King out into those strange places that he goes is that the man shows that he is really sort of crazy by the stuff that he tries. For instance, after that magnificent victory in the South, King is crazy enough to take seriously what he has said to the people. Those who talk about King the great orator, do not understand: King was not simply a great orator—he was a great mover of himself and others through terrible situations. He could orate because he had moved. "You've got to get into the Northern cities," he told them. By January 1966, he leaves Alabama and goes to Chicago. You know he's crazy. Anybody who goes to Chicago in January when she or he has the chance to be in Alabama must be a little bit off-center. But if you consider where the center of this country is now, and will be in the twenty-first century, you know we need as many eccentrics as possible. And that was King—off to Chicago in the winter. Off not just to the South side of Chicago, where some very important people lived, but off to West Lawndale, one of the toughest, most needy places you could find in Chicago. There we hear King speaking a word that is most unpopular at the end of the twentieth century: "I choose to identify with the underprivileged . . . I choose to identify with the poor . . . I choose to give my life for the hungry . . . for those who have been left out of the sunlight of opportunity . . . I choose to live for and with those for whom life is one long, desolate corridor with no exit sign. This is the way I'm going. If it means suffering a little, I'm going that way. If it means sacrifice, I'm going that way. And if it means dying for them, I'm going that way, because I heard a voice saying, do something for others."

When King made that decision—and it was a conscious decision—he caught the attention of a perceptive *New York Times* reporter, David Halberstam, who traveled with King for several weeks during that period. "King has decided to represent the ghettoes," he wrote. "He will work in them and speak for them but their voice is harsh and alienated. If King is to speak for them truly, then his voice must reflect their voice. It, too, must be alienated and it is likely to be increasingly at odds with the rest of American society." Halberstam was right—and the FBI and the CIA agreed. From that point on, they accelerated their attempt to subvert the life and work of one of the greatest lovers of American democracy that the nation has ever produced. At the same time, as we listen to the new voice of King and observe him carefully, we have to recognize that this man was dealing with deep hungers, deep needs, deep weaknesses in his own life. If we can look at him closely, avoid the voyeurism of modern television, and try to see him with both integrity and compassion, we realize that in one terrible motion he is both damning and redeeming himself again and again and again. That's the King I would like us to see; that's the King I would like us to know—no putty-like King, but a hard, difficult, life-true King.

I would next suggest that you see King toward the end of his life on the Meredith march in Mississippi as he walks side by side with Stokely Carmichael, knowing that Stokely wants the mass media to hear Black Power, and if he's walking with King, the media will be there. King knows this, but with generosity of spirit, he keeps walking with Stokely. And a young teenager comes up to King and says, "I hope you understand, now, Dr. King, you were trying to get us to love white people before we loved ourselves." We need to stay with King long enough to hear all of that. Because when King heard it, he must have also heard a friend of his saying, "Love your neighbor as you love yourself." He knew that black power and black consciousness and black self-love were a religious imperative, necessary for truly loving anybody, necessary for the future of America. Healthy self-love is a religious imperative.

When King began to speak out on Vietnam, it was not a popular movement. He risked a great deal—including, I am convinced, his life. But he had said, "I identify with the poor," and he was not willing to stop his identification at the borders of any country or any nationality. He knew that the poor of this country were being sent to destroy the poor of that country; he could not be silent in the face of such tragedy.

Finally, there are two more things that I want to suggest we must deal with as we move with King through the urban explosions of the late 1960s. As he was going through that experience, he had to figure out the question constantly: "Do I still believe in nonviolence?" And what became clearer and clearer was not that he believed in nonviolence as some kind of abstract concept; what he believed in more and more was the necessity for nonviolent revolution in America if the poor were going to be dealt with in justice and compassion. That's why King began calling on the Chicanos, the native Americans, the Appalachian whites, and saying, "Come on together with us black people and let's gather ourselves together around this issue of poverty. Through the Poor People's Campaign, let's challenge our government to change its ways." He asked them not be satisfied with testifying on behalf of policy documents. "No," he said, "let's organize ourselves so that we can be the policy makers, so that we can challenge the policy makers, not with other words, but with deeds." That was King, the voice, the vision, the way toward a compassionate nation.

I suspect the twenty-first century will need a lot of challenging of the policy makers, not with words but with deeds. So where else could King end up when somebody called to say, "Martin, the garbage workers are in trouble"? Where else can this Ph.D. in philosophical theology end up, but going to the garbage workers? Crazy man. Everybody else knows what Ph.D.s are for, but he apparently didn't. He thought that they were for serving garbage men. And I call your attention to that because, as Martin used to say, we need more Ph.D.s who will pay close attention to the deep issues of American life today and tomorrow in order to create a more perfect union.

The last word of all is in many ways the most painful one, but we must go with King far enough finally to be able to face the fact—the hard, necessary fact—that there is a very strong likelihood that the agencies of our own federal government were deeply involved in his assassination. Now what do you do with that? What do *we* do with that? For me it's clear that if you follow King that far, there's no chilling out, no selling out, no running out. There's work to do. And we are the ones who must do it. We the people must redeem our land and remake America—again and again and again. The whole future of America depends upon the impact and influence of Martin Luther King, through us, remaking America again and again.

Focusing on the Issues

Although suffering is limitless, I vow to end it

(The Boddhisatva Vow)

One of the most crucial elements in the critique of the religious left has been the pursuit of economic justice. As the gap between the poor and rich widens, the religious left has been outspoken in demands for redistribution of wealth and the continued support of a safety net for the poorest in our society. The Buddhist demand to work to end suffering reflects this perspective.

The Roman Catholic Church has certainly taken the lead in this endeavor. The National Conference of Catholic Bishops document, Economic Justice for All: Pastoral Letter on Catholic Social Teaching and the U.S. Economy *(1986), provided a blueprint for Catholic thinking on this issue. The letter underscored the biblical warrant for this perspective, and gave concrete examples of how the United States should approach taking care of those in society who lack resources.*

Ron Pasquariello presents a clear articulation of the position of the Protestant left on issues of economic justice and the growing disparity between rich and poor. Although the statistics in the article are now dated, they reflect trends toward a widening of the economic gap that have not changed since this article was published.

Catholics for a Free Choice take on the issue of welfare reform from the perspectives of Catholic teachings and feminism. This document also provides clear goals for how we as a people should deal with poverty among women, and how that poverty affects poor women's ability to make reproductive choices, as well as choices for themselves about work and child care.

Jeffrey Dekro and Lawrence Bush write from a Jewish perspective about how those who have benefited from the accumulation of wealth might themselves work on the issues of economic justice. Dekro and Bush also confront the economic stereotypes faced by Jews and how the assumptions this society makes about Jews and money have hindered the process of work on economic justice issues within the Jewish community.

Thomas Paprocki presents a dimension of this approach as it is expressed in the concept of a preference for the poor. Paprocki looks at the roots of this teaching in the life of Jesus, and focuses on how this concept can either be turned into action or reduced to platitudes.

These essays provide different perspectives on the need to rethink the growing economic divide in our country from religious perspectives. They underscore the importance of economic justice as part of the concerns of the religious left to repair the world.

Ronald D. Pasquariello

8 The Skewing of America: Disparities in Wealth and Income

The Federal Reserve Board reported some staggering news last summer: one-half of 1 percent of American families (just 419,590 out of a total of about 87 million households) possess 35 percent of this country's privately held wealth. As it turns out, the board had to rescind its study because a major error had been made. The new results are not yet available; they will not be as drastic, though they will show that the gap between the rich and the rest of us—stable until recently—has widened.

Private wealth is the value of an individual's or household's possessions. It includes real estate, homes, cars, stocks, trusts, savings and retirement accounts. Wealth is not income. Wealth is capital, stored-up economic power; it tends to be stable, and to grow. It is the cushion against the shocks of a mercurial economy. Income, on the other hand, is constituted primarily by wages and salaries (it also includes interest and dividends), and offers only as much economic stability as the job market does— which is very little.

The wealth concentrated in the hands of the very rich includes assets that confer economic power. In 1972, the top 5 percent of the population held 66.7 percent of the corporate stock and 93.6 percent of state and local bonds. This disparity, which has since widened, suggests that the very rich can control the decisions related to corporate and municipal assets.

The net worth of most Americans does not amount to much. Most families' forms of wealth are limited to homes, automobiles, furnishings, appliances and checking and savings accounts. For most, the family residence is the principal form of wealth. Except for money that may be raised by second mortgages, residences are not an available asset for most families. Furthermore, the value of a residence is subject to the capriciousness of the housing market. The fragile economic situation of most

Originally published in *Christian Century* (February 18, 1987), 164–166. Copyright 1987 Christian Century Foundation. Reprinted by permission from the February 18, 1987, issue of the *Christian Century*.

Americans has been starkly evident in communities where plants have closed or moved away. Many homeowners have been left jobless, with houses that are unsalable. As for savings, the average American has at most $5,000—hardly enough to support a family after unemployment benefits run out.

The gap between the rich and rest of us is also widening in terms of income. We have witnessed what Barry Bluestone and Ben Harrison have called "the Great U-Turn." Disparity in earnings declined from 1963 to 1978, but since then it has increased. By 1984 we had nearly returned to the income inequality of 1965.

Within the past decade, the median family income has leveled off and begun to decline. In 1979, 50 percent of two-parent families had an income of $26,299. Today 50 percent earn $24,556 or less. (There is a similar decrease for single-parent families.) The distribution of income among families has also become more unequal in recent years. The share of total income going to the bottom 60 percent of American families has declined, and the share going to the next 20 percent has increased negligibly, while the share going to the top 20 percent has increased by 2.5 percent.

The major reason for the decline in family income is the decline in real wages: most incomes are from wages, and average earnings have declined since peaking in 1973. Weekly wages have declined by 14.5 percent, hourly wages by 10.1 percent. Behind this decline is the loss of middle-income jobs as a result of the rise of the service economy and the failure of the minimum wage to keep pace with inflation.

According to statistics supplied by the Economic Policy Institute, a 25-year-old male worker in 1953 or 1963 could expect to more than double his income over a period of ten years. But in 1973, a 25-year-old male could expect a mere 16 percent increase in income by 1983. The average male who was 40 in 1973 actually saw a 14 percent decline in his income over ten years.

Practically all the households with annual incomes of more than $25,000 in 1983 were those of working couples. The traditional middle-class family with one wage-earner is no longer as economically feasible as it once was. Even in two-earner families incomes can stagnate, for women's wages still remain low relative to men's (so a woman's salary does not necessarily double the family income).

All of these figures indicate why there has been a decline in the proportional size of the middle class. Between 1973 and 1985, the proportion of American families with incomes between $20,000 and $50,000 dropped 5 percent. The sector of families earning less than $20,000 and $50,000 grew, but by only 1.8 percent. Meanwhile, poverty has been increasing among low-income persons. In 1978 about 24.5 million Americans lived below the poverty line, but by 1984 the number had climbed to 33.7 million. Moreover, the number of persons who work but are still unable to escape poverty has grown dramatically in recent years. The number of those aged 22 to 64 who work but are still poor has increased by more than 60 percent since 1978, according to the Center on Budget and Policy Priorities.

What conclusions can be drawn from all this? The most obvious is that it is more difficult for individuals to "make it" in our society than it once was. There has been excessive pressure on many American workers to take cuts in their wages or to take jobs well below their earning capacity. And many workers whose companies have folded or moved to greener (or foreign) pasture have lost health and retirement benefits.

Are there any specific forces responsible for this situation? For instance, what is the role of the current administration; is it to blame? The *Wall Street Journal* put it this way: "The Reagan administration's policies haven't narrowed the gap between rich and poor. The tax cuts in the first five years of Mr. Reagan's presidency favored the wealthy: reducing capital gains taxes benefited those with capital. Government programs aimed exclusively at the poor were trimmed, but others that help a broader group—Social Security and veterans' benefits, for instance—weren't" (September 22, 1986).

Though the skewing of America began before President Reagan took office, his policies have markedly accelerated the process. The Congressional Budget Office has indicated that budget and tax changes enacted from 1981 to 1983 have taken $20 billion from those with incomes below $20,000 a year and brought about a $35 billion increase for households with incomes of $80,000 or more.

Why should these facts concern Christians? First of all, because concentrations of wealth have important economic consequences. As was pointed out above, wealth translates into economic power and control through corporate stock and nonincorporated businesses, real estate and state and local bonds. Those who control these assets control how they are used and developed. The investment decisions of private companies, for example—decisions that affect how and where people work and what and how much they produce—are made in offices far removed from those workers or the general public. Those with wealth, who are closely tied to the banking community, govern capital accumulation and, with it, decisions about employment technology, income distribution, work organization, consumption patterns, and even our relations with other nations.

Consider the development of Harbor Place, a renovated waterfront area in Washington, D.C. All the decisions about how it should be built, what kind of establishment it should be, and to whom the site should cater were made almost entirely by the developers. Local residents who are worried about the effect on parking that the new 1,000-seat restaurant will cause were not consulted. In too many cases, decisions about which plants should be developed, which should be allowed to deteriorate, and which should be moved in pursuit of lower wages are made by corporate stockholders and their managers. Whole cities have been held hostage to large businesses, which threaten to withdraw if their demands are not met.

The concentration of wealth puts control of the not-really-free market in the hands of a relatively few families. Decisions about the quality of the food we eat, the goods we buy, the air we breathe, the prices we pay, the way work is divided and jobs defined, the kinds of transportation, recreation and entertainment available, the opinions and values that are supposed to be important, the kind of treatment we get in schools, clinics and hospitals—these are made by the people who control the economic resources.

The second reason for Christians to be concerned is that economic control also means political control. Thomas Jefferson feared that "an aristocracy of wealth [is] of more harm and danger than benefit to society." Those who control economic resources have the potential to control legislative decisions. Government is beholden to those who control the purse strings, and not only because of the dollars needed to run political campaigns. One of the functions of government is to ensure the stable operation of the economy, and to do so it must often defer to the wishes of those who control the means of production. A government that limited or disrupted economic growth, risking thereby the displeasure of the economic overlords, would also be putting the coherence of its polity at risk.

Finally, the concentration of wealth should be a concern because it is a cause of poverty. There is a tendency for Americans who think about the problem at all to consider poverty a problem of individuals. Individuals are poor because they lack certain social skills, or they lack intelligence or virtue, or they are inadequately educated, or have incongruous cultural values or have too many children. From this perspective, the solution to poverty is simply to let poor people feel the spur of their poverty, which should motivate them to alter their behavior. Usually those who urge the motivational value of privation are not themselves poor. When they get hungry, they go to the nearest restaurant. Nothing is more ludicrous than such criticism of the ill fed, ill housed and ill clothed by the well fed, well housed and well clothed.

Poverty ought to be viewed instead as an aspect of inequality, a facet of the maldistribution of wealth and income. It is the inevitable social byproduct of the concentration of wealth in the hands of a few. From this perspective, one does not pay primary attention to individuals, or propose programs aimed at correcting the deficiencies of individuals. For if inequality is the cause of poverty, the proper question is not "What is it about individuals that makes them poor?" but "What is it about the nature of the economy that creates poverty?" The case can be made that the current economic situation derives from our particular brand of American individualism. Individualism is healthy if it means the freedom to choose moral, political and cultural alternatives within a community of mutual concern. However, individualism has come to mean a solipsistic, acquisitive consumerism. Americans try to get what they can for themselves, by themselves, without being too troubled by the needs and problems of others. One works for oneself and leaves the rest of society to the workings of the "invisible hand." Indeed, according to this ideology it is by working for one's own advancement, without regard for other individuals or for the polity, that one does the greatest good for society.

What is lacking here is a true sense of the common good. Were programs and policies shaped by the obligation to contribute actively to the common good, the situation would be altered. Social responsibility, in this context, means being aware of and concerned about the impact of one's actions on others. If people saw themselves obligated to ensure that everyone has the essentials of life's opportunities, then the economic and political institutions of society would be structured differently.

Gross inequality is a direct contradiction of the will of God, the creator and sovereign over all nations and peoples. Creation is God's gift to all. We are collaborators in creation, our task being to shape the social and economic order according to God's intentions. To allow the appropriation of the world's resources by a small minority of persons betrays the gift of creation and the giver of the gift.

The prophets railed against the accumulation of land, and Israel's law provided for the Year of Jubilee, when land was returned to its original owners. The covenant established a community of mutual responsibility and care. Jesus, in keeping with this tradition, had a special concern for the poor, and opposed accumulation of possessions. He disdained the type of economic inequality which we are now witnessing. "A man's life does not consist in the abundance of his possessions," he declared (Luke 12:15) and he called the rich man who builds larger and larger barns in which to store his grain and other goods a fool, cautioning his listeners that "he who lays up treasure for himself . . . is not rich toward God" (12:16–21). As biblical scholar Richard J. Cassidy points out in *Jesus, Politics and Society* [Maryknoll, N.Y.: Orbis Books, 1978], that parable focuses on those who already have enough for their needs. The landowner does not seem to have acquired wealth unfairly or dishonestly; nevertheless, because he held on to more possessions than he needed, because he possessed wealth without regard to covenant community, he was declared a fool in the sight of God.

In the Bible, Walter Brueggemann says, justice means "to sort out what belongs to whom, and return it to them" ("Voices of the Night—Against Justice," *To Act Justly, Love Tenderly, Walk Humbly* [Mahwah, N.J.: Paulist Press, 1986], p. 5). There is a right distribution of goods and of access to the source of life. People have entitlements which must be respected. All this is implied in the great biblical vision of covenant and shalom, in which every family, clan, tribe and person has a place in which their God-given dignity is respected. This vision is not a romantic ideal; it calls for the transformation of unjust social systems. It is the obligation of churches to bring this biblical vision to bear on our complex economic and social world. They attempt this at some risk, of course, for it is not an easy message, and too many of the churches and those in the churches are dependent on the holders of wealth for their own economic being. But if the problem is not addressed by the ambassadors of the gospel, who will do so?

9 Poverty, Women, and Reproduction: Welfare Reform and Social Justice

> *The destruction of the poor is their poverty.*
> —[Proverbs 10:15]

The persistence of poverty is one of the most fundamental tragedies in the world. Hunger, homelessness, ignorance, sickness, and hopelessness are among its bitter fruits. As Catholics, we embrace and promote a Christian commitment to justice and an active concern for the poor. We recognize that the creation of an inclusive community demands special consideration for society's marginalized. Bearing in mind this preferential option for the poor, proponents of social justice must be diligent in examining the impact on the poor of legislative initiatives. Those who uphold the Catholic social justice tradition are called upon to vigorously oppose current political trends in the United States which seek to restrict or eliminate assistance to the poor on the basis of marital status, age, or childbearing decisions. In this paper, we raise some core questions about welfare, and examine welfare reform through the dual lenses of Catholic social justice teaching and a reproductive ethic based on women's well-being.

The Catholic Church, Social Justice, and the Poor

As policy makers look to reform our welfare system, they would be wise to reflect on the many valuable strands of thinking and writing about the poor, their needs, and their rights. In that vein, there is much that is instructive in Catholic social justice teaching. With almost universal accord, Catholic scholars and activists have maintained a central commitment to alleviating poverty. Catholic church teaching re-

Originally published in *Conscience* (Winter 1995/96), 16:25–32. Reprinted with the permission of *Conscience*.

garding the poor has been clear and consistent, and in many instances, the words of Catholic leaders have been courageous and ground-breaking. Specific, action-oriented care for the poor is, unarguably, a central theme of the Catholic social message throughout the twentieth century.

The Catholic church's modern advocacy for the poor dates back to Pope Leo XIII, who wrote the encyclical *Rerum Novarum* (On the Condition of Workers) in 1891. "Still, when there is question of protecting the rights of individuals," Leo wrote, "the poor and helpless have a claim to special consideration. The richer population have many ways of protecting themselves, and stand less in need of help from the State; those who are badly off have no resources of their own to fall back upon, and must chiefly rely upon the assistance of the State."[1] Leo confirmed not only the state's obligation to the poor, but also people's right to participate in decisions that shape their society.

In 1971, Pope Paul VI expanded upon Leo's words in *Octogesima Adveniens* (A Call to Action) by demanding of the well-off a selfless service to the poor: "the more fortunate should renounce some of their rights so as to place their goods more generously at the service of others."[2] In 1981, Pope John Paul II reaffirmed Leo's words and extended the hand of the church specifically to the poor, writing in *Laborem Exercens* (On Human Work) that the church considers solidarity with the poor "her mission, her service, a proof of her fidelity of Christ, so that she can truly be the 'church of the poor.'" John Paul continued by explaining that among the causes of poverty are that "a low value is put on work and the rights that flow from it, especially the right to a just wage and to the personal security of the worker and his or her family."[3]

The U.S. Catholic bishops defined the church's "preferential option for the poor" as an "empowerment" issue in their letter, *Economic Justice for All: Catholic Social Teaching and the U.S. Economy*, in 1986. "All members of society" the bishops wrote, "have a special obligation to the poor and vulnerable,"[4] whom they describe as "powerless, exiled, and oppressed."[5] And the new *Catechism* published in 1994, declares that "those who are oppressed by poverty are the object of a preferential love on the part of the church."[6]

The bishops went on in *Economic Justice* to outline four priorities for government in improving the lot of the poor. They recommended:

- Action on the premise that "the fulfillment of the basic needs of the poor is of the highest priority"[7];
- A high social priority for "increasing active participation in economic life of those who are presently excluded"[8];
- Directing "investment of wealth, talent and human energy . . . to benefit those who are poor or economically insecure"[9]; and
- The ongoing evaluation of "economic and social policies as well as the organization of the work world . . . in light of their impact on the strength and stability of family life."[10]

• • •

Women and Welfare

Views on welfare in the United States come out of a well of sentiment on race and gender. The welfare reform drive that dominated the first year of the current session of Congress has as much to do with the roles of women—especially poor women—as it does with welfare. While 300 thousand men receive public assistance under AFDC, and thousands of others benefit from other welfare programs, reform proposals—including family caps (limits on the number of a recipient's children for whom she can receive assistance), denial of benefits to mothers who are minors, time limits on receipt of benefits, "workfare," reimposition of abortion restrictions, dismantling of family planning services—all primarily affect women and women's ability to take charge of their lives. Women receiving aid also would be severely harmed by proposals to reduce the earned income tax credit. Conservative "reformers" paint a picture of welfare as an over-full trough at which increasingly promiscuous, greedy, and fecund women feed. This has never been the case, and it is a caricature that would be laughable were its impact not so devastating. The image of "welfare queen" taps into racist and sexist tendencies, both conscious and unconscious, in a broad segment of the population. Despite the stereotype, women on welfare are mostly white and have an average of two children. The majority of these women seek public assistance for periods of less than two years. Many of them work. Sometimes they are able to find only part-time employment, sometimes seasonal employment, and often their wages simply do not measure up.

More than 2.2 million adult, single, separated, widowed, or divorced women earned less in 1993 than the poverty level for a three-person household of $11,521, or $5.54 an hour at full-time, year-round wages. The median weekly pay for all women in 1992 was $295. This is barely half the median wage of $505 for all men. Further, the median weekly earnings for low-skilled jobs—usually held by women—were even lower: cashiers, $135; janitors and cleaners, $154; food preparation workers, $135; nursing aides, orderlies, and attendants, $222; textile sewing machine operators, $192; bus drivers, $214.13.[11]

Even with the best intentions of the state to place women in jobs, and with women's eagerness to work, those jobs by their nature simply do not provide adequate income. Half the participants who received job training and placement through New Jersey's acclaimed REACH jobs program remained below the poverty level even though they were earning more than minimum wage.[12] Former President Ronald Reagan declared late in his administration that his welfare proposals, in the form of the Family Support Act and Job Opportunities and Basic Skills Program, would effect a "lasting emancipation from welfare dependency." They did not. The Reagan years did not produce the much vaunted emancipation from welfare dependency, but instead the largest jump in welfare rolls in sixteen years. By 1993, the national rolls had swollen to 5 million families on AFDC from 1.3 million families in 1988.

Furthermore, the average AFDC grant, adjusted for inflation, has actually declined in the last twenty-three years from $676 a month to $373. This is an inflation-adjusted reduction of 45 percent. Part—and only part—of this reduction is due to the fact that AFDC families were getting smaller. AFDC families with no more than two children grew from just under half of the caseload, to almost three-quarters (72.7 percent) between 1969 and 1992. This is lower than the average for nonwelfare families. During roughly the same time period (1970 to 1993) the number of AFDC recipients rose from 1.9 million to 5 million individuals, while administrative costs for the program rose from $758 million to $2.87 billion, adjusted for inflation. The costs of running the program far outstripped other increases and contrast dismally with the overall inflation-adjusted levels of actual benefits paid.

Welfare and Reproduction

The current debate about welfare reform is only one chapter in the larger public discourse about cultural issues such as sex, marriage, procreation, and the family. With the notion that because welfare recipients accept public money, the public then has the right to dictate welfare recipients' behavior, welfare has become a hammer and anvil on which cultural conservatives aim to reshape behaviors among the poor. Their vision of how we ought to live our lives seems to be a greater good for these conservatives than helping the poor or eradicating poverty.

"America faces no problem greater than our skyrocketing illegitimacy rate," writes Lisa Schiffren, a former speech writer for Dan Quayle and a prominent member of the conservative Independent Women's Forum, in an op-ed column arguing that welfare reform should aim at teen-age mothers.[13] "Illegitimacy almost always sentences children to a life struggling against overwhelming odds that they will be poor."

While individual circumstances vary, most children fare better in a two-parent household—twice the adult attention, affection, guidance, resources, and sheer energy available for the demands of child raising—but we must ask ourselves if a male presence should be required for a child not to be poor. Even more to the point, we should ask if welfare policies should be the field on which the culture war is played out. All of us want to reduce the rate of teen pregnancy, for example, but many of us see the denial of already meager assistance to poor teenage mothers as unethical, punitive, and ineffectual.

The strong inclination among some policy makers to use the welfare system in an attempt to control reproduction deserves close scrutiny. Reproduction, located where public and private meet, is a likely target for those who are alarmed when poor people reproduce. (Public policies related to reproduction, both pronatalist and antinatalist, are not uncommon elsewhere in the world. Some western European countries encourage births through public policy. Other countries, most notably the People's Republic of China, use public policy to restrict births. In the United States, attempts to limit births are confined to the poor.) Not only is this tendency to engineer poor women's private decisions ethically questionable, but there is also strong evidence that these attempts will not achieve their goals. Recent studies show that the vast majority of pregnancies for women on welfare are unplanned. Denial or restriction of benefits will not reduce these unplanned events. But it will punish women for behavior that does not conform to prescribed patterns. And it will leave the children with no safety net at all.

Reproduction is both public and private. It is one of the most intimate human concerns, involving a couple's relationship to one another and a woman's relationship to her body. The decision to bring a new life into the world touches our deepest fears and reflects our best hopes for the future. But once a child is born, we as a society accept that we all bear some responsibility for the child, whose future actions will have consequences that transcend the bounds of his or her family. We all, regardless of whether we have children, contribute to public education, for example. Well-child programs, including nutrition programs for pregnant women and young children, help to insure that the next generation is prepared to compete in society. The taxpaying public should rightly be concerned about providing assistance to women who choose to bear children they cannot support. But proposals that would deny benefits for children born to women while on welfare would not encourage change. They would only make life harder for women who are raising children in already trying circumstances. There is a better way: We can provide opportunities for the poor to step out of poverty, and we can make quality sexual education and family planning accessible and available to everyone.

We should also be aware that public involvement in the private realm of reproductive decisions has consequences of its own. If we wish to protect the private nature of reproductive decisions—and the evidence is that we do—then we enter that sacred space with great risk. If we breach the private sphere, even with the best intentions, the next incursion may be made more routinely and with less reflection on the consequences. At a time when technological advances are making available increasing amounts of information about a developing fetus, we must ask if, as a society, we should be involved in deciding which children should be born. Where would we draw the line? Do we want, for instance, to prevent a woman from carrying a deformed fetus to term? Would only "perfect" babies who will not, presumably, draw inordinately on financial resources be permitted? This ethical morass can be avoided if we refuse to compromise individual freedom in reproductive decision making.

Summary and Action Recommendations

Our welfare system can and should be improved. However, certain reform recommendations have little to do with the commonly accepted goals of public assistance for the needy. Public opinion polls show that Americans solidly support the notion that the government should support poor women and their children, including extending some types of assistance beyond the point at which they now cease, just as recipients are getting back on their feet.[14] Nevertheless, many in this country believe that those currently receiving assistance are somehow undeserving. Misinformation about the nature of welfare and those who receive it creates a constituency for the ideologically prompted cuts currently proposed. Many proposals, including denial of benefits to children born to women on welfare and arbitrary time limits on receipt of assistance, are punitive at their core. Rather than dealing with the real problems of delivering appropriate financial and medical assistance to the needy, these proposals are designed to change certain behaviors.

In their first priority recommendation for government in improving the lot of the poor, the U.S. Catholic bishops packed their biggest punch: "The fulfillment of the basic needs of the poor [is] the highest government priority."[15] Before we buy the B-2, before we land on the moon, and certainly before we tell people how to behave, we should consider what poor people need and how we can provide it. The mission of a welfare system must be to provide the resources necessary to insure access to the basic needs, including shelter, food, clothing, education, and medical care. The system must provide these resources in a way that acknowledges and promotes the dignity of the individual. The system must provide services and support that will serve to ameliorate the underlying conditions that lead to and perpetuate poverty, including job training, life skills training, and appropriate child care.

The elimination of poverty does not, however, rest entirely within the welfare system as we know it. The government has a wider responsibility to ensure that jobs are available to women and men offering wages adequate to insure a decent standard of living. Government tax policies should use progressivity as a means of insuring that those who are closest to the edge are protected from slipping into poverty. Most categorical restrictions and limits such as child caps and time limits serve only to pit women against their children and drive families apart. While these measures create barriers that keep welfare rolls artificially low, their long-term impact is to create conditions that actually foster long-term poverty.

"Basic justice," the bishops wrote in *Economic Justice for All,* "calls for the establishment of a floor of material well-being on which all can stand."[16] Justice also "demands the establishment of minimum levels of participation in the life of the human community for all persons."[17]

A just welfare system would:

- Provide material sustenance to people—men, women, and children—who need it;
- Integrate the poor into solving the problem of poverty;
- Provide real help in finding good jobs for people and prepare them for work;
- Offer appropriate support during the transition from welfare to self-sufficiency;
- Encourage and facilitate reproductive choices in the form of sex education, reproductive services and counseling, and child care; and
- Offer hope to poor children.

Again, we look to Catholic social justice teaching as a guide. "As individuals and as a nation," the bishop wrote, "we are called to make a fundamental 'option for the poor.' The obligation to evaluate social and economic activity from the viewpoint of the poor and the powerless arise, from the radical command to love one's neighbor as oneself. . . . The prime purpose of this special commitment to the poor is to enable them to become active participants in the life of society. It is to enable all persons to share in and contribute to the common good."[18]

. . .

Notes

1. *Rerum Novarum* (On the Condition of Workers, 1891), 29.

2. *Octogesima Adveniens* (A Call to Action, 1971), 23.

3. *Laborem Exercens* (On Human Work, 1981), 8.

4. *Economic Justice for All: Catholic Social Teaching and the U.S. Economy*, 16.

5. Ibid., 49.

6. *Catechism of the Catholic Church* (Libreria Editrice Vaticana, 1994), 2448.

7. *Economic Justice for All*, 90.

8. Ibid., 91.

9. Ibid., 92.

10. Ibid., 93.

11. Linda Levine, "Jobs for Welfare Recipients: An Issue Overview," Congressional Research Service, Report 94-461 E, May 27, 1994.

12. Lee Seglem, "What to Do with Welfare," *State Legislatures*, May 1993.

13. Lisa Schiffren, "Penalize the Unwed Dad? Fat Chance," *New York Times*, Aug. 10, 1995.

14. American Public Welfare Association, *The Values of Welfare Reform* (Washington, D.C.: American Public Welfare Association, 1994), p. 4.

15. *Economic Justice for All*, 90.

16. Ibid., 74.

17. Ibid., 77.

18. Ibid, 87–88.

Lawrence Bush and Jeffrey Dekro

10   Jews, Money, and Social Responsibility

Rabbi Yishmael said: "One who wishes to acquire wisdom should study the way money works, for there is no greater area of Torah-study than this. It is like an everflowing stream. . . ."

—(Talmud, *Bava Batra* 175b)

The way money works is that everybody has problems with it. Everybody. This has become clear at each of the annual retreats for progressive Jewish funders hosted by The Shefa Fund, a Philadelphia-based public foundation that has, since 1989, been involved in grant-making and organizing money on behalf of Jewish spiritual and political causes. Pain abounds and tears invariably flow at these gatherings, at which people of wealth have an opportunity to interact in a supportive, intimate atmosphere. For those with inherited wealth, especially, money seems often undermining to their ambition and self-esteem, a constant source of political tension, and deeply commingled with their angriest or most mournful family memories. Adding insult to injury are the eat-the-rich prejudices and adore-the-rich objectifications in which most non-wealthy people indulge, creating obstacles to cross-class intimacy.

Why all this emotion about a mere tool of exchange? One answer, offered by Martha Ackelsberg, a professor of political science at Smith College, at The Shefa Fund's first retreat in 1989, is that money is obviously not merely a tool of exchange, but a measurement of power and status used to create rankings in society. These rankings are propped up by two myths: the myth of personal merit (that we "deserve what we have"), and the myth of individualism (that we succeed or fail exclusively on our own—indeed, that success is a process of differentiating ourselves from others). These myths are given substance and reinforcement by the class system's unequal

Originally published in *Tikkun* (September/October 1993), 8:33–36, 92. Reprinted from TIKKUN MAGAZINE, A BI-MONTHLY JEWISH CRITIQUE OF POLITICS, CULTURE, AND SOCIETY. Information and subscriptions are available from TIKKUN, 26 Fell Street, San Francisco, CA 94102.

opportunities and privileges, class-bound cultural identities, and cross-class prejudices, all of which ultimately serves, in Ackelsberg's words, to "legitimize vast inequalities of income, wealth and respect," while "generating feelings of isolation, powerlessness and inadequacy."

For The Shefa Fund conferees, such feelings of isolation are compounded by Jewish memory: memory of the classic anti-Semitic stereotypes that link us to greed and ill-begotten affluence, and memory of persecution and displacement, particularly in Europe, against which Jewish wealth (bribery) and professionalism (indispensability) were often our only available, though far from infallible, defenses. For Jews, money has been a tool not merely of status and power but of survival. ("'Choose life'—this refers to a craft or trade," says the Jerusalem Talmud, quoting the same, very practical-minded Rabbi Yishmael cited at the opening of this essay.) Anxiety therefore usually triumphs over pride as we contemplate our relative economic success in America, for we know, as Jews, that we have good reason to worry about visibly thriving within a system that is marred by inequity.

Estimates, for example, by Steven M. Cohen, a leading demographer of American Jewish life, that one third of American multimillionaires are Jews, as are 40–50 percent of elites in professions such as medicine, law, and the media, are apt to make most Jewish Americans nervous; these data appear to give credence to the rich Jew stereotype. On the other hand, a 1976 *Harvard Business Review* study of 444 top executives of major U.S. corporations that found only 5 percent were Jewish (although we make up a significantly higher percentage of college graduates), may relieve some of our anxiety—while leaving us vaguely alarmed about anti-Semitism in corporate life.

Given money's anxiety-making power, why would a Talmudic sage assert that "there is no greater area of Torah-Study" than "the way money works"—a statement that itself provokes Jewish fears, because of its potential for feeding anti-Semitic perceptions of Jews and Judaism?

We believe that Rabbi Yishmael's assertion about money is profoundly spiritual, and potentially far more empowering than the usual religious preachments that avoid confronting the complexities of wealth and poverty by simply dismissing money as "filthy lucre" and urging various degrees of asceticism. In fact, Judaism does very much concern itself with the holiness potential of nearly every aspect of daily living. Within Jewish thought, the challenge to human beings is either to actualize this holiness, and thus bring blessings, or to ignore it, and thus cause suffering. Either way—whether we render our economic life into a Torah of Money or into an idolatrous worship of the Almighty Dollar—Rabbi Yishmael is affirming that our choices will have consequences, from which a faithful observer can glean wisdom. What are the kernels of holiness that can render blessings rather than torments from our economic involvements? Central to the Torah of Money are teachings that reinforce human awareness of interdependence and mutual responsibility—an awareness that directly contradicts the preachments about personal merit and individualism that make the class system so painful. While Jewish covenantal history originates with a handful of individuals (Abraham, Sarah, Isaac, Rebekah, Jacob, Leah, Rachel), "it finds its fulfillment," writes Judith Plaskow in her Jewish feminist theology, *Stand-*

ing Again at Sinai, "only at Sinai when the whole congregation answers together, 'All that the Lord has spoken we will do'" (Exodus 19:8). Plaskow sees a link between feminism and Judaism in their shared, central assumption "that personhood is shaped, nourished and sustained in community. . . ."

In the economic sphere, this assumption is underlined by Judaism's emphasis on stewardship, rather than ownership, of wealth. "The Divine origin of wealth," writes Meir Tamari, former chief economist in the Office of the Governor of the Bank of Israel, "is the central practice of Jewish economic philosophy." Since Judaism is a community-oriented rather than an individual-oriented religion, this means that the group at all levels . . . is thereby made a partner in each individual's wealth."

Reinforcing this sense of stewardship are the Jewish cycles of work/acquisition and rest/restoration: the weekly sabbath, the sabbatical year, and the half-century Jubilee Release that are detailed in Leviticus 25:1–13. Stewardship is also the principle underlying the Jewish tradition of *tzedakah,* obligatory alms-giving, which acknowledges charity in its highest forms to be a process of social investment that redounds to the benefit of the donor, the recipient, and the whole community.

The Jewish holiday, prayer, and study cycles likewise contain sources for the development of a Torah of Money:

- The Sh'ma, for example, the best-known prayer of the Jewish liturgy, with its declaration of the unity of God and the cosmic significance of our deeds, can easily be extrapolated into a treatise on communally aware, environmentally responsible economics.
- The concepts of *beracha and kedusha* that before eating and performing other deeds we must consciously affirm a sense of being blessed ("Whoever enjoys the goods of this world without reciting a blessing is like a thief," declares the Talmud)—offers valuable guidance about limiting wasteful consumption.
- The concept of *s'yag l'Tora,* making "a fence for the Torah"—that is, establishing practices that would keep us from violating Torah teachings even accidentally, unwittingly, or under duress—can easily be taken as a basis for a ban on nuclear weaponry and nuclear power, the sheer toxicity and dangers of which threaten the very fabric of Creation.

There is no shortage of building blocks for the Torah of Money, since more than 100 of the 613 commandments of Jewish law deal with economic issues. Yet while Judaism has in modern history been idealized and appropriated as a paradigm by proponents of both capitalism and socialism, few modern Jews have in fact tried to develop a Jewish economic philosophy that is not an apologetic for either system, but a genuine alternative to both. Orthodox communities, as Guardians of the Halacha, have generally been too inward-looking and hostile to modern textual interpretation to propose a Torah of Money that might be broadly relevant to our socioeconomic lives: the liberal religious Jewish community has generally been unwilling to burden itself with Judaism's obligations and has contented itself with Louis Brandeis's famous claim that "The twentieth century ideals of America have been the ideals of the Jew for more than twenty centuries"; the secular Jewish community has rejected and eventually become ignorant of, Judaic wisdom because it seems dependent upon deity for its authority. Today, however, the collapse of communism and the increasing human and environmental toll of capitalism has created a pressing need for alternative economic models. Activists are renewing Martin Buber's search for what he called, in 1943, "a genuine third alternative . . . leading beyond individualism and collectivism, for the life decision of future generations." Such crises of our species as mass starvation, AIDS, unrestrained violence, and the degradation of our biosphere—crises that transcend economic systems, political dogmas and national boundaries—are bringing us face-to-face with questions about self-preservation and self-restraint, personal and communal responsibility, moral authority and political power, questions that are at the very core of the Jewish religious tradition. If divine authority offends contemporary sensibilities, the environmental imperatives of Creation carry implications of covenant that are as demanding as any divine commandments. In short, the "market value" of Judaism is at an all-time high in the ongoing enterprise of human liberation.

Of course, Judaism by no means has a patent on designs for a genuine third alternative in economic life. Among many other religious and secular voices for economic justice, there has been in the United States for well over twenty years a socially responsible money movement that has sought to make social change by using marketplace mechanisms that can reform corporate behavior, such as shareholder initiatives, socially screened investments, consumer boycotts, and selective shopping. Many Jews have been among the pioneers of this movement, including:

- Alice Tepper Marlin, founder of the Council on Economic Priorities, whose best-selling *Shopping for a Better World* has brought the notion of socially responsible money activism into nearly a million American households. Tepper Marlin began on this path when she was asked in 1968 to design an investment portfolio for a Boston synagogue seeking to exclude companies manufacturing weapons for use in Vietnam.

- Robert Zevin, manager of the Calvert Social Investment Fund at U.S. Trust, whose research helped establish that South Africa-free portfolios—comprising the major part of the $600 billion presently counted as socially screened investments—can be as profitable as the Standard & Poor 500.

- Ben Cohen and Jerry Greenfield of the Ben & Jerry's Ice Cream Co., who give 9 percent of their profits to socially progressive causes, maintain a 7:1 ratio within the company, and have succeeded at making one out of every 100 Vermonters a shareholder in their company. ("The community allows you to exist," Cohen has written. "People in the community buy your product. They provide the infrastructure; they provide all the resources that you use; they provide everything except the ideas.")

- Arnold Hiatt, chief executive officer for twenty-four years of the Stride Rite Corp. (maker of Keds, Sperry and Stride Rite shoes), a company that gives away 5 percent of its profits. "We look at public service as an investment," he told *Newsweek* on May 4, 1992, after he gave up his CEO status to head the Stride Rite Foundation.

"We believe that the well-being of a company cannot be separated from the well-being of the community. If we're not providing the community with access to day care and elder care, if we're not providing proper funding for education, then we're not investing properly in our business."

For these and many other notable Jewish activists within the social responsibility movement, however, political judgments seem rooted more consciously in the American peace, feminist, and civil rights movements of the past three decades than in any religious tradition. Although some individual activists may feel influenced by their Jewish values and tradition, few of them publicly bring to bear Jewish concepts or affirm their Jewish identities in the course of their work. Indeed, despite what we see as an exciting overlap between the goals and ideals of the social responsibility movement and the Torah of Money, the organized Jewish community and its articulated values and interests have been invisible within, or conspicuously absent from, the social responsibility movement, for reasons that we will explore.

For example, while nuclear power has been universally avoided by socially responsible investors, the National Jewish Community Relations Advisory Council (NJCRAC), representing the broadest coalition of national and local Jewish organizations, has consistently endorsed the development of nuclear energy, for fear of the influence of oil-producing (mostly Arab) nations. Only the National Council of Jewish Women and, most recently, the Reform movement, have stood for a moratorium on nuclear development.

Similarly, while the Council on Economic Priorities gives negative citations in its ratings books to companies that are deeply involved in weapons-related work (among them Bayer, Eastman Kodak, General Electric, and Ralston Purina, all with consumer products on the supermarket shelves), Jewish organizations, in contrast, have remained mostly mute about the sharp conventional arms buildup of the Carter-Reagan-Bush years in order to protect the steady flow of aid to Israel.

Nor have industries with a significant Jewish presence been subjected to the pressures that the organized Jewish community could bring to bear on behalf of social responsibility. The $3-billion toy industry, for example, includes a strong Jewish presence in Mattel, Hasbro, Ideal, and other major companies. This Jewish presence, in combination with the Jewish influence within the film and television industries, lends a particular opportunity to Jewish activists and organizations to act upon concerns about violence-linked toys and entertainment. That opportunity has not been pursued—perhaps, in part, because companies such as Hasbro, the makers of G.I. Joe, have been generous donors to Jewish Federation drives and communal organizations.

The most glaring Jewish absence, however, is in the realm of community development corporations and socially responsible banks, institutions that are *reinvesting* dollars in the name of social justice, rather than merely *divesting* or withholding dollars from socially irresponsible corporations. The National Association of Community Development Loan Funds (NACDLF), for example, has since 1985 gained more than forty member funds with approximately $80 million under management—dollars that have created at least 14,000 affordable housing units and 3,700 jobs, according to NACDLF, in communities that were redlined and denied credit by mainstream banks. Religious institutions have provided nearly $18 million of this investment capital—with less than $100,000 coming from Jewish institutional sources.

Similarly, when Brooklyn's Community Capital Bank, modelled on the notably successful South Shore Bank of Chicago, needed to raise $6 million in start-up capital, only five Jewishly identified investments were forthcoming—this in the city with the largest Jewish population of any in the world, and despite an outreach effort involving meetings, letters, personal briefings, and solicitations. Nationwide, approximately 5,000 Jewish family foundations have assets totaling billions of dollars. Many of these foundations were endowed from the fortunes of urban-based businesses, real estate developers, attorneys, etc. These monies should represent an abundant source of potential investment capital for community development activities in cities across the country. Moreover, the Jewish historical experience of exclusion from credit, which was compensated for by more than 500 Jewish credit unions and more than 2,000 fraternal organizations in the 1920s and 1930s, should serve to sensitize Jews to the plight of credit-starved minority communities. Why has the organized Jewish community shied away from the socially responsible money movement? We believe there are a number of explanations, which we will briefly outline.

First, despite the scope of American Jewish wealth, few Jewish organizations have historically had substantial monies available at the national level for investment. Most operate on cash-flow budgets, and the building of endowment funds is a relatively new development in Jewish organizational life.

Second, the community is highly decentralized. Within each organization, and from one locale to the next, diverse interests compete for the allegiance and resources of individual donors. Few opportunities exist to explore and develop policy, including philanthropic and investment policy, on issues other than those of direct and exclusive Jewish communal concern. These "direct and exclusive" Jewish concerns, moreover, are daunting. They include protection of Jews worldwide from anti-Semitism and physical threat; economic and political support for Israel; Jewish immigration and social welfare needs in the United States; promotion of Jewish education and culture; and maintenance of Jewish institutional networks, all this on the shoulders of fewer than six million people, a large plurality of whom are not even organizationally affiliated with the Jewish community.

Third, for all its vaunted clout, the Jewish community has a cautious and wary mind-set. Agitating loudly for reform in a corporate world that only recently has been cleared of charges of board room anti-Semitism would not be a natural course of action for most Jewish organizations. Our extreme sensitivity to anti-Semitism makes Jews particularly guarded, in fact, about publicly and forthrightly using money as a tool of political influence.

Fourth, Israel's historical alliance with the U.S. military-industrial complex has muted Jewish opposition to the bloated U.S. industry, whereas the social responsibility movement has deep roots in the opposition to that industry that arose during the Vietnam War. Although many Jews and some Jewish organizations (notably the Reform movement) actively opposed that war, there remains a Jewish fear that disinvestment in military-related corporations may threaten Israel's security. Thus, a certain distance persists between the Jewish community and the social responsibility community.

Finally, alienation between Jews and African Americans, fed by harsh Black anti-Semitism, has driven Jews away from many of the community development activities with which the social responsibility movement is directly involved. Jewish migration from cities to the suburbs, and into the ranks of the economically privileged, has also lessened the Jewish sense of stake in urban issues.

Despite these obstacles, there is still substantial agreement among American Jews about the need to overcome the poverty that torments 32 million American families and undermines the well-being of the United States as a whole. Motivated both by self-interest and by a well-preserved prophetic sensibility, the Jewish community as a whole remains one of America's most tenacious advocates of democracy, generosity, and open-mindedness, notwithstanding twelve years of conservative government. "When Ronald Reagan asked and George Bush echoed, 'Are you better off today than you were eight years ago,'" said Michael Pelavin, then-chair of NJCRAC, in a 1989 address, "the Jewish community answered not individually but collectively. While many of us may indeed be better of financially today than in 1980, we dispute the premise of the question. We ask today 'What is the state of America today compared to eight years ago?' . . . The strength of the Jewish community and its ability to survive in freedom bears a direct relationship to the quality of life of those around us. . . ."

Pelavin's affirmation of Jewish prosperity during the Reagan-Bush years is offset by the sense of downward mobility faced by many baby-boomer Jews, their younger siblings, and children. The white-collar recession of the past few years and the general stagnation of the middle class has hit Jews hard. Unemployment for college graduates, notes Rob Hoffman in the *International Jewish Monthly* of B'nai B'rith (May 1992), "rose from 5.2 percent to 6.9 percent in 1991, and two thirds [of college graduates] see job security as a first job's most important feature. . . . Law firms are among those hit hardest . . . starting with a 10–20 percent decline in recruitment by larger firms over the last two years." Likewise have the Jewish poor and elderly been particularly affected by the fraying of the social "safety net," although Jewish communal services have done an outstanding job at preventing their situation from deteriorating as badly as it has for other ethnic groups.

Building an alliance between the social responsibility movement and the organized Jewish community does not, therefore, necessitate politically converting American Jews. Individuals and institutions, rather, need to be emboldened to put their money where their values are. One such fortifying effort is the Tzedek Economic Development Campaign (TzEDeC) of The Shefa Fund, which is exploring ways for Jews and Jewish institutions to invest publicly and participate visibly in low-income community development throughout the United States. Toward this end, The Shefa Fund is convening a board of experts in business and finance, community economic development, social investment, philanthropy, and Jewish communal affairs, to develop a feasibility study of various strategies (such as community loan funds, housing development tax credits, and enterprise zones) that could be adopted to stimulate Jewish investment. This feasibility study will lead to a business plan to implement TzEDeC's goals within two years.

We believe an alliance between the Jewish community and the social responsibility movement would be of great mutual benefit. For the social responsibility movement, it would mean access to billions of new dollars, tremendous financial and political savvy, and a vocabulary of religious humanism that has great power and currency in modern American life. For the Jewish community, working with the social responsibility movement would help define an activist role for the consumer, investor, and contributor. This would expand the landscape of politics beyond the kinds of activism that mobilized Jews in the past as trade unionists, students, and community residents but have become less and less relevant to the daily lives of professional, suburbanized Jewish Americans today. Such an alliance would also mean bringing our Judaism and our Jewish selves into fruitful contact with issues of universal concern—issues with which many Jewish activists who make their home outside the organized Jewish community are already involved. Finally, it could help win for Judaism and for the Torah of Money a heightened investment from caring people for whom the "ism's" of the past century have exhausted their theoretical and prescriptive power.

Thomas J. Paprocki

11 Option for the Poor: Preference or Platitude?

For over 100 years now, a phenomenon has been emerging in the Catholic Church with increasingly greater sophistication—Catholic social teaching. It is unusual in that the emergence of this remarkable doctrine has not been confined to intellectual or academic ruminations, but can be observed in the practical settings of significant world events and movements. The National Conference of Catholic Bishops has described Catholic social teaching as a set of principles, a body of thought and a call to action. Its growing sophistication can be seen in the wisdom gleaned from years of taking these principles and teachings and putting them into action in labor movements, public policy, social action, economic development and the shift from dictatorship to democratic forms of government, especially in the third world countries of Latin America.

Despite its growing sophistication, Catholic social teaching has been called the best kept secret in the Roman Catholic Church in the United States. Whatever the reasons for this obscurity, there can be no doubt that Catholic social teaching defines itself as an essential component of the Catholic faith. This was best articulated by the 1971 Synod of Bishops in their statement, *Justice in the World:* "Action on behalf of justice and participation in the transformation of the world fully appear to us as a constitutive dimension of preaching the Gospel" (No. 6). Indeed, it is no exaggeration to say that this document, in fact, this one sentence, was the primary motivation for my decision as a priest to enter law school and establish the Chicago Legal Clinic to provide legal services for the poor.

Within the tradition itself, the phrase that has come to express and be identified with Catholic social teaching is "option for the poor." Of course, the underpinnings for this phrase are contained in the teachings of Jesus himself, his care for and attitude

Originally published in *America* (April 22, 1995), 172:11–14. Reprinted with the permission of Thomas J. Paprocki and America Press, Inc., 106 West 56th Street, New York, NY 10019.

towards the poor, and the poverty of his own life. The early Christian community showed a special respect for the poor, as can be seen in St. Paul's Letter to the Galatians, in which he wrote that the "pillars" of the church—James, Cephas (Peter) and John—gave the handclasp of fellowship to Paul and Barnabas and sent them to preach the Gospel to the Gentiles as well as to the Jews. But there was a condition: "The only stipulation was that we should be mindful of the poor—the one thing that I was making every effort to do" (Gal. 2:10).

The nascent elements of the contemporary option for the poor are found in the encyclical *Rerum Novarum* of Pope Leo XIII, who wrote in 1891, "In protecting the rights of private individuals, special consideration must be given to the weak and the poor" (No. 54). While Pope Leo's encyclical expresses *concern* for the poor, a specifically articulated *option* for the poor did not emerge until recent years. It is now a firmly established tenet of Catholic social thought, frequently invoked by Pope John Paul II himself.

Preferential but Not Exclusive

The very notion of an option for the poor has itself been a source of controversy. Some have tended to connect the term more with Marxism than with its true roots in the Bible; others, feeling threatened and perhaps guilty about their own commitment to the poor, respond defensively. Furthermore, the skepticism is compounded by the addition of a descriptive adjective to the term, as in *preferential* option for the poor. Such a description was made by the bishops of Latin America at their conference in Puebla, Mexico, in 1978.

Calling the option for the poor a preferential one raises all kinds of questions and doubts. Doesn't God's love and mercy reach all people, rich and poor alike? Should the church discriminate by attending to the poor and ignoring the rich? Will I be excluded from salvation if I am not sufficiently poor? Pope John Paul II sought to address such concerns by clarifying that this option was a call for a "preferential yet not exclusive love for the poor." This means that the church is to show a special solicitude for the poor, but not necessarily to the point of neglecting those who are not poor. All other things being equal, when choices must be made about the allocation of human and financial resources, including such resources as time and attention, priority should be given to the indigent. At the same time, everyone must be cared for somehow, if the church is to remain truly catholic in the broadest sense of that term.

Preference or Platitude?

What does this "preference" mean in practice? The word "preference" comes from the Latin verb *praeferre,* to put before. "Option" comes from the Latin word *optio,* a free choice. A "preferential option," then, is to make a free choice to put someone or something before another. Or, as the Rev. Louis Cameli of Mundelein Seminary puts it, "The option for the poor means giving poor people a break."

In an honest examination of the notion of our ethical obligation to make an option for the poor, we must ask whether we have made this choice a real preference or a mere platitude. Have we really chosen to prefer the poor in practical, concrete ways, or has the notion of an "option for the poor" become merely a trite phrase, invoked to offer obligatory homage to Catholic social theory?

The answer to this question requires a sort of examination of conscience. Since such examinations are best done in the private forum, the purpose in asking the question here is not to come up with public finger-pointing answers, but to assist our *consciences* by putting the matter squarely before our *consciousness*. (Both words, "conscience" and "conscious," come from the same Latin roots, *com* and *scire*, to know with or to share knowledge.) When making an examination of conscience, it is helpful at times to look at the lives of others, not in order to compare ourselves with them favorably or unfavorably, but to see how they have sought to put their beliefs into practice. Indeed, that is why we continue to read the lives of the saints, hoping to learn from and perhaps imitate their example.

A Real-Life Preferred Option

While it may be premature to declare this man a saint, Peter Bigelow was recently featured in *Chicago* magazine for his personal preferential option for the poor. Peter Bigelow is the owner of a $19 million homebuilding company, who recently sold his own luxurious home in suburban Rolling Meadows for $325,000. That in itself does not constitute an option for the poor. What is significant is the choice of location for his new home: North Lawndale, one the most impoverished neighborhoods on Chicago's West Side. If a white man is an anomaly in this African-American community, a *rich* white man choosing to live in North Lawndale, where the per capita annual income is $5,500, is practically incomprehensible. His purpose in moving to the West Side: to establish a not-for-profit housing venture and add his expertise to a variety of building projects providing desperately needed housing. He sums up his motivation succinctly: "I didn't know any poor people, but Jesus did."

Individual and Community Option

The story of Peter Bigelow is one example of an individual's choice to opt for the poor. Such choices can and should be made by the community as well. The fact that there are concurrent dimensions in which both the individual and the community respond to the Gospel can be seen in the Eucharist. We read and reflect on the Scriptures and pray and worship together as a group, but there is also an individual encounter when we receive the body and blood of Christ. So too, the option for the poor calls for a response by both the individual and the community.

The example of Peter Bigelow is a radical response, but there are other, less drastic ways for individuals and corporations to respond. Charles H. Shaw and Edward A. Brennan, for example, have not moved to North Lawndale, as Peter Bigelow did. But The Shaw Company (a real estate developer) and Sears, Roebuck and Company (the giant retailer of which Ed Brennan is C.E.O.) have chosen to develop the original site of Sears, Roebuck on the West Side of Chicago.

This joint venture between Shaw and Sears is an ambitious plan to build a community for low and moderate income people. The development will be both commercial and residential, since the goal is to build a neighborhood. There will be subsidies for the poor and a heavy emphasis on home ownership, which Shaw sees as crucial to bringing stability to a community. As he puts it, "You care more about the system if you own part of it." Shaw also hopes that this development will be a vessel for jobs by bringing employment opportunities back to North Lawndale.

Why would Charles Shaw get involved in something like this? He answers by explaining that when Ed Brennan asked him to enter into this joint venture, he said he tried to figure out the right thing to do. From this perspective, he knew that he should say yes to the proposal. Shaw says he believes strongly in the role of the private sector in developing our country. He also describes a spiritual reflection prompted by a very serious auto accident that almost cost him his life last year. While recuperating, he had time to reflect on what to do with his life and how best to use the limited time we have on earth. His conclusion: He now seeks to undertake projects where he thinks he can make a difference.

Undoubtedly Charles Shaw and Ed Brennan hope to make money on this development. But the hope of financial gain in their joint venture only underscores the point that the option for the poor does not necessarily mean taking a bath in red ink. In contrast to some real estate developers who might be interested only in wealthy communities, a conscious decision was made to invest in one of the most impoverished areas of Chicago. That is an option for the poor.

In the legal profession, with which I am more familiar, some attorneys opt to serve the poor as full-time providers of legal services for the indigent with government agencies or not-for-profit legal clinics. Others choose to remain in private practice and volunteer their services by taking two cases per year *pro bono publico.* Still other attorneys and business executives assist the poor by giving of their time and expertise to serve on boards of directors of charitable organizations which help the poor. For many, the easiest way to give is through financial contributions.

In addition to these individual responses, a corporate examination of conscience will ask to what extent the organization itself fosters an atmosphere of encouraging pro bono or charitable involvement. When members of the organization seek to do charitable work, are they told to do so on their own time? Or is that desire tolerated only grudgingly as an unwelcome intrusion into company time? Or are members of the organization actively encouraged to do some charitable or volunteer work even as part of their official responsibilities? In any organization or business, is there a corporate philosophy of philanthropic giving? Some law firms, for example, have taken helpful steps to be proactive in this regard by adopting policies that expressly encourage pro bono involvement. Many have even hired pro bono coordinators to act as liaison between the firms' attorneys and not-for-profit legal service providers.

In a parish setting, individuals are often asked to give to special collections for the poor, to serve in soup kitchens or help provide food baskets for the hungry and donate used clothing for the needy. But the parish as a community can and should look for ways to make a communal option for the poor. For example, as parish income grows, is any potential surplus eaten up by constantly hiring more staff members, so that the budget is never better than break-even? Or are some funds deliberately set aside to assist poorer parishes in the inner-city?

On a diocesan level, we typically expect to find institutions dedicated to helping the poor, such as Catholic Charities, the Campaign for Human Development and Catholic Relief Services. But we must also ask: Are "full-service" parishes possible only in those communities wealthy enough to hire sufficient staff to provide these services; or are resources allocated in such a way as to ensure that even the poorest parishes can offer the wide spectrum of services one would typically expect of a parish, such as youth ministry, religious education, ministry of care for the sick, music and liturgical ministry? In the sphere of Catholic health care, is there any real distinction between Catholic hospitals and for-profit medical centers in the availability of their services for the poor? Similarly, in Catholic higher education, is an intellectually talented but financially impoverished student any more likely to get a scholarship at a Catholic college than at a state university?

Authenticity

As with any examination of conscience, the responses of individuals and communities to the challenge of opting for the poor will vary. The question is whether the option for the poor is an authentic description of Catholic social teaching put into practice in the real world, or mere lip-service designed to enhance a theoretical doctrine with no basis in fact. The extent to which we bring that question to conscious deliberation and then make some deliberate choices in real life will determine whether the answer is truly a preferential option or merely a pious platitude.

The earth is the Lord's

(Psalm 24:1)

Often the Jewish, Christian, and Muslim traditions are seen as supporting the idea that human beings are "the crown of creation," and exhibiting an anthropocentric view of the world that focuses on mastery of nature and animals and their use for human need only. Yet these traditions, as well as Buddhist and Native American traditions, incorporate a reverence for the whole world, and a respect for the whole of creation. Psalm 24:1 declares: "The earth is the Lord's, and the fulness thereof; the world, and they that dwell therein." From this perspective, humans are required to use their physical and mental abilities to care for the planet on which they find themselves.

The three essays included here make strong religious cases for this perspective, based on their respective authoritative texts. The use of ancient texts to support these perspectives points to the ways in which those texts can be rediscovered and reinterpreted to connect to contemporary insights and visions of the future.

Kenneth Kraft writes about new American Buddhist practices that focus on issues of conservation of resources. These practices include reinterpretations of the teachings of the Buddha to focus attention on the earth and its needs. Kraft includes examples of practical suggestions for individual and collective Buddhist practices.

Andrew Linzey argues for animal rights based on his interpretation of Christian scriptural mandate. He focuses on the role of humans as humble servants who are set on earth to imitate Christ and identify with the diseased, poor, oppressed, and outcast, among which he includes the world's animals.

Arthur Waskow takes the biblical concept of Jubilee as his paradigm. The Hebrew Bible demands that the earth lie fallow every fiftieth year and that people give up their wealth. Waskow sees this command as a vision that suggests that humans learn about recycling wealth, rest from the demands of a cycle of producing and consuming, and decentralize resources. His vision speaks to a world that would be respectful of nature and the future of the planet.

Interest in ecology and the rights of animals has been an important dimension of the religious left's incorporation of new ideas and visions for the world's future. Of course, there are many other dimensions of environmentalism that concern the religious left: a strong interest in alternative fuel sources, recycling, and vegetarianism among them. Ecofeminism has developed extensive practices and protests around these issues, and religious groups are often involved in celebrations of Earth Day.

Kenneth Kraft

12 The Greening of Buddhist Practice

On January 5, 1993, a Japanese ship called the *Akatsuki Maru* returned to port with a controversial cargo: an estimated 1.5 metric tons of plutonium. Its 134-day voyage was the first step in a Japanese plan to send spent nuclear fuel to Europe to be reprocessed as plutonium, which will then be reused as fuel in nuclear reactors. However, the *Akatsuki Maru's* 20,000-mile round trip provoked expressions of concern in more than forty countries, including public demonstrations in France and Japan. Experts charged that such voyages could not adequately be shielded from the risks of a nuclear accident or a terrorist attack. Editorial writers questioned Japan's commitment to its own non-nuclear principles (reactor-grade plutonium can also be used to make nuclear weapons). Pointing to the nuclear aspirations of North Korea and other countries, some observers called for a worldwide halt in the recovery of plutonium from spent fuel.

Plutonium (named after Pluto, the Greek god of the underworld) is one of the deadliest substances known to humankind. A single speck ingested through the lungs or stomach is fatal. Plutonium-239 has a half-life of 24,400 years, but it continues to be dangerous for a quarter of a million years. If we think in terms of human generations, about twenty-five years, we are speaking of 10,000 generations that will be vulnerable unless the radioactivity is safely contained. In Buddhism, the number 10,000 is a concrete way of indicating something infinite. That may also be the unpleasant truth about plutonium: it is going to be with us forever.

The American scholar-activist Joanna Macy has suggested that our most enduring legacy to future generations may be the decisions we make about the production and disposal of radioactive materials. Our buildings and books may not survive us, but we will be held accountable for what we do with the toxic substances (nuclear and non-nuclear) that we continue to generate in such great quantities. Buddhists have long believed that the present, the past, and the future are inextricably linked and ultimately inseparable. "Just consider whether or not there are any conceivable be-

Originally published in *Cross Currents* (Summer 1994), 44:163–179. Reprinted with the permission of *Cross Currents*.

ings or any conceivable worlds which are not included in this present time," a thirteenth-century master asserted.[1] For human beings at least, to sabotage the future is also to ravage the past and undermine the present. Although the threat of nuclear holocaust appears to have abated, we are beginning to see that the ongoing degradation of the environment poses a threat of comparable danger. As the *Akatsuki Maru* ships plutonium to Japan, it is also carrying a radioactive cargo, a "poison fire," into our common future.

I am reminded of a Zen *koan* still used in the training of monks. The master says to the student: "See that boat moving way out there on the water? How do you stop it?" To give a proper answer the student must be able to demonstrate that he has "become one" with the boat. Just as one must penetrate deeply into a *koan* to solve it, Buddhists around the world have begun to immerse themselves in environmental issues, attempting to approach urgent problems from the inside as well as the outside. An increasing number of practitioner-activists believe that the only way to stop the boat of ecological disaster is to deepen our relationship to the planet and all life within it.

In this essay I would like to survey some of the ways in which Buddhists are responding to the environmental issues faced by so many countries today. I will concentrate on spiritual/religious practices and forms of activism that take place in a spiritual context. Although many Buddhists in Asia and elsewhere are becoming increasingly aware of ecology, I focus principally on North American Buddhists, who seem to be taking the lead in the "greening" of Buddhism. Of course, what we need most are *human* responses to the environmental crisis rather than "Buddhist" ones; when the Buddhist label is used here, it is almost always used in that spirit.

Individual Practices Related to the Environment

A list of individual practices must begin with traditional forms of Buddhist meditation (and closely related practices such as chanting). Meditation can serve as a vehicle for advancing several ends prized by environmentalists: it is supposed to reduce egoism, deepen appreciation of one's surroundings, foster empathy with other beings, clarify intention, prevent what is now called burnout, and ultimately lead to a profound sense of oneness with the entire universe. "I came to realize clearly," said a Japanese Zen master upon attaining enlightenment, "that Mind is not other than mountains and rivers and the great wide earth, the sun and the moon and the stars."[2]

For some Buddhists, meditation alone is regarded as a sufficient expression of ecological awareness. Others supplement time-honored forms of meditation with new meditative practices that incorporate nature imagery or environmental themes. For example, the following verse by the Vietnamese Zen teacher Thich Nhat Hanh is widely used by his American students, who recite it mentally in seated meditation:

> Breathing in, I know that I am breathing in.
> Breathing out, I know that I am breathing out.

> Breathing in, I see myself as a flower.
> Breathing out, I feel fresh.
>
> Breathing in, I see myself as a mountain.
> Breathing out, I feel solid.
>
> Breathing in, I see myself as still water.
> Breathing out, I reflect things as they are.
>
> Breathing in, I see myself as space.
> Breathing out, I feel free.[3]

Thich Nhat Hanh has helped to popularize another method of individual practice—short poems (*gatha*) that can prompt us to maintain awareness in daily life. Many of these "mindfulness verses" also function as reminders of our interconnectedness with the earth. The verses may be memorized or posted in appropriate locations. For example, when turning on a water faucet, a person following this practice will mentally recite:

> Water flows from high in the mountains.
> Water runs deep in the Earth.
> Miraculously, water comes to us,
> and sustains all life.

Washing one's hands can become an occasion for renewing one's dedication to the environment:

> Water flows over these hands.
> May I use them skillfully
> to preserve our precious planet.[4]

The following verse, meant to be used when getting into a car, again evokes a twofold mindfulness—for the moment and for interrelatedness:

> Entering this powerful car,
> I buckle my seatbelt
> and vow to protect all beings.[5]

The cultivation of intimacy with nature is a central aim for many Buddhist environmentalists. Buddhist activist Stephanie Kaza, who has written about her "conversations" with trees, suggests other ways to develop empathy with the natural environment:

One may engage in relationship with the moon, observing its waxing and waning cycle, position in the sky, and effect on one's moods and energy. One may cultivate relationships with migrating shorebirds, hatching dragonflies, or ancient redwoods. One may learn the topography of local rivers and mountains. These relations are not one-time encounters; rather they are ongoing friendships.[6]

The deepening sense of connectedness with our surroundings sometimes acquires an emotional intensity comparable to that of love or marriage. One practitioner writes, "This kind of in-love-ness—passionate, joyful—stimulates action in service to our imperiled planet. Walking in the world as if it were our lover leads inevitably to deep ecology."[7]

Group Practices

When we turn our attention to group practices, we find that new and diverse forms are being created at a rapid rate. For American Buddhists, the family has become fertile ground for the potential elaboration of spiritual practice in daily life, and environmental concerns are often addressed in this setting. A parent from Colorado treats recycling as a "family ecological ritual," using it "to bring out the meaning of inter-being."[8] At most American Buddhist centers, conservation of resources and reduction of waste is a conscious part of communal practice. The responsibilities of the "ecological officer" at one center include: "educating workers and management about waste, recycling, conservation, etc.; evaluating operational procedures in terms of waste and efficiency; and investigating ecologically correct product lines."[9]

The Zen Center of Rochester, New York, conducts an "earth relief ceremony" that includes chanting, circumambulation, devotional offerings, prostrations, and monetary donations. Buddhist rituals traditionally end with a chant that "transfers the merit" of the event to a designated recipient. The earth relief ceremony ends with the following invocation:

> Tonight we have offered candles, incense, fruit, and tea,
> Chanted sutras and *dharani.*
> Whatever merit comes to us from these offerings
> We now return to the earth, sea, and sky.
> May our air be left pure!
> May our waters be clean!
> May our earth be restored!
> May all beings attain Buddhahood![10]

The Rochester Zen Center also sponsors rites specifically on behalf of animals. Ducks and other animals are purchased from pet stores or breeders and released in their natural habitats, and relief ceremonies for endangered species are held.

In northern California the Ring of Bone Zendo has found ways to integrate backpacking, pilgrimage, and *sesshin,* the intensive meditation retreat that undergirds formal Zen training. First conceived by poet and Zen pioneer Gary Snyder in the 1970s, this "mountains and rivers *sesshin*" emphasizes long hours of silent, concentrated walking in the foothills of the Sierra Mountains. "The wilderness pilgrim's step-by-step breath-by-breath walk up a trail," writes Snyder, "is so ancient a set of gestures as to bring a profound sense of body-mind joy."[11] The daily schedule also includes morning and evening periods of seated meditation and a morning lecture by the teacher, who expounds on the "Mountains and Rivers Sutra" chapter of *The Treasury of the True Dharma Eye*, by Zen master Dōgen. This text includes the following passage:

> It is not just that there is water in the world; there are worlds in the realm of water. And this is so not only in water—there are also worlds of sentient beings in clouds, there are worlds of sentient beings in wind, there are worlds of sentient beings in fire, there are worlds of sentient beings in earth. . . . Where there are worlds of sentient beings, there must be the world of Buddhas and Zen adepts.[12]

The Ring of Bone Zendo conducts weeklong backpacking sessions twice a year, and the practice has spread to other West Coast Zen groups. In March 1991, Thich Nhat Hanh inaugurated another kind of group practice in a six-day meditation retreat specifically for environmentalists. The two hundred people who traveled to Malibu, California, for the event included members of Greenpeace, Earth First!, Earth Island Institute, Rainforest Action Network, Natural Resources Defense Council, and other environmental organizations. Some were practicing Buddhists; others had little previous exposure to Buddhism or meditation. The retreat interposed periods of meditation with lectures by Nhat Hanh, silent walks through the Malibu hills, and gentle singing. In his talks, Nhat Hanh stressed the value of "deep, inner peace" for environmental activists: "The best way to take care of the environment is to take care of the environmentalist."[13]

· · ·

Green Buddhism's Global Reach

With increased communication and cooperation among Buddhists around the globe, Buddhist-inspired environmentalism is also becoming manifest in national and international arenas. Thailand, for example, has been the source of several influential projects. The Buddhist Perception of Nature Project, founded in 1985, uses traditional Buddhist doctrines and practices to teach environmental principles to ordinary villagers and city-dwellers. The International Network of Engaged Buddhists (INEB), established in 1989 by Nobel Peace Prize nominee Sulak Sivaraksa, puts environmental concerns high on its agenda, with special emphasis on Third-World issues. In rural Thailand, environmentally conscious monks have helped protect endangered forests and watersheds by "ordaining" trees: villagers are loath to chop down trees that have been symbolically accepted into the Buddhist monastic order.

An unusual example of a Buddhist program with global repercussions is found in a successful baking business run by the Zen Community of Yonkers, New York. Since the late 1980s the Zen Community has cooperated with Ben and Jerry's ice cream company to produce Rainforest Crunch cookies. The product uses certain nuts and nut flour in an ecologically sustainable way, so it helps to protect Amazonian rain-forests and support Brazilian farming cooperatives. A percentage of profits is do-nated to groups like the Rainforest Action Network. With $1.6 million in annual sales (1991), the bakery has also provided employment to about two hundred local resi-dents, some of them formerly homeless. The advertising slogan for this popular prod-uct is a cheerful reminder of interconnectedness: "Eat a Cookie. Save a Tree."

The best-known international spokesperson for Buddhism, the Dalai Lama, has made many statements in support of environmental responsibility on a global scale. Strictly speaking, the Dalai Lama's teachings may not qualify as environmental "ac-tivism," but his ideas and his example are important sources of inspiration for so-cially engaged Buddhists. With his usual directness, he says, "The Earth, our Mother, is telling us to behave."[14] The Dalai Lama has proposed a five-point peace plan for Tibet that extends the notion of peace to the entire Tibetan ecosystem. He first pre-sented his peace plan in 1987, speaking before the United States Congress, and he restated it in his 1989 Nobel Peace Prize address and again at the 1992 Earth Summit in Rio. On these occasions he has said, in part:

> Prior to the Chinese invasion, Tibet was an unspoiled wilderness sanctuary in a unique natural environment. Sadly, in the past decades the wildlife and the forests of Tibet have been almost totally destroyed by the Chinese. The effects on Tibet's delicate environment have been devastating. . . .

> It is my dream that the entire Tibetan plateau should become a free refuge where hu-manity and nature can live in peace and in harmonious balance. . . . The Tibetan plateau would be transformed into the world's largest park or biosphere. Strict laws would be enforced to protect wildlife and plant life; the exploitation of natural resources would be carefully regulated so as not to damage relevant ecosystems; and a policy of sustainable development would be adopted in populated areas.[15]

A decade ago the Dalai Lama supported nuclear power as a possible way to improve living conditions for the world's poor, but since then his thinking has changed. As part of his peace plan, he now rejects any use of nuclear energy in Tibet, not to men-tion "China's use of Tibet for the production of nuclear weapons and the dumping of nuclear waste."[16]

Even if the Dalai Lama's ambitious plan seems unrealistic by the standards of re-alpolitik, his proposal has exposed a worldwide audience to a Buddhist vision of a desirable society. Central to that vision is the attempt to extend the ideal of nonvio-lence (*ahimsa*) to all forms of life. Some people come to embrace environmentalism as an extension of their commitment to nonviolence, just as others come to embrace nonviolence via their commitment to the environment.

A final example of Buddhist-inspired environmental activity that is finding expres-sion on a national and international scale is called the Nuclear Guardianship Project (NGP). Its targeted problem is radioactive waste, which brings us back to the *Akatsuki Maru* and its 1.5 metric tons of dangerous cargo. The concept of nuclear guardianship, advocated most forcefully by Joanna Macy, begins with the premise that current technological expertise does not offer a certifiably safe method for the disposal of nuclear waste: plans to bury the waste underground overlook known risks; transmutation and classification schemes have not yet been perfected; and other proposals (such as shooting the waste into space) are even less realistic. From these assumptions, Macy and other project participants argue that nuclear waste should be stored in an accessible manner using the best available technology, monitored with great care, and recontained in new ways as technology advances.

But the thinking of NGP strategists is not limited to scientific and political calculations. If we are to succeed in protecting future generations from lethal radioactivity, they claim, people must also be inspired mythically and spiritually. Without a grander vision and deeper motivation, we might not even be able to implement whatever technical solutions become available. For Macy, one possible way to foster new attitudes would be to turn each nuclear site into a center of activity related to guardianship. She describes the genesis of this idea:

> It started with a kind of vision I had in England in 1983, when I visited the peace camps that had spontaneously arisen around nuclear bases. . . . I sensed that I was on sacred ground. I had a feeling of *deja vu*. I thought, "Oh, maybe I'm being reminded of the monasteries that kept the flame of learning alive in the Middle Ages." People made pilgrimages to those places too. But then I realized, "No, this is about the *future*. This is how the radioactive remains are going to be guarded for the sake of future beings."[17]

Because such sights would require unwavering vigilance, they would entail a social version of the mindfulness practice that is so central to Buddhism. "We can contain the radioactivity if we pay attention to it," writes Macy. "That act of attention may be the last thing we want to do, but it is the one act that is required."[18] She goes on to suggest that surveillance communities built around today's nuclear facilities could also become centers for various activities beyond the technical process of containment: pilgrimage, meditation retreats, rituals "of acceptance and forgiveness," even a kind of monastic training. One hopeful NGP participant declares, "Let us build beautiful shrines, life-affirming shrines, with gardens and rooms for meditation."[19]

Not content merely to outline the possibilities, Macy and others are experimenting with ritual forms to be used in study groups and public workshops. They are even willing to modify the traditional four vows taken by Mahayana Buddhists, by adding a fifth vow:

Sentient beings are numberless; I'll do the best I can to save them.

Desires are inexhaustible; I'll do the best I can to put an end to them.

The Dharmas are boundless; I'll do the best I can to master them.

The Poison Fire lasts forever; I'll do the best I can to contain it.

The Buddha way is unsurpassable; I'll do the best I can to attain it.[20]

• • •

The Nuclear Guardianship Project is difficult to assess. It has not yet made inroads among nuclear engineers, much less been tested in the public domain. To some observers it seems wildly fanciful, because it expects to transform deep-seated psychological responses to nuclear waste: denial of responsibility ("not in my backyard") and denial of danger ("it's not making us sick"). The NGP must contend with lingering disagreement among scientists on technical issues, and it must deal with the economic realities of implementing accessible containment on a massive scale. However, the greatest source of resistance may be our apparent unwillingness to reduce our material standard of living voluntarily. The best way to limit future nuclear waste is simply to stop producing it, but that course would call for radical social changes that few citizens anywhere are willing to contemplate. It is one thing to recognize the risks of nuclear energy, but quite another to change the systems and personal habits that currently demand it.

Regardless of the NGP's potential to influence affairs in the political realm, the concept of nuclear guardianship is certainly intriguing as a religious vision. This is not the first time that Buddhists have believed that the world is coming to an end in some significant way, and that an unprecedented response is required. In past eras, predictions about the imminent disappearance of the Buddha's teachings led to a revitalization of religion and sometimes to major shifts in society. By directing attention to the distant future, Macy invites us to "reinhabit" a deep, mythological sense of time; such a perspective is a welcome antidote to the impoverished, constricted sense of time that prevails in industrial societies. In a similar manner, the NGP calls for a dramatic extension of our sense of ethical responsibility. The notion of guardianship begins with plutonium but goes on to embrace numberless unborn beings and the planet as a whole.

Points of Departure from Buddhism's Past

It is clear that an ecologically sensitive Buddhism exhibits significant continuities with traditional Buddhism, continuities that can be demonstrated textually, doctrinally, historically, and by other means. Sustained inquiry by scholars and practitioners will continue to elucidate those links. It is also instructive to consider the ways in which today's green Buddhism may depart from Buddhism's past. The individual and group activities surveyed here are not only innovative on the level of practice; in many cases they also embody consequential shifts in Buddhists' perceptions of nature and society.

In several contexts we have seen ecobuddhists struggling to think and act globally; that breadth of commitment is itself a trait that distinguishes today's activists from most of their Buddhist predecessors. Just as current environmental problems are planetary as well as local, present-day Buddhism has become international as well as regional. For centuries, classic Buddhist texts have depicted the universe as one interdependent whole, and elegant doctrines have laid the conceptual foundation for a "cosmic ecology."[21] Contemporary Buddhist environmentalists are seeking to actualize that vision with a concreteness that seems unprecedented in the history of Buddhism.

The increased awareness of the sociopolitical implications of spiritual practice is another feature that might qualify as a departure from earlier forms of Buddhism. Socially engaged Buddhism is one of the notable developments in late twentieth-century Buddhism, and environmental Buddhism is an important stream within this larger movement. There is a well-known Zen story in which a master rebukes a monk for discarding a single chopstick. The original point is that even if the chopstick's mate is lost, it still has intrinsic value and can be put to use in some other way. In today's world, the widespread use of disposable chopsticks might suggest other lessons about the far-reaching environmental impact of daily actions.[22] Green Buddhists no longer assume that spiritual practice can take place in a social or environmental vacuum. Moreover, they believe that an overly individualistic model of practice may actually impede cooperative efforts to improve social conditions.

The importance of women and of women's perspectives is another characteristic of ecobuddhism that distinguishes it from more traditional forms of Buddhism. Today's environmentally sensitive Buddhists want to free themselves and others from sexist patterns of thought, behavior, and language. Women, no less than men, are the leaders, creative thinkers, and grassroots activists of green Buddhism. The influence of women also manifests itself in an aversion to hierarchy, an appreciation of the full range of experience, and an emphasis on the richness of relationships (human and nonhuman). Out of this milieu, the notion of the world "as lover" has emerged as a model for a new bond between humanity and nature. The ancient Greek goddess Gaia, who has been reclaimed by many people as a symbol of the earth, is also embraced by Buddhist environmentalists, men and women alike. Even the Buddha is sometimes feminized, as in the following gatha by Thich Nhat Hanh:

> I entrust myself to Earth;
> Earth entrusts herself to me. I entrust myself to Buddha;
> Buddha entrusts herself to me."[23]

Shifting perceptions of nature denote another area in which past Buddhism and present Buddhism diverge. Buddhists have long been sensitive to the transitory nature of things. In Japan, for example, generations of poets have "grieved" over the falling of cherry blossoms. Yet according to the premodern Buddhist view, nature's impermanence is also natural, part of the way things are, so the process of extinction (in a paradoxical way) is also reassuring. The grief of Buddhist environmentalists is prompted not by falling cherry blossoms but by the actual loss of entire species of living beings, and by the continuing devastation of the planet. A new dimension of meaning has been added to the time-honored Buddhist notion of impermanence. Gary Snyder writes:

> The extinction of a species, each one a pilgrim of four billion years of evolution, is an irreversible loss. The ending of the lines of so many creatures with whom we have traveled this far is an occasion for profound sorrow and grief. . . . Some quote a Buddhist teaching back at us: "all is impermanent." Indeed. All the more reason to move gently and cause less harm.[24]

Perennial assumptions about nature's power to harm human beings have been augmented by a fresh appreciation of human's power to harm nature. In an early text the Buddha gives his monks a prayer which reads in part:

> My love to the footless, my love to the twofooted, my love to the fourfooted, my love to the manyfooted. Let not the footless harm me, let not the twofooted harm me, let not the fourfooted harm me, let not the manyfooted harm me. All sentient beings, all breathing things, creatures without exception, let them all see good things, may no evil befall them.[25]

This passage expresses generous concern for other beings, yet it also serves as a protective charm against dangerous animals (especially poisonous snakes)—if I don't harm them, they won't harm me. In contrast, the ceremonial texts from Green Gulch Farm or the Nuclear Guardianship Project are most concerned about human threats to nature. Religious power is invoked in each case, but in the new texts that power is summoned to protect the environment from us and to atone for our depredations.

In many Buddhist cultures, nature has functioned as the ideal setting in which to seek salvation. Traditionally, movement toward nature was regarded as a type of *withdrawal:* one retreated to the mountains or the jungle to be free of society's defilements and distractions. But for contemporary Buddhists a deepening relation with nature is usually associated with a spirit of *engagement.* Even if the experience of heightened intimacy with nature is private and contemplative, that experience is commonly interpreted as a call to action. In this new context nature nonetheless retains its potential soteric power. For many Buddhist activists, preservation of the environment doubles as a spiritual path to personal and planetary salvation.

Conclusion

Critics and supporters of contemporary Buddhist environmentalism have already raised a number of provocative questions. Seasoned Buddhist practitioners suspect that the comparisons between "ecological awakening" and a true enlightenment experience are too facile. Buddhist scholars in North America and Japan ask if there a point at which the distance from traditional Buddhism becomes so great that the Buddhist label is no longer appropriate. Others express concern about the New Age elements that seem to be part of ecobuddhism (such as NGP rituals evoking the future), and they are not sure how to assess such elements. Buddhist environmentalists take these issues seriously and raise further questions. In daily life, how can traditional Buddhist practices and new ecologically oriented practices be meaningfully integrated? To what degree can a modern environmental ethic be extrapolated from these individual and group practices? What is the relation of green Buddhism to other forms of environmentalism, including deep ecology? Such questions will continue to generate discussion and reflection as the various forms of socially engaged Buddhism evolve and mature.

From certain perspectives it may seem that Buddhist environmentalism is marginal, especially in the United States. After all, "green politics" has appealed only to a minority in the culture at large; Buddhism captures only a percentage point or two in the national religious census; and even within American Buddhist communities, not everyone is interested in environmental issues or their relation to practice. If there is a way to communicate the key ideas and basic practices of green Buddhism to a wider public, it has not yet been found. Granted, Buddhists may have affected the outcome in a number of local campaigns, saving an old-growth forest in Oregon, protecting a watershed in northern California, blocking a proposed nuclear dump in a California desert. In such cases, however, it is hard to isolate distinctively "Buddhist" influences.

The potential significance of green Buddhism can also be considered from a religious standpoint. Even if there is little visible evidence of impact, Buddhism may nonetheless be contributing to a shift in the lives of individuals or the conduct of certain groups. Some would argue that if only one person's life is changed through an ecological awakening, the repercussions of that transformation have important and continuing effects in realms seen and unseen. An abiding faith in the fundamental interconnectedness of all existence provides many individual activists with the energy and focus that enable them to stay the course. Simply to return to a unitive experience is often enough: "We don't need to call it Buddhism—or Dharma or Gaia. We need only to be still and open our senses to the world that presents itself to us moment to moment to moment." [26]

Notes

1. Dogen, in Philip Kapleau, *The Three Pillars of Zen*, rev. ed. (New York: Doubleday, 1989), 310.

2. Quoted in Kapleau, *The Three Pillars of Zen*, 215.

3. Thich Nhat Hanh, *Touching Peace: Practicing the Art of Mindful Living* (Berkeley: Parallax Press, 1992), 11–12.

4. Thich Nhat Hanh, *Present Moment, Wonderful Moment: Mindfulness Verses for Daily Living* (Berkeley: Parallax Press, 1990), 9, 10.

5. *The Mindfulness Bell* 1:3 (Autumn 1990), 16.

6. Stephanie Kaza, "Planting Seeds of Joy" (unpublished paper, 1992), 13.

7. Lenore Friedman, "Book Reviews," *Turning Wheel* (Fall 1991), 39.

8. *The Mindfulness Bell* 4 (Spring 1991), 17.

9. *The Ten Directions* 11:1 (Spring/Summer 1990), 15.

10. Rochester Zen Center, "Earth Relief Ceremony" (unpublished manual, 1992).

11. Gary Snyder, *The Practice of the Wild* (San Francisco: North Point Press, 1990), 94.

12. Thomas Cleary, trans., *Shōbōgenzō: Zen Essays by Dogen* (Honolulu: University of Hawaii Press, 1986), 98.

13. *The Mindfulness Bell* 7 (Summer/Fall 1992), 6.

14. Allan Hunt Badiner, *Dharma Gaia: A Harvest of Essays in Buddhism and Ecology* (Berkeley: Parallax Press, 1990), v.

15. The Dalai Lama, "Five-Point Peace Plan for Tibet," in Petra K. Kelly, Gert Bastian, and Pat Aiello, eds., *The Anguish of Tibet* (Berkeley: Parallax Press, 1991), 291; the Dalai Lama, "A Zone of Peace," in Martine Batchelor and Kerry Brown, eds., *Buddhism and Ecology* (London: Cassell, 1992), 112–13.

16. Kelly, Bastian, and Aiello, *The Anguish of Tibet,* 288.

17. "Guardians of the Future," *In Context* 28 (Spring 1991), 20.

18. "Technology and Mindfulness," *Nuclear Guardianship Forum* 1 (Spring 1992), 3.

19. N. Llyn Peabody, "A Summary of the Council Discussion," *Buddhist Peace Fellowship Newsletter* 3/4 (Fall 1988), 23.

20. "Buddhist Vows for Guardianship," *Nuclear Guardianship Forum* 1 (Spring 1992), 2.

21. Francis H. Cook, *Hua-yen Buddhism: The Jewel Net of Indra* (University Park: Pennsylvania State University Press, 1977), 2.

22. Even if disposable chopsticks do not contribute to the destruction of rainforests (experts disagree), comparable examples are abundant.

23. Nhat Hanh, *Present Moment, Wonderful Moment,* 59.

24. Snyder, *The Practice of the Wild,* 176.

25. Aṅguttara Nikāya, Pali Text Society Publications 2, 72–73.

26. Nina Wise, "Thâystock at Spirit Rock," *The Mindfulness Bell* 5 (Autumn 1991), 19.

Andrew Linzey

13   The Theological Basis of Animal Rights

Secretary of Health and Human Services Louis Sullivan recently told a Vatican conference that animal rights "extremists" threaten the future of health research and that churches "cannot remain on the periphery in this struggle. . . . Any assertion of moral equivalence between humans and animals is an issue that organized religion must refute vigorously and unambiguously." Sullivan went on to say that world religious leaders possess the authority to "affirm the necessity of appropriate and humane uses of animals in biomedical research."

At first sight, Sullivan has backed a winner. What better than conservative theology and who better than conservative churches to respond to the rallying call for human superiority over animals—even and especially if this "superiority" involves inflicting pain and suffering? Christian theology has, it must be admitted, served long and well the oppressors of slaves, women and animals. Only 131 years ago, William Henry Holcombe wrote confidently of slavery as the "Christianization of the dark races." It took 1900 years for theologians to question seriously the morality of slavery, and even longer the oppression of women. Keith Thomas reminds us that over the centuries theologians debated "half frivolously, half seriously, whether or not the female sex had souls, a discussion which closely paralleled the debate about animals." Apparently the Quaker George Fox encountered some who thought women had "no souls, no more than a goose."

Who better to look to then but the Roman Catholic Church, which in its approved *Dictionary of Moral Theology* of 1962 confidently proclaims that "Zoophilists often lose sight of the end for which animals, irrational creatures, were created by God, viz., the service and use of man. . . . In fact, Catholic moral doctrine teaches that animals have no rights on the part of man"? In practice, Catholic countries are among the worst in

Originally published in *Christian Century* (October 9, 1991), 906–909. Copyright 1991 Christian Century Foundation. Reprinted by permission from the October 9, 1991, issue of the *Christian Century*.

the world as far as animals are concerned. Bullfighting and the Spanish fiestas in which animals are gratuitously mutilated (with the compliance of priests and nuns) are examples of how historical theology lives on. Surely Sullivan could not have chosen a more agreeable ally in his fight against "extremists" who believe that animals have rights.

And yet, there are signs that Christian theology and Christian churches cannot be so easily counted upon to support the standard line that humans are morally free to do as they like with animals. Anglican Archbishop Donald Coggan in 1977 stated the unthinkable: "Animals, as part of God's creation, have rights which must be respected. It behooves us always to be sensitive to their needs and to the reality of their pain." Archbishop Robert Runcie went further in 1988 and specifically contradicted historical anthropocentrism. His words deserve to be savored:

> The temptation is that we will usurp God's place as Creator and exercise a *tyrannical* dominion over creation. . . . At the present time, when we are beginning to appreciate the wholeness and interrelatedness of all that is in the cosmos, preoccupation with humanity will seem distinctly parochial. . . . Too often our theology of creation, especially, here in the so-called "developed" world, has been distorted by being too man-centered. We need to maintain the value, the preciousness of the human by affirming the preciousness of the nonhuman also—of all that is. For our concept of God forbids the idea of a *cheap creation*, of a throwaway universe in which everything is expendable save human existence. . . . The value, the worth of natural things is not found in Man's view of himself but in the goodness of God who made all things good and precious in his sight. . . . As Barbara Ward used to say, "We have only one earth." Is it not worth our love? ["Address to the Global Forum of Spiritual and Parliamentary Leaders on Human Survival" (his emphases).]

Even at the very center of conservative theology there are indications of movement. The pope's 1984 encyclical *Solicitudo Rei Socialis* speaks of the need to respect "the nature of each being" within creation. It underlines the modern view that the "dominion granted to man . . . is not an absolute power, nor can one speak of a freedom to use and misuse or to dispose of things as one pleases."

It would be silly to pretend that Pope John Paul II and Archbishops Coggan and Runcie are card-carrying members of the animal rights movement (there are no membership cards in any case). Yet for Sullivan, desperately hoping for moral assurance in the face of animal rights "extremists," these cannot be encouraging signs. Is the ecclesiastical bastion of human moral exclusivity really going to tumble? Might there be, in 50 or 100 years, a Roman encyclical defending the worth, dignity and rights of the nonhuman world? The *National Catholic Reporter* noted that Pope John Paul II had only "cautiously" defended animal experimentation. In 1982, the paper recalled, the pope argued that "the diminution of experimentation on animals, which has progressively been made ever less necessary, corresponds to the plan and well-being of all creation." The true reading of Sullivan's overture might be not confidence but desperation. Perhaps the most worrying thing for Sullivan is that the churches *won't* remain on the periphery in this struggle.

Sullivan has a counterpart in the United Kingdom: agriculture minister and fellow

Anglican John Selwyn Gummer, who tried to bolster the meat trade by asserting that vegetarianism is a "wholly unnatural" practice. Like Sullivan he thought Christian theology would be of some help—in his case, against 5 million British vegetarians. "I consider meat to be an essential part of the diet," argued Gummer. "The Bible tells us that we are masters of the fowls of the air, and the beasts of the field and we very properly eat them."

Alas, biblical theology cannot be so easily wheeled in to rescue the minister of agriculture. The creation saga in Genesis I does indeed give humans dominion over animals (v. 28) but just one verse later commands vegetarianism (vv. 29–31). As Karl Barth observed: "Whether or not we find it practicable and desirable, the diet assigned to men and beasts by God the Creator is vegetarian" (*Church Dogmatics,* III/1, p. 208). Bystanders may marvel at how Gummer could in all innocence hurl himself not at the weakest but the strongest part of his enemy's armor.

Sullivan and Gummer seem united in the view that if theology is to speak on animal rights, it will speak not on the side of the oppressed but on behalf of the oppressor. Indeed, the view somehow seems to have got about that there can be no mainstream theological basis for animal rights. As well as accusing the movement of being "philosophically flawed and obscurantistic—based on ignorance and emotion, not reason and knowledge—and antihuman and even antianimal," the magazine *Eternity* produced by Evangelical Ministries Inc., claimed in 1985 that "the true religious underpinning of animal-rights consists is a kind of vague neopantheism" (Lloyd Billingsley, "Save the Beasts, Not the Children? The Dangerous Premises of the Animal-Rights Crusade," February 1985).

To begin to construct an adequate theological understanding of animals, we should recall Runcie's statement about the "value, the preciousness of the nonhuman." Secular thinkers are free to be agnostic about the value of the nonhuman creation. They could argue, for example, that creation has value only insofar as humankind is benefited or insofar as other creatures can be classed as utilities. Not so, however, for Christians. If, as Runcie observes, "our concept of God forbids the idea of a cheap creation" because "the whole universe is a work of love" and "nothing which is made in love is cheap," Christians are precluded from a purely humanistic, utilitarian view of animals. This point will sound elementary, but its implications are profound.

At its most basic it means that animals must not be viewed simply as commodities, resources, tools, utilities for human use. If we are to grapple with real theology, we must abandon purely humanocentric perspectives on animals. What may be the use of animals to us is a totally separate question from what their value is to almighty God. To argue that the value and significance of animals in the world can be circumscribed by their value and significance to human beings is simply untheological. I make the point strongly because there seems to be the misconception—even and especially prevalent among the doctrinal advocates of Christian faith—that theological ethics can be best expressed by a well-meaning, ethically enlightened humanism. Not so. To attempt a theological understanding must involve a fundamental break with humanism, secular and religious. God alone is the source of the value of all living beings.

This argument is usually countered in one of two ways. The first is to say that if this is so, it should follow that all creation has value, so we cannot rate animals of greater value than rocks or vegetables, let alone insects or viruses. Increasingly this argument seems to be made by "conservationists" and "green thinkers" who want to exclude animals from special moral consideration. They argue that the value of animals, and therefore what we owe them, is really on a par with the value of natural objects such as trees or rivers. One can immediately see how this view falls in neatly with the emerging green view of "holistic interdependence" and holistic appeals to respect "earth as a whole." God loves the whole creation holistically, so it is claimed.

But is it true that God loves everything equally? Not so, I think. Christian tradition clearly makes a distinction between humans and animals, and also between animals and vegetables. Scholars eager to establish the preeminence of humans in Scripture have simply overlooked ways in which animals exist alongside humans within the covenant relationship. The Spirit is itself the "breath of life" (Gen. 1:30) of both humans and animals. The Torah delineates animals within its notion of moral community. After having surveyed the ways in which animals are specifically associated, if not identified, with humans themselves, Barth concludes: "'O Lord, thou preservest man and beast' (Ps. 36:6) is a thread running through the whole of the Bible; and it first emerges in a way which is unmistakable when the creation of man is classified in Gen. 1:24f with that of the land animals" (*Church Dogmatics,* III/1, p. 181n).

The second way in which my argument may be countered is by proposing that while animals have some value, it is incontestably less than the special value of humans. But this objection only adds fuel to my thesis. I, for one, do not want to deny that humans are unique, superior, even, in a sense, of "special value" in creation. Some secular animal rightists, it is true, have argued in ways that appear to eclipse the uniqueness of humanity. But Christian animal rights advocates are not interested in dethroning humanity. On the contrary, the animal rights thesis requires the re-enthroning of humanity.

The key question is, What kind of king is to be reenthroned? Gummer's utterances show only too well how "dominion" has come to mean little more than despotism. But the kingly rule of which we are, according to Genesis, the vice-regents or representatives is not the brutalizing regime of a tyrant. Rather, God elects humanity to represent and actualize the loving divine will for all creatures. Humanity is the one species chosen to look after the cosmic garden (Gen. 2:15). This involves having power over animals. But the issue is not whether we have power over animals but how we are to use it.

It is here that we reach the christological parting of the ways. Secularists may claim that power is itself the sufficient justification for our use of it. But Christians are not so free. No appeal to the power of God can be sufficient without reference to the revelation of that power exemplified in Jesus Christ. Much of what Jesus said or did about slaves, women or animals remains historically opaque. But we know the contours even if many of the details are missing. The power of God is Jesus is expressed in *katabasis,* humility, self-sacrifice, powerlessness. The power of God is redefined in Jesus as practical costly service extending to those who are beyond the normal boundaries of human concern: the diseased, the poor, the oppressed, the outcast. If humans claim a lordship over creation, then it can only be a lordship of service. There can be no lordship without service.

According to the theological doctrine of animal rights, then, humans are to be the servant species: the species given power, opportunity and privilege to give themselves, nay sacrifice themselves, for the weaker, suffering creatures. According to Sullivan, the churches must refute "any assertion of moral equivalence between humans and animals." But I, for one, have never claimed any strict moral equality between humans and animals. I have always been a bit worried by Peter Singer's view that animal liberation consists in accepting "equal consideration of interests" between humans and animals. In my view, what we owe animals is more than equal consideration, equal treatment or equal concern. The weak, the powerless, the disadvantaged, the oppressed should not have equal moral priority but greater moral priority. When we minister to the least of all we minister to Christ himself. To follow Jesus is to accept axiomatically that the weak have moral priority. Our special value as a species consists in being of special value for others.

No one has enumerated this doctrine better than that 19th-century pioneer of social reform for both humans and animals, the seventh Earl of Shaftesbury:

> I was convinced that God had called me to devote whatever advantages He might have bestowed upon me to the cause of the weak, the helpless, both man and beast, and those who had none to help them. . . . What I have done has been given to me; what I have done I was enabled to do; and all happy results (if any there be) must be credited, not to the servant, but to the great Master, who led and sustained him.

The relevance of such theology to animal rights should be clear. Readers will have noticed I have assiduously used the term "animal rights" rather than "animal welfare" or "animal protection." Some Christians are still apt to regard "rights" terminology as a secular import into moral theology. They are mistaken. The notion of rights was first used in explicitly theological contexts. Moreover, animal rights is explicitly a problem of Christian moral theology for this reason: Catholic scholasticism has specifically and repeatedly repudiated animal rights. It is the tradition, not its so-called modern detractors, that insists on the relevance of the concept of rights. The problem is only now compounded because, unaware of history, Christians want to talk boldly of human rights yet quibble about the language when it comes to animals. For me the theological basis of rights is compelling. God is the source of rights, and indeed the whole debate about animals is precisely about the rights of the Creator. For this reason in *Christianity and the Rights of Animals* (New York: Crossroad, 1987) I used the ugly but effective term "theos-rights." Animal rights language conceptualizes what is objectively owed the Creator of animals. From a theological perspective, rights are not something awarded, granted, won or lost but something recognized. To recognize animal rights is to recognize the intrinsic value of God-given life.

I do not deny that the rights view involves a fundamental reorientation. This is one of its merits. The value of living beings is not something to be determined by human beings alone. Part of the reason rights language is so controversial is that people sense from the very outset that recognizing animal rights must involve personal and social change. Whatever else animal rights means it cannot mean that we can go on consuming their flesh, destroying their habitats, wearing their dead skins and inflicting suffering. Quite disingenuously some church people say that they do not "know" what "animal rights" are. Meanwhile, by steadfastly refusing to change their lifestyles, they show a precise understanding of what animal rights are.

Earlier I compared the oppression of slaves and women to that of animals. Some may regard that comparison as exaggerated, even offensive. But at the heart of each movement of reform has been a simple yet fundamental change of perception. Slaves should not be thought of as property but as human beings with dignity and rights. Women should not be regarded as second-class humans but as humans with dignity and rights. At the heart of the animal rights movement is a change of moral perception, simple, yet profound: animals are not our property or utilities but living beings with dignity and rights.

To recognize animal rights is a spiritual experience and a spiritual struggle. One homely example may suffice. The university where I work is situated amid acres of 18th-century parkland. Wildlife abounds. From my study window I observe families of wild rabbits. Looking up from my word processor from time to time, I gaze in wonder, awe and astonishment at these beautiful creatures. I sometimes say half-jokingly, "It is worth coming to the university for the rabbits." Occasionally I invite visitors to observe them. Some pause in conversation and say something like, "Oh yes," as though I had pointed out the dust on my bookshelves or the color of my carpet. What they see is not rabbits. Perhaps they see machines on four legs, "pests" that should be controlled, perhaps just other "things." It is difficult to believe that such spiritual blindness and impoverishment is the best that the superior species can manage.

Sullivan makes free with calling animal rightists "extremists." The reality is, however, that moral theology would hardly advance at all without visionaries and extremists, people who see things differently from others and plead God's cause even in matters that others judge insignificant. I don't think there are many moderates in heaven.

Arthur Waskow

14   From Compassion to Jubilee

Three related illnesses are eating at the heart of America:

- an increasingly damaging and unjust distribution of wealth;
- a deepening threat to the environment;
- a collapse of social solidarity—what has been called both *fraternite* and sister-hood—at the levels of family, neighborhood, workplace, and society.

For several years now, *Tikkun* has insisted that society cannot expect to deal with the first two of these symptoms without addressing the third. Economistic proposals for redistributing wealth or healing the poisoned environment are not powerful enough to counter the old destructive ways that have proved profitable and job-producing in American society. It will take empathy for Mother Earth herself as well as for the victims of environmental cancer and immune-system collapse to give new energy to movements for economic and environmental change.

Creating such a politically informed empathy requires the development of a shared rhetoric, a language of vision and change. Such a language would take us beyond the conventional "shared" American myth of individualism, which is not about shar-ing, and which makes serious concern for other human beings and for the earth impossible.

The very absence of a myth that affirms our common interest proves the severity of our problem. I do think, however, that we have the beginnings of a shared lan-guage. It is contained within an extraordinary passage from the Bible—but more on that passage in a moment.

Originally published in *Tikkun* (March/April 1990), 5:78–81. Reprinted from TIKKUN MAGAZINE, A BI-MONTHLY JEWISH CRITIQUE OF POLITICS, CULTURE, AND SOCIETY. Information and subscrip-tions are available from TIKKUN, 26 Fell Street, San Francisco, CA 94102. Copyright © 1990 by (Rabbi) Arthur Waskow. Waskow is director of the Shalom Center and author of *Godwrestling—Round 2* (Jewish Lights Publishing, Woodstock, Vermont), among other works of Jewish renewal and progressive religion.

What dybbuk would possess me even to think of the Bible as a source of social solidarity in this world of secularized intellectuals and weakened religious institutions? Am I setting us up for a successful return of the religious Right, just as it is losing its steam? It seems to me that the Bible remains the only element of "high culture" with which large numbers of Americans feel any connection, and the only one that both white and Black workers have in common. It attracts figures such as Robert Alter and Geoffrey Hartman on the one hand, and great masses of less intellectual Americans on the other. In part this explains why Jesse Jackson, a preacher, appeals to people across lines of race and, to some extent, class.

Even if Jews and Catholics and Protestants mean different things when they say "the Bible"—even if Muslims, Buddhists, Native Americans, secularists, and some feminist spiritualists are skeptical of the Bible altogether—the cultural wisdom contained in the Bible still speaks to more Americans than does any other expression of compassion, community, and sharing.

I think we are wrong to assume that all American social critics and activists are staunch secularists. Is it an accident that the head of SANE/Freeze is a clergyman? Is it an accident that the most respected leader of the movements of the sixties, Martin Luther King, Jr., the first American since George Washington to be honored with a national holiday, was a preacher? But—some will say—the proof of the pudding is in the program. The Bible may teach compassion toward the poor, but surely—some will say—this advocates a kind of welfare handout, the sort we know doesn't work. And what of the Bible's sense of empathy for the earth? "Fill up the earth and subdue it," it instructs us.

Not so.

One of our culture's most remarkable expressions of empathy for the land and its people also encodes a program for compassion. I mean the biblical passage about the Sabbatical and Jubilee years, contained in Leviticus 25.

That passage outlines a specific program, with three related elements:

- redistribution of the land, so that all families can periodically start over at a common economic level;
- a year-long rest period for the land, meant to ensure protection of the earth;
- celebrations designed to strengthen local clans and tribes.

All these elements of the program for compassion are understood as expressions of love.

The Bible's Jubilee program is rooted in the conception of sacred time that inspires the Sabbath tradition of rest, contemplation, and sharing on the seventh day of every week. The program institutes a moratorium on everyday customs every seventh and fiftieth year (the year after the seventh seventh year). The Jubilee year is a pause for contemplation and reorganization.

Every seventh year all debts are canceled. The land rests from organized cultivation and harvest, and whatever freely grows from it may be gathered by any family for food. Meanwhile, food that has been lying in storage is shared. In the fiftieth year the land rests again, and every family returns to the equal share of productive land that it was allotted when Israelite society began. The poor become equal to the rich, who give up the extra wealth they have accumulated.

All this was to be done not by a central government's taxation or police power, but by the direct action of each family, each clan, each tribe in its own region. When it was not done, an Isaiah (chapters 58 and 61) or a Jeremiah (chapter 34) or a Jesus (Luke 4) would arise to demand that the program be implemented.

What in our society would it mean to draw on this biblical teaching in order to create a program that could address our economic, environmental, and emotional woes—three symptoms of our modern illness? And what would it mean to make this not only a program but a strategy—to build a movement or constituency around a Jubilee program that would harness more energy and political power than ordinary secular progressive coalitions?

Most of us might not have the biblical chutzpah to propose shutting down the whole society one year out of every seven. But let us *imagine* three major structural reforms as elements of a possible Jubilee program:

- venture capital recycling;
- sabbaticals on research and development;
- celebrations of neighborhood empowerment.

Such a contemporary Jubilee program would involve a continuous recycling process in the society rather than a blanket moratorium at a given time.

Venture Capital Recycling

The policy goal is to shift massive amounts of investment capital from the control of giant, long-established corporations to grass-roots businesses—especially those that are owned and operated by workers, consumers, families, or neighborhoods.

How to do this? By very high taxes on the wealth (not merely the income) of very large, old businesses such as DuPont Chemical Company, the great global oil companies, and Chase Manhattan Bank. The proceeds of this capital recycling tax would go not to the general treasury but directly to a number of publicly controlled banks that would make loans available to help workers buy their factories, farms, and insurance companies, and to help neighborhood associations, churches and synagogues, and other grass-roots groups start cooperative food stores, restaurants, pharmacies, bicycle factories, fish hatcheries, and solar power stations.

To prevent liquidity problems, corporations could pay this capital recycling tax not in money but by turning over to a Community Ownership Trust a portion of their ownership rights (for example, stock certificates). The Trust would then transfer ownership rights to workers or communities.

The primary requirement for receipt of these venture capital loans and ownership rights would be the recipient's proof that they represent a particular community—

whether of co-workers in a single workplace, students and faculty at a specific school, or members of a neighborhood association, a religious congregation, or a family.

Favorable interest rates would be offered to firms that both use recycled materials in production and recycle their own waste products, as well as those that use renewable energy sources and otherwise demonstrate respect for the environment.

Low interest rates would also be made available to groups whose average income and wealth fall below a specific cutoff point. In this way, the white poor would not be excluded in favor of other disadvantaged groups such as women, Blacks, and Hispanics. "Disadvantage" would be understood as an economic condition, rather than one determined by ethnicity or gender. Because recipients would need to prove that they represent an existing community, the program would empower rather than shatter ethnic and racial communities. Such a wealth-recycling program would address one of the major problems posed by conventional tax-reform proposals and welfare programs. That problem involves the need for investment capital. Many people fear that a program which taxes large corporations too heavily will keep these corporations from investing in the economy, and thus precipitate depression. At the same time people fear that national investment, through projects such as the Tennessee Valley Authority or outright welfare grants, will inevitably create a large, unresponsive bureaucracy and a disempowered, irresponsible underclass.

If investment capital were taxed from corporations and recycled not through giant bureaucracies but rather through grass-roots community-controlled enterprises, we could avoid such dilemmas. The capital recycling tax would encourage investment—indeed, it would stimulate creative forms of investment by shifting capital to new hands—and empower, rather than subjugate, the recipients. It would strengthen community rather than the culture of individualism.

Sabbaticals on Research and Development

Most government programs that focus on the environment have concentrated on the end products of industrial activity—how to recycle and clean up waste. Very little attention has been paid to the decisions society makes about what to produce. The biblical Jubilee program, however, teaches us to confront issues around production. In an agricultural, pastoral society this entailed pausing from production altogether. But what would the Jubilee program mean for a technological, scientific society such as our own?

I offer two proposals, both of which draw on the Jubilee notion of pausing from production for a period of sacred, reflective time. Both proposals are intended to prevent us from treating production and technology as ends in themselves, and to train ourselves to reconsider them in the light of their environmental and social effects.

First, all corporate investments of more than a specific amount—one billion dollars?—stated for a single program, such as the production of a new car, or the invention of a new pesticide, would be subject to a one-year "sabbatical" delay while a public review studied the effect of the proposed program on society and the environment.

Second, all-scientific and technological research and development would halt one year out of every seven, and society would provide a real sabbatical for scientists and engineers.

What do I mean by a real sabbatical? It would be a time for scientists, engineers, and those who allocate capital to reevaluate our use of technology. The intent of this real sabbatical is not to stop technological development, but to interrupt it periodically, so that it can be reconsidered in terms of purpose and effect.

Both proposed sabbaticals would help us catch our breath and would soon bring about both physical changes in the environment and profound effects on our culture. In the physical sphere, the sabbaticals would slow down our invasion of the web of planetary life and perhaps encourage a change of direction. Culturally, these pauses (and the campaigns to get them adopted) would teach society that there are values other than producing, making, doing; and indeed that even the values of producers need to be governed by larger issues of long-term effects on human beings, the earth, and community.

Celebration of Neighborhood Empowerment

The provisions of Leviticus 25 are designed to strengthen grass-roots communities: in ancient times, such communities took the form of clans within a tribal region. For us, community is probably best represented by the concept of neighborhood.

Public policy has not been shaped with an eye to strengthening community or compassion. Just one example: all the efforts to cut down demand for drugs have focused on creating more fear—despite (or because of?) the likelihood that more fear and despair are quite likely to encourage more drug use. What would it mean for public policy to focus on creating stronger communities, rather than greater fear?

A Jubilee-style proposal: empower neighborhoods to choose one day a month, one week a year, for a neighborly celebration. Give seed-grants to neighborhood institutions to plan such events. Make this folk festival a decentralized but universal event.

Create a national "Sabbath," on at least two occasions a year—July 4 and New Year's Day? Or on the newer, more globally and environmentally conscious occasions of Hiroshima Day and Martin Luther King Day? or a revitalized Earth Day? Shut down all but life-preserving emergency services; close highways, hotels, television stations, newspapers, factories, offices; suspend train, bus, airline services. Let us rediscover walking and talking, singing and cooking. Let us rediscover our neighbors. Better than a day or two would be an entire week, so that we can experience the meaning of rest and celebration.

These three proposals make up a Jubilee program. What about a strategy to bring them about? All the proposals challenge powerful institutions in our society. Without the empowerment of people at the grass roots, none of it will be possible. How to begin?

It seems to me that the initiators of a Jubilee program should be the churches and synagogues, partly because the approach comes from the biblical tradition but not only because of this. Also because we know that religious communities can be great sources of empowerment and change—as some churches were the seeds and some synagogues the support of the civil rights movement, as some churches and synagogues nurtured the antiwar movement of the sixties and the disarmament movement of the eighties, as some religious communities helped antislavery efforts and were the defenders of the labor movement.

To organize well means, at very best, to infuse the means with the end. In this case, synagogues and churches might begin by creating in miniature the Jubilee program that we envision, as a sort of demonstration project that would help us organize the broader Jubilee program.

What is a miniature Jubilee?

In a particular city, for perhaps the nine days from one Friday night to the following week's Sunday, a cluster of synagogues and churches could hold a Jubilee festival. The festival would encourage economic renewal in the city and its neighborhoods by inviting co-ops, worker-managed firms, and innovative small businesses to explain their work; by demonstrating equipment for energy conservation and the local generation of solar energy; by turning empty lots or a part of church or synagogue grounds into communal vegetable gardens; by holding workshops on how tenants can buy apartment houses and turn them into co-ops; and by setting up a temporary food co-op and helping people organize a more permanent one.

The festival would address the psychological and cultural renewal of the neighborhood through song, dance, storytelling, and the sharing of food. It would encourage all the people in the neighborhood to pool and exchange their talents, skills, and memories.

The Jubilee as a whole would help empower people politically by instituting town meetings, at which people could discuss some of the major issues of our society—energy, jobs, environment, family, and the cost of living.

Obviously this miniature Jubilee would not be a re-enactment of the biblical Jubilee so much as an experiment in reinterpreting the Jubilee program for modern times. Approaches that began or were stimulated by the Jubilee festival would continue and grow through the year. Their work would intertwine the day-to-day problems of people in the neighborhood with study of both the biblically rooted religious traditions and the modern analytical knowledge of social relations. In this way, the Jubilee festival would create the context for a North American equivalent of the *communidades de base* that have revivified and renewed the church in Brazil and other parts of Latin America.

People who experience the miniature Jubilee could use that moment to begin imagining how to translate the Jubilee program into postmodern practice, which sees productivity as only part of a larger process that includes rest, and institutionalization as part of a process that includes decentralization. And they could start developing the political power that could bring about the kinds of change that they imagine.

How to get the Jubilee festival process going? In a given city, some of the rabbis, ministers, priests—and also the lay members of synagogues, *havurot*, churches, mosques—probably know who in the various religious communities shares this vision. They can create local Jubilee committees, asking congregations to agree to host or sponsor a Jubilee festival. Soon the project would grow through outreach to co-ops, labor unions, innovative businesses, and to singers, dancers, cooks, and story-tellers of the local traditions.

In all these practical proposals, there is an underlying thread of belief: that "ritual" and "politics" should be intertwined, not separated one from the other. This may seem fuzzy-minded to the practical politician, and irreverent to the ritually observant, but such responses are both symptoms of the modern age which has split politics off from any notion of the spiritual. Through the passages on the Jubilee, Leviticus teaches us that the most effective politics has a potent ritual element in it, engaging not only material interests but deep emotional, intellectual, and spiritual energies. Only when ritual focuses on reality does it become fully communal. Only then can it emerge as politics.

Am I my brother's keeper?

(Genesis 4:9)

The Hebrew Bible tells the story of Cain and Abel, two brothers who were different from one another based on their occupations of farming and animal husbandry. Because of this difference they were set apart. When God chose the sacrifice of Abel, the herder, over the sacrifice of Cain, the latter grew violent and killed his brother. When God asked Cain about Abel's whereabouts, his answer was a question: "Am I my brother's keeper?"

Those on the religious left answer that question in the affirmative, believing that despite human differences and animosities, we are responsible for one another. In this section, we look at the ways in which that responsibility expresses itself around the globe. The essays in this section represent discussions about three areas of the world that concern religious leftists in the United States: Latin America, Africa, and the Middle East. Of course, other areas might have been chosen for this section. U.S. relationships with countries in Asia continue to change, and religious issues there (for example, the tensions in Malaysia, relationships with Japan, the Pakistan-India conflict, the freeing of Tibet) have strong and compelling interest for the religious left. The section might have also included discussion of the response of the religious left to the conflict in Northern Ireland or genocide in Eastern Europe. But issues related to Africa, Latin America, and the Middle East represent significant areas of work for the religious left over the last two decades. The essays in this part illustrate both how much has changed, and how intractable many of these problems are.

James Evans writes about his experience of being denied an opportunity to visit South Africa to protest apartheid. He looks at apartheid from the perspective of Christian responsibility and the need for Christian witness. Todd Salzman takes a similar approach in his telling of the story of colonialism and the responsibility of the church in Rwanda for creating the internal antagonisms there today. Both rely on Christian scripture to underscore the values of liberation and the church to provide a witness to the struggle for freedom and peace.

Arthur Waskow uses the biblical story of Hagar, Abraham's first wife and ancestor of the founder of Islam, to think through a reconciliation of Jew and Muslim, Israeli and Palestinian.

Waskow's essay was written before the Oslo accord, and focuses on getting Israelis and Palestinians to negotiate. Unfortunately, there is still a need for negotiation.

Daniel Berrigan's essay reminds us of the tragic fate of Catholic clergy and laity in El Salvador, and focuses on the question of martyrdom in its relation to witnessing. The essay includes accounts of those who went to El Salvador to witness the events of the war there, and to call the U.S. government to account for its role. Barbara Holmes writes of the current issues on the Mexican-U.S. border and about how her experiences traveling across the border brought her back to her biblical commitment to social justice.

Taken together, these essays look at some of the more troubled areas in the world over the past two decades. They provide a powerful picture of the direct involvement of the religious left in writing and witnessing, and in speaking out on behalf of the prophetic values that require those on the religious left to make their voices heard even when the values they espouse are not popular. They insist on drawing the attention of the United States to the evils of colonialism and conquest, and of religious people to the problems of interreligious and ethnic conflict and the need to speak out against oppressive regimes in the name of religious liberty.

James H. Evans

15 Apartheid as Idolatry

In the fall of 1979 a group of civic, academic and religious leaders of the city of Rochester, N.Y., began planning a study tour of South Africa that was to begin in May 1980. At the last moment, however, the South African Government denied their visa applications, giving no reason. The group resubmitted the applications in February 1981, offering to take into account any suggestions from the Government that might improve the chances of approval. A consular official submitted a number of proposals; after discussion, the group amended its plans accordingly. But no response came from the Government until the day of the scheduled departure, May 16; the message was that a decision would be forthcoming in two weeks. The group's plane took off without them, and the members of the group then called off the tour in the conviction that South African officials were merely toying with them. By coincidence, on that same May weekend President Reagan was entertaining Prime Minister P. W. Botha of South Africa in the White House.

The episode roused indignation in Rochester, and even in Johannesburg, where the normally pro-Government newspaper Beeld chided the authorities for their behavior. But one member of the group— James H. Evans of the faculty of Colgate/Rochester Divinity School—was led to reflect not on the discourtesies shown to the Americans but on the far more serious suffering imposed on black people in South Africa under the apartheid system. The following article is a revised version of part of a paper he delivered in September at a theological conference in Buffalo.

White south Africans have perpetuated the myth that the history of South Africa begins in 1652, the year the Dutch East India Company established a station at the Cape Peninsula for its crews. According to the myth the land was empty when the white settlers arrived and it was only after their arrival that the African peoples began to move into the region. This is the myth. The reality, however, is that African peoples were farmers and herdsmen in Southern Africa as early as the third century A.D. Further scientific evidence supports the conclusion that African peoples have lived in the region since the early stages of the evolutionary cycle.

Why does the white myth of South Africa differ so widely from the black reality?

Originally published in *Christianity and Crisis* (December 14, 1981), 347–350. Reprinted with the permission of *Christianity and Crisis*.

Part of the reason is that the white invaders found it necessary to justify, historically, their conquest of a large portion of a black continent. By controlling the history of the region, they could control its black inhabitants. Today, a white minority in South Africa sits atop a despotic political and military regime, the sole aim of which is to keep the black majority in slavery.

To understand this system called apartheid, it is important to look at the history of its development. Whites have seized the history of South Africa and continue to do so by not allowing that history to be told from the perspective of the indigenous black peoples. From that perspective it can be seen that the history of apartheid is the history of the white invaders' worship of a false god. Apartheid is an idolatry. There are three specific historical events that illuminate this finding.

First, there is "The Great Trek" of 1834. In the 1820s, the white Afrikaners along the Eastern Cape Frontier in Southern Africa became disenchanted with the "liberal" treatment afforded the Africans by the British administration. Responding to the burgeoning Enlightenment movement in Europe, the British abolished slavery in 1833. The white Dutch Boers saw this act as contrary to the will of God. For they believed that God's providence demanded that black people be forever the servants of whites. The freedom of the slaves, for them, was a sin. Further, the British declared that, as Christians, the Africans were the equal to all who confessed Christ and believed in God. This, also, the Dutch Boers found to be contrary to their understanding of the will of God for them and the rest of humanity.

In 1834, then, these Dutch Boers "trekked" into the interior, beyond the reach of British rule, there to establish the Kingdom of God; a kingdom in which the white man would fulfill his destiny as ruler of the land, and black people would accept their lot as "hewers of wood and drawers of water." But there was more to the "Great Trek" than this. There was also the hidden motive of economics. In the interior there were free land and slave labor. The conquest of the interior by the whites was valiantly resisted by kings and warriors of the African peoples. But the whites, equipped with superior arms, eventually crushed the black resistance. Once the land was seized and the blacks enslaved, the whites were able to defeat the British economically, if not militarily. The enormous wealth accumulated by the Dutch Boers, and the methods used in attaining it, needed justification. This was step one on the road to apartheid.

Separate and Unequal Development

Second, there is the concept of "separate development." Separate development was the term used to convey the idea that white South Africans had a destiny and historical role, separate from that of the indigenous peoples. According to the white South Africans, the Bible demanded "ethnic diversity" among peoples as the will of God. Because different ethnic groups had different destinies, their paths to those destinies were also different. Whites, then, whose destiny it was to rule the land, were to work and live separately, as far as possible, from blacks. Whites were to have the best housing, education and employment because this was consistent with their destiny. Blacks, on the other hand, needed only the bare minimum for survival. The question here is "Who decided that ethnic diversity meant white supremacy?" This needed justification. This was step two on the road to apartheid.

Apartheid was instituted as official policy in 1948, when the National Party came to power in South Africa. Here the pseudo-theological ideas of racial segregation, and white supremacy become the ideological foundation for political policy. Apartheid prohibited all but the most necessary contacts between blacks and whites. It also instituted a caste system in which the Africans were at the bottom of the scale, the "Coloureds" in the middle, and, of course, the whites solidly in control at the top. By creating false distinctions among the oppressed, the whites hoped to prevent any political cohesion among them. But oppression, like fear, creates its own unity. It also breeds the desire for liberation. In 1960, blacks in Sharpeville, a small town in the Transvaal, peacefully protested against the law which required them to have a written pass in order to pass through certain neighborhoods. On March 21, 1960, the South African police killed 69 blacks and wounded 186 others. Sixteen years later in the township of Soweto, blacks protested the required use of the Afrikaners' language, "Afrikaans," in the teaching of high school subjects. Police swept through the township killing and injuring hundreds of women and children, many of them shot in the back. These events culminated in 1977 in the death in prison of the black leader, Steve Biko.

This is part of the history of South Africa. This history is summed up from a black perspective by the South African black theologian, Mokgethi Motlhabi, in an essay published in 1974:

> The history of the process of racism in South Africa would run something like this. When the land-hungry white invaders reached the southern tip of Africa they encountered the blacks who regarded the land as their own. Very soon, therefore, conflicts arose over the land. But black technology was unable to match white technology in the art of warfare and so black resistance collapsed. The white victors now came to own the land and thus had access to the largest slice of the wealth of the country. This they liked so much that almost every politically important decision that has been taken since then has been to ensure the wealth and power privilege of the whites, and to reduce the threat of any competition for wealth and power from the blacks.

Apartheid as the official policy of racism in South Africa is not only a political ideology, it is also a religious idolatry. Perhaps the clearest statement on racism and idolatry comes from George D. Kelsey (1965):

> Racism is a faith. It is a form of idolatry. . . . In its early modern beginnings, racism was a justificatory device. It did not emerge as a faith. It arose as an ideological justification for the constellations of political and economic power which were expressed in colonialism and slavery. But gradually the idea of the superior race was heightened and deepened in meaning and value so that it pointed beyond the historical structures of relation, in which

it emerged, to human existence itself. The alleged superior race became and now persists as a center of value and an object of devotion. Multitudes of [people] gain their sense of "the power of being" from their membership in the superior race.

Apartheid as a form of racism is an idolatry. It is a heresy. It is a gospel which purports to worship God, but, in reality, seeks only to sustain itself.

The Gospel and Liberation

In spite of the oppressive nature of apartheid, there are those who are proclaiming the liberating Gospel of Christ in the very midst of oppression. In 1968 at a conference held by the South African Council of Churches, a theological commission published a report entitled "Message to the People of South Africa." This report stated in part:

> There are alarming signs that this doctrine of separation has become, for many, a false faith, a novel gospel which offers happiness and peace for the community and for the individual. It holds out to [people] a security built not on Christ but on the theory of separation and the preservation of racial identity. It presents separate development of our race groups as a way for the people of South Africa to save themselves. Such a claim inevitably conflicts with the Christian Gospel, which offers salvation, both social and individual, through faith in Christ alone.

This statement drew from the South African Government threats of reprisals if the churches ever followed the implications of the "Message" to their logical conclusion. Three years later, the University Christian Movement held a series of seminars in South Africa, in which young black theologians presented their views on the relation between the Gospel and human liberation. These essays were "banned" by the Government and the leaders of the project were arrested or exiled.

Within these essays there are four related themes, all of which start from the basic assumption that true Christian theology in South Africa must be black theology. The first theme is that any adequate understanding of the relation between the Gospel and human liberation must come from those whose freedom is being denied. Black theology is theology done from the bottom. This means, according to Manas Buthelezi, that black theology begins, not with abstract concerns, but with real, living African people. It begins with black people; their sorrows and joys, their hopes and aspirations; indeed with their blackness itself:

> A genuine theology grows out of the dynamic forces in life, forces which are decisive for the shaping of everyday life. . . . Black theology is nothing but a methodological formula whose genius consists in paying tribute to the fact that theological honesty cannot but recognize the peculiarity of the black [person's] situation.

This means that blackness is not contrary to personhood. Indeed, the subjectivity of Africans, of which their blackness is a part, is a source of the truth about themselves and God.

The fact that black theology is done from the bottom also means, according to Ananias Mpunzi, that it is a theology of freedom. That freedom has two aspects. It is an individual freedom, which allows each person to express his/her uniqueness as a creation of God. It is also a communal freedom, which allows each person to experience acceptance as part of a tribe, race or group. Both aspects begin with the message of radical freedom that is the heart of the Christian Gospel. The fact that black theology is done from the bottom means, finally, that it is a theology from the viewpoint of those who suffer, according to Mokgethi Motlhabi. Black theology is not a new gospel, but a re-evaluation of the gospel message. It is an authentic expression or reflection on God in light of black experience.

The second theme is the doctrine of God. Black South Africans have had to cope with the Western concept of God, which implies that God is a white, male tyrant who is, at best, unconcerned about the oppression that black people experience, or is actually a party to it. Black theologians question this view of God because it conflicts with their understanding of the Gospel, and it is essentially foreign to their African heritage. For them, God is not to be identified with those who oppress them. God is not white if whiteness means that God is not active in the struggle for black liberation. God is not male if maleness means that there is no equity, justice or partnership between women and men in God's sight. The struggle for liberation includes the black woman and the black man. God's omnipotence does not make God a tyrant. Indeed, God's power is the will of God for the abundant life for all creation. Sabelo Ntwasa states:

> God is freedom. God is the freedom made known in our history. God is the freedom fleetingly and incompletely known in our own experience. But God is also the freedom beyond anything we have yet known, the freedom that calls us out of our chains of oppression into a wholeness of life.

The third theme is that of humanity. Black people in South Africa live in a situation in which their humanity is denied because of their blackness. Thus, the theological question for black South Africans is, according to Manas Buthelezi, "Can I realize my authentic humanity in the medium of my blackness? Is my blackness some fatalistic roadblock in life or a context within which God has made it possible for me to be an authentic person?" Part of the strategy of apartheid and all forms of racism is to set the humanity of black people over against their blackness. That is, the aim is to convince black people that it is impossible to be both black and human at the same time. It follows, then, that if black people accept this lie, then they will be forced to either give up their blackness for the sake of their humanity, or sacrifice their humanity for the sake of their blackness. Black consciousness, however, demands that we affirm both. Black consciousness is an integral part of the struggle for black liberation, Steve Biko has reminded us, because "the most potent weapon in the hands of the oppressor is the mind of the oppressed." To be fully human is not to deny our blackness, but to affirm it. This is the view of humanity from the bottom.

Unity in Struggle

Black South African theologians have solidly demonstrated their conviction that the Gospel of Christ is related to their struggle for human liberation. This they share with their black brothers and sisters in North America and the Caribbean. According to Bishop Desmond Tutu, there are three bonds which unite us. First, we are united by our blackness. Our blackness is something which we can, at times, deny but which we cannot escape. It is part of our being and existence. It is an ontological fact. It does not matter where we are, in Paris, New York or Lagos, it conditions our responses to the world around us and it conditions the responses of others to us.

Second, we are all bound to mother Africa. Whether we are in captivity in our own land or in exile in a foreign place, there are invisible ties linking us to the primordial soil from which we sprang. It has been argued that slavery in America "de-Africanized" the black slave. Bondage may have destroyed or altered many of the cultural manifestations of our heritage, but it did not and could not eliminate the racial memory and consciousness that binds us to our native land. The ties that link us to Africa are more psychological and spiritual than they are physical.

Third, black Christians in South Africa and the U.S. share a unity in Christ. As believers and as members of the people of God, Christ has called us together as his body. This is the unity that no amount of oppression can break. For Christ himself has declared, "What God has joined together let no one put asunder."

These things we share. But we also have a common mission, the liberation of humanity. That is what the Gospel demands from us in terms of our witness in the world. For in the latter day we, as individuals and as a people, will have to stand before the throne of judgment. There, in the words of Manas Buthelezi, "God will say to black [people]: 'Where were you when the white man did this to my Gospel?'" In the words of the old Negro spiritual, "Were you there when they crucified my Lord?"

Arthur Waskow

16   Pesach and the Palestinians

The last few months have poignantly called the Jewish people to learn more deeply from our tradition.

Many of us have found it painful to respond to a massive popular uprising of a people over whom the Jewish state rules and who have made unmistakably clear their firm intention to rule over themselves: the Palestinian people of the West Bank and Gaza. It has been especially painful for us to see a Jewish army seeming to behave toward others as our own lore tells us oppressors have behaved toward us.

The uprising began close to Hanukah, and there are many ironies in the theme of unarmed or ill-armed bands of farmers, students, artisans, shopkeepers, using strikes, boycotts, road-closings, slingshots, rocks, to face the well-equipped army of an occupying power; the weak demanding their freedom as a people, the strong refusing in order to protect their own victorious culture. Jews are taught to know that the end of the Hanukah story was that the weak won victory—a learning that was not unimportant in causing us discomfort. But there is even more powerful and more frightening teaching for us in the story of Pesach than the story of Hanukah—Pesach, our great central archetype of the liberation from slavery in *Mitzrayim,* the narrow place. For in the light of Pesach we realize that the pain we are feeling is really two pains. One is the pain of the present suffering of people, including children who are not only created in the image of God like all human beings but who in some ways are part of our own larger *mishpocha* (family). The other is our painful fear of the future: that if Israeli policy toward the Palestinians does not change, then upon Israel itself and the Jewish people may be visited such plagues as the Torah reports grew from the hardheartedness of Pharaoh.

Why might we see the Palestinians as in some ways part of our own larger *mishpocha*? Because our own tradition and theirs teach that both peoples are co-descendants

Originally published in *Genesis* 2 (Spring 1988), 19:8–12. Copyright © 1988 by (Rabbi) Arthur Waskow. Waskow is director of the Shalom Center and author of *Godwrestling—Round 2* (Jewish Lights Publishing, Woodstock, Vermont), among other works of Jewish renewal and progressive religion.

from Avraham/Ibrahim our Father. And because the Torah teaches that when Sarah tried to explain to Avraham why his other wife Hagar and her son Ishmael had to be sent out from the family, she said Ishmael "mitzacheyk"—was laughing at, or toward or from—her own son Yitzchak, Isaac, whose name meant Laughing Boy. Somehow the two sons were so much like each other—not identical, but similar—that each of them had become a cloudy mirror to the other, each mocking the other's identity so that neither could grow into his own. They needed to live apart. Only when their father Avraham died could they be reconciled.

This is not only a matter of legend, history, archetype; we can see today, with our own eyes, that the Palestinians and the Israelis bear an uncanny resemblance (not identity) to each other. The root of that resemblance is that each people loves the same land, and until now each people has refused to see the other's connection to that land—each fearing that if it recognized the other's connection it would be denying its own legitimacy. In our very collision we are so deeply the same, and not the same: *mishpocha!*

And our resemblance does not end there. In our long Jewish exile in Europe we experienced both pogroms and "making it"—success in the most avant-garde, inventive aspects of commerce, culture, politics. In their more recent wanderings through the Arab world, so have the Palestinians been the most excluded, the victims of sieges and starvation in Lebanon, of massacres in Jordan—yet the most educated, the most mobile. Not for nothing are they called the Jews of the Middle East. In the archetypal tale of Ishmael and Isaac, the fate of the two is intertwined. Abraham sends Ishmael out into the desert where he almost dies. Having endangered the life of one son, Abraham is commanded to offer up the life of the other, Isaac. Today we can see that the futures of our two peoples are intertwined: that every rejection or oppression that either imposes on the other comes back to haunt the imposer.

There is an important connection between the Hagar-Ishmael story and the one of our slavery in Egypt. Hagar is called *"Hagar hamitzria"*—"the stranger who is an Egyptian." It is no accident that we become what the Torah calls *"gerim b'eretz mitzrayim"*—"strangers in the land of Egypt"—and that the Torah warns us over and over again that we must love and respect the stranger in our own land, precisely because we were strangers in the land of Egypt and from that experience learned to know the heart of the stranger.

Hagar, "the stranger," was the beginning of this spiral of pain, and it is Hagar, the stranger, whom we must learn to treat decently when we meet again in our own land. In our third effort to govern ourselves in the Land of Israel by wrestling to discern the truly holy sparks in our ancient teachings, we find ourselves once again meeting up with Hagar and Ishmael. What to do?

"One teaching, one torah, shall there be for the homeborn and for the stranger who lives-as-a-stranger (*v'la-ger hagar*) among you," says the very passage of the Exodus story which commands us to celebrate the Exodus each year at Pesach.

What would it mean to respond to Hagar and Ishmael, this time, in accord with that basic rule—with neither expulsion nor an effort to subject them to Israeli rule?

To answer this, we need to look away for a moment from the teaching, the Torah, that is encoded in the texts of our tradition, and look at the torah that confronts us in the present. It is only in this wrestle that sparks of light fly up from the parchment— which, let us remember, is itself the record of our forebears' efforts to wrestle with painful issues similar to ours. What makes the record sacred is that their wrestlings were so profound as to be God-wrestlings.

What alternatives are there? At bottom, only four:

1. Expel the Palestinians from the West Bank and Gaza, as Kahane urges. Would the world permit this? Could the Jewish state remain Jewish in ethos if it did this?
2. Absorb the West Bank and Gaza into Israel and make the Palestinians full citizens. If this "worked" and the two peoples lived in peace under one government, sharing resources, writing laws, etc., Israel would no longer be a Jewish state. If it did not work—and as of now it is clear that both peoples distrust each other, neither wants the other to have a hand in governing it—the state would disintegrate like Lebanon, in a constant chaos of civil war.
3. Keep the status quo. Strikes, demonstrations, riots, shootings, beatings, deaths.
4. Let the Palestinians govern themselves on the West Bank and Gaza, either on their own or in a confederation with Jordan, as they decide—on the sole condition that they live in peace with Israel, under arrangements (such as demilitarization) that guarantee that the peace will be real.

The fourth option alone means neither expulsion of Hagar and Ishmael, nor their subjugation, nor an attempt to digest them into the Israeli body politic. The "one torah" for homeborn and stranger would be simply the most basic torah of relations between peoples: equality of self-determination, in a context of peace.

Are there risks involved in a self-governing Palestinian people? Yes. The main one is that the West Bank would become a staging point for military attack on Israel. That is why control over arms there, joint Israeli-Palestinian-Jordanian patrols on the Jordan River, and similar arrangements would be so necessary.

Are these risks as great as those stemming from the other three alternatives? Judge for yourself.

So much for the way we are supposed to treat the Palestinians. But what if we do not? After all, it *is* hard:

Their official leadership has not behaved like Moses, Miriam and Aaron. The leaders of our Exodus did not begin by demanding the shattering of Egypt. They proposed a form of liberation that would have left Egyptian society intact. But the Palestinian leadership began by explicitly rejecting the legitimacy of Jewish liberation and has never made a clear offer of peace and security to Israel, in exchange for Palestinian self-government. (There have in fact been some unclear offers, which an Israeli diplomacy that desired this result would have vigorously explored—but not clear ones.) What is worse, various branches of the Palestinian nationalist movement have made few distinctions between quasi-military attacks on Israeli soldiers and terrorist attacks on Israeli civilians—let alone distinctions between violence and nonviolence. (Even Palestinians like Mubarak Awad who have called for nonviolence have refused to oppose and criticize the use of violence as Gandhi and King did.) So those who say there are no Palestinians who are willing to negotiate with Israel may have been partly right.

Does this difficulty give us a license to settle into the status quo? *Not if the status quo is dangerous to us, to our own interests, to our own being.* If the status quo is dangerous to us, and we can find no one with whom to negotiate to end it, then we must figure out a way to end it ourselves, without a negotiating partner.

So let us ask. Is the status quo dangerous to us? Suppose Israel tries to preserve it on the grounds that it is too hard to do anything else—especially to negotiate. What then?

The Torah teaches us that once this dynamic of the birth of a new people has really begun, there is no status quo. One way or another, the birth goes forward—and an effort to prevent it brings plagues down upon the whole society that stands in the way.

What is the career of Pharaoh? At first he hardens his own heart against the sufferings of the Israelites and the Egyptians. When demonstrators come to him to say, "Let our people go!," he responds with a more bitter subjugation: "Go make bricks without straw." When they persist and when God—the very Truth and Power of the universe—closes in upon him with the first few plagues, he hardens his heart still more.

And then God takes over. Pharaoh loses his ability to choose. Even when his advisors say to him, "Don't you understand that you are destroying Egypt?" he cannot change. Now God is hardening his heart. It is as if he had been smoking crack—once, twice, thrice, he still is choosing—and then the addiction takes over. From then on Pharaoh is doomed—and not only Pharaoh. For the death of the first-born descends upon every Egyptian family.

Usually we Jews read this story with an eye to the Pharaohs of the other peoples, who have oppressed us and brought plagues upon themselves. Some of us (some Hasidic rebbes, for example) have occasionally read the tale as a more inward teaching—looking at "Pharaoh" within each of us, the impulse toward evil in every individual that must be resisted with God's help, lest it take over and destroy us. This teaching reminds us that we are less likely to act like Pharaoh outwardly, towards others, if we face clearly the fact that Pharaoh is within us, too—not only in "those others."

But rarely, if ever, have we faced a situation in which the danger is that the leaders of the Jewish people might use political power in a Pharaonic way—that we may find "pharaohitude" within us, not in an individual spiritual sense alone, but as a spiritual and political community. Rarely, if ever, have we found ourselves as a body politic needing to see that some aspect of Pharaoh is within us if we are to prevent ourselves from acting like Pharaoh outwardly.

Yet that is now our danger. When the Prime Minister of Israel calls on Jewish settlers on the West Bank to be "strong" and on the Palestinians to be "quiet," he is hardening his heart. When the Defense Minister orders the cracking of bones, he is risking becoming addicted to "cracking."

We have already begun to see the first plagues threaten Israel itself. When Israeli Arabs, who until now have been integrating themselves into the political and even social fabric of Israel (despite the particular economic and cultural barriers between them and Jewish Israelis) respond to the physical pain and death and political torment of their families on the West Bank and Gaza with the first unravelings of that fabric, that is a plague coming down on Israel itself. When some Israelis form vigilante groups to expel Arabs and threaten Jews with whom they don't agree, that is a plague coming down on Israel itself. When the U.S. public and government begin to distance themselves from Israel's policy and behavior, that is a plague coming down on Israel itself.

All these plagues are self-induced. The Nile was not to blame for turning bloody, the Pharaoh was.

And the plagues are likely to grow worse. Moral and economic exhaustion, rates of emigration, internal strife and violence, are likely to grow. Those among the Palestinian leadership who are most hostile to negotiation will more and more strongly insist that Israel will be weaker and its allies less supportive the longer the process goes on.

If we want to prevent the recent *choices* of hard-heartedness from becoming an *addiction* to hard-heartedness, the addiction that brings down worse plagues upon us, what must we do? We must do more than Pharaoh's advisors, who protested too late and too perfunctorily. We must actually get the policies of the Israeli government to change, to become open-hearted. *We must do this for our own sake, as well as the sake of the Palestinians.* For the sake of our bodies, not of our souls alone. For the sake of preventing plagues from descending on our own land and people.

What would be an open-hearted policy on the government's behalf? Let us sketch three; there may well be others.

1. To welcome an international peace conference, with the proviso that Palestinians who take part specify their commitment to the goal of making peace with Israel, and with the commitment on Israel's side that its goal is to achieve peace with a self-governing Palestinian entity on the West Bank and Gaza; *or*
2. To invite the very same Palestinians whom Israel has arrested as leaders of the uprising to meet and choose ten of their number to undertake negotiations with Israel, with the two goals stated above; *or*
3. To move Israeli troops to the Jordan River and other secure perimeters around the West Bank and Gaza, withdraw them from all settled Palestinian areas, and let the Palestinians choose their own authorities.

What could we do to press the Israeli government to take such initiatives as these?

We could send money and messages of support to Israeli organizations that support such views.

We could hold open learn-ins in our congregations and other organizations, inviting speakers who take such views to present them. We could contact groups to provide speakers for such learn-ins.

We could ask our congregations to put these questions on their formal agenda and vote for resolutions embodying such approaches, and send these resolutions to members of Knesset.

We could place ads in Jewish and/or general newspapers espousing such positions.

We could create delegations of rabbis, Jewish teachers and professionals, and other active Jews, to visit Israeli consulates, embassies and missions to explain their position.

We could introduce into our liturgies special moments to focus prayer for peace—not in general and vaguely, but specifically between Israel and the Palestinians. For example, at the end of the *Oseh Shalom* prayer, which ends the *Kaddish* and which asks God to make peace "among us and among all Israel," we could add "all Ishmael" so that the Hebrew would end, *"v'al kol Yisrael v'al kol Yishmael."* As another example, we could work out some way of memorializing Palestinians who were killed while engaged in nonviolent actions seeking their people's self-determination. (Some communities have already used the recitation of *Kaddish* or the lighting of *yortzeit* candles in this way, and some Jews have objected that these are special marks of memory for the Jewish dead. So those who wish to do memorials should think through how they feel about this, and whether these or other forms are more appropriate.)

We could work with any number of groups that have organized Jewish-Arab dialogues in the U.S. Most experience is that such continuing dialogues are difficult but not impossible and have sometimes resulted in much deeper understanding on both sides.

We could begin to refocus donations of money to Israel through the New Israel Fund, which has an explicit policy of supporting groups in Israel that seek peace and dialogue between Israel and the Palestinians and between Israeli Jews and Israeli Arabs.

In deciding whether to take any of these actions, we will need to take into account three serious questions:

- Is Israel already beyond the point of no return? Is there simply no way to gather the political strength and the far-sighted planning necessary to turn toward a policy along these lines?
- Do Jews outside Israel have the right to use any of these forms of persuasion, pressure, or assistance to change Israeli policy? Since Israelis live much more directly with the consequences of their acts than do other Jews, are they not the best judges of what will best protect them?
- Will public criticism of Israel by American Jews signal to other Americans that it is "open season" on Israel and lead to consequences the critics would oppose, e.g., cuts in U.S. aid to Israel?

In regard to the first, the tradition teaches that the Prophets spoke almost always to what would happen *if*—if the people acted in such and such a way. They rarely asserted that history had become determined—that the people had no choice.

There were some moments when a sage concluded that all choices had been thrown away. One such moment came when Yochanan ben Zacchai concluded that the Zealots who were in command of the defense of the Holy Temple when it was besieged by the Roman Tenth Legion had gone crazy in their militance. (They had burned the food in order to force a strategy of attack, instead of the defense that was succeeding.)

So Yochanan said, "I must get out of this place," and pretended to have died in order to get permission for his corpse to leave the Temple grounds. Then he begged the Romans to spare the Temple. Only when they refused did he ask, and win, their permission to open an academy in Yavneh that became the training ground for all the future generations of the rabbis. Thus he pretended to die in order to give birth to a new form of Judaism. For any serious Jew who is prepared to take on the heavy burden of concluding that Israel has passed the point of no return, the message is clear: devote yourself utterly to the remaking of Judaism in the Diaspora, with all your creativity and vigor. And even so, even at the last moment, try to save the situation in Israel.

In regard to the second question, it is clear that Israelis have much more power than anyone else to decide what their government will or will not do. Both politically and ethically, that fact stems from their reality of being on the ground and being much more affected than other Jews by what happens on the ground.

But does that mean other Jews have no stake in what happens there? If that were true, other Jews would not be sending money to Israel, visiting there, creating complex organizational ties with Israeli groups, looking for stories about Israel in the morning paper, teaching its history and geography in Jewish schools, and so on.

Perhaps a fair criterion is that American Jews do have and are entitled to have as much voice in Israel as stems from their degree of involvement in Israel's success. Those who have little involvement will in fact have little voice, because Israelis will pay them little attention. Those people and organizations that are deeply involved will be heard loud and clear.

As for the third question, on the impact of American Jewish criticism on other Americans: One of the prices of living in the new kind of Diaspora that is America— one of the costs of not living in a ghetto—is that we are not isolated from others. What we say, even among ourselves, is overheard.

This entails risks. How do we estimate them? A question to ask ourselves: Do we think support for Israel in American society is so brittle that crucial material support for Israel's basic security and economy will vanish if there is widespread belief that the occupation is wrong?

Criticism may also give benefits. Others, for example, may be somewhat more likely to believe what we say when we praise Israel if they know that on occasion we criticize it.

But still, there are risks. These risks must be weighed against the risks of not speaking out.

And here we must come back to the Torah-story of Pharaoh. How great are the risks that the Israeli government is hardening its heart in such a way that soon—but not yet—it will have no choice and will march like an addict to its doom? What would we do to prevent a beloved sister or brother from becoming addicted to crack? What risks would we run?

We are back to the basic question, the question in which practical politics and religious ethics fuse into a single burning question as the Prophets always said they would.

What can we do that will not leave us as impotent as Pharaoh's key advisors, imploring him to listen as he marched on, deaf, to swallow up his country in disaster?

This is the fourth question of the Hagadah of our liberation, in the Pesach of 5748.

Daniel Berrigan

17 The Martyrs' Living Witness:
A Call to Honor and Challenge

In San Salvador, on the 16th of November 1989, as is known around the world, six Jesuit priests, together with their cook and her daughter, were dragged from their beds and murdered. The event was hardly unforeseen or even unchosen by the priests.

For at least four years, they had dwelt under the livid threat that at length broke through their doors and called in a debt of blood. At one point several years ago, an ultimatum was issued against them; 30 days to leave the country or be killed. They chose to remain and take their chances. The word of the Spirit, one concludes, was: Remain.

Instead of leaving, the Jesuits sent a modest appeal to their brothers around the world. Please be apprised of our predicament. Please come if possible to El Salvador. International attention is our only hope. A slight interference, the presence of outsiders, might, just might, delay discharge of guns already cocked and aimed.

It was at this point that another New York Jesuit and I resolved to go. In the course of our visit, we met all those who were subsequently murdered. It occurred to me at the time that it might also be useful to publish a small account of the journey, of the friendships we formed, of the dangers and complications of life in that tormented country. I did so. But nothing we could do availed, as we were to learn to our horror and grief.

The reality of the situation of the Jesuits required neither drama nor dramaturge. Day after day, year after year, as the guns resounded to and fro like mad metronomes, the mortal danger wherein the priests stood—what form the end might take—could hardly have been made more vivid to them. Certainly not by their unclairvoyant visitors from *el Norte*.

Originally published in *Sojourners* (April 1990), 19:22–26. Reprinted with permission from *Sojourners*, 2401 15th Street NW, Washington, DC 20009; (202) 328-8842/(800) 714-7474.

The priests had no need of a drama, a play within their play. Why should someone seize the cincture of one among them, bind himself over, and so declare their plight? The Spirit, one might conclude, had spoken to them; a circuit of doom and glory bound them, each to each. One in life and work and consequence: Remain.

Agabus declared through the symbolic binding certain boundaries of knowledge of the future and its form (Acts 21:10–11). The prospective binding of Paul could only signify the drastic curtailing, if not the end, of his extraordinary mission. The response of the community to this dire likelihood is a spontaneous outcry, it is beyond bearing that Paul be taken prisoner. Yet again, friends are appalled. They beg him to stay free, while he is yet able, from bonds whose very prospect is a throttling of hope.

And he will not. He will counter their dread by introducing a larger, more awful threat and embracing that. "Why these tears, why try to weaken my resolution? I am ready not only to be bound, but to die in Jerusalem for the name of the Lord Jesus" (Acts 21:13).

What friend willingly consents in mind to the suffering of a friend, no matter the nobility of the cause? The office of friendship, we think, is to act counter to intemperate heroism. And in discharging that office with all one's might, as the heart drums insistently, the friend acts all the more nobly. Friendship cries in protest, weakens, warns, declares null and void the hot will of the one who runs to death. "Let this cross be far from you."

The outburst of Peter in the face of Jesus' announcement of his death—so heartfelt and altruistic, so right (and so wrong), so in accord with the heart's deep welling, so weakening and delaying what must be—is coldly received, perceived only as an assault on invincible will. And it is rejected in tones brusque, final, scandalous: "Stand aside, Satan."

Thus the friend, protesting, impeding, standing athwart, is locked in combat with the beloved one. "Simon, son of John, do you love me?" Friendship, and then vocation. How shall a sedulous friend resolve the dilemma? How do we stand with the other, and still pay respect to the friend's vocation?

The solution is hardly a relief, it is a multiplying of sorrow. It implies agreement with the determination of a friend, that he go where he must go, where he is quite literally and beforehand "bound." And then the new agreement is sealed in blood. It is the blood of an all but unimaginable pact.

The friend imagines, then leaps the void that lies between friendship and vocation. It is quite simple and final. He joins his friend in death. "In very truth I tell you, . . . when you are old you will stretch out your arms and a stranger will bind you fast and bring you where you have no wish to go" (John 21:18).

They all came to this in the early gathering. One, their friend, preceded them; the others were tardy, but eventually grew hardy in purpose. It was a gathering of death and rising from death.

"So, as Paul would not be dissuaded, we gave in and said, 'The Lord's will be done. . . .'" (Acts 21:14). Now we have something more than friendship, as the world would understand it. We have a community standing on the shore, not in farewell but in an accompanying spirit. The wind in his sails bears them along in a gale; all are bent on the same errand, the journey toward Jerusalem. Friend and friends, they are bound over. They stretch forth their hands and feet in one direction. More, they bend their necks to Paul's will, "To die in Jerusalem for the name of the Lord Jesus."

The members are well advised not to doubt the worst, to embrace the darkness of their own foreboding. And this for Paul's sake, that he not go alone on his dolorous way. And for their own also. The journey is theirs, and the binding over; and eventually, in likely prospect, the martyrdom as well.

The martyrs test the church. The church knows itself, which is to say it has mapped its journey toward Jerusalem and calculated the consequence of the journey. But this only insofar as it knows, embraces, honors, exonerates the martyrs.

This attitude and activity in regard to our own can only be called crucial. It implies at the same time that the church rejects the ideology which the state invariably, for its own perverse delight and to cover its crimes, attaches to the believers whom it marks for martyrdom. This is an insulting tag attached to a noble corpse: ideologue, or troublesome priest, or disturber of public order.

Thus the sequence: The state executes the martyrs, then denigrates their deaths behind a meticulous (or foolish) scrim of duplicity and doubt.

It was thus in the case of Jesus. He must not only die, but Roman law must be vindicated in his death (and he dishonored, his memory smirched) by charges of subversion, threats of destruction of the temple, endangerment of law and order.

In his death we have something more shameful even. We have the classic instance of religion abandoning the martyr, joining the vile secular chorus of dishonor. Worse and worse, it supplies out of its own foxy canons a philistine logic to conceal its implication in the crime: "One of them, Caiaphas, who was high priest that year, said, 'You have no grasp at all of the situation; you do not realize this: It is more to your interest that one man should die for the people than that the whole nation should be destroyed. . . .'" (John 11:49–50).

Martyrdom is included in the church's catechesis, for the church knows why martyrs die, and says so. More, in certain circumstances, the church makes it clear that such death is the only honorable witness and outcome.

Then, their deaths accomplished, the church's task continues. It raises them to the altar for holy emulation. For they are, after Christ and Mary, the church's chief glory. The church knows it and at least sometimes says it boldly, sternly defending the martyrs. The defense is risky. Often guns again are lowered, the terror continues, and others are placed at danger. The mere declaration of how and why the martyrs perished heightens the immemorial struggle between the church and the worldly powers—a struggle that the martyrs personify to the highest and noblest degree.

In San Salvador as elsewhere, noble tongues are silenced, but the truth must continue to be told. The truth of their death, the cruelty and injustice of it, the precious connection between their death and the integrity of the gospel. This is judgment, the heavy tolling, not of a passing bell, but a presentiment of the last day itself. The bell tolls for the defeat here and now of the violent victors, for the triumph of the victims.

The martyrs, all said, have stood surrogate for Christ and the church. Their crime is their firm withstanding on behalf of an irresistible word of love. In this they have spoken for the whole body of Christ.

Then, death accomplished, their community takes up the task, not solely to justify the innocent death, nor to seek justice. That's an impossible task in most cases, since the unjust and violent sit also in the courts. The task is otherwise: to confront the powers with judgment and a call to repentance. Even murderers, and the powers that impel them, must be salvaged. Even those who are furthest from the saving truth, from the mercy and compassion they have sought to extinguish.

This is the consonance between church and martyr: the martyr standing witness for the church, the church vindicating and honoring the martyr.

An ordination photo of Father Ellacuria, murdered Jesuit of El Salvador, shows him vested, prostrate on the sanctuary floor while the litany of saints is chanted over the new priests. A photo dated Thursday, November 16, 1989, shows Father Ellacuria murdered, prostrate outside the Jesuit house. He is in exactly the position of his ordination rite.

The church from time to time (and wondrously in our own time) earns the name church of martyrs. It does not mean, obviously, that all the faithful perish, it signifies the living consonance between the witness of those who die and those who survive. Both speak up, both pay dearly; some in blood, some in the bearing of infamy and danger.

This continuing burden of truth telling is, it would seem (and here one speaks with trepidation), mainly a matter laid upon the local church. The situation could hardly be called ideal. When the highest authorities of the church refuse to vindicate our martyrs, and thus refuse to confront the powers clearly and unequivocally, only the local community of faith can supply for the moral deficit.

The situation implies a kind of vexed and sorrowful logic. A given community has nourished the faith of the martyr with word and sacrament. A kind of holy ampelopsis has joined the holy one to the body of Christ. It seems only fitting (though regrettable as well) that after death, both the good repute of the martyr and the continuing witness against the powers should lie in the hands of those (invariably the poor) who survive and mourn. Let the great be silent, or mouth platitudes, or introduce absurd political innuendo. It is the humble who know, who speak; their tears are eloquent.

In the great world, and the great worldly church, other concerns are in the air. The blood and torment are distant. They are carried on the airwaves and tubes, a phenomenon known fatuously as "international news." There the images of the dead are seized, impeded, manipulated, shuffled about.

Add to this the political and economic interests of ecclesiastical headquarters. Suppose for a moment (one need not suppose!) that those who died perished for speaking on behalf of inarticulate, powerless Christians and others. Their deaths occurred in a minor, indeed inconsiderable, land, worlds distant from the highly "developed" church and its special concern and interest in the "developed" superstates.

The situation does not invite moral clarity. A conclusion is reached in exalted circles (and this in fact is the rub) that the murdered Christians defended no recondite or required dogma. They did not die for the integrity of, say, the doctrine of Eucharist, the virginity of Mary, the bodily resurrection of Christ. A mutter is heard from influential lips. The victims died in a politically volatile situation; it is reported that they took sides, that they were defenders of one ideology or another.

It could be conceded perhaps that they died for the sake of the powerless and poor. But this hardly suffices to grant them the entitlement of martyrs. So it is thought and said. Or is not said, but the silence wears a frown of thunder.

Let us be as clear as might be. Innumerable sisters and brothers have died in our lifetime for the sake of the powerless and poor. Let us think in consequence of this of a scriptural teaching baptized again and again in a sea of blood. A teaching, let it be added, generally neglected in high ecclesiastical circles—the teaching of the body of Christ.

Paul writes of the mutuality and integrity of all members of the body, the consonance of the lowliest with the most honored. "So that there might be no division in the body, but that all its parts might feel concern for one another. If one part suffers, all suffer together; if one flourishes, all rejoice together" (I Corinthians 12:25–26).

Bishops and others, we beg you, take notice of this passion for the integrity of the body, this rejection of the rejection of the lowly. Behold the scripture on behalf of which a host of martyrs in your lifetime and mine have staked their lives.

In the face of the ambivalent speech (and the even more ambivalent silence) of authorities, the harmless pieties, the intertwining of profane and church interests, are we not justified in insisting that those appointed to speak for the universal church speak clearly, passionately, in defense of our martyrs? That they clarify issues of faithful political witness, that their words resound with the same truth that at a crack of gunfire turned mortal bodies to pentecostal flame?

This is unpleasant and, to the mind of many, unfortunate; and, all said, true. Faith is a political matter, inevitably. So is martyrdom, in most cases. The task is to separate out, in mind and heart, the political content of a given death (one's dying for the poor, who themselves are joined to political parties of revolution, thus means taking sides). This political implication must be separated from another lurking issue—that of ideology: high and low, ecclesiastical or secular; the itch and appetite of special interest pursuits, hankerings; and, above all, the appetite for power, control, secrecy, nonaccountability.

Thus the death of the martyrs urges a scrutiny of conscience on the part of all. This includes a self-scrutiny of authority, of its ideology and behavior—especially an ideology that inhibits speaking the truth concerning the murder of our sons and daughters, the honor and dishonor of their deaths.

Let us, for Christ's sake, hear loud and clear, let the assassins hear, and let the faceless politicos and oligarchs hear why our martyrs stood where they did ("the standpoint is the viewpoint"), why in consequence they, known and anonymous, were eliminated. Let us hear praise of the martyrs. Let us hear an unambiguous call to the faithful, that the holy dead be emulated by the living.

Imitating the Martyrs: Voices for Peace

A Call to Action

I remember the living quarters of the murdered Jesuit priests and the two women—the blood-stained walls, the shattered glass, the bullet holes in the concrete walls. The blood-stained floors of the individual rooms were a stark contrast to the sitting room of the living area, where rocking chairs still encircled a table that held cups of unfinished coffee and ashtrays with crushed-out cigarette butts, representing an evening of conversation and closing evening prayer.

For me, it was in those moments of hearing the detailed story of the night of murder and violence that the impact of those eight murders—and the 75,000 other murders—finally was stored in my heart and soul.

I'd seen death, pain, and destruction in many other situations; but this, in a place of peace broken by the horror of evil, was once again a reminder of people's inhumanity to people. Yet it was also a reminder of the incredible power of the gospel message of freedom and liberation.

As I struggled to control the throbbing in my heart, someone showed me one of the bullets that investigators had found at the site—and on it was stamped "Made in the U.S.A."

Maybe it was later, or maybe it was at that moment, but I was struck by the depth of responsibility that we as U.S. citizens and as U.S. churches carry in this bloody conflict—and the need for us as church people to call for repentance for our complicity in the ongoing terror, death, and destruction of the Salvadoran people.

It is a call that comes from the understanding that out of the depths of great pain and human destruction come life, celebration, and salvation. Yet often when we in the First World call for repentance, we repent, we weep, we are sorrowful; and just as quickly we move on to celebration and salvation. We often forget the final step which is the call to action.

At a commemoration service for the martyred, which also marked the first time the ecumenical community in El Salvador had been together since the deaths of the Jesuits and the women, I heard stories of persecution interwoven with words of hope and celebration. After all the moving stories and uplifting music, a teen-age woman representing the youth of the Lutheran Church in El Salvador got up and said, "All has been said, all stories have been told. I cannot tell any more, but I do have one final reflection. I have learned and believe the words 'Do not weep for the martyrs, but rather imitate them.'"

It is these simple words that are a call to action for us. This is our call in the United States to become witnesses for the martyred, our opportunity to imitate them, to imitate the witness of the churches in El Salvador.

We need to be clear to our government officials so that they know that the religious community does not define itself by national boundaries, and that the persecution of one body of the community is felt by the whole. It's as if we were all under that persecution.

Now is the time. We—the powerful religious communities of the North—are called to be imitators of the prophetic churches serving the poor in the South. We are called to use all of our resources to stop our country from supplying military aid, and call for a politically negotiated settlement.

We are called to use all of our resources to speak out against the persecution of the church, to demand that justice be served in violations of human rights and the innocent deaths of thousands. We are called, as imitators of our brothers and sisters in El Salvador, to accompany them whenever they ask and whenever is needed.

The question for us, my friends, is, Are we ready to repent and be forgiven? For, indeed, it is in that forgiveness that we are free to respond to this call for action.

—Christine Grumm

Christine Grumm, vice president of the Evangelical Lutheran Church of America, accompanied Lutheran Bishop Medardo Gomez on a trip to El Salvador in January 1990. This reflection was offered at a convocation of U.S. and Salvadoran religious leaders in Washington, D.C., on January 23, 1990.

The Promise of the Resurrection

I am daily inspired by the words of a Salvadoran friend and union leader. I asked him once if he never felt despair, never felt like giving up. After some thought he turned to me and said, "No, Karen; because despair is a First World luxury."

It is our responsibility as the world's wealthy, my friend Oscar pointed out, not to despair, but to have the sufficient imagination to walk in the struggle with our brothers and sisters for whom justice is an issue of life and death. Not to give up until they do—and they will never give up. For they know that justice is inevitable, that unjust structures cannot forever withstand a people's hunger for freedom and dignity.

We of the First World are simply left with a choice: We can turn our backs and walk away from a challenge, or we can have the imagination to walk with the Salvadorans to the end of their struggle.

Our presence may bring that closer and lessen the suffering and the blood spilled. But with or without us, it is inevitable—that *is* the promise of the resurrection.

—Karen Ridd

Karen Ridd, a Canadian volunteer for Peace Brigades International in El Salvador, was deported from the country after being picked up during a November raid on a church shelter by Salvadorian security forces.

Go and Tell Them. . . .

The persecution against the church became very strong after the rebel offensive began in November, but many church leaders who had been targeted did not want to leave our country. The experience of being away makes us very sad, because we are very far away from our people.

We resisted having to leave. But it was even our own people that came to us and begged us to leave. They said, "Save your life; we need you later." But probably what convinced us most is when they said, "Go and tell people in the United States our message: We beg of you, we want peace."

On another occasion I visited the refugee camp of Mesa Grande in Honduras. Our brothers and sisters had prepared a great reception, with large banners that read: "Welcome Bishop Gomez. We want peace."

I asked the brothers and sisters at Mesa Grande, "Why do you ask me to bring peace if I am not the one to bring peace?" But they said, "No, you can bring us peace."

I said, "I don't know how to do that. Tell me, what can I do to bring peace?" And they said, "You can travel, Brother Gomez. You can travel to the United States. Go there and tell our brothers and sisters that we want peace."

Peace in our country means simply the following: No to the military aid. Peace in our country means a more humane policy than the current U.S. policy. And this peace can be constructed with your accompaniment.

Peace means that delegations of your groups would come to El Salvador, that you would become closer to us, more knowledgeable of our reality. Peace means all of the prayer and the solidarity actions that you carry out for us.

I am very grateful to God for each one of you. The Bible, the Word of God, continues to be written. And the scripture is written with all of the solidarity actions that are carried out on our behalf. May God bless you, brothers and sisters, for your great love.

—Medardo Gomez

Medardo Gomez, bishop of the Salvadoran Lutheran Church, was forced into exile last November. This reflection was offered at a convocation of U.S. and Salvadoran religious leaders in Washington, D.C., on January 23, 1990.

We Have Right on Our Side

We are a hard-working people, and our children deserve a better today and a much better tomorrow. Yet our rivers, our lakes, and our mountains are stained with blood.

We are a people who want liberty, who want an authentic democracy. We are against the forces of death, and we want a truly prosperous country that we construct with the work of all. For all these reasons, my brothers and sisters, in the name of the Salvadoran people, and in the name of our Lord Jesus Christ, I urge you to continue your struggle together until we have peace with social justice in El Salvador.

Until we tear down and destroy that position which has been shown to have failed over the last 10 years—the position of a military victory—we must turn to the only possible alternative. Now with moral strength, with all that we are, we say no more war. We want negotiation, and we want peace.

And that, beloved brothers and sisters, we will achieve as one part of the body of Christ; because we have right on our side. This is what we believe, because we believe that the reign of God has come down, through the efforts of the Lord and through our own efforts. Let us continue on in the struggle.

—Edgar Palacios

Edgar Palacios is pastor of Shalom Baptist church in San Salvador and the coordinator of the Permanent Commission of the National Debate for Peace in El Salvador. This reflection was offered at a vigil of U.S. and Salvadoran religious leaders on the steps of the U.S. Capitol on January 29, 1990.

Those Who Long for Peace

Peace should not be left in the hands of those for whom party interests are more important than the needs of the people, but should be in the hands of those who truly long for peace. We need a humanization of peace.

We need to work for peace from the perspective of the suffering of the orphans and widows, and the tragedy of the assassinated and disappeared. We must keep our eyes on the God of Jesus Christ, the God of life, the God of the poor, and not on the idols, or the gods of death, that devour everything.

More compelling than spoken words, the reality of El Salvador—the 75,000 dead, the 7,000 disappeared, the widows and the orphans, the 1.5 million displaced people and refugees, and the millions of impoverished Salvadorans—cries out for peace.

—Ignacio Ellacuria

Ignacio Ellacuria, the rector of the Central American University in San Salvador, was one of the six Jesuit priests murdered by Salvadoran armed forces in November. These comments were made at a march for peace in San Salvador on March 4, 1989, and are included in El Salvador: A Spring Whose Waters Never Run Dry.

All of Us Can Do Something

We have been told by the faithful of El Salvador to weep no more, and instead to imitate the actions of the martyrs. And yet we've discovered that sometimes we cannot stop the tears.

At times like this, we remember not only our brothers and sisters who have lost their lives, but those who are being deprived of freedom right now. Parish workers from my community were tortured for 15 days at the hands of the security forces before they were allegedly handed over to the civil judiciary system.

While President Cristiani talks about a judicial system in El Salvador that works, in reference to the case of the murdered Jesuits, hundreds and hundreds of political prisoners in El Salvador right now are outside of any legal system. They have never been charged. So part of our weeping is not only for those deceased, those who have been murdered, but for those who continue to suffer in the prisons and the barrios of El Salvador.

To those of you who have seen the pain of the Salvadoran people, you cannot wait until the tears are no more; you march with your tears. You don't wait until you have conquered your fear; you walk with the fear. You don't wait until the anger has subsided; you speak with the anger.

The day that he was assassinated, Archbishop Oscar Romero, in his last sermon, spoke at a memorial service for a woman who had died the previous year. In that service he told stories about what this simple woman had done. And then he said, "All of us can do something."

Whether this day we are doing civil disobedience, speaking with truth and anger to congressional representatives, praying and fasting, or writing still another letter— all of us can do something; all of us can do something; all of us can do something.

—Jim Barnett

Jim Barnett, a Dominican priest, served four and a half years in a parish of displaced people near San Salvador. He left the country last November under threat of death. This reflection was offered at a vigil of U.S. and Salvadoran religious leaders on the U.S. Capitol steps on January 23, 1990.

Barbara Holmes

18 Back to the Dust: How I Rediscovered the Power of Scripture

Until a recent trip to the Mexican border, I didn't realize what was missing from my biblical reflections. I didn't realize the power that was waiting to be grasped.

Maybe I'm unusual, but I suspect not. As a child, the Bible stories I heard were pathways to a world I could enter at will. I raced toward the field to ward off the trouble that had long been brewing between Cain and Abel. I stood nearby as David faced Goliath, holding a few extra rocks, just in case. Day after day, I felt the sun on my face, the dust in my throat—and God's hand on my life.

I entered the biblical world through the archway of stories, told and retold. I heard them around the dining-room table and in Sunday school classes at a Congregational church in New Haven, Connecticut.

That plain but sturdy church had been a "way station" in the underground railroad. Runaway slaves escaping to Canada had sought sanctuary there. Decades later, between hymns, you could still hear the sounds of feet "runnin' for free." There was a relatedness in that place. Melodic, richly interwoven voices of witnesses past and present attested to a trustworthy—and free-spirited—God.

With a beaming grin, the God of my childhood would pop up in burning bushes— and surprise folk with babies and deliverance, just when they least expected it. The best part, of course, was that God loved the whole world. Especially ten-year-old me.

I don't know how or when, but somewhere between Sunday school and adulthood, I lost the grit and reality of the Bible. The loss seemed small, for I still loved the God of the narrative. I was still entranced by the words of Scripture. Indeed, year by year, a poetic holiness stuck to my innards, drawing me from law practice to ministry.

Originally published in *The Other Side* (Jan/Feb 1997), 33:9–11, 37. Reprinted with the permission of *The Other Side*.

As an adult, there were times when urban church experiences would stir historical memories. I would be transported, once again, to a time when the biblical text was a road anyone could walk. On such occasions, the roads of deliverance from Egypt couldn't be distinguished from marches in Selma. The Song of Miriam—and the songs of Mahalia—would lilt through shared space.

Such moments, however, became few and far between. During most of my adult life, the Bible was a period piece in which everyone was in costume but me.

I wasn't the only one, however, viewing the action from a distance. Much of the church of Jesus Christ seemed to join me in the race for upward mobility.

Just as I pursued the phantom of worldly success through career choices, churches everywhere developed business plans and increased their financial holdings. I dressed for success, and so did the church.

After a while we were both so far away that we could barely see Jesus and his motley band as they walked through chapter and verse. The Bible became a book to be discussed or debated—not a place to dwell.

I suppose some of my changed perspective can be attributed to the onset of adolescence. But history reminds me that the erosion of my spiritual imagination coincided with a national loss of innocence.

The openness of spirit that allowed me to freely inhabit kingdom spaces—and inspired my generation to creatively imagine a just and righteous nation—also left us vulnerable to dream killers. After the assassinations of John, Martin, Robert, and Malcolm, and after the horror at Kent State and the deaths of so many civil-rights workers, it seemed prudent to me—and perhaps to the church—to retreat to our own backyards.

I accepted this limit that life had imposed until a Tucson-based group called BorderLinks offered a unique opportunity. I and others would spend two weeks crossing biblical and cultural boundaries. The group would be made up of theological students from diverse areas of the United States, Catholic nuns, and Mexican lay women.

BorderLinks trips are experiential travel seminars, providing opportunities to meet and converse with people from other cultures. A typical day consists of shared meals, reflection, and the opportunity to dialogue with persons directly affected by major social-policy decisions. Such persons can include Central American refugees, Mexicans living along the border, church workers, and government officials.

The first half of most seminars is spent in Tucson, the second half in Mexico in a border community. Participants grapple with the history of cultural conflict between the United States and Mexico, as well as the economic and theological implications of the issues presented. The intent is to juxtapose the realities that we encounter on the border with the lives that we live and the God that we claim.

I was excited as I flew to Tucson, Arizona. Here was a new chance to push against the closed passageways of the biblical text. I would wedge myself into the biblical world of covenant and calamity, undaunted by the always narrow space between mystery and revelation. This time, I said, I would clearly mark the path to en-lightenment.

As it turned out, however, no bread crumbs were needed. Jesus and his women disciples in Agua Prieta, Mexico—working in their own way—opened a doorway of insight for me into the biblical text. And they opened it so wide that I can't imagine it ever being closed again.

What blew through that doorway? Dust. The precious dust of Agua Prieta. And the precious dust, says Scripture, of which we all have been made.

We didn't go to Agua Prieta immediately. We spent our first week on the U.S. side of the border, confronting the intersection of faith and social justice. A series of meetings and daily readings from the Gospel of Mark served as a catalyst for our discussions.

Each day, we were to stop three times to read a selected biblical passage. Our task: to reflect and listen. No interpretation or exegesis. No lurching to mental pews to hear the story from a distance.

At first, it seemed a strange assignment. But the repetition soon drew me into that "nowness" where I AM THAT I AM lives. Each reading peeled back layers of com-placency and cynicism, exposing the raw and radical message shaded in every word.

Through our readings and discussions, we became more self-aware. We saw how personal, political, and theological disappointments had eroded our faith in "now." Postmodernity had offered us immediacies. But they had shown themselves transi-tory—and dangerous. In such a context, a disembodied future can seem oddly safe and solid.

It was difficult to admit that most of us had substituted the idolatrous icon of I Will BE for the God of Ages' I AM.

We were still in Tucson, preparing for the border crossing. But we had already begun to cross the self-constructed personal and spiritual boundaries that separated us from God, the text, and one another.

After that first week of unmediated textual encounters and personal reflection, we no longer felt bewitched by the seductive potential of "not yet." On day trips into the desert, we reveled in the sands like wilderness children sustained by the thin, vapor-ous, already-gone "now."

Scripture had become a conduit that led beyond self-reflection toward the needs of others. We began to confront our culpability for the pain and poverty that grips many of our Mexican brothers and sisters. As an African American, I bristled at times at the naiveté of my companions. Tears shed for poverty at a cultural distance seem to dry up quickly when the same poverty is familiar and racially allocated.

Still, a community of sorts began to jell as we jostled against one another, unsettling cultural suppositions, tweaking prejudices, and hearing text against the tapestry of human indifference, economic villainy, and the enduring power of God's love.

Finally, it was time for us to cross the border. There, on "the other side," we would read with the women of Agua Prieta.

As we drove toward the hills of Sonora, Mexico, we contemplated our daily encounters with a living God. And as we drove, we heard the loving but painful question posed to Paul—and to us: "Why do you persecute me?" (Acts 9:4).

A week in Tucson had opened our ears to the plight of border communities, a plight we could hear but not see. So we groped our way to a town just a fence away, much as Paul must have groped his way to Ananias.

And we found that there is something about the dust and verve of Agua Prieta, Mexico, that removes scales from stunned eyes. The unpaved road leading into the town sends billows of dust heavenward like a cloud of glory.

We were led to private homes and shared family meals. We worshiped in a local jail and visited the squatter community of Colonia Las Brisas. Finally, we gathered in the open courtyard of the Catholic church. Here was a chance to see God's realm through others' eyes, a chance to listen to the women disciples in whose care we had been placed.

We sat in a circle. A brisk wind sent a harsh chill through the afternoon air. But in the determined light of a steady sun, the women of Agua Prieta led us in Bible study. They opened to us the text—the text of the Book and the text of their lives.

As they spoke with us about the value of ordinary things, I realized there is grace in the dust. Jesus kneels and writes our shortcomings on a temporary slate that can be blown clean. There is also protection in the dust, for it allows a woman with an issue of blood to evade the ecclesial powers that would have marginalized and thwarted her attempt to grasp the healing power in Jesus' hem.

For me, the lesson became clear, just as it is clear to the women of Agua Prieta. Participation in the biblical text is always available to those who live in the liberative and grounded space of love. God's power, sought on exalted altars, is offered instead in the dry earth that swirls around the feet of the faithful.

With tears and laughter, the women of Agua Prieta brought me home. They renewed a link I had lost for too long.

As I watched these women stand with Scripture amidst their daily realities, the pathway back to living text became joyfully apparent. For the women of Agua Prieta, the road of life runs through the middle of biblical promise and biblical lament. They cannot watch Scripture as a drama on a stage, for they see and understand that they too are part of the story.

In talking with those of us who had come from north of the border, they were honest about the harm that insatiable consumerism and divisive public policies inevitably inflict upon their lives. They were pensive when talking about human indifference to suffering.

But never did they accuse. They were faithful and prophetic witnesses precisely because they were unwilling to distance themselves from the text—or from us.

In so doing, they reminded me of a truth that I hope I shall never forget: that the mysteries of God are always ordinary when they are lived. It is only from the outside—from an uninvolved distance—that the mysteries become impenetrable.

The reclamation of "now" is more than a theological reconsideration. It is a reminder that the call to enact God's love cannot be postponed until we have more time or more resources.

We must use what we have. The important thing is to see ourselves as interconnected and responsive parts of the whole body of Christ. We must be willing to inhabit the centers of human suffering as faithfully as we serve the pastor's aid committee and as energetically as we participate in the gospel choir. Living in the "now" of Scripture means embracing the addicted and the disheveled as fully as we embrace our families. For text comes to life in the dust and grit of agape love.

When we left Agua Prieta, a cloud of dust flowed behind us in protective swirls, blocking the town from all backward glances. Like others in our group, I rejoiced, for I had reoccupied a promised space. The scales had fallen from my eyes. My ears were open. And I was ready to beckon others to enter.

Today, in one-on-one ministry encounters, the lessons learned in Agua Prieta seem easy to share. More challenging are my efforts to lovingly guide the church itself from an infatuation with worldly acquisitions.

Still, I press on. For on the border between wealth and poverty, on the border between "then" and "now," it became clearer for me than it ever had been before. The story is my story. And our story.

I'm reading the Bible these days with power and strength. I'm reading with dust swirling through my nostrils.

The path may feel uncertain. But I no longer walk alone. For the dust that swirls around me is the dust raised by the Holy One who walks beside me. And I pray that that dust—that precious dust—will ever keep me from looking back.

Todd Salzman

19 Catholics and Colonialism: The Church's Failure in Rwanda

On April 6, 1994, two ground-to-air missiles struck the jet carrying Presidents Juvenal Habyarimana of Rwanda and Cyprien Ntaryamira of Burundi. All on board were killed. Within hours, a killing rampage erupted in Rwanda that, over the next three months, would leave between half a million and a million dead. It is by no means insignificant that some of the first victims were Catholic priests, lay workers, and young retreatants at the *Centre Christus* in Kigali, Rwanda, and that attacks on the church continued throughout the massacres. Startlingly, a majority of the killings in the genocide even took place *within* church buildings: Hutu militia turned these traditional places of refuge into mass Tutsi graves; the buildings were also frequently desecrated. As a result, analyses initially focused on a persecuted church. But since approximately 90 percent of the Rwandan population is Christian—Tutsi and Hutu alike—the focus has turned to the question of a church of persecutors.

Clearly, many Christians participated in the massacres. There were also, however, many priests, nuns, and lay people who risked their lives or died protecting those in danger. The church, therefore, was one of both saints and sinners. But did it sin more than it was sinned against? It is my contention that, in Rwanda, ethnicity—and not Christianity—was the principal factor driving the killings. But the church was guilty of complicity whenever it sharpened ethnic division through educational bias or political preference for a clearly racist regime, or remained silent before clear discrimination and violations of social justice. Perhaps what the Rwandan genocide calls most into question concerning the role of the church is its method of evangelization and the ethnic divisions it hardened and perpetuated. This complicity made it a target for disdain and retribution. The evolution of ethnicity and the distinction between Hutu and Tutsi is a central factor of Rwandan history and was the predominant impetus for the genocide. These divisions, however, were not entrenched

Originally published in *Commonweal* (May 23, 1997), 124:17–19. Copyright © Commonweal Foundation 1997.

in precolonial Rwandan society. The earliest observers recognized two predominant groups, the cattle-owning Tutsi and the farming Hutu. Although these two groups shared the same language and culture, the Tutsi were considered the elite in Rwandan society, as cattle were a sign of wealth. The minority Tutsi, who arrived in present-day Rwanda around the thirteenth century, gradually established monarchical control over the majority Hutu. But to preserve the peace, certain Hutu were allowed to function within the monarchy. Strict differentiation along ethnic lines developed only after the arrival of German and Belgian colonialists in the late nineteenth and early twentieth centuries.

The colonialists justified and consolidated the rule of the Tutsi elite; they did not create the distinction between Hutu and Tutsi, but aggravated it. Following the defeat of Germany in World War I, the League of Nations gave Rwanda to Belgium as a "gift" to administer. Belgium decided upon a policy of indirect rule and favored the Tutsi—taller, thinner, and lighter in color—over the Hutu. The Belgians centralized power in a single chief and gave the Tutsi control of the judicial system. As a result, the majority Hutu were excluded from participation in Rwandan politics. The ideology supporting this ethnic differentiation was that certain races were born to rule whereas others were born to be ruled. Known as the "Hamitic theory," it was based on a tradition of Old Testament exegesis identifying the descendants of Ham—Noah's son cursed for his sinfulness—as dark-skinned Africans. The "Hamitic theory" was originally used to justify slavery and racism against all blacks, but revised to justify favoritism by the colonial powers—and the church—of the lighter-skinned Tutsi. They were cast as divinely instituted rulers.

The first missionaries of Africa, the White Fathers, had arrived to a lukewarm welcome in Nyanza, Rwanda, in 1900. The Tutsi chiefs and policy makers were agreed that the missionaries should be limited to interaction with the Hutu; in fact, not until the mid-1920s did a single member of the ruling Tutsi class convert, and the early converts to Christianity were predominantly Hutu peasants. But this process of evangelization went against the White Fathers' mandate to evangelize from the top down—to convert the purportedly superior Tutsi first. For the Catholic missionaries, this topdown approach was the typical method of evangelization; that it did not work in Rwanda was a frustration and a challenge.

Initially, the Tutsi perceived the missionaries as a threat to their established power. In 1907, however, this perception began to shift with the arrival in Rwanda of White Father Leon Classe, a staunch advocate of the hierarchical method of evangelization. Classe believed that the success of the Rwandan mission depended upon the conversion of the Tutsi; though he did not oppose Hutu advancement *per se,* in his stance for a Tutsi-led church he applied the "Hamitic theory" to theology. When tensions arose within the mission itself over its responsibilities, Classe's argument was decisive: "You must choose the [Tutsi] . . . because the government will probably refuse [Hutu] teachers. . . . In the government the positions in every branch of the administration, even the unimportant ones, will be reserved henceforth for young [Tutsi]." Classe's statement foreshadows the marriage between church and state that was destined to aggravate growing ethnic divisions in Rwanda. The means of bringing about this marriage was, principally, education.

Prior to Classe's arrival, the White Fathers had resigned themselves to establishing an indigenous Hutu church—a goal which required educated clergy. But though there were Hutu ordinations, the vast majority of candidates abandoned the seminaries. With their education, however, many Hutu were able to attain positions as teachers and administrators within the colonial system, thus upsetting the social hierarchy and legitimating Tutsi suspicion of the missions. This might have been the legacy—or the end—of Christianity in Rwanda; but the conversion and enthronement of Tutsi King Mutara Rudahigwa as Mutara III in 1931 quelled social instability and set church and state on another course.

Rudahigwa's conversion sparked *la tornade,* the rush of Tutsi converts to Christianity. With his conversion, conditions turned favorable for evangelization through the chiefs to the masses. Rwanda's social structure was conducive to this method: Once the leaders converted, there was social pressure for the masses to convert as well. As the sociologist Ian Linden has noted, "[I]n a remarkable way, Catholicism became 'traditional' the moment the Tutsi were baptized in large numbers." And not only did it become traditional, but it also became the state religion. In a short period of time the Hutu-Catholic church of the poor became the Tutsi-Catholic church of the ruling elite.

As a consequence of this state of affairs, many of the converts were ill-prepared and drawn into the church for questionable motives such as social and economic benefits. The Catholic church took control of education in the 1930s and exercised a clear bias for the Tutsi, who thereby acquired a monopoly on positions of authority and control, not only in industry but in the political bureaucracy as well. The sociologist Catherine Newbury has affirmed that this educational policy resulted in "clear discrimination against Hutu in most of Rwanda's Catholic mission schools." The alliance between church and state "introduced a more marked stratification between ethnic groups than had existed in the past. And as stratification was intensified, ethnic distinctions were sharpened." The mission schools' bias in favor of the Tutsi against the Hutu—sometimes even minimal height levels were enforced—was a major factor in hardening ethnic divisions and spurring resentment.

The Tutsi church-state alliance started to come apart after World War II, when colonial political and religious support for the Tutsi was gradually transferred to the Hutu. Several factors account for this shift. First, Belgium's exploitation of Rwanda during the war generated anticolonialist sentiment, and the empowered Tutsi began to rail at their colonial yoke. Because of the alliance between church and state, the church was also implicated in this discontent. Second, the champion of a Tutsi-dominated church, Father Classe, died in 1945. (According to the historian Gerard Prunier, Classe was "almost a national monument" for his influence on Rwandan politics.) He was replaced by the White Father Laurent Deprimoz, who began to address the divisive nature of ethnicity within the Rwandan church. Perhaps inevitably, however, Deprimoz's efforts backfired and only made these divisions more strident.

Third, the number of indigenous clergy, the majority of whom were Tutsi, came to equal the number of European clergy, and a struggle broke out for control of the church. The imbalance of power between the White Fathers and indigenous clergy caused no little resentment among the latter. This struggle was intensified by new Belgian missionaries who, Flemish rather than Walloon and from humbler social classes, did not sympathize with the aristocratic Tutsi but encouraged the downtrodden Hutu.

The final vestiges of colonial control over Rwanda were shattered with the death of King Rudahigwa in 1959 and the investiture of his successor, Jean-Baptiste Ndahindurwa, who took the name Kigeri V. This transition of power precipitated a civil war; Tutsi and Hutu formed factions poised against one another. Pushed by Tutsi clergy, Bishop Aloys Bigirumwami of the Nyundo vicarate became the symbolic figurehead of the Tutsi faction, the *Union Nationale Rwandaise,* and Bishop Andre Perraudin of Kabgayi was perceived as the champion of the oppressed Hutu for his insistence on the church's social teaching. Though they had issued a joint letter calling for peace, the bishops—and church—were swept into the emerging violence.

This powder keg exploded in November 1959, after the brutal attack of a Hutu activist. A peasant revolt (*Jacquerie*) broke out leaving hundreds dead and thousands displaced. Thereafter, through political guile and propaganda, the Hutu nationalist movement gained support and momentum, culminating in a call for independence and the popular election of Gregoire Kayibanda as *de facto* president of a new republic on January 28, 1961. Belgium formally recognized Rwanda's independence on July 1, 1962, but independence brought only deeper wounds. Following it, the Hutu took over governmental positions from the Tutsi, and the oppressed rapidly became oppressors. The Hutu turned the "Hamitic theory" against the Tutsi, who were recast as "Hamitic invaders" and colonialists. Many Tutsi fled north into Uganda from where they staged raids on the Hutu, who retaliated in turn. From December 1963 to January 1964, the new Hutu government killed between 10,000 and 12,000 Tutsi. Extended over thirty years, this fighting and repression constituted a long fuse to the 1994 explosion.

On November 21, 1991, the Catholic bishops of Rwanda issued a letter to priests and religious on the "Pastoral Role in Rebuilding Rwanda." A central theme of this letter was the need to overcome ethnic divisions. Thaddee Nsengiyumva, bishop of Kabgayi and president of the Rwandan Episcopal Conference, acknowledged the church's complicity in perpetuating these divisions by declaring, in a public letter dated December 1, 1991, that "the church is sick." Too little, too late? Certainly too little to prevent the genocide of 1994, when President Habyarimana's murder gave Hutu extremists within his regime free reign to execute their "final solution."

Proclaim liberty throughout the land

(Leviticus 25:10)

The book of Leviticus in the Hebrew Bible contains the words that are written on the Liberty Bell: "Proclaim liberty throughout the land and to all the inhabitants thereof." This idea is part of the support that the religious left has for those individuals and groups who have been denied their right to speak through imprisonment and unjust treatment.

George Tinker writes about the liberation of Native people from their oppression in the United States. He critiques the Western bias of liberation theology, and tells about the ways in which Native theologies are the basis upon which Native Americans speak about and understand their struggle for land and liberation from both the domination of Western civilization and its ideology.

Helen Prejean and Mumia Abu-Jamal look at how capital punishment limits rights, and focus on the variety of biblical teachings that do not support this kind of punishment. Abu-Jamal also stresses the ways in which sentencing is related to race in this country.

Valentín-Castañón discusses the history of Puerto Rico and its relationship to the rest of the United States. He examines the situation of Puerto Rican political prisoners, and also looks at New Testament roots for fighting for the liberation of those imprisoned unjustly.

David Fredrickson underscores the importance of persuasive, public argument as a Christian concept, and provides the arguments to suggest that Paul was a leading exponent of free speech. Fredrickson argues that political speech is fundamental both to our social context in the United States, and to the Christian way of life. For a society to be free, all viewpoints must be given voice.

These essays focus on some of the issues that receive less attention in the media, and point to the need to liberate those who are held captive so that they may have the opportunity to speak for themselves.

George Tinker

20 The Full Circle of Liberation: An American Indian Theology of Place

This is a challenge to hear the voices of indigenous peoples. We make up a Fourth World, if you will, oppressed both by the powerful nations and by the so-called developing nations. As Fourth World peoples we share with our Third World relatives the hunger, poverty, and repression that have been the continuing common experience of those overpowered by the expansionism of European adventurers and their missionaries 500 years ago.

What distinguishes Fourth World indigenous peoples from Third World peoples, however, are deeper, more hidden, but no less deadly effects of colonialism that impact our distinct cultures in dramatically different ways. These effects are especially felt in the indigenous spiritual experience, and our struggle for liberation is within the context of this distinctive spirituality. Our liberation struggle has been overlooked, until recently, in Third World liberation theology models of social change, which often remained inappropriate and ineffective in the struggle of indigenous people for self-determination. In fact, most liberation theologies' themes were derived from the very modes of discourse of the Western academy against which indigenous peoples have struggled for centuries. These modes—whether theological, legal, political, economic, or even the so-called social sciences—have shaped colonial, neo-colonial, and now Marxist regimes that, in the name of development, modernization, or even solidarity, have inflicted spiritual genocide on Fourth World peoples.

Gustavo Gutierrez, the foremost thinker on liberation theology, argues four important points: (1) liberation theology should focus on the "non-person" rather than on the non-believer; (2) liberation theology is a historical project that sees god as revealed in history; (3) liberation theology makes a revolutionary socialist choice on behalf of the poor, and (4) liberation theology emerges out of the praxis of the people.

Originally published in *Sojourners* (October 1992), 21 : 12–17. Reprinted with Permission from *Sojourners*, 2401 15th Street NW, Washington, DC 20009; (202) 328-8842 /(800) 714-7474.

The latter emphasis on praxis is perhaps the most enduring and pervasive gift of liberation theology.

However, a Native American theology finds the emphasis on the historical unsuitable and begins with a much different understanding of Gutierrez' category of the non-person. Moreover, Native American culture and spirituality implies different political solutions from those currently imposed by any socialist paradigm. In the context of these differences, my hope is for constructive dialogue leading to a mutual understanding and solidarity between Third and Fourth World peoples and an advance of genuine and wholistic liberation.

Resistance to Class Categories

In an early essay in the progressive theology journal *Concilium*, Gutierrez described the meaning of the "non-person" in language that strongly distinguished the concern of liberation theology from the rest of modern theology:

> Much contemporary theology seems to start from the challenge of the non-believer. He [or she] questions our religious world and faces it with a demand for profound purification and renewal. . . . This challenge in a continent like Latin America does not come primarily from the man [or woman] who does not believe, but from the man who is not a man, who is not recognized as such by the existing social order: He is in the ranks of the poor, the exploited; he is the man who is systematically and legally despoiled of his being as a man, who scarcely knows that he is a man. His challenge is not aimed first at our religious world, but at our economic, social, political and cultural world; therefore it is an appeal for the revolutionary transformation of the very bases of a dehumanizing society. . . . What is implied in telling this man who is not a man that he is a son of God?

This powerful statement names the alienation of marginalized poor and oppressed peoples and the impetus for a liberation theology response to people who suffer under unjust systems. However, it falls short in naming the particularities of indigenous peoples' suffering of non-personhood. The very affirmation of Third World "non-persons" tends to continue what has been, in praxis, a disaffirmation of indigenous people for now 500 years in the Americas.

While he avoids the language of explicit political programs, Gutierrez, like other Latin American theologians, explicitly and implicitly identifies the preferential option for the poor with socialist and even implied Marxist solutions that analyze the poor in terms of social class structure. This overlooks the crucial point that indigenous peoples experience their very personhood in terms of their relationship to the land. These theologians' analyses are powerful and effective to a point, but by reducing the non-person to a class of people that share certain universal attributes, some more telling attributes are disregarded.

Native American peoples resist categorization in terms of class structure. Instead, we insist on being recognized as "peoples," even nations, with a claim to national sovereignty based on ancient title to our land. Classification, whether as "working class" or "the poor," continues the erosion of our cultural integrity and national agenda. As much as capitalist economic structures—including the church (missionaries) and the academy (anthropologists)—have reduced Native American peoples to non-personhood, so too the Marxist agenda fails finally to recognize our distinct personhood.

Reducing our nationness to classness imposes upon us a particular culture of poverty and especially a culture of labor. It begs the question as to whether indigenous peoples desire production in the modern economic sense in the first place. To put the means of production into the hands of the poor eventually makes the poor exploiters of indigenous peoples and their natural resources. Finally, it seriously risks violating the very spiritual values that hold an indigenous cultural group together as a people.

This is not to suggest simply discarding Marxist or other tools of analysis. Rather, this is a constructive critique of these tools and the implicit hegemony they exercise in much of our midst in the Third World.

The failure to recognize the distinct personhood of Native American peoples has a history as long as the history of European colonialism and missionary outreach in the Americas. In particular, it should be noted that the church's failure to recognize the personhood of Native Americans was the most devastating. Less direct than the military (yet always accompanied by it), missionaries consistently confused the gospel of Jesus Christ with the gospel of European cultural values and social structures. They saw our cultures and our social structures as inadequate and needing to be replaced with what they called a "Christian civilization."

Many liberation theology and socialist movements in general promise no better than the continued cultural genocide of indigenous peoples. From an American Indian perspective, the problem with modern liberation theology, as with Marxist political movements, is that class analysis gets in the way of recognizing cultural discreetness and even personhood. Small but culturally unique communities stand to be swallowed up by the vision of a classless society, of an international workers' movement, or of a burgeoning majority of Third World urban poor. This too is cultural genocide and signifies that indigenous peoples are yet non-persons, even in the light of the gospel of liberation.

God in Place and Time

In the Power of the Poor in History, Gutierrez argues that God reveals God's self in history. I assert that this is not only *not* a self-evident truth, but that Native American theology that is true to our culture must begin with a confession that is both dramatically different from and exclusive of Gutierrez' starting point. Essentially, a Native American theology must argue out of spiritual experience and praxis that God reveals God's self in creation, in space or place and not in time.

The Western sense of history as a linear temporal process means that those who heard the gospel first have and always maintain a critical advantage over those of us who hear it later and have to rely on those who heard it first to give us a full interpretation. This has been our consistent experience with the gospel as it has been preached to us by the missionaries of all the denominations, just as it has been our experience with the political visions proclaimed to us by the revolutionaries.

The problem, from 16th-century historian Las Casas to Marx, is the assumption of a hegemonic trajectory through history that fails to recognize cultural distinctions. With the best of intentions, solutions to oppressed peoples' suffering are proposed as exclusive programs that don't allow for diverse possibilities.

Whatever the conqueror's commitment to evangelization and conversion or to military subjugation and destruction, it was necessary to make the conquest decisive—at military, political, economic, social, legal, and religious levels. And just as the conquest had to be decisive, so too must modern revolutions be decisive. They allow no room for peoples who consider themselves distinct—economically, politically, socially, and culturally—to find their own revolution or liberation. A prime example was the situation of the Miskito Indians in Nicaragua during the Sandinista revolution. Summarily relocated from their coastal territories, where they had self-sustaining local economies, to high-altitude communal coffee plantations, Miskito peoples were forced to labor as culturally amorphous workers with no regard to the abject cultural dislocation they had suffered. The Miskito Indians had been a people; the removal from their land reduced them to a class whose cultural identity could not be a factor.

Whether in capitalist or socialist guise, then, history and temporality reign supreme in the West. On the other hand, Native American spirituality and values, social and political structures, and even ethics are rooted not in some temporal notion of history but in spatiality. This is perhaps the most dramatic (and largely unnoticed) cultural difference between Native American thought and the Western intellectual tradition.

The question is not whether time or space is missing in one culture or the other, but which is dominant. Of course Native Americans have a temporal awareness, but it is subordinate to our sense of place. Likewise, the Western tradition has a spatial awareness, but it lacks the priority of the temporal. Hence, progress, history, development, evolution, and process become key notions that invade all academic discourse in the West, from science and economics to philosophy and theology. History becomes the quintessential Western intellectual device.

If Marxist thinking and the notion of a historical dialectic were finally proven correct, then American Indian people and all indigenous peoples would be doomed. Our cultures and value systems, our spirituality, and even our social structures, would give way to an emergent socialist structure that would impose a notion of the good on all people regardless of ethnicity or culture.

Drawn Together in Creation

One could argue with Native American peoples that we must learn to compromise with the "real world," that to pursue our own cultural affectations is to swim upstream against the current of the modern socioeconomic world system. When rightists or capitalists assert this, I know they are arguing the self-interest of prerogatives of those who own the system. When Third or Forth World peoples make the argument, I am curious how readily some of us concede to Western categories of discourse. How easily we internalize the assumption that Western, Euro-American philosophical, theological, economic, social, spiritual, and political systems are necessarily definitive of any and all conceivable "real" worlds.

Native Americans think that our perception of the world is just as adequate, perhaps more satisfying, and certainly more egalitarian than the West's. In order to sense the power of our culturally integrated structures of cognition, a beginning understanding of Native American spirituality is necessary, for all of existence is spiritual for us. That is our universal starting point, even though we represent a multitude of related cultures, with a great variety of tribal ceremonial structures expressing that spirituality.

That the primary metaphor of existence for Native Americans is spatial does much to explain the fact that American Indian spirituality and American Indian existence itself are deeply rooted in the land, and why our conquest and removal from our lands was so culturally and genocidally destructive to our tribes. There is, however, a more subtle level to this sense of spatiality and land rootedness. It shows up in nearly all aspects of our existence, in our ceremonial structures, our symbols, our architecture, and in the symbolic parameters of a tribe's universe.

The fundamental symbol of Plains Indians existence is the circle, a symbol signifying the family, the clan, the tribe, and eventually all of creation. Because it has no beginning and no end, all in the circle are of equal value.

In its form as a medicine wheel with two lines forming a cross inscribed vertically and horizontally across its whole, the circle can symbolize the four directions of the Earth, and more important, the four manifestations of Wakonta (the Sacred Mystery, Creator, God) that come to us from these directions. Native American egalitarian tendencies are worked out in this spatial symbol in ways that go far beyond the classless egalitarianism of socialism.

In one layer of meaning, these four directions hold together in the same equal balance the four nations of Two leggeds, Four leggeds, Wingeds, and Living-moving Things—encompassing all that is created, the trees and rocks, mountains and rivers, as well as animals. Human beings lost their status of primacy and "dominion." In other words, American Indians are driven implicitly and explicitly by their culture and spirituality to recognize the personhood of all "things" in creation. When the Lakota peoples of North America pray *Mitakuye ouyasin*, "For all my relatives," they understand relatives to include not just tribal members, but all of creation.

This matrix of cultural response to the world that we might call spirituality continues to have life today in North America among our various Indian Tribes, even for those who remain in the church and continue to call themselves Christian. More and more frequently today, Indian Christians are holding on to the old traditions as their way of life and claiming the freedom of the gospel to honor and practice them as integral to their inculturated expression of Christianity.

Today there can be no genuine American Indian theology that does not take our indigenous traditions seriously. This means, of course, that our reading of the gospel and our understanding of faithfulness will represent a radical disjuncture from the theologies and histories of the Western churches of Europe and America—as we pay attention to our stories and memories instead of to theirs.

This inculturation of an indigenous theology is symbolic of American Indian resistance and struggle today. More than symbolic, it gives life to the people. However, we also see the possibility that our interpretations can prove renewing, redeeming, and salvific for Western theology and ecclesiology.

An American Indian theology coupled with an American Indian reading of the gospel might provide the theological imagination to generate a more immediate and attainable vision of a just and peaceful world. Respect for creation must necessarily result in justice, just as genuine justice necessarily is the achievement of peace.

We understand repentance as a call to be liberated from our perceived need to be God and instead to assume our rightful place in the world as humble human beings in the circle of creation with all the other created. While Euro-cultural scholars have offered consistently temporal interpretations of the gospel concept *basileia* ("kingdom") of God, an American Indian interpretation builds on a spatial understanding rooted in creation. If *basileia* has to do with God's hegemony, where else is God actually to reign if not in the entirety of the place that God has created?

While God revealing God's self in history holds out some promise for achieving justice and peace in some eventual future moment, the historical/temporal impetus must necessarily delay any full realization of the *basileia* of God. Instead, American Indian spirituality calls us to imagine ourselves here and now as mere participants in the whole of creation, with respect for and reciprocity with all of creation, and not somehow apart from it and free to use it up at will. The latter is a mistake that was and is epidemic in both the First and Second Worlds and has been recklessly imposed on the rest of us in the name of development.

This understanding of *basileia* and repentance mandates new social and political structures, genuinely different from those created by either of the dominant Euro-cultural structures of capitalism or socialism. The competition generated by Western individualism, temporality, and paradigms of history, progress, and development must give way to the communal notion of inter-relatedness and reciprocity.

I am not espousing a value-neutral creation theology in the style of Matthew Fox or a New Age spirituality of feel-good individualism. Rather, ultimately this is an expression of a "theology of community" that must generate a consistent interest in justice and peace.

If I image myself as a vital part of a community, indeed as a part of many communities, it becomes more difficult for me to act in ways that are destructive of these communities. The desire or perceived necessity for exerting social, political, economic, or spiritual control over each other gives way to mutual respect, not just for individuals, but for our culturally distinct communities.

If we believe we are all relatives in this world, then we must live together differently than we have. Justice and peace, in this context, emerge almost naturally out of a self-imaging as part of the whole, as part of an ever-expanding community that begins with family and tribe, but is finally inclusive of all human beings and all of creation. Such is the spirit of hope that marks the American Indian struggle of resistance in the midst of a world of pain.

Helen Prejean

---

21 The Upward Mobility of the Gospel

When people ask me how I got involved with people on death row, I smile and say, "The upward mobility of the gospel." It's true. It's one thing to read about the "least" of these in our gold-edged Bibles. It's quite another to associate with the real, live human beings considered by society as "disposable human waste."

It did not take long for me to discover, when I lived and worked in an almost all-black public housing project in New Orleans, Louisiana, that the road was short from poverty to prison to death row. I moved into the housing project on June 1, 1981, because my religious community had made a commitment to "stand in solidarity with the poor of the world and to work for justice," and I was seeking to personalize that commitment. I didn't realize that the road I was taking would lead me straight into Louisiana's execution chamber where I would be a witness to death by electrocution of three human beings.

Nor did I dream when I got involved in the lives of poor people and death row inmates that I would get involved with murder victims' families as well. Involvement with the death penalty thrust me up against victims' families. I say against, not because it was my choice but because so many people feel that if you are against executions, you must be against victims.

In New Orleans there is a group called "Survive" whose sole purpose is to minister to murder victims' families. It was the death penalty abolitionists of Louisiana who initiated the group.

Following Jesus stretches us. When I see Jesus' arms outstretched on the cross, I see him—and us—embracing victims and perpetrators alike. Surely the merciful, compassionate Jesus about whom we sing so beautifully on Sundays would embrace both the sorrowing, shattered victims and the "scum" condemned to death by the state.

Embrace the perpetrators, do not condone their violent deeds. Condone never. Do

Originally published in *Christian Social Action* (November, 1990), 3:36–37. Reprinted with permission from *Christian Social Action* magazine, November 1990; copyright 1990 by the General Board of Church and Society of the United Methodist Church.

not condone their deeds, but uphold their innate dignity as human beings. Otherwise, we place ourselves in the untenable positions of deciding who is worthy of living and who can be "eliminated."

We shrink from the word. We know that's what Hitler and the Nazis did. We want to justify that the death penalty is categorically "different" from what the Nazis did to the Jews, the gypsies and gay persons.

Nazi victims were innocent, we say, murderers aren't. But looking at roots of things gives us pause. The Nazis did not flower without soil to grow in. Their soil was the Weimar Republic, the German Democratic Republic, one of the most democratic in Western Europe. The Weimar doctors, not the Nazi doctors, wrote the book called *The Defense of Destruction of Life Without Value.*

In the execution chamber, I have watched three human beings put to death. I was with them in the last months, days, hours of their lives. They were very alive. They were very dead. I carry the flaming memories of those experiences like stigmata.

I watched them as they were strapped—arms, legs, trunk—into a wooden chair, their jaws clamped shut by a tight chin strap, electrodes placed on their skull, their legs. Each of them I had known as a human being. Each had a heart, a mind, a personality, a past, a family, children of their own.

Which of us would like the task of representing the state and bearing the message to the child of the executed: "We killed your father this morning?" Who would like to look into that child's eyes and explain why "it was expedient that one man die for the good of all?" That just happened in Louisiana in May. Dalton Prejean was executed. Someone bore the news to his nine-year-old son. Looking into a child's eyes sometimes reveals our own hearts to us.

Why do so many people, even those who claim to believe in Jesus Christ, say they support the death penalty? To put it as simply as I can, I think we do so for two main reasons:

- We're scared to death. We're scared of crime, scared of violence. We buy into state killing as a way of trying to protect ourselves.
- The death penalty is removed from us. We don't watch anyone die. We only read about executions in a tiny little blip on page 10 of the newspaper. Executing criminals isn't big media news anymore. It's getting old. We're "used" to it now. It's easy to kill a statistic. It's easy to kill someone who's not "human like us," an animal, a monster.

If citizens witnessed executions, we would eliminate the death penalty.

As people are brought close to the death penalty through education, support for it drops radically. And recent, nuanced polls (not simply the question: Are you for or against the death penalty?) show that when people are given a real alternative to death—life imprisonment without parole or even a minimum of 25 years imprisonment for first degree murder—support for the death penalty falls below 50 percent.

There is a 25-minute videotape titled "The Religious Community Confronts the Death Penalty" that gives surprising information about the death penalty. There are at least seven facts about the way the death penalty is applied in this country that are not common knowledge.

But the videotape does more than just give facts. It brings you face to face with a real person who was executed after the reinstatement of the death penalty in 1976. The videotape was smuggled out of the prison. Watch the videotape. Apply the rhetoric you hear about the death penalty. Consider again the deepest values of Jesus Christ. Search your own heart. Then answer this most fundamental moral question: Are you for life, or are you for death?

22 Between Brick and Steel

Woe to the city that is filthy and polluted, to the oppressing city!
—Zephaniah 3:1

Some events in the life of a city define it for generations to come, indelibly marking it within consciousness and memory. The riots in Los Angeles. Oakland's earthquake. The Kennedy assassination in Dallas. The Milwaukee mass murders.

Before being confined between brick and steel on Pennsylvania's death row, I lived in Philadelphia, a city infamous for the events of May 13, 1985. On that day, my city destroyed one of its own neighborhoods, bombing the stretch of Osage Avenue where the homes and headquarters of the largely African American naturalist group MOVE were located. This unleashed an urban holocaust which incinerated eleven human beings. "The City of Brotherly Love" demonstrated that day that killing is perfectly acceptable if those killed are African American and perceived as radical.

Here on Pennsylvania's death row, where executions are one at a time rather than wholesale, the same racial politics come into play. While the state's African American population barely tops 9 percent, 62 percent of those on death row here are of African descent. National statistics are equally grim. African Americans make up only 12.1 percent of the U.S. population, but nearly 40 percent of those on death row are black.

Most Blacks on Pennsylvania's death row are from Philadelphia. Over 38 percent of those on death row from Philadelphia County were sentenced by Senior Judge Albert F. Sabo. Only two of the twenty-four people Sabo had sentenced to death as of April 1990 were White. While the city was recently forced to terminate Sabo's paid position due to budget restrictions, he has elected to continue his "public service" without pay.

Due to a variety of factors, Blacks are 23 percent more likely to be sentenced to death in Philadelphia than elsewhere in the United States. Clearly the city which

Originally printed in *The Other Side* (September/October 1992), 28:32–34. Reprinted with the permission of *The Other Side*.

bills itself as "the cradle of liberty" sings a different tune for its African American population.

> From heaven did the Lord behold the earth, to hear the groaning of the prisoner; to loose those that are appointed to death. (Psalm 102:19–20)

A voice rises from a cell near mine: "Alllaaaaah Hu Akbar, Ullaaaaahhh, Hu Akbir; Alllaaaaah Hu Akbar, Ullaaaaahhh, Hu Akbir; Laaa-Illa Ha-Illl-Ullahhh!" (Allah is the greatest! Allah is the greatest! There is no God but Allah!)

The voice is thick, throaty, smoky, melodious, and identifiably African. It bounces, soars aloft, drops, and vibrates from brick to steel, from wall to bar. It is a *cri de coeur,* an Islamic call to prayer, a plea to God for deliverance for the grandsons of slaves who remain strangers in a strange land.

This *is* a strange land. The largest group of Pennsylvania's inmates are housed in the middle of the state's rural and rustic heartland. The area surrounding the prison is 98 percent White and, except for the prison and the jobs it offers, economically depressed.

The contrast between prisoner and guard here could not be more striking. One is urban, hip-hop, rap and Africanic; the other is rural, country, tobacco-chewing, and Germanic. One is a captive; the other, captor. It's a recipe for conflict.

On the street, some of the imprisoned were hustlers, stick-up boys, rapists, and ruthless criminals. But here, all search for solace amidst loss, for divinity on the brink of the abyss. In this quintessential abode of alienation and hostility, they seek peace— and find it in disparate ways.

Some find release from this managed and man-made hell through religion, through faith in a force greater than themselves. Others seek escape through sports on television or in the illusory psycho-sex of pornography. Some escape through extreme introversion and self-imposed isolation; others find release in madness, cloaked under clouds of psychotropic drugs.

> Let the sighing of the prisoner come before thee; according to the greatness of thy power preserve Thou those that are appointed to die. (Psalm 79:11)

By state design, there is no "life" here on death row in Pennsylvania. People live only in this sense: their breath leaves and returns, and blood pumps through their bodies. But the elements which define life for many other prisoners—the touch of one's beloved, the cuddle of one's child, a hug of reassurance, a brief, yet enabling, kiss—are not to be found. Noncontact visits are the regulation, due to an executive order by former governor Richard Thornburgh. For twenty-two hours a day, men are held in a six-by-eight-foot single cell. Their only other option is to "recreate" for a short period in an "individual exercise unit," a nine-by-twelve-foot outdoor cage made of Cyclone fence. Visitors are met in a small room with a table where a floor-to-ceiling, steelwire-enforced, Plexiglass divider makes human touch an impossibility, even if one were not handcuffed.

This is "life" for about 145 people in Pennsylvania, and for more than twenty-six hundred people on death row across the United States.

The Spirit of the Lord God is upon me; because the Lord has anointed me to preach good tidings to the meek, God has sent me to bind up the broken-hearted, to proclaim liberty to the captives, and the opening of the prison to them that are bound. (Isaiah 61:1)

Jesus read this verse in the synagogue to explain his mission (Luke 4:18), but it has hardly been the guiding mission of U.S. Christianity. The United States, a largely Christian nation, leads the so-called civilized world in imprisoning its citizens and its stubborn adherence to the death penalty. The Bureau of Justice Statistics Report on Correctional Populations of October 1991 reports that more than four million persons, or 2.2 percent of the total adult U.S. population, is currently under correctional supervision. Thirty-seven percent (1,489,000) are African American. The proportion of the Black male population imprisoned in the United States is nearly four times that of the outlawed apartheid regime of South Africa. In spite of our "tough on crime" policies, we are the most violent nation on earth, showing that executions and incarcerations do more to continue the cycle of societal violence than to prevent it.

I remember the prosecutor at my trial asking me: "Do you remember saying, 'Political power grows out of the barrel of a gun?'" I replied, "It is America which has seized political power from the Indian race, not by God, not by Christianity, not by goodness, but by the barrel of the gun." While the truth of such an observation is evident, I wouldn't always recommend pointing it out. Particularly if you are an African American capital defendant charged with the premeditated murder of a White cop, standing before an all-White (and presumably mostly Christian) jury.

For the letter kills,
but the Spirit gives life. (2 Corinthians 3:6)

It's been said that "law is simply politics by other means." Such an assertion is certainly borne out by the ragged judicial history of the MOVE cases. To date, no politician, no police officer, no official of city, state, or federal government has ever been charged with criminal activity related to the events of May 13, 1985. Only MOVE member Ramona Africa, who watched her family slaughtered, incinerated, and dismembered—and was herself burned and scarred for life—was imprisoned. Incredibly, the city convicted her of conspiracy. Conspiracy to bomb her own house?

A similar pronounced discrimination is seen in death-penalty cases. Faced with a Black defendant in a capital case, state prosecutors play on the fears and prejudices of the mostly White jury, painting the defendant as the incarnation of evil itself.

A recent case featured this argument from the district attorney to the jury: "The Bible speaks of the Prince of Darkness, the personification of evil. All of our cultures, ancient and modern, primitive and civilized, have symbols for the presence of evil. . . . Adolph Hitler is the personification of evil. Six million people were killed. . . . There is evil among us . . . and I suggest to you . . . that this defendant is such a person."

The justices in this case called it a "fair argument" and "legitimate."

As I live, saith the Lord God,
I have no pleasure in the death of

The wicked, but rather that they turn
From their ways and live. (Ezekiel 33:11)

A recent case in New Mexico illustrates the disparate sentencing in capital cases. A twenty-nine-year-old White ex-construction worker was tried for seven killings. He was convicted on four counts of first-degree murder, two counts of second-degree murder, and one count of manslaughter. The nature of the victims (a state trooper, a deputy sheriff, three women, and a baby among them) made a sentence of death almost a foregone conclusion.

The jury refused to return the death sentence, causing the defendant's lawyer to comment, "The jurors could see he was a good man who had a terrible time." One wonders if the jury would have found him worthy of life if he were African American. Would he have been called a good man—or a monster?

Race, of assailant and victim, continues to skew conviction, sentencing, and even length of time served. Case after case proves that Black defendants are convicted more often—and given harsher sentences. In a sense, all Blacks on death row are political prisoners, in that they suffer from a corrupted policy which makes race a major factor in capital cases.

Those who say they love God but hate
their brothers and sisters are liars. (1 John 4:20)

Images from the MOVE bombing of May 13, 1985, still haunt me: the wicked lick of flames leaping into the pre-Mother's Day sky; the bound and burned Ramona Africa being taken captive; the sneering taunts of the police officers. I will never forget watching the grim visage of a Black mayor proclaiming, "I would do the same thing again!" even as the charred remains of the bodies were being sifted from the smoking debris.

But the triumph of politics over the realm of the Spirit on that day was perhaps most clearly exemplified by Philadelphia's Black clergy, who stood tall beside the city's first African American mayor, symbolically sprinkling holy water over the carnage and destruction. For too long, Christians have sprinkled this same holy water on the abominable horror of the death penalty.

The death penalty must be abolished. For Whites, the death penalty is a lottery of chance which has little to do with the crime committed. For Blacks, the lottery is rigged, infused with a racism that subverts justice. That the death penalty is entirely unchristian is beyond debate. Whether the judicial system—in Philadelphia, Pennsylvania, or the entire United States—is *capable* of radical transformation is the beginning of one.

Eliezer Valentín-Castañón

23 Release the Prisoners!

Since 1980 a number of Puerto Rican political prisoners have been incarcerated in the U.S. federal prison system. Their struggle is not new, but many persons still are not aware of their situation and the request for their freedom. As the resolution adopted by the 1996 General Conference states, "the call for the release of these prisoners enjoys wide support in the United States, Puerto Rico and internationally." That resolution also indicates that "we, as Christians have been called to identify with the prisoners and their needs."

An Historical Background

In 1898, as a result of the Spanish-American War the island and the people of Puerto Rico were given to the U.S. government as a war booty. This was part of the Treaty of Paris, a peace agreement signed on December 10, 1898. The treaty was the culmination of a long and well-thought-out process that had as its goal the acquisition of Puerto Rico as part of a U.S. defense and economic strategy.

General Nelson Miles, officer in command of the U.S. invasion troops, fulfilled part of the dream of Captain Alfred T. Mahan, U.S. naval geopolitical strategic adviser. Mahan's ideas found fertile soil in the Monroe Doctrine, or what we know as "Manifest Destiny," and were quickly embraced by yet another powerful figure, Theodore Roosevelt, who strongly sought to make the dream a reality.

Mahan's strategy was to acquire control over some "militarily strategic" areas of the Pacific, Central America, and the Caribbean: Panama, Cuba (Guantanamo), and Puerto Rico among others. These, he argued, would guarantee the U.S. safety from enemy countries, since " . . . it would be very difficult for a transatlantic state to

Originally published in *Christian Social Action* (December 1996), 9:12–16. Reprinted with permission from *Christian Social Action* magazine, December 1996; copyright 1996 by the General Board of Church and Society of the United Methodist Church.

maintain operations in the western Caribbean with a United States fleet based upon Puerto Rico and the adjacent islands."

However, military hegemony was not the only reason for invasion. Philip C. Hana, the last U.S. counsel in Puerto Rico, stated clearly, "The trade of Puerto Rico is of more value to the United States than is the trade of many of the South and Central American countries." In terms of exports, Puerto Rico was the tenth market for American goods, with a favorable trade balance of nearly $2.5 million. Mahan's strategy offered the U.S. economy the possibility of an ample market for a growing capitalist economy. What Puerto Rico had to offer to the United States politically, militarily, and economically was of too great value to let it pass. As President Roosevelt wrote, in March 1898, to his good friend Senator Henry Cabot Lodge: "Do not make peace until we get Puerto Rico. . . ."

Thus, the rationale given for the invasion clashes dramatically with General Miles' promise of liberty, a promise suggested in the first official proclamation presented once he was in control of the island: "We have not come to make war upon the people of a country that for centuries has been oppressed, but, on the contrary, to bring you protection, not only to yourselves but to your property, to promote your prosperity, and to bestow upon you the immunities and blessings of the liberal institutions of our government."

Hence, in order to accomplish the goal of total control of the island, Congress in 1900 approved the Foraker Act. It sought to tighten its control over Puerto Rico by controlling all aspects of the economy and by imposing all education in English. This strategy sought the ideological and cultural unification of Puerto Rico to the United States.

The governor and his cabinet were appointed by the President of the United States, as well as the secretary of education. Then, in 1917 U.S. citizenship was imposed by Congress via the Jones Act, thus enabling the drafting of Puerto Ricans to serve in the U.S. army.

After 50 years of direct colonial rule by the United States, Puerto Rico's colonial status was modified on July 7, 1952. The current political definition of the island began when the U.S. Congress adopted Public Law 447, setting up a "Free Associated State" commonly known as "The Commonwealth of Puerto Rico." In a "creative" way the United States opened the door for a new definition of the colonial experience.

Colonial Rule Solidified

When Congress approved the "Free Associated State," it also adopted the Constitution of Puerto Rico, which had to be framed as the Constitution of the United States. These actions only achieved the strengthening and solidification of the colonial control of the United States over Puerto Rico. However, these Congressional actions were then presented to the international community as the U.S. solution to the colonial status of the island.

Notwithstanding this U.S. interpretation, the control over *this "U.S. territory"* has been in the hands of neither the Puerto Rican government nor the Puerto Rican people, but, rather, in the hands of the U.S. Congress. To put it more bluntly, Puerto Rico has never ceased to be a colony of the United States.

In a recent case before the 11th Circuit Court of Appeals (U.S. vs. Sánchez, 992F2d 1143, June 4, 1994), the court concluded that Puerto Rico remains a *U.S. territory.* The court sustained that Congress has the power to revoke unilaterally or derogate the Constitution of Puerto Rico and the statutes that regulate the relationship between the United States and its territory.

More recently, the subcommittee on Indian and Insular Affairs of the House of Representatives rejected the inclusion of the current political status of Puerto Rico in a new referendum for considering that the current formula is "clearly colonial," the same formula Congress adopted in 1952. The above information suggests that the struggle of Puerto Ricans for self-determination and freedom is within the scope of the United Nations' resolutions on decolonization. The international organization has clearly established that colonialism is a crime, and it recognizes a colonized people's right to end colonialism. The United Nations also recognizes that these resolutions and laws apply to Puerto Rico. For many years the UN Decolonization Committee has approved resolutions recognizing the inalienable right of the people of Puerto Rico to independence and self-determination.

Injustice Suffered under Colonialism

The injustice suffered under Puerto Rico's colonial reality cannot be overlooked. During his tenure as President, George Bush admitted that Puerto Rico's people have never been consulted as equals on their political status. In pursuit of President Bush's idea, Congressman Don Young (R-AL) introduced the "United States–Puerto Rico Political Status Act" (H.R. 3024). The supporters of the bill affirmed that "for the first time since the Treaty of Paris entered into force" Puerto Ricans would freely express their wishes regarding their political status.

As with any people of one nation dominated by another, some Puerto Ricans have resisted the U.S. government's control of their nation's sovereignty. Their resistance, whether the mere advocacy for independence or the taking up of arms against the colonizer, has been censored and criminalized, punished throughout the years by harassment, surveillance, imprisonment, and even execution.

In Puerto Rico's history several executions have taken place. In 1935, the police killed four Nationalists in the town of Rio Piedras. In 1937, the governor of Puerto Rico, Blanton S. Winship ordered the police to massacre a group of Nationalists who were in a peaceful demonstration in the town of Ponce. The death count was 22. In 1978, in a very resounding case, Puerto Rico's police department was involved in the murders of two young "independentistas" (people seeking Puerto Rico's independence).

Charges of Seditious Conspiracy

In 1985, some 300 FBI agents, members of the U.S. Special Forces, and the U.S. National Guard in Puerto Rico, armed with automatic weapons, removed 16 Puerto Ricans from their homes and charged them with conspiracy to derogate the U.S. government and arms possessions. At that time, not even the governor of Puerto Rico was notified of the operation. From 1980 to 1985 about 30 Puerto Ricans were charged with seditious conspiracy to overthrow the U.S. government, possession of stolen vehicles and arms possession.

Of those 30 persons, 16 refused to participate in the U.S. court system because of their belief that the U.S. government, as the colonizer, is the enemy power. They requested a war court trial in accordance with UN General Assembly Resolution 3103. Their petition was denied, and some of these 30 have served their sentences, while others were released because no valid case could be brought against them.

Today we still have 14 Puerto Rican political prisoners in the U.S. prison system. It is important to point out that none of the 14 political prisoners was charged with causing any deaths, as has been claimed by the Institute for Religion and Democracy and other voices. These men and women received excessive and onerous sentences geared, first of all, towards punishing political activity more than the stated crimes. They are also being punished for refusing to participate in the U.S. judicial system, because they considered it inappropriate for the colonizing power they opposed to be the one to hear their plea for justice and freedom.

The sentences imposed on the Puerto Rican political prisoners are of a political nature, which becomes evident when considering the length of their imprisonment. The average length of time served in general in federal prisons, for all offenses between 1979 and 1980, was 3.6 years. The highest time served for crimes such as rape and kidnapping, for the same period of time, was 11.5 years. The average time served by federal prisoners until their first release (1985–1990) for all offenses ranged from 1.2 years in 1985 to 1.6 years in 1990. For kidnapping the highest time served before release was 8.6 years.

The Puerto Rican political prisoners have already served more than 13 years longer than the longest average time served by federal and state prisoners convicted of violent crimes, including homicide and kidnapping; longer than the time rapists and brutal killers are made to serve. The average sentence among this group is 71.6 years for the men, and 72.8 years for the women.

Fighting for Freedom and Independence

The actions of the 14 Puerto Rican political prisoners are comparable to those of American patriots, who by the standards of the British empire were considered criminals. Our patriots denounced the tyranny of British control over their colonies and committed acts that in those days, and even today, could be considered "terrorist acts." They fought for the principles of freedom and self-determination to gain their independence from British rule.

Similarly, the U.S. government recognized that Nelson Mandela's imprisonment by the South African *apartheid* government was unjust, even if legally correct. Mandela was jailed for 27 years on charges of attempting to overthrow the *apartheid* government through violent means. Many in the United States sought to pressure the South African government to free Mandela because his captivity was based on his political convictions. Today we are holding 14 prisoners like Mandela because of their efforts to gain independence for their country, Puerto Rico. Like the American patriots and Mandela, the Puerto Rican political prisoners are conscientious activists who have struggled for the principles of freedom and democracy and self-determination. They are not criminals.

Regardless of their political and ideological perspectives, the call for their release enjoys wide support in the United States, Puerto Rico, and the international community. The governor of Puerto Rico, the Honorable Pedro Roselló (of the pro-statehood party), has stated his belief that the prisoners have already served a reasonable amount of time. Former governor, the Honorable Rafael Hernández Colón (of the pro-status quo party), also supports their release. Among the House of Representatives members of Puerto Rico lineage who have called for their release are Luis Gutiérrez, José Serrano, and Nydia Velázquez.

Many civic and religious organizations have also joined in the effort, including: Puerto Rico Bar Association, National Conference of Black Lawyers, National Lawyers Guild, United Church of Christ, United Methodist Church, Baptist Peace Fellowship, Episcopal Church of Puerto Rico, Methodist Church of Puerto Rico, City Council of the City of New York, and many municipal governments throughout Puerto Rico. Support has also come from international organizations such as the Brehon Law Society, the Australian Parliamentarians, and a number of faculty members of the University of South Africa.

Biblical-Theological Undergirdings

Scripture teaches us to identify with prisoners and to work for the release of those unjustly held captive (Psalm 146:6–7, Isaiah 61:1). We see in Scripture how some of our greatest spiritual heroes spent time in jail for political reasons. Jesus was persecuted and sought by the authorities of his time because his beliefs and actions were seen as threatening to the dominant sectors of Jewish society and the colonist power of Rome (see Luke 4:28; Matthew 12:9–14, 21:45). As Orlando Costas, author of *Liberating News: A Theology of Contextual Evangelism* [Grand Rapids, Mich.: Eerdmans, 1989], so eloquently stated:

> The gospel makes "somebody" out of "nobodies" of society. . . . [W]hen this occurs, the powers and principalities are threatened because business can no longer be done as usual. (pp. 62, 66)

Peter was persecuted, imprisoned and sought by the authorities as well (Acts 4: 23–30, 5:17–33), and Paul also experienced persecution and imprisonments (Acts 16: 16–24, 17:13, 19:23–39; 2 Corinthians 11:16–26). All of them were seen as subversives and as enemies of the public good by the colonizing powers.

Scripture shows that Jesus' battles were ideological and spiritual rather than military—but they did involve profound conflict with the ruling powers. The arrest and assassination of John the Baptist prompted Jesus to begin his public ministry in isolated areas (Mark 1:4), and Jesus' cleansing of the temple (Matthew 21:12–17, Mark 11:15–19, and parallel passages) dramatically challenged the economic, political, and religious control of the authorities over the "Laos" (people) of God.

Jesus was considered a threat by the state, charged with "perverting our nation" (Luke 23:5). He endured both "state" and "federal" trials where he refused to defend himself (Matthew 27:1–2, 11–14; Luke 23:1–12; John 18:28–38; and parallel passages). By his silence he rejected the authority and jurisdiction of the colonial power or simply recognized the futility of a legal defense in courts run by the very forces he had been speaking against. Like today's prisoners, who are repeatedly strip-searched, he was stripped and humiliated; ultimately he received the harshest possible sentence—that reserved for political dissidents—a horrible death on a cross.

Our theological tradition, on many occasions, has condemned the use of violence to solve political struggles. However, the use of arms in the interest of a just cause has been a matter of a completely different category (e.g., the War for Independence, Civil War, World War I and World War II). However, what our theological tradition has clearly condemned is the use of military power to subjugate others, to advance economic adventures, and to impose our will over others (Korea, Vietnam, Grenada, and the many interventions in Latin America and the Caribbean).

Calling for the Prisoners' Release

Considering the historical background and the biblical witness moves us to question: Why are Mandela and Arafat, fighters for the freedom and self-determination of their people who were once regarded by the U.S. government as terrorists, now welcomed to the White House while the Puerto Rican prisoners who struggle for the same right of freedom and self-determination of their people languish in jail with excessive sentences?

If we use common-sense moral standards to consider that question, the plight of the Puerto Rican prisoners seems absurd. We, as Christians, have been asked to pass judgement on neither the political prisoners' goal (Puerto Rico's independence) nor on their means (including the possible use of arms). Instead, we are joining people from Puerto Rico, the United States, and around the world, who are calling for the release of these prisoners in light of how much time they have already served for their actions. We are acting in the recognition that the release of political prisoners must be a part of any genuine resolution of conflict in a colonial situation, as is the case of Puerto Rico. The only true crime of these men and women has been their commitment to work towards realizing Puerto Rico's independence, which has had a long history. The prisoners' ideology and their means of acting should not preclude them from receiving justice.

We, as United Methodists, have been called to identify with prisoners and their needs. We have been called to bring justice to them when injustice has taken place (Luke 4:18, Matthew 25:36). This is one of those times when injustice has taken place. Therefore, The United Methodist Church has joined thousands of people from around the world who are calling for release of these prisoners.

Editor's Note: In September 1999 President Clinton granted clemency to eleven Puerto Rican nationalist prisoners.

David Fredrickson

24 Free Speech in Pauline Political Theology

Thy words, Stranger, lack a city.
  —Plutarch, *Life of Lysander*

Since we have such hope, we use much free speech.
  —St. Paul, *The Second Letter to the Corinthians*

I. Free Speech and the Church as *Ekklēsia*

Although it is generally recognized today that Paul's faith was not a religion of subjectivity, some may nevertheless object to the notion that the apostle's theology has a political dimension. Surely, it may be said, the sectarian communities which Paul nurtured with the stark contrasts of "outsiders" and "insiders" did not think that their task was to influence public policy in the cities of the Roman empire. While it is of course preposterous to think that the early Christians had Caesar's ear, influencing public policy is only one way of engaging in politics.

There is another way of being political: creating an alternative public space through speech.[1] This way has the possibility of unmasking and criticizing the injustice of the dominant political expression while anticipating, embodying, and proclaiming God's transformation of the whole of political life in church and society.[2] In this way Paul's letters were political. He did everything he could to persuade his hearers that the gospel of the death of Jesus and the resurrection of the humiliated and crucified One had deep implications for political life, since it carried the promise of a unified humanity.

Originally published in *Word and World* (Fall 1992), 12:345–351. © *Word and World*. Reprinted with permission. All rights reserved.

It was not the case that Paul argued that unity in diversity is a worthy goal for enlightened minds to pursue or powerful generals to impose. Unlike some of the philosophers, he did not operate with an ideal of the unity of humankind based upon universal reason. Rather, his program was a political theology, because he claimed that God in Jesus through the Spirit is creating a new human community through the proclamation of the gospel in which difference is not collapsed or intimidated into sameness but woven together in unity.[3] Furthermore, unlike the philosophers of the first century who despised rhetoric for its claim to find truth within persuasion and who instead sought to undergird political and social institutions with eternal truths,[4] Paul relied heavily on public argumentation for the preservation of the communities.

There is no lack of evidence for a political framework in Paul's theology. One obvious place to look is the term *ekklēsia*, which is generally translated "church" but to a first-century Greek speaker would have been heard as the assembly of free citizens called together to draw upon their right and obligation to speak freely and deliberate publicly matters of life and justice in their city.[5] Did Paul understand the church to be such a deliberative body which shaped its future through rhetoric? The very fact that he participated in this deliberation through his letters implies that he did, to say nothing of the fact that much of his writing utilized the classical techniques of deliberative rhetoric. New Testament scholars are just beginning to discover the intensity of mutual exhortation in the life of the earliest churches[6] and the importance of rhetoric in mission and community formation.[7] Paul himself in 2 Corinthians 5:11 summarizes his ministry in the words "we persuade people (*anthrōpous peithomen*)" — an appeal to one widely recognized definition of rhetoric in antiquity.[8]

Let us assume, then, that Paul shared the classical ideal of a political body shaping itself through persuasive speech and not through violence or the dictates of an institutionalized hierarchy. Yet, if for Paul each community gathered in Jesus' name was an *ekklēsia*, how did he avoid the classism and sexism of this social institution in which only citizens (freeborn males) were permitted to speak their minds, since only they, as I will point out below, possessed the right of free speech? Paul certainly could not avoid this issue, since, as recent studies of early Christian communities have emphasized, the churches were characterized by a high level of social stratification.[9] Rather than a haven for the poor and oppressed, these churches were microcosms of society in the sense that, aside from the aristocracy, all levels of social and economic power were represented. The question must have been intense: Would all be allowed to speak?

This sociological profile of the Pauline communities accentuates the problem of access to free speech and helps us appreciate the theological dimensions of the issue. If the *ekklēsia* of classical Athens is a model for the church in terms of its emphasis on free speech for the preservation of the community, would the church follow its model all the way and permit only the elite within the church to speak? Would the church take as its organizing metaphor the full-fledged city, where slaves, women, and foreigners labored without voice so that the free males could be at leisure (the root meaning of freedom) to express their thoughts and shape the community? Or would the

Spirit free all and entitle all within the community to speak freely and to become the *ekklēsia*?

How Paul argued against elitism within the church and opened free speech to all should be an important issue for those interested in discovering, interpreting, and finally confessing the apostle's political theology. I will confine my examination to a reading of 2 Corinthians 3:7–18, although the issue of free speech is found in the rest of this letter and in all of his writings.[10] This passage, however, provides the most extensive theological argumentation for God's liberation of speech in the Christian community. Here we find the classical association of free speech (3:12) and freedom (3:17). In order to grasp fully the theological character of the legitimation of free speech in 2 Corinthians 3, I will first sketch the place of free speech in Greek political and moral philosophy, arguing that Paul adopts, but, more importantly, also adapts the classical tradition.

II. The Legitimation of Free Speech (*parrēsia*)

In the ancient Greek city, free speech was the exclusive right of citizens. This meant that women, aliens, and slaves were not permitted to speak freely. We gain a sense of how important participation through speech in public life was when we observe that the loss of *parrēsia* was considered the most grievous misfortune that could be suffered by a freeborn male.[11] Without free speech one was reduced to the lot of a slave.[12] Freedom of action and freedom of speech were two sides of the same coin, but this coin could be possessed only by the citizens of the city.

Yet the influence of the city on social life was doomed. As political power became more concentrated in the hands of the successors of Alexander the Great and eventually in Rome, daily life in the cities was determined less and less by the free speech of local citizens.[13] Free speech no longer found its legitimation in communal terms. Now philosophic discussions took up the theme that the legitimate basis of the philosopher's *parrēsia* was his personal freedom. The "city" becomes a metaphor for the wise person's moral virtue. For example, the Stoic philosopher Musonius Rufus, a contemporary of Paul, used the freedom of the Athenian citizen as a metaphor of the individual philosopher's moral independence, which in turn granted *parrēsia*. The reasonable person

> does not value or despise any place as the cause of his happiness or unhappiness, but he makes the whole matter depend upon himself and considers himself a citizen of the city of God (*politēs tēs tou Dios poleōs*) which is made up of men and gods.[14]

Since the philosopher's charter of freedom in the city of God is written in his own soul, he can be deprived of his freedom by nothing external. The philosopher's *parrēsia* resides not in his political status but in his freedom from fear and his ability to make all things depend upon himself. Moral freedom at an individual level has replaced political freedom as the basis of *parrēsia*.

Free speech was legitimated also from the perspective of the benefits it bestowed on the common good. Free speech was the cornerstone of Athenian democracy, the goad which compelled citizens to do their duty, and the most effective means of preserving the city's safety.[15] Orators exploited the assumption that free speech was necessary for the well-being of the city. Isocrates was adept at portraying the benefits of his *parrēsia*.[16] He contrasts himself with flattering orators who speak for the pleasure but not the benefit of their hearers.[17] As a matter of duty he hides nothing and speaks words that may cause pain but in fact are aimed at the public's well-being:

> It is, therefore, my duty and the duty of all who care about the welfare of the state to choose, not those discourses which are agreeable to you, but those which are profitable for you to hear. And you, for your part, ought to realize, in the first place, that while many treatments of all kinds have been discovered by physicians for the ills of our bodies, there exists no remedy for souls which are ignorant of the truth and are filled with base desires other than the kind of discourse which boldly rebukes the sins which they commit, and, in the second place, that it is absurd to submit to the cauteries and cuttings of the physicians in order that we may be relieved of greater pains and yet refuse to hear discourses before knowing clearly whether or not they have the power to benefit their hearers. I have said these things at the outset because in the rest of my discourse I am going to speak without reserve and with complete frankness.[18]

This tradition of free speech in service of the preservation of the city was entrusted to philosophers, but they lost sight of the public dimension. As the city was surpassed by larger political units and individuals were thrown more frequently upon themselves to define and live out the good, free speech was reduced to an ideal for the preservation of individual morality. Medical imagery underscores the movement of free speech from city to soul-care. The physician stands for the philosopher, medical instruments and drugs for bold words, incisions for hurt feelings, and physical healing for moral transformation.[19] The view that *parrēsia* healed erring individuals was as widespread as the notion of the philosopher as physician.

We have seen how during the decline of the Greek city-state free speech moved from the political sphere to the arena of soul-care. We have also seen how in this period legitimation of free speech ceased to be a matter of political right and the intent to preserve the city and rested instead on personal moral virtue and the intent to reform individual souls. In 2 Corinthians 3, Paul does two things. First, he restores the public dimension of free speech. Second, he finds the legitimation of free speech not in citizenship or moral virtue but in the transforming power of the Spirit.

III. Free Speech in 2 Corinthians 3:7–18

Modern exegetes have erroneously interpreted *parrēsia* in 3:12 as a reference to Paul's psychological disposition.[20] Thus, they have translated the verse in ways which obscure the claim that Paul makes about the rhetorical character of his mission and ministry practice. In this passage, *chrēsthai parrēsia* clearly amounts to speaking one's mind without fear, just as orators and political leaders of ancient Athens in *ekklēsia* used free speech to save the city from imprudent action.

Our task is to determine how Paul returns free speech to a political sphere and how he speaks of his own free speech in a way that demonstrates to his readers that all in the church have access to it. According to 3:12, Paul bases his use of free speech on hope. This in itself is remarkable, since the reigning political philosophy of the day, Stoicism, regarded hope as a moral disease which the wise man removes from his soul. The content of Paul's hope is developed in 3:7–11, and here we see the public focus of his argument concerning free speech. The dichotomy of letter and spirit which controls this portion of the argument is a political, not a hermeneutical, distinction.[21] Ancient political writers pointed out that written law coerces[22] and cannot elicit justice in human communities.[23] In this tradition of political thought, the main point of 3:7–11 is the superiority of the new ministry based upon its source, the Spirit, and its effect, the creation of justice. The contrast between a ministry which condemns and one which transforms is found in 3:9: *hē diakonia tēs katakriseōs* and *hē diakonia tēs dikaiosunēs*. Paul portrays his ministry as one which fosters transformation, unlike the ministry of the old covenant which kills and condemns. His confidence to use *parrēsia* is based, therefore, on his hope in the life-giving and justice-creating power of the ministry in which he participates.[24] He has returned free speech to public purposes: justice and life.

Since this eschatological hope in the Spirit's transforming power and purpose is the possession of all in the community without distinction, all are entitled to free speech. Paul drives this point home in 3:13–18. Here he treats the problem of shame and its relationship to freedom. It was widely recognized in antiquity that shame was the greatest enemy of free speech.[25] Paul argues in 3:13–18 that where the Spirit is, there is no shame, only freedom.

Moses' veiling himself suggests that he hides himself from a sense of shame,[26] since in ancient philosophy and literature there was a frequent connection between shame and concealment.[27] Bad conscience requires hiding.[28] Moses' inability to withstand the gaze of the sons of Israel and his wearing of a veil indicate his shame, a result of the old covenant (*to telos tou katargoumenou*) whose ministry condemns even the one who is its minister.

Nevertheless, the fact that Moses' veil is removed signifies an end to his shame, and he comes to exemplify freedom (*eleutheria*). The connection between Moses' unveiled face and freedom is made intelligible by the commonplace in philosophy, hellenistic Judaism, and early Christianity that freedom was dependent upon a good conscience.[29] Free speech, in turn, finds its legitimate basis in the freedom granted by a good conscience.[30] The person having no cause to be ashamed was empowered to use free speech. In short, Paul's imaginative interpretation of Exodus 34:29–35 serves to illustrate the freeing and transforming activity of the Spirit in the church where there is now no need for concealment, since "we all" ([2 Cor.] 3:18) are being transformed into the same image, the Lord, at whom we gaze as if in a mirror.

IV. Conclusion

One of the pressing political needs of the church today is to imagine new ways for unity in the midst of cultural diversity, moral reasoning, and differences in race, gender, sexual orientation, and social class. Political theology should seek to bring about community in diversity without coercion, subordination, or the imposition of the liberal ideal of toleration, which is itself based upon the dangerous notion that we are all the same under the surface. In short, political theology must help us imagine the church as a place of speech, where all voices are free to make arguments, to seek to persuade others, and to receive evaluation as to whether that which is freely said promotes justice and life—all for the sake of the church's unity and mission and all without the threat of shame and exclusion.

Paul's political theology of free speech goes to the heart of the matter. All have a voice; no one may be silenced; no one may speak for someone else; and all speech must build up the community. As risky as it may sound, because of the hope in the Spirit's justifying and transforming presence, everyone in the church is entitled to speak with complete freedom. Because of the Spirit's granting of freedom, no one may be shamed into silence. Either local churches will embrace this theology and move forward in mission as communities of moral discourse (that is, really becoming churches in the Pauline sense of the word), shaping their futures through persuasion, or they face the possibility of dying away as they protect themselves from difference and conflict by stifling the voices of all the people—those who "with unveiled face, beholding the glory of the Lord, are being changed into his likeness from one degree of glory to another."

Notes

1. D. Georgi (*Theocracy in Paul's Praxis and Theology* [Minneapolis: Fortress, 1991]) also asserts that Paul's theology is political and describes the church as alternative utopia. Nevertheless, I wish to draw a clear line between Georgi's position and my own. Whereas I emphasize the church as a place where deliberation occurs by all through free speech, Georgi thinks the Pauline letters are repositories of Paul's idea system which inverted the patriarchal God and promoted the value of solidarity. Not only do I disagree with his view that Pauline letters are codes to be cracked for the ideology they contain, I also question the value of solidarity when it is not accompanied by an even greater emphasis on free speech shared by all. Solidarity implies an underlying likeness and a willingness of the powerful to speak "on behalf of" the powerless. For a critique of solidarity isolated from rhetoric, see G. M. Simpson, "*Theologia Crucis* and the Forensically Fraught World: Engaging Helmut Peukert and Jurgen Habermas," *Journal of the American Academy of Religion* 57 (1989) 509–541.

2. Like contemporary critical theorists, Paul presupposes an ideal speech situation in light of which he criticizes present social conditions. Among recent philosophers, this method of critique has been most ardently advocated by Jurgen Habermas. See T. McCarthy, *The Critical Theory of Jurgen Habermas* (Cambridge, MA: MIT, 1978) 75–125, 272–357.

3. E. Castelli (*Imitating Paul: A Discourse of Power* [Louisville: Westminster/John Knox, 1991]) offers a radically different interpretation, since she detects in Paul's rhetoric the beginning of the master Western narrative which reduces all difference to sameness. Although her insistence that Paul's letters were simultaneously political and rhetorical (an improvement over Georgi), her deeply suspicious hermeneutic, inspired by the work of Michel Foucault, reduces all claims of truth to moves for power.

4. See especially J. de Romilly, *Magic and Rhetoric in Ancient Greece* (Cambridge, MA: Harvard, 1975).

5. See W. Meeks, *The First Urban Christians: The Social World of the Apostle Paul* (New Haven: Yale, 1983) 108. For the origin in the ancient Greek city of other moral values important for early Christianity, see W. Meeks, *The Moral World of the First Christians* (Philadelphia: Westminster, 1986) 19–39.

6. A. Malherbe, "'Pastoral Care' in the Thessalonian Church," *New Testament Studies* 36 (1990) 375–391.

7. H. D. Betz, "The Problem of Rhetoric and Theology according to the Apostle Paul," in *L'Apotre Paul: Personnalite, style et conception du ministere*, ed. A. Vanhoye (Louvain: Louvain University, 1986) 16–48; W. Wuellner, "Greek Rhetoric and Pauline Argumentation," in *Early Christian Literature and the Classical Intellectual Tradition: In Honorem Robert M. Grant*, eds. W. Schoedel and R. Wilkin (Paris: Editions Beauchesne, 1979) 177–188.

8. Cicero, *De Oratore* 1.31.138.

9. A. Malherbe, *Social Aspects of Early Christianity*, 2nd ed. (Philadelphia: Fortress, 1983) 113–122.

10. See S. Marrow, "Parrhesia and The New Testament," *Catholic Biblical Quarterly* 44 (1982) 431–446.

11. Demosthenes, Fragment 21.

12. Euripides, *Phoenissae* 390–392.

13. For the shift from cities to empire as the locus of decision making and the Stoic legitimation of this transition, see B. D. Shaw, "The Divine Economy: Stoicism as Ideology," *Latomus* 44 (1985) 16–54.

14. Fragment 9. Text and translation by C. E. Lutz, *Musonius Rufus "The Roman Socrates"* (New Haven: Yale, 1947) 68–69.

15. Demosthenes, *Orations* 13.15; 60.25–26.

16. Isocrates, *Oration* 8.5, 10.

17. Isocrates, *Oration* 8.3–5.

18. Isocrates, *Oration* 8.39–41; trans. by George Nortin, *Isocrates*, vol. 2 (Cambridge, MA: Harvard, 1982) 33.

19. For the ubiquity of medical imagery in the moral exhortation of the philosophers, see A. Malherbe, *Paul and the Popular Philosophers* (Minneapolis: Fortress, 1989) 127–130.

20. Only W. C. van Unnik ("The Semitic Background of *parrēsia* in the New Testament," in *Sparsa Collecta II: The Collected Essays of W. C. Van Unnik* [Leiden: E. J. Brill, 1980] 293 n. 7) has examined the phrase *chrēsthai parrēsia*. Yet even he continues to translate "we are very bold." V. Furnish's insistence in Anchor Bible (*II Corinthians* [Garden City, NY: Doubleday, 1984] 206, 230) to translate *chrēsthai* as "to act" is dubious, since it lacks strong and independent lexical support. John Chrysostom (*Hom. 7 in 2 Cor. 2* [J. Migne, *Patrologia graeca* 61.444]), on the other hand, recognized that Paul refers to the manner of his speaking.

21. The Pauline antithesis between letter and spirit should be understood in the light of

widespread philosophic reflection on the nature of written law and its inability to bring about freedom. This approach is brusquely rejected by E. Kasemann ("The Spirit and the Letter," in *Perspectives on Paul* [Philadelphia: Fortress, 1971] 144–145). Yet other exegetes have seen the relevance of the distinction for the interpretation of 2 Corinthians 3:6. See especially S. Vollenweider, *Freiheit als neue Schopfung: Eine Untersuchung zur Eleutheria bei Paulus und in seiner Umvelt* (Gottingen: Vandenhoeck & Ruprecht, 1989) 87–96, 265–269. For the ancient period, see John Chrysostom, *Hom. 6 in 2 Cor. 2* (*Patrologia graeca* 61.438–439).

22. Aristotle, *Rhetoric* 1.14.7, Ps.-Crates, *Epistle* 5; Philo, *The Special Laws* 4.150; Plutarch, *Life of Lycurgus* 13.1; Seneca, *Epistle* 94.37.

23. Isocrates, *Oration* 7.41; Ps.-Heraclitus, *Epistle* 7. 10; Dio Chrysostom, *Oration* 69.8; Plutarch, *Life of Solon* 5.2.

24. For a recent treatment of the political consequences of Christian hope, see J. Moltmann, *On Human Dignity: Political Theology and Ethics* (Philadelphia: Fortress, 1984) 97–112.

25. See, for example, Philo, *The Special Laws* 1.202–204.

26. Origen (*Hom. 5 in Jer. 8–9* [*Patrologia graeca* 13.305–308]) recognized the connection between veil and shame in 3:13. Although van Unnik ("'With Unveiled Face,' an Exegesis of 2 Corinthians iii 12–18" in *Sparsa Collecta I: The Collected Essays of W. C. van Unnik* [Leiden: E. J. Brill, 1973] 202) notes the association, he does not sufficiently explore the philosophic background. He gives extensive evidence of the connection in Jewish tradition in his "The Semitic Background," 294–304.

27. Xenophon, *Agesilaus* 9.1; Plato, *Phaedrus* 243B; Philo, *Mut.* 198–199; Epictetus, *Diss.* 3.22.15–16. Paul reiterates the connection between shame and concealment in 4:2: *ta krupta tēs aischunēs*.

28. Isocrates, *Orations* 1.16; 3.52; Philo, *Joseph* 68; *The Special Laws* 3.54; 4.6.

29. Periander (Stobacus, *Florigelium* 3.24.12) aptly puts the relationship: "When Periander was asked 'What is freedom?' he replied: 'a good conscience.'"

30. Philo (*Every Good Man is Free* 99) remarks that "freedom of speech, genuine without taint of bastardy, and proceeding from a pure conscience, befits the nobly born."

There is neither male nor female for you are all one

(Galatians 3:28)

The religious right has framed the societal debate about religious issues in terms of two agenda items. They seek a return to a society that spoke in a single Christian voice in public. And they desire a society where that Christian voice espouses the values of patriarchy. They imagine a world of families with men as heads of household and women taking the role of their "helpers." Their analysis argues that once this bedrock family as described by the religious right is reestablished throughout our society, all social problems will disappear. To that end, the religious right has targeted abortion, same-sex relationships, and women's rights to independence as the crucial factors that need change. And they support their teachings based on references to Christian scripture.

In the essays that follow, those ideas are challenged from the perspective of the religious left. Much energy of the religious left has been devoted to countering the ideas of the religious right about family and about doctrinal views of abortion and homosexuality. While it has been problematic for the religious left to constantly fight the right on these issues, the results have been a powerful set of statements about the rights of women, gay men, and lesbians to their freedom and dignity.

Laila Al-Marayati looks at the role of women and family in Islam, making the argument that the Qur'an views women as whole, independent human beings rather than exclusively as wives and mothers. Mary Pellauer writes about the importance of the religious witness against domestic violence and the necessity for churches, synagogues, and mosques to take active roles in creating environments that condemn violence and support equality. Many of Pellauer's recommendations have been implemented in religious groups that speak out against domestic violence.

Alpert and McNeill look from Jewish and Christian perspectives respectively at what it means to identify as gay and religious in the religious world today. For both authors it means making a connection to Scripture by questioning both the text and the interpretations of it that have been used to make a wedge against gay and lesbian people in the Jewish and Christian worlds.

Rosemary Ruether explores the ways in which the family has changed over time, and focuses in particular on Jesus' teachings that reconceptualize family as the community of believers. She also comments on the role of patriarchy in the lives of women in the church.

Hunt and Kissling describe the challenges made to the Roman Catholic Church by the clergy and laity who dissent from the church's stance against abortion. They present a valuable case study of how religious feminists succeed and fail at making change, and examine the role of public protest for social change. Helen Tworkov writes about abortion from the perspective of Buddhism. Her willingness to "take both sides" exemplifies much of the religious discussion surrounding abortion today.

These essays represent the opportunity for those on the religious left to speak in their own voices about subjects that are an important part of their vision of a world of justice and freedom.

Laila Al-Marayati

25   The Worth of a Woman

In traditionalist Islam, a woman's ability to bear and raise children is simultaneously cause for reverence and subjugation. As wife and mother, a Muslim woman's main function is to produce righteous Muslim children; she is the primary caretaker, in charge of the household, and the chief supporter of her husband. She is allowed to participate in other activities only to the extent that they do not detract from her primary duties. Thus, a Muslim woman who is not a mother is not fulfilling her proper role in life. She is deficient. This pronatalist view of a woman's worth depending on her child-bearing and -rearing capacities, however, is not clearly spelled out in Islamic texts. Exposing the lack of evidence for a pronatalist and patriarchal view of Islam is crucial. Revisiting the original texts and alternative interpretations which focus on the celebration of the partnership of men and women in all aspects of life, including reproduction, is the first step toward enabling Muslim women to challenge the status quo. Islam, which means submission to the will of God, originated in Mecca in Saudi Arabia in the seventh century of the common era when, over a period of twenty-three years, Muhammad, an unlettered merchant, received revelation from God in the form of the Holy Qur'an. Because the Arabic text was memorized immediately and then written down in a single version within forty years of the Prophet Mohammed's death, Muslims regard the Qur'an as the word of God in the original version in which it was revealed. While the text of the Qur'an is considered sacred, authentic, unadulterated, and thus immutable, humankind's understanding and interpretation of it varies. The next important source of information is the body of work known as Hadith, the sayings and actions of the Prophet Muhammad collected over time by a variety of individuals and first documented in written form approximately two hundred years after his death.

The Qur'an was meant for all people for all time, to be read and understood by any individual. Over the years, Muslim religious scholarship evolved in areas such as theology, exegesis, and jurisprudence, resulting in a variety of interpretations of the Qur'an. While differing views were expressed and tolerated on a wide range of is-

Originally published in *Conscience* (Spring 1997), 18:22–25. Reprinted with the permission of the author.

sues, the understanding of the role of women remained decidedly static. Relying on male religious authority to present a singular version or interpretation of the Qur'an regarding women in general and women's sexuality in particular has interfered with women's ability to achieve their full capacity as Muslims and human beings. Those who question the prevailing view that women's primary role is to serve others are accused of caving into Western cultural domination.

Looking closely at some of the verses of the Qur'an will enable us to come to a different conclusion regarding the role of Muslim women. Contrary to what some might think, the Qur'an does not state that a woman's most important and valuable position in life is that of mother, or more precisely, a bearer of children. The definition of a true believer and righteous servant of God is the same for men and women and ultimately determines the worth or value of an individual in the eyes of God:

> True piety does not consist in turning your faces towards the east or the west—but truly pious is the one who believes in God, and the Last Day, and the angels and revelation, and the prophets; and spends of his substance—however much he may cherish it—upon his near of kin, and the orphans, and the needy and the wayfarer, and the beggars and for the freeing of human beings from bondage; and is constant in prayer, and renders the purifying dues; and [the truly pious are] they who keep their promises whenever they promise, and are patient in misfortune and hardship and in time of peril: it is they who have proved themselves true, and it is they, they who are conscious of God. (Qur'an, Chapter 2: verse 177)

> And the believers, both men and women, are close to one another: they enjoin the doing of what is right and forbid the doing of what is wrong and are constant in prayer, and render the purifying dues, and pay heed unto God and His Apostle. It is they upon whom God will bestow His grace: verily, God is almighty, wise. (9:71)

The Qur'an also stresses the importance of the parent-child relationship with an emphasis on the duty of children to honor and respect their parents:

> And [God says]: We have enjoined upon man goodness towards his parents: his mother bore him by bearing strain upon strain, and his utter dependence on her lasted two years, [hence, oh man], be grateful to Me and to your parents [and remember that] with Me is all journey's end. (31:14)

From the pronatalist point of view, having children is both a means of achieving righteousness by fulfilling a certain role and a blessing from God. Indeed, the Muslim prays: "Oh our Sustainer! Grant that our spouses and our offspring be a joy to our eyes, and cause us to be foremost among those who are conscious of Thee!" (25:74). Also, for some, having many children can be considered a claim to fame, especially in patriarchal cultures that emphasize large families as indicative of a man's prowess and stature in the community. God warns us against such an attitude in the following verse:

> Wealth and children are an adornment of this world's life: but good deeds, the fruit whereof endures forever, are of far greater merit in your Sustainer's sight, and a far better source of hope. (18:46)

Islam emphasizes accountability and responsibility in all relationships. Thus, a parent cannot neglect obligations to her or his children. One is not rewarded for simply producing a child; one must rear her properly as well. This applies to both parents, married or divorced, who are advised to consult with one another about the best choices for their children:

> And if both [parents] decide, by mutual consent and counsel, upon weaning, they will incur no sin [thereby]; and if you decide to entrust your children to foster-mothers, you will incur no sin, provided you ensure, in a fair manner, the safety of the child which you are handing over. (2:233)

The unique role of a woman in going through childbirth and then nursing a child is cause for God to emphasize the obligation of her grown children to honor, respect, and love her. Again, being a parent is valuable, but a Muslim's worth is not dependent on whether or not or she actually ever occupies that position.

Other verses in the Qur'an which are relevant to motherhood involve specific individuals who are considered to be proper examples for Muslim women to follow. Mary, the mother of Jesus, is the most well known, traditionally valued because of her maternal assignment. While her importance in that regard is not disputed, Mary was virtuous in her own right, based on her own unique, devoted relationship to God:

> And Lo! The angels said: "Oh Mary! Behold, God has elected you and made you pure, and raised you above all the women of the world. Oh Mary! Remain thou truly devout unto thy Sustainer, and prostrate thyself in worship, and bow down with those who bow down [before Him]." (3:42–43)

And while Mary is commonly cited as an example for Muslim women to follow, again identifying with her role as the mother of a messenger, the Qur'an clearly states that her devotion to God is a reminder for all Muslims:

> And [for those who have attained to faith, We have propounded another parable of God-consciousness in the story of] Mary, the daughter of Imran, who guarded her chastity, whereupon We breathed of Our spirit into that [which was in her womb], and who accepted the truth of her Sustainer's words—and of His revelations—and was one of the truly devout. (66:12)

Another argument against Islamic pronatalism is that, of the Prophet Mohammed's wives after his first marriage, only one bore him a child (who died by the age of two). He was married to his first wife Khadijah for twenty-five years during which time they had six children. When Khadijah died, Muhammad married nine other women over the next ten years. (Polygamy was common at that time.) Although only one of these wives bore him a child, one is extremely hard-pressed to find a hadith (saying) reflecting the Prophet's remorse, regret, or even concern about this fact. Each woman was valued on her own merit and much is written about all of his wives. God in the Qur'an refer to them collectively as the "Mothers of the Believers" and the Muslim community has always viewed them with a great respect and reverence which has never been associated with their reproductive status. Finally, the issue of contraception is relevant to this discussion: if woman's primary role is that of wife and mother, then, contraception would be discouraged. Sex would naturally be important only in terms of reproduction. Yet contraception is not forbidden, as is noted in several hadith, and, the Qur'an says the sexual relationship between a husband and wife serves mainly to strengthen the bond of love in the marriage:

> It is lawful for you to go in unto your wives during the night preceding the [day's] fast [during the month of Ramadan]: they are as a garment for you, and you are as a garment for them . . . you may lie with them skin to skin, and avail yourselves of that which God has ordained for you. . . . (2:187)

And while Muslims pray for the blessings from God in the event that they conceive, the purpose of the sexual relationship encompasses more than procreation.

In God's view, as expressed in the Qur'an, " . . . the best of you in the sight of God is the one who is most deeply conscious of Him. . . ." (49:13). Clearly, this is not a result of one's biology or physical nature over which there is no control. Conscious and conscientious commitment to God and Islam is what distinguishes the righteous Muslim. As reiterated in the Qur'an, God is absolutely just. To devalue an individual based on something over which she has no control is not consistent with the notion of a just God, who ascribes value and judges mankind based on intentions and deeds. The fact that "He gives both male and female [offspring to whomever he wills], and leaves barren whomever He wills . . ." (42:50) indicates that God's will ultimately prevails regarding childbearing. Thus, a woman is not punished or rewarded for having or not having children.

Exposing the lack of evidence for a pronatalist Islamic view is crucial, because many Muslim women are still strongly attached to this understanding. The value of fertility is often culturally based, but many individuals feel that this value is reinforced by their religion. The childless woman can have difficult relationships with her husband and in-laws, with other family members, and with the community at large. Her supposed defectiveness can lead to divorce, polygamy, abuse, and numerous psycho-social problems that damage her self-esteem and can be potentially debilitating. While social rejection and criticism of the childless woman is not unique to Islam, understanding that the connection between child-bearing and a woman's worth is cultural, not religious, can help Muslim women value themselves based on their willful behavior, choices, and beliefs. Although pronatalist views often prevail today in many Muslim communities, an alternative focus emerges after study of the primary texts. Women and men are valued based on their individual behavior and beliefs. Parenthood is considered a blessing and a challenge for both mothers and fathers. Muslims are commanded to honor and respect their parents because of the great effort involved in bearing and rearing them. The reproductive capability of women is only one part of their identity and therefore cannot represent their total worth.

Challenging a view that enjoys widespread support is unpopular at best and threatening at worst. Fears of truly dismantling an entrenched hierarchy in which each individual occupies a well-defined position may prevent open discussion and change of the pronatalist approach. Indeed, my arguments might be dismissed as simply reflecting a Western feminist point of view, not based on Islam. But by realizing that there may not be one single view and by allowing for diversity of opinions on this and other matters, Muslims can adapt to change that will not only improve our lives and the society in which we live, but that will enhance our understanding of Islam.

Mary Pellauer

26 Violence against Women: The Theological Dimension

. . .

I became interested in women's history about ten years ago. Reading about the women's suffrage movement, that piece of American life which nobody had ever told me about before, I felt both empowerment and despair. Empowerment, because these women were my feminist foremothers; here, at last, was *my* tradition. Despair, because the struggles, arguments, and claims of the last women's movement were astonishingly like our more recent ones. I became haunted by a sense that we were repeating ourselves.

One day I stumbled across early feminist attacks on the "rule of thumb"—the judicial precedent, based on English common law, that a husband might beat his wife provided that the rod used was no thicker than his thumb. I was devastated to find the origins of this piece of our language. But I also remember thinking: Here at last is some *progress.* Here, surely, is a relic of a barbarian past left behind as we became more "modern."

The Shock of Recognition

My complacency was shattered when the women's movement discovered battered women. Over the past years, the growing literature regarding violence against women circled what became a familiar theme, virtually a litany: No one had ever studied this material or asked these questions before. No one asked, for example, whether the women Freud saw might genuinely have been victims of incest. No one asked the women in primitive cultures what they thought about the ritual rape male anthropologists shrugged off so easily. No one asked whether being beaten by one's husband was a private trouble or a public issue.

It took some months, nearly a year, in the earliest stages of my discovery of battered women, for me to *realize,* to *remember,* that as a child I had seen battering in my own

Originally published in *Christianity and Crisis* (May 30, 1983), 206–212. Reprinted with the permission of *Christianity and Crisis.*

home. I had seen my father lunge at my mother with a butcher knife. I had seen her pick up a big black frying pan to fend him off. I stood paralyzed in the door to the stairs watching this swift and passionate duel. I stood in the door to the living room. I sat on a kitchen chair: I had seen it more than once. I had seen him slap and hit, seen him after her with a baseball bat, heard the endless reams of abusive language that spilled from my father's lips.

I had taken it for granted—just as had the police, the school system, the newspapers we read, the books in the public library, the social workers. I believed that this was just the way it was for women. While I had a hard time dealing with those memories, I had an even harder time dealing with the fact that I had *forgotten*, forgotten so effectively that I never connected my own personal experiences of those stark and terrifying tussles in my home with the women's history I had read, or even with the testimony of contemporary battered women.

I recall too that when our pastor came to call, we all sat about properly on our chairs, smiled stiffly, and said: "Yes, everything is fine, fine, just fine."

In those same early 1970s while in graduate school, I began teaching in several Chicago-area seminaries. Once at a Christmas party, a male faculty friend wandered over, a glass of Scandinavian glogg in his hand, to mention that he was counseling a seminarian who was beating his wife. I was thunderstruck, shaken to the core of my confidence in Christianity—I looked around at the seminarians I taught with eyes even more suspicious and wary than a stiff dose of Mary Daly's *Beyond God the Father* had previously made them. And I found connections. Even the friends I admired and trusted knew almost nothing about rape and battering. Worse, they took these abuses for granted in the same casual way our culture as a whole did. Those who became concerned often acted as though it were a problem "out there," somewhere beyond the churches. They did not believe that these were issues which they would find, starkly, in their own parishes. Such things do not happen to "Christian women."

This combination of personal experience and perceived need led me to develop and co-teach, with Lois Gehr Livezey, a course on "Violence and Violation." We were glad for each other's company, for neither of us was very sure that these were *really* theological issues. More than once we scared ourselves with the novelty of what we were saying. Nowhere in any traditional theological books could we find guidance on such topics. In the following ten years I *never* taught this course without finding among my students women who were prey to these forms of abuse.

Over the past decade, some things *have* changed. There are now rape crisis centers and hotlines, as well as a sizable battered-women's movement, with a national coalition to share information and strategy. Attention has focused on other forms of abuse—pornography, sexual harassment on the job, strip-searches of women by police, sterilization abuse, to name but a few.

This movement, however, is just beginning to have an impact on Christian ministry and our churches. Thanks to ground-breaking work by the United Methodist Women in Crisis project, we now *know* that our local parishes include sizable numbers of victims of these forms of violence. But so far, church agencies and sociologists of religion have not been very interested in whether, or how many, victims turn to their clergy for support. Nor do we have anything beyond anecdotal evidence on how clergy treat abused women who do turn to them. Feminist grassroots groups may be wary of clergy because victims all too frequently report that their minister or priest exacerbated the victim's plight. ("This is a cross you must learn to bear" or "turn the other cheek" can be deadly dimensions of traditional Christian piety in this context.) Occasionally one does meet pastors who are aware, compassionate, and active in co-alition building for structural change, but we don't know how typical they are.

As increasing numbers of women enter seminaries, consciousness of such abuse has increased among ministers. This may be due to the unspoken solidarity among women, since many of us will never be comfortable telling a man about these intimate wounds. It may be due to the fact that women in ministry are more aware of the threats and menaces against all women, and hence willing to speak about them, to communicate understanding and openness. It may also be a function of the sheer novelty of women in ministry: because the bonds of congregational expectations are not yet solidified, new roles are possible for women clergy.

But women in ministry are few and far between, and overextended. For change to occur, therefore, clergymen also must hear and respond in new ways. They must become convinced that violence against women is literally a life-and-death issue; they must learn to respond from the new knowledge of such abuses rather than from old stereotypes, and to engage in the social analysis that embeds our understandings of violence against women in larger understandings of sexism. Clergymen must be transformed, personally and theologically, as women have been. If men in the clergy learn nothing more than to refer to women's agencies, to support shelters and rape crisis lines, it will be a gain.

In order for us all to take serious and effective steps toward eradicating these abuses, I propose three broad guidelines for ministry.

1. *Churches must break the dynamics of silence surrounding rape, battering, and sexual abuse of children.* Taken most simply, this means information and education, tasks that have been integral to our churches' lives. We have Sunday schools, bulletins, books, devotional guides, memoranda, denominational statements, study guides. They must now be used to spread the word. This process has already begun: Thanks to its Commission on Women and the Churches, the United Presbyterian Church in the U.S.A. has submitted materials regarding sexual violence to its General Assembly. The United Methodist Office of Women in Crisis has become an important center for collecting and distributing information. Magazines such as *The Lutheran* have in the last year published articles on rape, incest, battering, and pornography.

But most essential is our communication at *the local parish* level, for that is where U.S. churches and the Christian faith live and move and have their being, to para-phrase the liturgy. There, it is human interaction which is crucial. And it is here, I fear, that we most frequently fall short.

Like my family, many victims may never take these wounds to their ministers. This may be realistic, especially when so few clergy know how to deal with these evils. But I do not believe that there is a parish anywhere in this nation that does not include victims of domestic and sexual violence. The parish clergy may or may not know who they are, particularly in the "last taboo" of father-daughter sexual abuse. Even should the clergy know, the congregation may not. Obviously, it is fundamental to guard the privacy of each victim, whose right alone it is to decide with whom to share their story. But it is nonetheless important for a congregation to understand that it is *likely* to include such people. Our silence reinforces and perpetuates the inhibitions and taboos that contribute to the suffering of the victim; it allows many myths and stereotypes regarding such victimization to undermine each woman's movement towards health. Furthermore, our silence contributes to the sense that churches are places where people go when all is well, when we have on our best clothes, where we smile at each other and say, "things are fine, fine, just fine," where we act out the pretence that we are in control of our lives.

Such dynamics may vary among social classes, ethnic groups, and denominations. Perhaps the glazed smile is most in evidence in those circles where keeping up appearances is most prized. But among other groups different dynamics may function to the same end, such as in my lower-class family who perceived the pastor as a primary authority figure.

Other dynamics also undermine our ministry to the victims of abuse. The notion that anger is not a Christian virtue, for example, or the fear of conflict. I would add also the suspicion that both the less happy and the extravagant emotions do not belong in church—melancholy, tears, fear, anxiety, panic, urgency, deep need, insecurity.

Once when I was speaking on these topics to a middle-class congregation, a member said to me, "Why do you dwell on these matters? It will just make you unhappy." This reaction may not be unusual, though that person was unusually honest in saying aloud what many seem to believe. I have some sympathy with this reaction. But I am not just "unhappy" about rape and battering and child sexual abuse; I am furious, agonized—and determined. What the women's movement has made us see, however, is not simply the massive pain of sexual and domestic violence. It has made us see that these conditions are not the will of God or the inevitable workings of nature, but that they can and must be changed. It has made us see that our pain and anger are legitimate and that they can become sources of energy to change the world.

Averting our eyes from the agonizing realities does more than guard our individual "peace" of mind. It *ensures* that we will not participate in the struggles of social transformation that are required. Ministry occurs when the skin of the soul is rubbed raw. If we turn our eyes from the pain of such issues, we turn away from the deepest work of our Christian calling to ministry, and away from the real locus of its power and beauty.

What can churches begin to do? The presence of congregations in every corner of the nation suggests that they would be an ideal network of safe homes. Seminaries need courses to help students deal with such issues. We need more organizations such as the Center for the Prevention of Sexual and Domestic Violence under the pioneering leadership of Rev. Marie Fortune, who first made me aware of the theological questions asked by rape victims. Synodical bodies need to take some steps such as that of the Minnesota Council of Churches, which employs the Rev. Joy Bussert (LCA) to provide clergy continuing education regarding rape, battering, and child sexual abuse. Sunday schools and women's groups can provide basic self-defense classes for women. . . . We need to generate liturgical resources, songs and prayers, sermons and rituals, for weeping and lamenting these pains, and for celebrating true wholeness for abused women. However, we barely begin to understand ministry regarding sexual and domestic violence when we consider such issues primarily as they relate to churches, congregations, and clergy.

2. *Adequate ministry on sexual and domestic violence requires moving toward full-scale social justice.* Many rape victims, battered women, and sexually abused children have no contact with a church. Our responsibilities do not end with those with whom we come face to face. Nor is humane and informed counseling of victims, however necessary, enough. We must address ourselves to structural changes in the institutions of the social order, so that we can prevent abuse.

Adequate ministry to women who are already victimized itself requires sweeping changes in our institutions. Until recently, hospitals, police, court systems, laws, schools and churches were virtually united in what I can only call organized thoughtlessness and *organized mercilessness* toward abused women. Over the last few years, some have changed; others have not. Government budget cuts and inflation endanger even the few programs in existence. To ensure their permanence, such changes need to reach into the medical school, the law school, the police academy, the graduate department of psychology or education, the theological seminary, where images of women are distorted. All these institutions need to be scrutinized, to be called and pressured to offer victims compassionate treatment that enhances the healing of their physical, psychic, and spiritual wounds, and to ensure that offenders are treated with a moral seriousness that demands their transformation.

Such changes will require thoughtful and strategic coalition with feminists rather than the defensiveness which often characterizes our behavior as churches. Here I fear that it is we who are churchpeople who will need to prove our credentials and our seriousness, rather than the other way around. We in the churches have not been the pioneers of the movement against violence against women.

Prevention is even harder. Sexual and domestic violence does not have a single, tidy cause that can be readily isolated in one set of practices, beliefs or institutions. Rather, it is part of a massive social pattern of our common life: sexism. These dramatic abuses are related to the less dramatic dimensions of the patriarchal order: to an advertising industry that sells products with pictures of women chained astraddle chairs or with precocious hip-bumping gyrations of preadolescent girls; to a clothing industry that produces and markets garments reinforcing images of women as sexual objects and actively encouraging our physical helplessness; to segregated labor mar-

VIOLENCE AGAINST WOMEN 213

kets that price women's work at 59 percent of men's; to structures in which so many of us learn to accept or to inflict violence; to movies and television that portray male violence as attractive and desirable. Precisely because violence against women is so deeply embedded in this patriarchal whole, many feminists believe talk of prevention to be a utopian dream. Indeed, if we could get reliable and institutionalized guarantees of understanding, thoughtfulness, and mercy for victims, we might be a long way toward utopia. I for one find that I need to hold on to a small piece of that utopianism, that piece which lives in our longing for "justice that flows like living water," not intermittent justice, but a continuous flow, a mighty flood.

3. *Adequate ministry on sexual and domestic violence requires a theological reconstruction in a feminist vein.* The last ten years have witnessed a deepening and widening of the streams of feminist theology. There is more than one theological reconstruction required of us if we are to come seriously and critically to terms with sexual and domestic violence. Historical theology and biblical criticism, for example, must grapple with those traditional stories and comments which explicitly portray or perpetuate abuse against women. Pastoral care courses in seminary after seminary must rework their psychological and spiritual perspectives so that they can both cease perpetuating notions that take such abuses for granted, and also reconstruct their perspectives toward healing and health of the victims.

We need both new words and new actions, new concepts and new institutions, as integral parts of this theological reconstruction. It is our theological creativity, in thought and feeling and action, that is at stake for me here. This creativity both depends upon and enhances our creativity in ministry—just as the misogynous neglect of abused women in our tradition perversely reinforces itself in theology and ministry.

We need, for example, to listen with new ears for the ringing sounds of God's voice rippling through the voices of women as they come up against rape, battering, and child sexual abuse. When women who are raped speak of it as a life-threatening experience, we need new words—words surely that can replace the silly, brutalizing old words—which said implicitly that rape was barely important, if they did not say explicitly that nobody should kick about being given a good time.

We need new words that can express the ultimate dimension that can be a part of rape as women come face to face with an evil meant to them. We need to listen to the rape victim who goes home in a daze to wash herself, and we need to wonder whether she is expressing a spontaneous theology, a theology which asserts that the violation of the body is a fundamental, perhaps an *ontological* violation. (One of the meanings of "violate" suggests this: "to profane, to desecrate.") In short, we need to learn to do theology *from the body.* This may be difficult for a tradition with body-mind dualisms as deeply embedded as ours. But a theology that takes rape, battering, and child sexual abuse seriously will be a fresh one, fed by new insights into the victim's perspective, enhancing our abilities to do justice and love mercy.

A feminist theology involves us directly with power and sisterhood, both central to theological movement in the midst of sexual and domestic violence. Like anger, these are not comfortable topics to address in the context of ministry. Many themes in our tradition imply that the abnegation of power is good, especially for women. With the separation of church and state, and with massive industrialization, power has largely departed for "secular" realms.

But it is power that keeps sexual violence in place. When we women stand up for ourselves, learning self-defense, rejecting passivity, affirming our own thinking, speaking, and feeling, fighting back in whatever way we can, remembering our own experience even when our tradition tells us it isn't so, then we undercut the cycles of sexism and its violence. A feminist theology that takes women's power and sisterhood as a theological resource is a small but luminous gift we may have yet to offer to the women's movement; and to our churches.

Sisters

Sisterhood is sisterhood wherever it occurs—within or outside the church. Where there is sisterhood, there is a women's movement. It is in sisterhood that empowerment of women happens: by the stroke of a hand on a back, by the ear listening at the other end of the telephone, by the voice saying exactly what I have felt but could not bring myself to admit, by the occasional confrontation that we can accept from one who knows our experience, by the anger gathering, the tears mingling. Slowly, we learn to think theologically about those tears. We learn to affirm that the tears we shed are God's tears. As our anger burns within us, it turns into determination. As our determined anger strikes sparks off others, we learn to affirm that a small fire is struck in God, who has been waiting for that small flame. She begins to wake, to shake herself, to turn tears and anger into determination. She comes to join us.

As we learn to work together, as we gather power, our voices converge in our own speech. As we speak our new words, she teaches us to learn to hope again, to be born in and to be borne on a slender hope, that in the end we may sing a new song.

We are not there yet, in that new epoch, singing that new song. But as we begin to understand the abuse of women—and understanding we begin to act, and acting we begin to understand—we gather strength and courage and the capabilities to transform our situation. As we gather in the resources of a whole ministry—resources of theology, of action, of institution-building—in cooperation with the women's movement, we may yet, God willing, live in that day.

And she *is* willing.

Rebecca T. Alpert

---

27 In God's Image:
Coming to Terms with Leviticus

Joan and Leslie have been lovers for the past five years. This year, they decided to go home for the Jewish holidays to Joan's family in upstate New York. It was an important milestone. Joan's parents had become more comfortable with their daughter's lesbian lifestyle and lover; this would be a way of acknowledging the growth in the relationships among Leslie, Joan, her parents, and her younger brother.

Joan's family is deeply involved in their local Conservative synagogue, and it was truly an act of courage for all of them to go to Kol Nidre services together. Joan was excited—proud of her family and eager to reenter the Jewish life she had left behind. Leslie was scared, but interested in learning more about involvement in the Jewish community. Although Leslie's parents are Jewish, she was raised without religious training.

Yom Kippur evening turned out to be a good experience. The congregants were friendly and welcoming to Joan and her "friend." Religiously, too, the women were moved by the powerful experience of communal prayer. They decided that night to spend the entire next day in shul, continuing their fasting and waiting for the stirring blast of the *shofar* to bring an end to the day.

All went well until the afternoon service. The rabbi explained that for the Torah portion, they would be reading from the book of Leviticus, chapter 18, a description of forbidden sexual practices. Why read that on the holiest day of the year? No explanation was offered. As the Torah was read, Joan and Leslie followed along in the translation until they read the words: "Do not lie with a male as one lies with a woman; it is an abomination."[1]

Joan and Leslie froze, recognizing the meaning for them as lesbians, even though

From *Twice Blessed: On Being Lesbian or Gay and Jewish.* Edited by Christie Balka and Andrew Rose (Boston: Beacon Press), pp. 61–70. © 1989 by Christie Balka and Andrew Rose. Reprinted by permission of Beacon Press, Boston.

the language refers only to men. They looked at one another, disappointment spreading across Joan's face while a tear formed in the corner of Leslie's eye, as if to say, "This place is really not for us, after all."

Three times a year, on Yom Kippur afternoon and then twice during the annual cycle of Torah readings, every year for the past 2,500 years, Jews around the world have listened to the public reading of the words of Leviticus declaring a sexual act between two men "an abomination." When the prohibition is read from Leviticus 20, during the third yearly reading, it is declared not only an abomination, but also a capital crime.

What could be more profoundly alienating than to know that the most sacred text of your people, read aloud on the holiest day of the year, calls that which is central to your life an abomination? What could be more terrifying than to know that what for you is a sacred loving act was considered by your ancestors to be punishable by death?

Coming to terms with Leviticus may be the greatest single struggle facing gay men and lesbians seeking to find a religious home within the Jewish community. Before we examine strategies for all of us to cope with this dilemma, we must understand the power and authority of this text: What is Leviticus, and why is it so important?

Leviticus is the third book of the Pentateuch, the five books of Moses. These books comprise the story of the birth of our people and the beginnings of the Jewish legal system. Traditionally, they are understood as revelation—God's words, written down by Moses, God's prophet, on Mt. Sinai. Thus, these words are considered not only a record of our past, but God's explanation of God's will for the people of Israel as well. Laws codified in these books are the ultimate source of authority and are the starting point for the later development of Jewish civilization. According to strict interpretation of Jewish law, no law stated in the Torah can ever be nullified or abrogated.

Beyond its implications for the Jewish legal system, the Torah has deep symbolic power. It is preserved on a handwritten parchment scroll. It is kept in the ark, a sacred space at the front or center of every synagogue, under a flame that burns perpetually. It is adorned with a special cover and ornaments. It is removed from the ark with great pageantry to be chanted aloud three times weekly. The public reading of Torah is the central event of the Sabbath morning service. To be called to the Torah to recite the blessing for reading from the scroll is a great honor. Blessing and reading from the Torah forms the central experience of the bar/bat mitzvah ceremony. (Imagine, if you will, the adolescent who thinks he or she might be gay having to read from Leviticus 18 or 20 at the rite of passage!)

Clearly, the words of the Torah cannot be dismissed lightly, nor would we wish them to be. The Torah contains concepts that are vital to us: that we should love our neighbors as ourselves and deal respectfully with the stranger, the poor, and the lonely in society. The Torah instructs us to all see ourselves as having been created in God's image, and therefore as the bearers of holiness in the world. It also contains wonderful and challenging stories of the world's beginnings and our people's journey from slavery to freedom. Those of us who choose to remain identified with the Jewish tradition do so in part because of the foundation laid by Torah. We cannot simply excise what we do not like; it is our heritage and the primary text of our people. Yet a piercing question arises and reverberates through our lives: How do we live as Jews when the same text that tells us we were created in God's image also tells us that our sacred loving acts are punishable by death by decree of that same God?

This question may impel us to deny the power of Leviticus, but in truth we cannot. For all of us involved in any way in Jewish life, this text has authority. It has authority in that it is used by others to support the belief that homosexuality is wrong. (Of course, this is true not only for Jews. Leviticus is quoted by right-wing Christian religious groups to the same end.) And whether we ourselves consciously accept the authority of the text or not, we would be foolish to think that it does not affect us deeply, sometimes in subtle or insidious ways. For those of us who are lesbian or gay, it can undermine our pride in ourselves, feeding our own homophobia as well as that of others.

Let me suggest, then, three methods of coming to terms with Leviticus. We can, as did our ancestors, interpret the text to enable us to function with it on its own terms. We can, like biblical scholars, treat the text as a historical record and draw conclusions based on the way it functions in a given context. Or we can encounter the text directly with our emotions and our self-knowledge, allowing it to move us to anger, and then beyond anger, to action.

Each method comes to terms with the text's authority in a different way. Through interpreting the text we stay within the system and redirect it. Through historical reasoning we place limits on the text's authority by examining it with the lens of another system. Through encountering the text emotionally, we confront it and therefore use it as an instrument of transformation.

The Interpretive Method

Midrash—the process of making commentary to interpret the text—is a vital aspect of attempts throughout Jewish history to make the Bible come alive. Throughout the generations, interpreters have sought to make the text accessible to their contemporaries who may not understand its original meaning. The text may be ambiguous, unclear, or redundant. A word or custom may be unfamiliar and need explanation. One part of the text may contradict another part, and a resolution of the conflict is necessary. The same word or phrase may be repeated, seemingly without purpose, and commentators have sought to explain these repetitions by assigning different meanings to them. Finally, there are cases in which the grammar or syntax is unusual and lends itself to providing a new interpretation.

While interpretive methods are legitimate and widely practiced, it should be noted that many would claim that the text is not really in need of interpretation. It stands on its own as God's word.

With this understanding as our background, let us look at how Leviticus 18:22 and 20:13 have been interpreted by traditional Jewish commentators. We find that this prohibition is mentioned less often than others in the Torah. Some have assumed that this lack of discussion is due to the fact that homosexuality was not common among Jews. Suffice it to say that we can only speculate about the extent of homosexual practice, but we can say with certainty that the subject was not considered problematic enough to require extensive public discussion. For whatever reason, to be sure, homosexuality was not a visible issue in the Jewish world until contemporary times.

Most of the interpretations of Leviticus 18:22 hinge on an unclear word—*to'evah*—which is generally translated as "abomination." In fact, the meaning of this word is obscure. Therefore, interpreters have taken the opportunity to translate it in ways that explain the prohibition. After all, the text never tells us why lying with a man is *to'evah*, but only that it is.

What might *to'evah* mean? According to the second-century commentator Bar Kapparah, it means "*to'eh ata ba*—you go astray because of it" (see Babylonian Talmud, Nedarim 51b). This play on words has been taken to mean that it is not intrinsically an evil to engage in homosexual acts, but rather that they have negative consequences. Bar Kapparah did not spell out those negative consequences—rather, it was left to later commentators to interpret his interpretation.

Certain medieval texts suggest that one is being led astray from the main function of sexual behavior, namely procreation. Some Rabbinic commentators assume that to go astray means to abandon your wife and to disrupt family life. This interpretation is reinforced by medieval commentator Saadiah Gaon's general pronouncement that the Bible's moral legislation is directed at preserving the structure of the family (*Emunot ve-Deot* 3:1). Finally, modern commentator R. Baruch haLevi Epstein, author of the commentary *Torah Temimah*, suggests that going astray means not following the anatomically appropriate manner of sexual union.[2]

The most well-known biblical commentator, Rashi, who lived in eleventh-century France, had but one comment on the subject. Wanting to make the text clearer to his readers, he explained rather graphically the meaning of the phrase, "as with a woman": "He enters as the painting stick is inserted in the tube."

In the contemporary era, traditional Jews have had to come to terms with the fact that gay men and lesbians have made ourselves a presence in the Jewish community. The most serious and thorough traditional response on the subject has been made by Norman Lamm.[3] Lamm affirms the text as it is simply understood—a strong prohibition against homosexuality. While he claims interpretation to be unnecessary to explain the text, in fact, he makes an interpretation of his own of the meaning of *to'evah*: "The very variety of interpretations of *to'evah* points to a far more fundamental meaning, namely, that an act characterized as an abomination is prima facie disgusting and cannot be further defined or explained."[4] While the term *to'evah* is not a problem for Lamm, the fact that this is considered a capital crime is at least distressing. But since capital punishment was one of the things the rabbis interpreted out of existence by making it impossible to convict someone of a capital crime, Lamm does oppose penalizing homosexual behavior.

It is not only Orthodox Jews who assert interpretations to substantiate their anti-homosexual points of view. Note the following response by the well-known Reform rabbi, Solomon Freehof: "In Scripture (Leviticus 18:22) homosexuality is considered to be an 'abomination.' So too in Leviticus 20:13. If Scripture calls it an abomination, it means that it is more than a violation of a mere legal enactment, it reveals a deep-rooted ethical attitude."[5]

So far, we have examined traditional interpretations of the text. These interpretations either support the plain meaning of the text, explain difficult or unclear words in the verse, or use the text to create legal pronouncements on unrelated subjects.

Yet the interpretive method is also used to alter the meaning of other biblical verses, sometimes even contravening the original meaning. This fact creates an opportunity among contemporary commentators to alter or expand the meaning of our verse.

Contemporary commentators in the first instance see a contradiction between Leviticus 18:22 and the idea as stated in Genesis that we were all created in God's image. This contradiction must be resolved. We must assume that those of us who were created lesbian and gay are also in God's image, and that acts central to our identity cannot therefore be an abomination.[6]

In another interpretation, it is pointed out that the text refers only to certain sexual acts, not to same-sex love relationships. Therefore, the text is not relevant to a style of life and love and family of which it was ignorant.

It has often been pointed out that lesbians are not included in the Leviticus prohibition. This fact has led to a variety of interpretations: that women's sexual activities don't matter, that lesbian activity is acceptable, or that the absence of this rule makes the ruling against gay men invalid.

Perhaps the text is addressing the issue of sexual experimentation. According to this interpretation, straight men who are considering a "fling" and in the process hurting their current partner should refrain from doing so.

Another contemporary commentator, Arthur Waskow, has suggested that the text is only trying to tell us not to make love to a male as if he were a female—that is to say, gay love and straight love are indeed different.[7] One should not be confused with the other. (The acts do not evoke the same feelings or fulfill the same commandments.)

To some readers, this whole process of textual interpretation may seem irrational and unnecessary, and even amusing. Why go to the trouble to validate this text? Why play by these rules? There are many gay and lesbian Jews who feel compelled by the absolute authority and immutability of the Torah text. For them this is the only solution that will enable them to affirm both their gay and Jewish selves, and help them to feel whole. And for all of us, as noted earlier, the traditional interpretations affect us in subtle and destructive ways. It is for these reasons that more creative work needs to take place in the area of interpreting the text.

Biblical Criticism

A little more than one hundred years ago, Jewish and Christian thinkers began to study the Bible as a document created by human hands. The early biblical critics' questioning of divine authorship is viewed as commonplace today, but in their times their views were heretical.

Biblical scholars sought to place the Bible in its context in the Ancient Near East. They explained much of what was unclear in the biblical text by reference to practices in other cultures. They explained redundancies as the result of compilation of documents by multiple authors. They introduced the concept of evolution and attempted to date biblical materials. Biblical critics developed sensitivity to the nuances of the text, developing concerns about linguistic and literary patterns.

The viewpoint of biblical criticism enables us to look at our verse in its historical, linguistic, and cultural context and understand it in a new, more objective light. Of course, we must bear in mind that complete objectivity is unattainable. Even looking at the text from outside, we are bound by our own cultural norms and expectations. In truth, we are looking at our verse through another kind of lens. While we think the approach of biblical criticism is a valid way to look at the text, we do not think that we have found in this method a way of obtaining "the truth."

From this perspective we certainly see the simple meaning of the text—that in biblical times, homosexual acts were forbidden. Yet this method does not require that we affirm the truth of that reality for today. We can, as biblical critics, acknowledge the need for a reexamination of biblical norms. (After all, the Bible also countenanced other things we no longer accept as moral—slavery and a second-class status for women and people with disabilities, for example.)

Furthermore, we can explain why homosexual acts were considered to'evah from a different perspective, by examining parallel linguistic uses of the word. We discover that to'evah is actually a technical term used to refer to a forbidden idolatrous act. From this information, we may conclude that the references in Leviticus are specific to cultic practices of homosexuality, and not sexual relationships as we know them today. This explanation is supported by reference to the other legal condemnation of homosexuality in Deuteronomy, which directly interdicts homosexual practices related to cultic worship.

Second, we understand that much of the Bible is an effort to make the separations between acts considered holy and those considered profane, to create an ordered perception of the universe. Accordingly, the sexual prohibitions described fit into the larger category of laws about kosher foods, the separation of the sexes and their clothing, and the prohibitions against plowing with two types of animals and of mixing certain types of fabric. We can reexamine, today, which of these separations are still meaningful. Looking at the text from the outside also enables us to explain the repetition of the law as being derived from two different sources, written at different times. So the death penalty may have been applied at one period in biblical history, but not at another time.

Through this approach, we are able to step back from the text and ask questions about how the text functioned. We can see from some of the suggestions above that the text functioned to keep order and define it and to separate the Israelite people from the practices of their neighbors. This gives us the opportunity to conclude that values may be disengaged from specific laws, and that there may be other means of perpetuating values if we indeed still share them today. Further, if we are not bound by the assumptions of divine authorship, we can assert that while the prohibition against homosexual acts functioned in its time, it is no longer appropriate to our ethical sensibilities today.

Encountering the Text

There is one last approach for coping with Leviticus. In this method, we confront the text directly. We do not look to the midrashist or the scholar to interpret the text for us. Rather we face the text in its immediacy—seeking its meaning in our lives, coming to terms with all that implies, and then going beyond it.

To face the simple meaning of Leviticus is to acknowledge the source of much of lesbian and gay oppression. The Bible does tell us that sexual acts between people of the same sex are *to'evah*—an abomination—and that they are punishable by death. And we know very well that this text has given generations the permission to find those of us who are lesbian or gay disgusting, to use Norman Lamm's word; to hate us; and even to do violence against us.

In our encounter with Leviticus, we experience the pain and terror and anger that this statement arouses in us. We imagine the untold damage done to generations of men, women, and children who experienced same-sex feelings and were forced to cloak or repress them. We reflect on those who acted on those feelings and were forced to feel shame and guilt and to fear for their lives. We remember how we felt when we first heard those words and knew their holy source. And we get angry—at the power these words have had over our lives, at the pain we have experienced in no small part because of these words.

Then, if we can, we grow beyond the rage. We begin to see these words as tools with which to educate people about the deep-rooted history of lesbian and gay oppression. We begin to use these very words to begin to break down the silence that surrounds us.

We proclaim the two consecutive weeks in the spring during which these words are read (*Parshat Ahare Mot* and *Parshat Kedoshim*) as Jewish Lesbian and Gay Awareness Weeks. During this time we urge that Torah study sessions be held in every synagogue to open the discussion of the role of gay and lesbian Jews in the community. Those of us who can take the risks of visibility must make ourselves available to tell our stories—of our alienation from the community, and of our desire to return. Each of us can tell the story of what this prohibition has meant in our lives—how we have struggled with it, and where we are on the road to resolution. And we expect to be listened to, with full attention and respect, as we do so.

In this way, we can transform Torah from a stumbling block to an entry path. We become more honest with ourselves and with our community about the barriers to our involvement, about our need for separate places to worship, and about our demand to be accepted as an integral part of Jewish life.

Whether we try interpreting, criticizing, or confronting, there are no easy answers for coming to terms with Leviticus. But we cannot desist from the challenge of finding creative solutions to deal with this dimension of our oppression. To be whole as Jewish lesbians and gay men we must acknowledge with what great difficulty those pieces of our lives fit together. But we must also demand—of ourselves and of our community—that those pieces be made to fit.

We marvel at the fact that words written thousands of years ago still have so much power to affect our lives. Words are powerful. Now it is up to us to make the words that will transform our lives and give new meaning to our existence as gay and lesbian Jews.

Notes

1. Although the Leviticus text specifically refers to relationships between men, lesbians experience the power of this prohibition in reference to themselves as well.

2. I am indebted to Norman Lamm's essay, "Judaism and the Modern Attitude towards Homosexuality," *Encyclopedia Judaica Yearbook* (1974), pp. 194–205, for the citations of these interpretations.

3. Ibid. Lamm gives an extensive presentation of all traditional discussion of the subject of homosexuality, not only that which pertains to Leviticus.

4. Ibid., p. 198.

5. "Judaism and Homosexuality: A Response," *Central Conference of American Rabbis Journal* (Summer 1973), p. 31.

6. I am indebted to the writings of Rabbi Hershel Matt (of blessed memory) for this interpretation.

7. Waskow suggested this interpretation in a private conversation.

John J. McNeill

28   Homosexuality:
Challenging the Church to Grow

It has been more than ten years since I wrote *The Church and the Homosexual* (Sheed Andrews & McMeel, 1976). I wrote the book out of love for and loyalty to the Christian tradition in general and the Roman Catholic Church in particular, and out of a desire to support the church's moral authority. I felt what I had to do as a trained professional moral theologian was to play the role of a critical lover and loving critic and try to help the church realize a viable ethic concerning homosexuality. I also wrote it out of love for and loyalty to the homosexual community.

Certainly one of the major motivating factors behind my work for the past 20 years—in research, writing and psychotherapy, and in the pastoral activities of preaching, leading retreats and giving lectures and workshops to gay people—is the fact that I myself am a homosexual. It was with great struggle and pain that I gradually learned to accept that essential aspect of myself and learned to live with it with a certain degree of peace, joy and even pride. I have wanted to share that grace with as many people as possible. I agree with Meister Eckardt: "The fruitfulness of a gift is the only true way to show gratitude for the gift."

Most importantly, I wrote *The Church and the Homosexual* because of my increasing awareness of the enormous amount of unjust suffering in the Christian gay community. I observed that many, if not most, lesbian women and homosexual men felt caught in a dilemma: to accept themselves and to affirm their sexuality, they believed that they must leave the church and even give up their faith; and to affirm their Christian faith, they felt that they had to repress and deny their sexuality and lead a life devoid of any sexual intimacy. The evidence was clear to me that both solutions led to an unhappy and unhealthy life. I was convinced that what is bad psychologically has to be bad theologically and that, inversely, whatever is good theologically is cer-

Originally published in *Christian Century* (March 11, 1987), 242–246. Copyright 1987 Christian Century Foundation. Reprinted by permission from the March 11, 1987, issue of the *Christian Century*.

tainly good psychologically. For as St. Irenaeus claimed, "The glory of God are humans fully alive."

In *The Church and the Homosexual* I sought to overturn three traditional stances taken by the Christian community regarding lesbian and homosexual relationships. I opposed, first of all, the view that God intends all human beings to be heterosexual, and that therefore a failure to be heterosexual represents a deviation from God's creative plan—a deviation that demands an explanation usually given in terms of sin or, more recently, in terms of sickness. According to this view, those who find themselves to be homosexual must change their orientation through prayer and counseling or, failing that, live totally chaste and sexually loveless lives. This is the position held in the Vatican letter "On the Pastoral Care of Homosexual Persons" issued last October [1986] to all the bishops of the world. This letter was deemed necessary to offset "deceitful propaganda" coming from gay Christian groups challenging the church's tradition and its interpretation of Scripture. According to this position, sexual fulfillment is exclusively the right of the heterosexual.

I proposed instead that God so created humans that they develop with a great variety of both gender identities and sexual-object choices. Consequently, the attempt to force humans into narrow heterosexist categories of what it means to be a man or a woman can destroy the great riches and variety of God's creation. Always and everywhere a certain percentage of men and women develop as homosexuals or lesbians. They should be considered as part of God's creative plan. Their sexual orientation has no necessary connection with sin, sickness or failure; rather, it is a gift from God to be accepted and lived out with gratitude. God does not despise anything that God created.

It should be stressed here, in opposition to certain current views, that human beings do not choose their sexual orientation; they discover it as something given. To pray for a change in sexual orientation is about as meaningful as to pray for a change from blue eyes to brown. Furthermore, there is no healthy way to reverse or change sexual orientation once it is established. The claim of certain groups to be able to change homosexuals into heterosexuals has been shown to be spurious and frequently based on homophobia (cf. Ralph Blair's pamphlet "Ex-Gay" [HCCC Inc., 1982]). The usual technique used to bring about this pseudo-change involves helping gay persons internalize self-hatred, an approach that frequently causes great psychological harm and suffering. The Christian communities that make use of this sort of ministry usually do so to avoid any challenge to their traditional attitude and to avoid any dialogue with self-accepting gays and truly professional psychotherapists. (The psychotherapists whom these churches frequently cite are generally very conservative and homophobic in their orientation.) The real choice that faces lesbians and homosexuals is not between heterosexuality and homosexuality but between a homosexual relationship or no relational intimacy whatsoever.

Other churches have confined their official ministries to helping gay people live out celibate lives. According to Christian tradition, celibacy is a special gift of God given to a certain few for the sake of the kingdom. The occasional homosexual who receives this gift is, indeed, blessed. Clergy choose a celibate lifestyle voluntarily, lay-people are given no choice; they are told they must live celibate lives. But there is no reason to believe that God grants this gift to everyone who is lesbian or homosexual. On the contrary, empirical studies have shown the vast majority of gay people who have attempted a celibate lifestyle end up acting out their sexual needs in promiscuous and self-destructive ways. Every human being has a God-given right to sexual love and intimacy. Anyone who would deny this right to any individual must prove without a doubt the grounds for this denial. The healthy and holy Christian response to a homosexual orientation is to learn to accept it and live it out in a way that is consonant with Christian values.

The second thesis of my book was that homosexuals, rather than being somehow a menace to the values of society and the family, as Christians have tended to assume, have, as a part of God's creative plan, special gifts and qualities and a very positive contribution to make to the development of society (cf. also my article "Homosexuality, Lesbianism, and the Future: The Creative Role of the Gay Community in Building a More Humane Society," in A *Challenge to Love: Gay and Lesbian Catholics in the Church*, edited by Robert Nugent [Crossroad, 1984]). Indeed, if lesbians and homosexuals were to disappear, the further development of society toward greater humanness could be seriously endangered. Consequently, I am convinced that there is a special providence in the emergence of visible gay communities within the Christian churches at this point in history.

The third thesis of my book was perhaps the most controversial. The traditional position has been that since every homosexual act is sinful and contrary to God's plan, the love that exists between gay people is a sinful love which alienates the lovers from God. I argued that the love between two lesbians or two homosexuals, assuming that it is a constructive human love, is not sinful nor does it alienate the lovers from God's plan, but can be a holy love, mediating God's presence in the human community as effectively as heterosexual love.

I fully appreciated how controversial my arguments were. But I pointed out that there was new evidence from biblical studies and from various empirical studies in the human sciences, especially psychology and sociology—that completely undermined the traditional understanding of homosexuality as a chosen and changeable state. Examples of recent psychological data come from new insights into psychosexual development, e.g., (a) one has no choice about sexual orientation; (b) the only healthy reaction to being homosexual is to accept it. And, above all else, there was new evidence coming from the collective experience of lesbians and homosexuals who as committed Christians were seeking to live their lives in conformity with Christian faith and Christian values. All this evidence should give every Christian community serious reason to reconsider its understanding of homosexuality.

I hoped that my book would open up a serious moral debate in the churches concerning homosexuality. But in ten years no such debate has taken place. My own church's response was to try to silence the messenger rather then debate the message. One year after my book's publication, the Vatican Congregation for the Doctrine of the Faith ordered me to be silent on the issue of homosexuality and sexual ethics, forbidding me to publish anything further in the field. For nine years I obeyed that order to be silent. However, the recent letter on pastoral care of homosexuals (already referred to), as well as the demand by the Vatican that ethicist Charles Curran retract his position on homosexuality and other sexual moral issues, or relinquish his position as a Catholic theologian, and its more recent order to me that I give up all ministry to homosexual persons, have convinced me that I can no longer in conscience remain silent.

It is the AIDS crisis that above all else makes it clear that churches do not have the luxury of time in dealing with homosexuality. In the U.S. alone as of February 9, [1987] there had already been 30,632 recorded cases of AIDS and 17,542 recorded fatalities, a majority of them gay men. It is predicted that in the next decade there may be as many as 200,000 victims. I am convinced that the churches will not respond properly to this crisis until they resolve the underlying moral issues. The Catholic Church in its recent pastoral letter has taken a dogmatic stance, allowing no room for debate or dialogue. But my ultimate religious obedience must be to truth, justice and the will of God as revealed in the sufferings of the Christian gay community. Therefore, with the publication of this article, I am making my first detailed public statement in ten years on the issue of homosexuality.

I find the absence of a serious moral debate within American churches on homosexuality truly puzzling. Robert Bellah and his associates throw some general light on this absence in their recent sociological study of American culture, *Habits of the Heart: Individualism and Commitment in American Life* (Harper & Row, 1985). They point out that the liberal middle class has a therapeutic mentality which is uncomfortable with moral argument. Those who share the therapeutic attitude embrace pluralism and the uniqueness of the individual, and conclude that there is no common moral ground and no publicly relevant morality. They tend to see moral debate as leading inevitably to irresolvable conflict or coercion.

Bellah and his co-authors acknowledge that the therapeutic critique of traditional morality is frequently legitimate. "Where standards of right and wrong are asserted with dogmatic certainty and are not open to discussion, and, even worse, where these standards merely express the interests of the stronger party in a relationship while clothing those interests in moralistic language, then that criticism is indeed justified" (p. 140). Most gay people share this distrust of morality. Having been the victims of moralistic condemnation and control, they eagerly adopt the therapeutic live-and-let-live stance.

The mainline Protestant churches, too, share the therapeutic mentality. In place of the moral question, Is this right or wrong? they pose the therapeutic question, Is this going to work? The liberal churches tend to assert individual autonomy and freedom, and the right to do your own thing. However, this therapeutic attitude is usually accompanied by an institutional search for compromise on moral issues. For example, some churches, in the face of psychological evidence that sexual orientation is not freely chosen, have begun to distinguish between homosexual orientation—

which, they agree, is not morally culpable—and homosexual activity which is always morally wrong insofar as it is freely chosen. This compromise is intrinsically unstable. It reminds me of the nursery ditty: "Mother may I go out to swim?" "Yes, my darling daughter. Hang your clothes on the hickory bush, but don't go near the water!"

Only a sadistic God would create hundreds of thousands of humans to be inherently homosexual and then deny them the right to sexual intimacy. I, for one, would prefer to believe that the church is wrong about homosexual activity than that this sadistic, superego God has any true relation to the God of love revealed by Jesus.

Conservative and fundamentalist churches, for their part, also do not engage in moral debate. They feel they have a clear and direct revelation of God's will concerning homosexuality, and they vigorously condemn it on the basis of biblical fundamentalism and a conservative acceptance of certain cultural mores, especially in the sexual realm (such as the dominance of men over women).

Christians opposed to gay rights frequently cite Genesis 19, the story of Sodom. The history of the interpretation of this passage displays how prejudice and homophobia have distorted the message of Scripture. Throughout the Old and New Testaments, the sin of Sodom was never understood as homosexuality. Rather, that sin was understood as selfishness, pride, neglect of the poor and inhospitality to strangers. (In the desert context of these passages, inhospitality to a stranger meant certain death.) For example, Ezekiel writes, "Behold, this was the sin of your sister Sodom: she and her daughters lived in pride, plenty and thoughtless ease; they supported not the poor and the needy; they grew haughty and committed abominations [sexual orgies to bring fertility] before me. So I swept them away. . . ." (16:49–50). And every time Jesus refers to Sodom he identifies the sin of that city as inhospitality to strangers. For example, in Luke, Jesus says of those towns that were inhospitable to disciples: "I tell you on that day Sodom will fare better than that town" (10:12).

In *The Church and the Homosexual* I trace the interesting historical process by which the biblical condemnation of inhospitality was transformed into a condemnation of homosexuality. Here is one of the supreme ironies of history: for thousands of years in the Christian West, homosexuals have been the victims of inhospitable treatment—the true crime of Sodom—in the name of a mistaken understanding of Sodom's crime. Inhospitality, the crime that cries out to God for vengeance, has been and continues to be repeated every day. Who in our midst lives in pride and plenty and thoughtless ease, neglecting the poor, being inhospitable to refugees and persecuting those who, like Lot, offer them sanctuary? They indeed are the sodomites!

The absence of serious moral debate leaves conservative and even reactionary moral forces as the only voice on the subject of homosexuality. When a crisis comes, such as when gays fall ill with AIDS, they can easily be victimized by traditional homophobia disguised as moral judgment and, as a result, fall back into self-condemnation and self-hatred. As noted, self-hatred and internalized homophobia undermine gay relationships and tempt gay people to act out sexual needs in self-destructive ways. In the age of AIDS, only two choices are really open to Christian gay people in conformity with Christian values: abstaining from all sexual activity—a response which the majority find impossible—or entering a monogamous relationship. However, to have a stable, healthy relationship, one needs to have a healthy self-love and self-acceptance, which is psychologically possible only when one can accept one's sexuality as morally good and, in a Christian context, compatible with God's love.

A striking example of the negative result of the absence of an open debate on the moral meaning of homosexuality is the recent U.S. Supreme Court decision upholding the rights of states to outlaw sodomy. In the majority opinion, Justice Byron White argued that the right to privacy does not extend to same-gender sexual activity, even when confined to the home. He accepted the state of Georgia's argument that sodomy laws can be justified by the need to protect morality. Chief Justice Warren Burger concurred with Justice White that "to establish a fundamental right to homosexual sodomy would be to cast aside millennia of moral teaching."

Here is an example of traditional homophobia disguised as moral judgment and the will of God. Even the court's dissenting opinion, expressed by Justice Harry Blackmun, entirely avoids the moral issue. "That certain, but by no means all, religious groups condemn the behavior at issue," wrote Blackmun, "gives the state no license to impose [its] judgment on the entire citizenry. The legitimacy of legislation depends instead on whether the state can advance some justification for its law beyond its conformity to religious doctrine." Blackmun's position to the law is based on the right to "the most comprehensive of rights and the most valued by civilized men, [namely] the right to be left alone."

Both gay people and the liberal churches are wrong to steer clear of moral debate, or to think that moral standards are, as described in *Habits of the Heart*, "inherently authoritarian and in the service of domination." On the contrary, there are standards of right and wrong within Christian tradition concerning human sexuality, based in human nature and biblical revelation which are acceptable to homosexual and heterosexuals alike, and which can form the moral basis of public policy.

In light of the gay Christian experience, however, two fundamental issues of sexual morality must be reexamined. The first issue is what makes a sexual act fully human; the second is the biblical understanding of homosexual acts.

Christian tradition has always emphasized that human sexuality has two primary functions—it provides an experience of loving intimacy ("It is not good that a human be alone. Every human has need of a companion" [Gen. 2:18]); and it is the means of procreation. What is unique to human sexuality is the fusion that God has made of biological sexuality with the uniquely human vocation to, and capacity for, love.

The debate over birth control some years ago led liberal churches to conclude that the relational aspect of sexuality has primacy and, when appropriate, can be separated from the procreational aspect. Even the Catholic Church acknowledged the value of heterosexual activity exclusively as an expression of love when it approved the rhythm method of birth control. At that moment, if the church had been logical and free of homophobia, it would have re-examined the value of homosexual activity as an expression of human love and companionship.

What does Scripture have to say about homosexuality? The Christian community now possesses for the first time some excellent scholarly works on the treatment of homosexuality in Scripture, such as Robin Scroggs's *The New Testament and Homosexuality* (Fortress, 1984) and George Edwards's *Gay/Lesbian Liberation: A Biblical Perspective* (Pilgrim, 1984). We also have an excellent study of the development of Christian tradition regarding homosexuality: John Boswell's *Christianity, Social Tolerance, and Homosexuality: Gay People in Western Europe from the Beginning of the Christian Era to the Fourteenth Century* (University of Chicago Press, 1980). And there are some very good theological reflections on human sexuality in the light of Christian revelation; see James Nelson's, *Embodiment: An Approach to Sexuality and Christian Theology* (Pilgrim, 1978) and *Between Two Gardens: Reflections on Sexuality and Religious Experience* (Pilgrim, 1983).

These scholars conclude that nowhere in Scripture is there a clear condemnation of a loving sexual relationship between two gay persons. Homosexuality is never mentioned in the Four Gospels' accounts of the ministry of Jesus—a silence that would be inexplicable if this were the "most heinous crime," as tradition claims. Scriptural authors never deal with homosexual orientation, and when they do treat homosexual activity, they never do so in the context of a loving relationship. They presuppose that they are dealing with lustful activity freely chosen by heterosexuals (as in Romans 1), or they deal with a humanly destructive activity in the context of idolatry, prostitution, promiscuity, violent rape, seduction of children or violation of guests' rights.

There can be no valid moral debate on these issues that does not include lesbian and gay people as full participants. The Holy Spirit has something to say to the churches in and through the experience of lesbian and homosexual Christians. A truly extraordinary witness to the kind of full human love that can exist between two gay persons is being manifested daily by AIDS victims and their lovers and friends. The exceptional fidelity, self-sacrifice and affection, as well as the pain, grief and sorrow and the deep spiritual response to the suffering and bereavement that is being expressed, is a sign to the churches of the presence of the Spirit of love in these relationships. "See how they love one another!"

The recent paper produced by Lutherans Concerned, "A Call for Dialogue: Gay and Lesbian Christians and the Ministry of the Lutheran Church," is an example of the eloquent theological reflections that are coming from gay Christians. Similar statements have been made by the Catholic gay group, Dignity; the Episcopal group, Integrity; the Methodist group, Metropolitan Community Church; Evangelicals Concerned; and others.

Lutherans Concerned summarizes its theological reflection with the following observation: "Indeed, gay and lesbian Christians, like any other Christians who have had deep encounters with the word of the Gospel, are able to see the word speaking directly and profoundly to their own experience. Lesbians and gay men will be bold enough to offer new insight into the Gospel to the whole community of Christ. They will claim the biblical word for themselves, in the experience of hoping and believing in the Gospel, of trusting in one's own conscience, even in the face of opposition. . . . Ultimately, lesbian and gay people within the church will make a great contribution to construction of relational ethics and to evangelical outreach, which we pray will draw many others who are estranged, alienated or unloved, to Jesus Christ, to the household of faith, and into the reconciliation which has begun."

All in all, this is a great moment to be gay and Christian. This is the age when the Holy Spirit is fulfilling the promise made in Isaiah (56:2–8) that after the Messiah comes and the new covenant is established, those who are sexually different, who were formerly excluded from the community of God, will have a special place in house of the Lord and "an everlasting name which shall not be cut off." The fulfillment of this prophecy was foreshadowed when the Holy Spirit led the apostle Philip to encounter the eunuch, who was reading Isaiah (Acts 8:26–40). The author of Acts intended to show how under the new covenant the church, led by the Holy Spirit, would reach out to include all those who were excluded by the Old Testament's procreational covenant. The eunuch symbolizes all those excluded from the Old Testament community because they were sexually different. The eunuch believed in Christ as the Messiah, was baptized, received the Spirit and went off "full of joy."

"My house," God says through Isaiah, "shall be called a house of prayer for all people." The gay Christian movement is continuing this initiative of the Holy Spirit, offering the Christian churches a challenge and an opportunity to grow to the full stature of the human family.

Rosemary Radford Ruether

29 Searching Scripture for a Model of the Family

Conservative American Christians are very concerned about the need to restore what they say is the biblical view of the family: a male-dominated nuclear family consisting of a working husband, a nonworking wife who is a full-time mother, and several dependent children. It is as if the Bible endorses a version of the late Victorian, Anglo-Saxon patriarchal family as the model of family life proposed in the Scriptures. It is taken for granted that this Victorian ideal of the patriarchal nuclear family was created in the Garden of Eden and remained static until a recent, and unhappy, period in the 20th century when it began to be "undermined" by feminists, gay people, and delinquent children. Since conservative rhetoric about the "biblical view of the family" lacks any sense of the socioeconomic history of the family over the past three to four thousand years, it is not necessary for its proponents to reflect upon the norm itself or the forces that are challenging it, but simply to restore what is presumed to have always been, as the expression of God's will.

In reality, in biblical times no such nuclear family existed. Rather, the Bible presents several different perspectives on the family, none of which readily corresponds to the modern nuclear family, a relatively recent development in history.

If by the biblical view of the family one means, for example, the sort of family envisioned in the earliest strata of the Old Testament, restoring it would mean restoring an entire tribal form of economics. Such a family, in fact, a clan or small tribe, consisted of several hundred people headed by a patriarch who was the clan sheik. His family consisted of several wives, as well as concubines, their children, his slaves, and their children, other relatives such as his mother, and friends, and hangers-on. His authority also extended over his married sons and his daughters-in-law, his sons' concubines and slaves and their children and married daughters and sons-in-law and

Originally published in *Conscience* (March/April 1984), 5(2):1, 3–6. Reprinted with permission of the author.

their dependents. Such a large clan unit was first based on desert nomadic shepherding, and later adapted itself to settled agricultural life.

Although dependent in legal matters, women of this Hebrew family were by no means shut up in a harem, nor did their role consist solely in child nurture and housekeeping. Rather, they were valued as economic workers who produced many of the goods consumed by the family. In the book of Proverbs, the "good wife" is praised, not for her good looks or her mothering qualities, but for her efficiency as the manager of this domestic industry. She is described as like "a merchant vessel who brings her goods from afar." She considers a field and buys it, and plants a vineyard from her own earnings. She manages a large household of servants who spin and weave the clothes worn by the family. The wife also sells the goods produced in her household to merchants and derives further income. She is clothed in fine linen and purple. Her arms are strong, and she is filled with dignity and strength so that she can laugh at the days ahead.

Nothing is said about her husband's activities, except that he is "known at the city gates where he takes his place with the elders of the land." The wife is, in effect, the primary income producer, whose work frees her husband for political activity. Such a woman was indeed a formidable personality, so much so that the book of Proverbs constructs a theological metaphor that compares her to God. She is like God's immanent wisdom which creates, rules, and reconciles the universe. Presumably when our contemporary, conservative Christians talk about restoring the biblical model of the family, they do not have in mind the polygamous slave-holding clan of the patriarchal narratives nor the powerful economic manager of the book of Proverbs.

When we turn to the New Testament, written over a far shorter period of time than the Hebrew Scriptures, the situation is no less complex. Many of the New Testament writings, particularly the Gospels and the historical Paul, were subversive toward the patriarchal family as it existed in Jewish and Greco-Roman cultures. In the Christianity reflected in these texts the church functioned as a countercultural community that claimed priority in the lives of its members and dissolved the primacy of commitment to the family. In order to follow Jesus, one must "hate," or put aside the primary commitment to one's mother and father, spouse and children.

In a story found in all three synoptic Gospels, the church, as the true family of Jesus' followers, is contrasted with the blood-related family and kinship group. In this story, Jesus' mother and brothers come to where he is preaching and demand to speak to him. But Jesus repudiates this claim of the kinship family upon him with the words:

> "Who are my mother and my brothers?" And looking around on those who sat about him, he said, "Here are my mother and my brothers! Whoever does the will of God is my brother and sister and mother." (Mk. 3:31–35; cf. Lk. 8:19–21 and Mt. 12:46–50)

Here the Christian community is seen as a new kind of family, a voluntary community gathered by personal faith, which stands in tension with the natural family or kinship group.

The Tension between Kingdoms

This tension between church and family continues in Paul. Paul does not demand that his followers remain unmarried, but he would prefer that all Christians remain as he is; namely, unmarried (I Cor. 7:7). For Paul, the appointed time of world history is drawing to a close and the Kingdom of God is at hand. Concern about the business of marriage and procreation, which are the affairs of the world, draws primary attention away from one's relationship to God. In the coming Kingdom all family relations will be dissolved, so they should not claim primacy in Christian concerns in the here and now. Paul is also concerned with the problems of households divided when one spouse becomes Christian while the other remains an unbeliever.

In both the Jewish and Greco-Roman worlds, it was axiomatic that the religion of the household was that of the head of the family. A family was not simply a social unit, but also a religious entity united around its household ancestral gods. The family religion, in turn, tied the household to the public order or the state. The public cult, rooted in the household gods of the tribes that came together to make the city or the nation, represented a joint household religion linking all the families together in one community. Therefore, for a person to depart from his or her family religion, the religion of ancestors and the nation, was to engage in an act of subversion toward the family and the public order. This was doubly heinous when dependents in the patriarchal family, a wife, daughter or son, or a slave, departed from the family cult and followed a different religion.

Christianity heightened this conflict since it did not allow its followers to be initiated into its cult and still follow in the old religion, as the mystery religions did. As an exclusive faith, Christianity declared other religions to be false and their gods mere idols or even demons. Such exclusivity was also found in Judaism, but, for the people of the Greco-Roman world, Judaism was the ancestral religion of a particular ethos, or nation. So its particularities could be tolerated within its own community, provided that it did not take the form of political rebellion against the Roman superstate. Christianity was different; it was both exclusive and universal. It had rejected its ethnic roots. The religion of no particular national group, it made its claims upon individuals regardless of family or nation. *This* concept of religion was inherently subversive, disrupting the order of both household and state.

It is important to see the close connection between the family and the state. We are familiar with the idea that Christianity was persecuted as a religion subversive to the state, although we tend to think of this as a mistake, since Christianity's claim was spiritual, not political. But we have failed to see the equally important fact that Christianity disrupted the family, because household and state were so closely linked in ancient society. To follow a religion contrary to that of the family—a religion, moreover, which declared the official religion to be false and demonic—was to strike at the heart of the social order of both the family and the state. It meant that wives could dissolve their allegiance to their households, children to their parents, slaves to their masters. These persons, in turn, no longer reverenced the state whose prosperity was founded on the favor of the ancestral gods. Thus we should not minimize the seriousness of the assault on society posed by early Christianity. Most Christians in the first and second century believed that this conflict between Christian faith and the family and state should be expressed boldly and unequivocally. The Christian should be ready to die, if necessary, rather than to concede the claims of the household and state gods.

In I Corinthians 7, Paul replies to a series of questions occasioned by this kind of ascetic and apocalyptic Christianity. Should Christians not yet married get married? Should those who are married abstain from sexual relations? Should the wife or husband married to an unbeliever separate and divorce? Paul is hard put to reply to these questions since, in fact, he shares much of the perspective of the militant ascetic and apocalyptic faith from which these questions come. But he is also concerned to modify the confrontation between this faith and the family. So he suggests a series of compromises, often tentatively and eschewing full claims of authority. It would be better for married Christians to abstain from sex, but, since this might lead to immorality by the nonbelieving partner, one should concede to the demands of sex, although also allowing for times of abstinence as well. Still, complete celibacy would be the ideal. If one is unmarried, better not to marry. If yoked to an unbeliever, stay with him or her, if the spouse consents. However, if the nonbelieving partner desires to separate, it is right to do so. A sister or brother is not bound to the nonbelieving spouse.

Post-Pauline Polarizations

Paul's efforts to find a middle ground between the claims of family and the claims of faith were not successful. Instead, we see in Christian literature of the next several generations a polarization between two positions, one exalting the claims of faith against family and state, and the other increasingly modifying the early radical vision of faith in order to accommodate the claims of the family and the state.

The first or radical position is reflected in the Gospel as well as in the martyr literature and the popular Acts of the Apostles that I have just mentioned. This literature, as we have seen, affirmed the primacy of the claims of the faith against those of the family and the state. The individual is absolved of his or her dependency and loyalty to these institutions in order to be faithful to a higher loyalty. The mother may deny the claims of an infant son upon her; a daughter may repudiate the demands of a father; a bride-to-be those of her parents and her husband. In some of these popular stories women who are already married are depicted as leaving their husbands in order to follow Christ.

Having departed from the family and the conventional social institutions, women, youth, and slaves join a new community of equals. The hierarchical ties of family and society are done away with. There is no more master and slave, no more dominance of male over female. The differences among ethnic groups, Jew and Greek, Greek and Scythian, are dissolved. All are one in a new family, a new humanity defined by Christ. Thus not only is the Roman matron, Perpetua, praised for rejecting her family and the state, but the social gap between her and her slave woman is overcome as well. The free-born Perpetua and the slave woman, Felicitas, became equals and sisters.

It is not accidental that many of these stories revolve around women, women as wives, as daughters, and as slaves. For the first four centuries of its existence Christianity moved up the social ladder primarily through women, children and slaves. Male heads of families were the last to be converted precisely because, for them, the claims of the ancestral religion of city and state were the religious base of their authority and public offices. Families in which all members were Christian began to develop in the lower ranks of society; in contrast, among the upper classes, even in the fourth century, it was common for the women and female children to be Christian, while the husband and older son remained pagan. Thus the conflict between the Christian faith and the pagan world continued to divide, not just Christians as a group from the outside world, but households as well, separating Christian wives, daughters, and slaves, from pagan heads of family. The pagan paranoia toward Christianity, which flared up in waves of persecution in these centuries, was rooted in this fear that Christianity subverted the social order, not just in its public political form, but at its most intimate base in the family.

Over against that radical Christianity, which affirmed and even exalted in this conflict, urging Christians to remain firm against state and family even to death, there arose a more conservative view which sought to modify the conflict. Not surprisingly, this more conservative view reflects the position of a growing established leadership associated with bishops and with a patriarchal conception of established order in both society and the church. One finds this conservative voice of the institutional church reflected in the apologists of the second century and also in the household codes of the post-Pauline strata of the New Testament.

The apologists seek to modify the confrontation with the state by lifting up an ideal of Christians as ideal private citizens. The Christian is docile and obedient to the state. The Christian is scrupulously moral in all business dealings. He or she observes the strictest code of sexual morality. Therefore, the state should not see the Christian as subversive, but as the ideal citizen whose good private morality is the ideal base of public virtue. The apologists do not deny that Christians reject the public cult and its gods as false and demonic, but they seek to privatize this religious difference. They veil or conceal the apocalyptic vision of Christianity which saw the present world order as soon to be overthrown by God.

This effort to privatize the religious differences between pagan and Christian, while claiming personal morality as public virtue, did not entirely succeed. The pagan world continued to believe that Christianity was politically subversive precisely because it did not separate the private from the public. For pagans, religious belief was a public political act of allegiance to the gods upon whom the prosperity of the state rested. To deny the existence or divinity of those gods was to subvert the transcendent foundations of the state. Moreover, the stance of the apologists contained a kind of concealed contradiction, since they continued, privately, to hold on to an apocalyptic faith that denied the official gods and hoped for an imminent intervention of God to overthrow the pagan state.

The household codes of the New Testament attempt a similar compromise between the claims of faith and the claims of family. It is important to recognize that the original context of these codes did not have in mind the Christian family, but rather the divided household in which a Christian wife, daughter, son, or slave was in potential conflict with the claims of authority of the non-Christian head of the household as father, husband, and master. Like the apologists, the household codes seek to modify this conflict by depoliticizing or spiritualizing it. The Christian woman or slave is seen as inwardly free. The equality of male and female, slave and free, is exalted to the spiritual and eschatological plane. But, on the social level, the wife, daughter, or slave should express this new spiritual freedom by redoubled submission to the patriarchal authority of husband, father, or master.

As the First Epistle of Peter puts it, Christians, although aliens and exiles in this world, should all the more maintain the strictest conformity to outward standards of conduct so that the gentiles (or pagans) will not accuse them of wrongdoing. "Be subject for the Lord's sake to every human institution," whether emperor or governor. Servants be submissive to your masters, not only to the kind and gentle, but also those who are harsh and cruel. Likewise, wives obey your husbands, so that those who are unbelievers may be won over by the good behavior of their wives. Clearly what is in view in these texts is not the Christian household, but the household divided and potentially disrupted by Christian wives and slaves asserting their liberty against pagan masters and husbands.

However, like apologists, the efforts of the household codes to privatize and spiritualize the radical character of the Christian vision were only partially successful. No matter how docile and submissive the wife or slave might be outwardly, she was nevertheless in spiritual revolt against the authority of her master or husband by choosing a religion which was not only different from his, but which made her regard herself as an alien and an exile in this world awaiting an imminent overthrow of his social system. Good outward moral behavior could assuage this contradiction, but not ultimately change the perception of pagan society that such a Christian faith struck at the root of its authority. The wife or slave who conceded, however assiduously, the outward claims of obedience, had nevertheless removed herself inwardly from all claims of this authority upon her life.

Resolutions Unresolved

As Christianity moved from the late first to the fourth century, this conflict between faith and family resolved in opposite, but complementary ways. On the one hand, the radical vision of an egalitarian Christian counterculture is institutionalized in monastic Christianity. Here Christian women, as well as men, continue to claim that faith takes precedence over all worldly institutions of state and family. They dissolve the ties of marriage, reject procreation or worldly occupations, and live apart in a separate community where all become equal and share in a communal lifestyle. But such an ideal of life is not longer proposed to all Christians, but only to an ascetic elite.

On the other hand, we see in the household codes of the New Testament, and in the political theology of the Constantinian state, the Christianization of the patriarchal family and the Roman empire. The hierarchy of husband over wife, master over slave, emperor over subject, is taken in to the Christian community itself and sanctified by Christian theology. In Ephesians 5, the headship of husband over wife becomes a symbol of the headship of Christ over the church. The wife should submit to her husband, as to Christ. The husband should love his wife as Christ loves the church. Such "love patriarchalism," while it modifies traditional patriarchy by proposing a high ideal of husbandly benevolence toward dependents, nevertheless fundamentally discards the original Christian vision of equality in Christ. Its pattern is paternalistic, not mutual. The exhortation to the husband to "love your wife as Christ loves the church" is not paralleled by the exhortation to the wife to love her husband in like manner, but rather by a command to submit to her husband as the church submits to Christ.

A similar pattern is suggested in the relationship of slaves to masters. If the husband and master is not kind and loving, but harsh and cruel, this does not allow his dependents to criticize or rebel against his authority. Rather, the sufferings of Christ now become a model for patient endurance of unjust violence:

> For one is approved if, mindful of God, he or she endures pain while suffering unjustly. . . . For to this you have been called, because Christ also suffered for you, leaving you an example, that you should follow in his steps. (I Pet. 2:18–25)

In these texts we see the revolutionary suffering of the cross of Christ converted into a theology of voluntary victimization. The cross of Christ is no longer a symbol of truth and justice which enables the Christian to stand against an unjust world, but it has become an example of patient and unprotesting acceptance of unjust suffering. This corruption of the theology of the cross into a theology of victimization takes place at the most intimate level, in the relationship of women and slaves to the patriarchal head of the family. Starting with the most intimate of relationships, the cross becomes a symbol of unprotesting submission to unjust violence and oppression, rather than a protest against it in the name of an alternative human community. The Kingdom of God becomes an antidote and compensation for this endurance of suffering, rather than a vision of an alternative world. In a similar way, Eusebius of Caesarea, in the fourth century, Christianized the relationship of emperor and subjects. The emperor becomes the political representative of the Word of God, the vicar of Christ on earth. The Christian should obey the emperor as a visible embodiment of the reign of Christ over the world. In this Christianization of the patriarchal family and the Roman emperor, the Christian church ceases to stand against the dominant social order as a representative of an alternative human community where "God's will shall be done on earth." The radical egalitarianism of early Christianity is spiritualized in the first circumstance, as a reward to be enjoyed after death, or it is marginalized in the second into a separate, elite, monastic community set apart from the historical order of family and state.

Thus the hierarchical patterns of power of family, state, and social class fail to be transformed by Christianity, but rather are resacralized as expressions of obedience to Christ. By making the Christian egalitarian counterculture a monastic elite, outside of and unrelated to the family, the Christian church retrenched from the possibility that this radical vision itself could lay claims upon and transform the power relationships of society and family.

And yet, despite conservative efforts to appropriate *the* biblical view of the family, the church remains the main depository in our culture for the values of community life; for the ethic of mutuality and mutual service. In its Scriptures, the church enshrines the early Christian vision of the church as a new kind of community, a new kind of humanity, overcoming the divisions of patriarchal society, of male over female, master over slave, racial group against racial group. But this vision of the church as a new community, a new family, has either been interpreted as a celibate community over against the family, or else distorted into sacralizing the traditional patriarchal family. The challenge to create a new understanding of family as committed communities of mutual service, taking a variety of forms, can also offer the church a new opportunity to reinterpret this ancient Christian vision of the redeemed society as a new community of equals.

Mary E. Hunt and Frances Kissling

30 The *New York Times* Ad: A Case Study in Religious Feminism

The publication of the Catholic Statement on Pluralism and Abortion, popularly referred to as the *New York Times* ad, sparked a historic religious controversy. It marked a milestone in the gradual and controversial effort to bring feminist values to bear on the Roman Catholic church. Not surprisingly, given the delicacy and complexity of this case, little critical analysis has emerged from the Roman Catholic feminist community.

The variety of responses to the ad, especially the virulent attacks by the Vatican, make the story a dramatic example of feminist theo-politics. Even as we write, three of the women in canonical communities who signed the ad, Barbara Ferraro and Patricia Hussey of the Sisters of Notre Dame de Namur, and Rose Dominic Trapasso of the Maryknoll Sisters, are in danger of being dismissed from their canonical congregations. We write as active participants in the controversy. Our commitment to praxis as the base for all theological reflection leaves us not disinterested observers, but advocates for women's well-being. We will explain the history and activities surrounding the ad, sketch the significance of the case for Roman Catholic feminists, and conclude with suggestions for new models of relationships and accountability among religious feminists. We understand this kind of analysis to be an essential part of the critical work necessary for the "feministization" of any patriarchal institution. By feministization we mean the process by which values of inclusivity and mutuality, justice and equality are made manifest in previously patriarchal, that is, hierarchical, gender-, class-, race-stratified organizations.

Originally published in *Journal of Feminist Studies in Religion* (Spring 1987), 3:115–127. Reprinted with permission from the *Journal of Feminist Studies in Religion*.

History

The ad began as a Catholic Statement on Pluralism and Abortion written in 1983 by Daniel Maguire and Frances Kissling. It was circulated to twenty Roman Catholic ethicists for critique. Early signers agreed to serve as the sponsoring committee and to allow their names to be used in seeking other signers.

At that point, the process of circulating the statement came to a standstill. The committee had neither funds nor staff to assist in sending it out. In May 1983, the board of directors of Catholics for a Free Choice [CFFC] considered a request for a grant of up to $5,000 to assist the committee in circulating the statement to various professional societies. Some board members objected that the statement was too moderate; it took no position on the morality of abortion and paid no more than lip service to a legal right to choose abortion. Others objected that it was aimed at a scholarly rather than a grass-roots community.

Despite this discussion, the CFFC board voted to make funds available to the sponsoring group, the Catholic Committee on Pluralism and Abortion. The committee, made up of the writers and several other theologians, then circulated the statement to the membership of the Catholic Theological Society of America and the College Theology Society. CFFC's financial support was acknowledged, and persons were asked to sign the statement with the awareness that their names might be made public. No special attempt was made to seek signatures from members of canonical communities, though several signed the statement in response to these mailings.

It was the 1984 presidential elections that prompted publication of the statement as an ad in the *New York Times*. Geraldine Ferraro, Democratic candidate for vice president, and a prochoice Catholic, was singled out by conservative bishops, especially Bernard Law of Boston and John O'Connor of New York, for special criticism. The bishops made clear their opposition to Ferraro's candidacy because of her position on abortion, even though the candidate reiterated her personal opposition to abortion. Political observers noted that Catholic male candidates for office, such as Edward Kennedy and Mario Cuomo, whose positions on abortion were virtually identical to Ferraro's, had never been publicly attacked by such high church officials. It was in this context that the Catholic Committee on Pluralism and Abortion decided to publish the piece as a full-page ad in the *New York Times* on Sunday, October 7, 1984—at the height of the presidential campaign.

The informal network of progressive Roman Catholic women in canonical communities acted at this point. Some signed the statement precisely because it would appear in the *New York Times*. Several sent telegrams to the CFFC office in a desire to beat the deadline. A few were spared the pain of the last two years simply because their letter or telegram arrived a day or two late. Some signed the statement even after Catholic papers had published the fact that Anne Carr, a canonical signer whose name had been released at a September press conference, had "resigned" (at the express request of Bishop Joseph Imesch) from the women's advisory committee to the U.S. Catholic bishops' committee on the proposed pastoral letter on women.

The ninety-seven signers of the ad included twenty-six women belonging to fourteen canonical communities, one diocesan and one order priest, two brothers, and sixty-seven other signers. Initial responses in the press drew attention to the fact that committed Catholics were speaking out on abortion although church officials considered the matter closed to debate. As church officials see it, raising questions about abortion constitutes dissent.

The National Conference of Catholic Bishops' Committee on Doctrine, under the signature of its chair Archbishop John Quinn, issued the first institutional church response on November 14, 1984. Quinn stated that the signers had presented "a personal opinion which directly contradicts the clear and constant teaching of the church about abortion, a teaching which they as Catholics are obliged to accept."

Archbishop Quinn's response was never really accorded any serious consideration for several reasons. First, as many well-respected theologians have made clear, it is difficult to prove that the current teaching on abortion is a "clear and constant teaching of the church." Second, this argument would seem to call for some disciplinary action, e.g., excommunication, against all the signers, not just threats of dismissal for signers in canonical communities and priests, who are, canonically speaking, the most vulnerable. Such action was never mentioned, probably because even church officials know that 79 percent of all U.S. Catholics approve of abortion under certain circumstances, though most reiterate that abortion is always a tragic choice. Hence the Quinn statement can be seen as little more than the pro forma response of a national episcopacy in its capacity as the local representative of the institutional church. The more problematic response became public on November 30, 1984, when Cardinal Jean Jerome Hamer of the Congregation for Religious and Secular Institutes (CRIS) sent letters to most of the presidents of the canonical communities requesting that they direct the signers "to make a public retraction." If such retractions were not forthcoming, the letters continued, the superiors were "to warn the religious with an explicit threat of dismissal from their community." Similar word was sent by the appropriate agencies to the bishop of the diocesan priest, and eventually to the Maryknoll Sisters, who come under the Congregation for the Evangelization of the Peoples, not CRIS.

Negotiations

The letters set in motion a series of meetings, negotiations, and maneuverings which reveal how a patriarchal organization like the Roman Catholic church uses an issue like abortion to shore up and maintain its authoritarian structures. Obedience and not principle (i.e., alleged concern over fetal life) seemed to be at stake. How else does one explain the move to make examples of the priests and members of canonical communities over whom the hierarchy has more jurisdiction, rather than demand that all signers retract? The latter strategy might have convinced the public that a moral rather than theo-political issue was involved.

Three of the four male signers who were priests or members of canonical communities issued public retractions and affirmed church teachings by late December 1984. The fourth did so shortly thereafter, although it was not reported publicly until May 1985. Few observers missed the fact that the men all rapidly "regularized" their situations with Rome. A characteristic of a patriarchal organization like the Roman Catholic church is that it oppresses men as well as women. For priests, the penalty of dismissal from the priesthood could have been swift. This case shows that patriarchy oppresses men by subtly and surely influencing them to internalize its expectations. Hence most men—and the signers of the *New York Times* ad were no exception—find it impossible to engage in the transformation of patriarchy from within.

A series of painful and protracted negotiations began between the canonical signers' superiors and the Vatican in December 1984. These negotiations continue at this writing since three cases remain unresolved. (Note that the language of "superiors" and "members" is a distinction made by the Vatican and accepted by the canonical communities in the negotiations with Rome.)

Most of the communities made initial steps to oppose the Vatican's demands. They cited principles of subsidiarity and freedom of conscience in their internal discussions. They saw the Roman move, especially since it was directed to the superiors and not to the members themselves, as a negation of the strides made since Vatican II to empower members of canonical communities as agents of their own lives.

Rome had quite a different perspective. CRIS officials claimed that by virtue of their membership in canonical communities, the women, both superiors and members, were subject to obedience. Further, by virtue to their public vows, they were "public" members of the church and therefore were expected to adhere to its teachings in the public arena. The sharp difference in perception between the canonical communities and Rome clarified that the period of experimentation begun at Vatican II was over for canonical communities. The ability of the Vatican to demand and eventually receive "clarifications" from most of the women in canonical communities also showed that the strenuous efforts by women to act justly and equitably toward each other are finally inadequate when their lives (in canonical communities) are circumscribed by the strictures of a patriarchal pyramid like the Roman Catholic church.

This insight was a product of the wrenching and time consuming meetings held between superiors and the members of canonical communities, as well by the sixty-seven signers and the canonical signers. It must be remembered that because they are not ordained members of the clergy, the women in canonical communities, including the superiors, are technically lay people in the church. Yet this chapter in church history proved that women in canonical communities exist in a kind of limbo with all of the obligations of the laity and none of the so-called privileges of the clergy. Seemingly unconscious of this reality—namely that all Catholic women are Lay women until the first one is ordained—and limiting their concerns to the preservation of their members in their communities, the superiors repeatedly rejected invitations to meet with the other signers to develop joint strategies. The superiors' group, the Committee of Concerned Leadership (CCL, not to be confused with the Conference of Catholic Lesbians founded in 1983) met periodically.

Although public reports of these meetings do not exist, it can be assumed from the unilateral actions taken by each of the superiors on behalf of her member(s), that the superiors were unable to agree among themselves on concerted efforts. Common strategies would have shown that the bonding of women from various communities can help to change a patriarchal church. Likewise, in cases where conflicts arose between the interests of the individual signers and the maintenance of the communities, our information leads us to conclude that the individuals were consistently passed over for "the good of the whole."

Concerted action might have helped to overcome the false split between women based on membership in a canonical community, a split which serves the ends of a patriarchal church. Joint decision-making and sharing of information among all signers and the so-called superiors, in our judgment, represented the only hope the women in canonical communities had for standing firm against unjust Vatican demands.

The fact that the CCL chose to cooperate on the Vatican's terms, with a case-by-case settlement, instead of taking a united stand against the intrusion of Vatican officials on their membership, meant that the terms of the debate never changed. While it is true and laudable that some superiors pushed harder than Rome expected, we think overall they made a strategic mistake: that is, the failure to join publicly with all their sisters and to develop strategies with the other signers that would have shown the strength of a new, feminist model of church, one that invites participation and respects difference. We hope that they now know for the next time.

Not only did the superiors not take a public stand, but it is also reported that something of a deal was worked out during the August 1985 visit of Cardinal Hamer. The language of "clarification" eventually replaced "retraction" as the minimum the Vatican would accept to close the cases. Despite the warning from signers that such "clarifications" would later be called retractions by the Vatican (something that happened at least twice subsequently), this compromise solution was seen as the most they could hope for.

Unfortunately, they missed the fact that, finally, Rome's request was not for doctrinal purity. Some of the "clarifications" said little if anything about adherence to the institutional church's position on abortion. Rather, Rome was seeking to solidify obedience within a clearly delineated hierarchical chain of command. That these women "clarified," and that the superiors could and would make them do it, was all that Rome really wanted this time around.

This conclusion is borne out by the fact that the Congregation for the Evangelization of the Peoples later followed the same procedure in dealing with the Maryknoll superiors over the case of Rose Dominic Trapasso. Likewise, in the even more prolonged cases of Barbara Ferraro and Patricia Hussey, the Sisters of Notre Dame de Namur have continued to demand, cajole, and embarrass them into some form of public compliance with the Vatican requests. These two women have been clear from the beginning that they are pro-choice, come what may. Yet their superiors persist in requesting some action that will demonstrate their adherence to church teachings, i.e., show their obedience.

That the superiors refused to make common cause with the signers is regrettable. But what is worse is that, even at this writing, there are some members of canonical communities who do not yet have written or oral details of the clarifications which were made in their names. Indeed, we are told that Marjorie Tuite went to her grave without ever seeing the letter her superior wrote to Rome on her behalf. This behavior of the superiors is totally inconsistent with any definition of feminism. And apparently little has been learned over the course of the controversy since at this writing, the Central Governing Board of the Maryknoll Sisters consistently refuses to provide Rose Dominic Trapasso with a copy of the Vatican's letter outlining its requests in her case.

Another characteristic of a patriarchal system is the horizontal violence it depends on and engenders, in this case nun versus nun, albeit superior versus member. In addition, such a system depends on self-censorship as an added guarantee that the oppressed will finally get the oppressors' job done. Regrettably, these too are part of the history in this case.

By May 1986 fourteen of the women in canonical communities had "clarified" their positions and their cases were closed. In conversation with many of the signers we have been told how most of these cases were resolved. A few, very few, signers do agree with the absolute prohibition on abortion and so informed their superiors who communicated this to CRIS. Others, who interpret the magisterial teaching in a more nuanced way than the magisterium, relied on their own interpretation and with their superiors' formulated wording that meant one thing to them but was likely to be interpreted by CRIS as adherence to the strict magisterial teaching. In one instance the Catholic Statement on Pluralism and Abortion was rewritten, leaving out the offending sentence, "There is the mistaken belief in American society that this is the only legitimate Catholic position." Finally, some superiors, we are reliably informed, after being told by their members that they, in fact, do not agree with the magisterial teaching on abortion, took it upon themselves to inform CRIS that, in the superior's opinion, the member was in agreement with the teaching.

At this point, pressure was put on the Vatican to settle the remaining ten cases quickly. This pressure came from two sources. First, at a March 1–3, 1986, meeting of the International Right-to-Life Committee, held in Rome, leaders of the movement stressed to Vatican officials the importance of settling these cases. They claimed that the ambiguity that remained damaged the political efforts of the U.S. right-to-life movement.

The second source of pressure was the Committee of Concerned Catholics, a group of signers of the ad who engaged in educational outreach and grassroots organizing in response to the reprisals that followed the ad. The committee decided to mount a second ad campaign, this time a "Declaration of Solidarity" with those whose rights had been violated after signing the first ad. More than one thousand signatures were gathered from Catholics in seventeen countries, including at least five priests and forty women in canonical communities. Note that this is almost double the number of clerical/canonical signers, and ten times the number of original signers.

The declaration, published on March 2, 1984 in another full-page ad in the *New York Times* stated that:

> Such reprisals consciously or unconsciously have a chilling effect on the right to responsible dissent within the church; on academic freedom in Catholic colleges and universities; and the right to free speech and participation in the U.S. political process.

It went on to say:

> We believe that Catholics who in good conscience take positions on the difficult questions of legal abortion and other controversial issues that differ from the official hierarchical positions are within their rights and responsibilities as Catholics and as citizens.

These pressures led CRIS to dispatch its second-in-command, Archbishop Vincenzo Fagiolo, to meet with the ten canonical signers whose cases remained. His trivializing manipulation (including asking two of them what their "mommies and daddies" thought of their actions) resulted in eight more "clarifications." While *none of* these was a full-fledged antiabortion statement, some contained language like, "We hold as we have in the past, that human life is sacred and inviolable." This was enough prolife tone and content to please the Vatican. Given the fact that the statements were varied and somewhat ambiguous gave the canonical members a measure of self-respect in a difficult situation.

Those who chose not to clarify, namely Ferraro and Hussey, were then cast as uncooperative at best, unsisterly at worst. They were unwilling to act in the role that had been assigned to them as members of a canonical community. Unfortunately, they were the ultimate victims in a divide and conquer strategy instituted by the Vatican and carried out community by community, down to the last member.

Related Incidents

Meanwhile, many other signers suffered personal and professional repercussions because of their actions. Professor Daniel Maguire was "disinvited" from several college lectureships. Lawyer-theologian Jan Via was "disinvited" from speaking to other Catholic lawyers in her home diocese of San Diego. Several signers were denied jobs, promotions, and/or tenure in various incidents that can be traced to their signing the ad. Still another signer was called to confer with her local bishop in a conversation that was aimed at putting her tenured position at a Catholic university in jeopardy.

Emboldened by their success with the Vatican 24/97, and conscious that dissent and disaffection run high among U.S. Catholics, the Vatican continued its campaign to restore its eroded authority. Mary Ann Sorrentino, executive director of Planned

Parenthood in Rhode Island, was told by her bishop that she was automatically ex-communicated because her job involved procuring abortions. Sorrentino, a signer of the "Declaration of Solidarity," was used by local authorities—with clear Vatican approval—to give a direct message to all Catholics who participate in abortion-related activities. A young woman, Sarabeth Eason, age twelve, was recently dismissed from a Catholic grade school for her prochoice stance. Such are examples of Vatican overkill.

The revoking of Professor Charles Curran's canonical license to teach as a Catholic theologian at the Catholic University of America follows in the same strategic line. Curran's position on abortion is cited as among the reasons why he may no longer teach theology in any Catholic institution. However, it must be noted that he neither signed the ad nor publicly supported those who did. Curran, unlike the Vatican 24/97, received widespread support from hundreds of Catholic theologians and ethicists, even though he holds a relatively permissive view of abortion. He considers abortion morally acceptable when the life of the mother, or values commensurate with life, are at stake.

The transfer of some episcopal power from Archbishop Raymond Hunthausen to Auxiliary Bishop Donald Wuerl in Seattle, Washington, though not directly related to the case in question, can be seen as part of the same pattern. Hunthausen's pastoral openness on other sexual issues, including allowing members of Dignity, a Catholic gay/lesbian group, to celebrate the eucharist in the Seattle cathedral, and not expressly forbidding sterilizations in Catholic hospitals in the Archdiocese (a situation that is now said to have been remedied), was seen as a dissenting position. While the Vatican never expected the groundswell of popular support for Hunthausen that continues to grow, they did expect the U.S. Catholic bishops to support the hierarchy's action. This is exactly what happened at a recent meeting of the National Conference of Catholic Bishops. Hence, an example has been made of Hunthausen. All of the bishops must scamper back to their dioceses and put their own houses in order lest the same fate befall them. This is an effective use of self-censorship by the Vatican.

Significance for Roman Catholic Feminists

These events have had a number of serious and negative consequences for the individuals involved, and for Roman Catholic feminism in general. But they have also had a positive impact on the roles played by Roman Catholic feminists in the broader feminist movement and in the public debate on reproductive rights.

First, the ad and the resulting dispute effectively and finally put to rest the myth that Catholics, especially professional Catholics (i.e., those whose identity is tied to church positions, or whose lives and/or social support is founded on the institutional church) share the belief of the Vatican and the U.S. bishops that abortion is to be absolutely prohibited both legally and morally.

Second, the *New York Times* ad ended the hegemony of both bishops and male clerics as the public interpreters of Catholic teaching, belief, values and practice. This is true not only in the abortion arena, but in all areas of public interest. In the two years since the ad appeared, it has become common practice for electronic and print media to seek the views of Catholic feminists on all major news events concerning Roman Catholicism. Many of the signers have been quoted widely in major print media. They have appeared frequently on television, and have given hundreds of radio interviews and speeches. They have been featured and honored in such publications as *Esquire, Vogue, New Woman, Ms., The Nation,* and *The Washington Post Sunday Magazine.* In each instance they have been able to put forth strong, intelligent, theologically sophisticated feminist perspectives as Catholics on issues of reproductive rights, authority and dissent in the church, and related concerns. Likewise, Catholics are doing new feminist liberation theological work on these issues in journals, books, university courses and professional meetings.

Third, the signers of the *New York Times* ad have been a source of hope and inspiration for women whose religious feminism is just beginning to take root. They have said to women who have had abortions that they too are moral agents with a right and responsibility to make choices about their own bodies.

Fourth, the signers have created new links between religious and secular feminists. They have aroused new interest and respect for religious feminism among leading secular feminists. One wrote recently that it is religious feminists who have transformed the abortion question, making it more than a proabortion versus antiabortion deadlock, finally bringing the nuances of ethics and theology to such discussions.

Fifth, the Vatican threat to canonical communities, and the long period during which signers belonging to these communities refused to clarify their positions, forced many communities and members to study the question of abortion, some for the first time. They were invited to consider the concept of women's reproductive freedom alongside their own concept of freedom as members of canonical communities. It is safe to say that the result of this inquiry is a significant increase in the number of prochoice women in canonical communities.

These examples of public good are in stark contrast to the private difficulties and severe strains the Vatican threat and the responses of canonical signers and their superiors have created within the community of committed Catholic feminists. All parties have had to confront, or are avoiding confronting, hard truths about themselves, their commitments to each other, and to all women. In the absence of a willingness to expose and analyze these problems, the wounds will not heal.

The canonical signers whose cases have been settled are deeply demoralized. As one wrote, "I know of no signer who feels good about the settlement of her case." The signers are severely disappointed in themselves. They see that they are significantly less able to resist, to maintain full integrity, to stand firm in their beliefs, and to stand with each other than they believed themselves to be. This demoralization has severely limited their ability effectively to support the three remaining canonical signers. Indeed, there is substantial guilt among these signers, many of whom understand that the private settlement of their cases has created greater difficulties for Ferraro and

Hussey (and now Rose Dominic Trapasso), who have refused to comply with the demand for clarification.

Without exception, the leadership of all of the communities involved violated the principles of open exchange and dialogue that were thought to exist within the communities. For example, to greater and lesser degrees, they held meetings concerning the canonical signers, but without their assent and without informing them. They kept secret from the signers verbal and written communications with the Vatican. These acts have created distance and distrust between many of the canonical signers and their leadership. The canonical signers were also stung by the open and formal support that the Leadership Conference of Women Religious offered to Charles Curran, in contrast to the total absence of public formal or informal support for them. In short, the canonical signers felt betrayed.

The rest of the signers also felt betrayed. The actions of the superiors have shown them that canonical communities do not see themselves in the service of the whole church, particularly women. Rather, they are self-serving institutions in which survival, the maintenance of property, canonical status, and power, however marginal, are more important than the integrity of individual members or a broader sense of church.

While the other signers are somewhat more sympathetic to the canonical signers, there is still the feeling that when faced with the tough choices between solidarity with all women and loyalty to their congregations (hence to a part of the institutional church) they will choose their congregations. Many women have told us that the ability of the canonical signers or their communities to serve as leaders in the religious feminist movement within Roman Catholicism has been severely compromised by these events.

As a result of this, and as a consequence of the deepening bonds among signers, there is a noticeable shift in leadership. What was once a movement of women in the church led by canonically connected women is increasingly becoming a movement called Women-Church, which includes all women and men who are committed to a "discipleship of equals." Women-Church, rejecting the divisiveness of patriarchal Catholicism's hierarchies, makes no distinctions between secular and religious, lay and clergy. Insofar as the *New York Times* ad had helped to bring about a deepening and broadening of this base, the pain and problems have been useful.

New Models for Religious Feminists

This episode in current Catholic history sparks us to suggest three issues which all religious feminists may find relevant to their concerns. We hope that readers will respond to this piece, drawing out additional insights that they find in the case.

1. Conflicts of interest and struggles for ideological and personal survival will emerge as we try to transform patriarchal religions. We suggest that religious

feminists give serious attention to creative forms of conflict resolution. We caution against the claim that "sisterhood" requires an uncritical acceptance and affirmation of all strategies women choose in resisting patriarchal institutions. We need to take strict account of the power dynamics involved among us, analyzing the places in which we find ourselves in the structures in which we live. Knowing that problems will arise, we call for a willingness to come to the table and discuss such issues as women, even when it is clear that we do not agree and/or that our various social locations will make us what Lois Kirkwood calls "structural enemies." Only a commitment to keep talking with each other will signal trajectories of accountability to women and not finally to patriarchal institutions.

2. It seems clear to us that the days of canonical religious communities, or other analogous women's auxiliaries bound to patriarchal organizations on these organizations' terms, is over. The structures of domination which place men over women simply cannot be replicated to place some women over other women on the basis of freely chosen commitment to canonically domesticated groups. This is the painful lesson of the *New York Times* ad, something that many women in canonical communities have already recognized and are trying to remedy. This does not mean that women should not form deep bonds and even organize their relationships into economically and spiritually supportive communities. But such groups simply cannot be part of a patriarchal structure if women are to commit ourselves fully to a "discipleship of equals." While it is beyond the scope of this essay to draw out the implications of this assertion for ordained ministry for women, it does raise interesting questions about the value of women's ordination. It seems that even ordination gives some women a kind of position that is contingent on patriarchal approval.

3. The heart of the matter is the question of accountability to the whole church instead of to a segment of it. If religious feminists wish to make changes in particular units of a religious organization, the key is that we see these as structurally connected to the whole. Each local expression of church needs to exist with a measure of autonomy as well as a measure of connectedness. Hence, women's groups will find any separatism difficult to justify, especially if it is separatism from other women. Likewise, commitment to dialogue and respect for pluralism will be hallmarks of any feminist religious quest. This, after all, is what the *New York Times* ad was all about.

Editor's note, 1993: None of the signers' cases is being pursued any longer. On June 1, 1988, the leadership of the Sisters of Notre Dame de Namur dropped dismissal proceedings against Patricia Hussey and Barbara Ferraro. In mid-July, having defended their right to belong to the community, the pair resigned, citing the impossibility of repairing relationships with many community members and affirming their commitment to pursuing justice work as Catholic lay women.

Helen Tworkov

31   Antiabortion/Prochoice: Taking Both Sides

Everything important about life is important about abortion. "The Great Matter of Life and Death"—as the Zen texts put it—haunts every nuance of the battles between men and women, rich and poor, fetal rights versus mothers' rights, or states' rights versus federal rights. Yet the abortion debate has become so politicized and polarized that both sides view inquiry as betrayal. Politics may promise yes or no answers, but abortion is a no-win situation which confronts humanity with its own greatest mysteries.

Ambivalence about abortion is common, but rarely voiced, and for those women and men committed to individual rights for adults, any discussion that compromises prochoice approaches heresy. Yet ambivalence, confusion, and conflict come with the territory, for abortion poses questions that cannot be answered by doctors, priests, senators, or moral philosophers, or settled by dogma.

"This is not an intellectual issue," says a white middle-class therapist and former staff member of a New York City abortion clinic where the average clients were thirteen-year-old black girls. "I wanted to work there," she continued. "I believed in abortion; it was a feminist issue. But the first time I witnessed an operation, something came up from deep inside me. I couldn't take it." After three months, she resigned but today remains a dedicated proponent of the right to choose. "In terms of a woman's entire life, abortion is usually a pretty awful experience, but that doesn't mean it's the wrong choice."

As the 1992 elections heat up, everyone wants to figure out which side to be on, but the subject of abortion demands more than that. According to Sho Ishikawa, a thirty-year-old former Zen monk from Japan who currently attends Brown University, "Because of the political issue, you have to take a stand: abortion is right or wrong. But that's just a conventional sense of right and wrong. It's never the whole story. Espe-

Originally published in *Tricycle: The Buddhist Review,* Vol. 1, No. 3 (Spring 1992): 60–69. Reprinted with permission from *Tricycle: The Buddhist Review.*

cially with abortion." Buddhists are often asked to explain their view of abortion by those who incorrectly assume that Buddhism has its own version of papal authority. Though Buddhism has no cohesive platform, its primary views provide alternatives to the current abortion debate. In Judaism and Christianity, human life has been the focus of the Biblical injunction, "Thou shalt not kill." Like the first commandment, the first precept of the Buddhist ethical code also prohibits killing. In Buddhism, the most severe karmic consequences arise from killing humans, but no form of life escapes the first precept. Buddhists take vows "to save all sentient beings." Without doubt this includes cows and carrots. Yet there are Zen teachers who apply "sentient" to any form that comes into and passes out of this sphere of existence, and that can include nonorganic objects such as teacups and toothbrushes and art works. We vow to "save" them through care and attention. While East-West dialogues tend to stress common values, Buddhism does offer very clear alternatives to our own anthropocentric traditions. From the all-encompassing life-view of Buddhism, the religious wing of the antiabortion movement fails to communicate a sacred regard for creation by limiting its arguments to human life alone. When prolife politics excludes trees, oceans, animals, or victims of AIDS, warfare, and capital punishment, religious language may amount to nothing more than slogans that play well in the media.

In the American debate, President Bush's support for abortion in cases of rape and incest exemplifies the secular manipulation of religious sentiment. If the morality of the antichoice platform is based on protecting the fetus, then it is illogical and irreverent to suggest that any fetus qualifies for the death sentence. Also, in those communities where antiabortion sentiment prevails, these "exceptions" create their own twisted morality for those women who become pregnant through rape or incest. As witnessed by the support for Clarence Thomas and William Kennedy Smith, men and women in this society still view the violated woman as the victim of her own folly; therefore, to sanction abortion for cases of rape or incest further burdens the stigmatized woman with the responsibility of cleansing her defilement. This benign dispensation—as we are asked to see it—has nothing to do with protecting the unborn. Furthermore, the criminal, who often receives leniency in the court system, is morally censured by licensing the death of his offspring. In the name of protection we get punishment. These "exceptions" reinforce ancient patterns of control. As a necessary compromise to get votes and appear reasonable, the exceptions champion a political platform, not an objective morality. What we have here may point to an older and deeper issue: since men cannot deny to women their power to give life, they will try—as they have done historically—to deny to women the power to take it.

Public Debate, Private Considerations

Prochoice advocates also embrace the anthropocentric reliance on interpreting "the great matter of life and death" in terms of human values alone. They, too, trim the terms of debate to satisfy their constituencies. Based on a litany of sexist and secular injustices, this platform denies any dimension that threatens the political affirmation of adult rights, including the messy, emotional investigation of whether abortion is killing or not. Unfortunately, however, the public debate conditions private considerations. While denying "the great matter" may advance political success, it is detrimental to women who must face the very choice that this platform represents. Influenced by prochoice rhetoric, too many women face "the great matter" after choosing abortion. But only in the political arena does the belief that abortion is the taking of life threaten the prochoice platform. In actual lives and experiences it does not. For this reason, in the past few years many people, Buddhist practitioners and others, have arrived at what might be called a prochoice/antiabortion position.

This logic supports women's right to choose abortion and refuses to allow the mostly male legislature to control their lives. But prochoice/antiabortion indicates an acceptance of how painful and problematic abortion so often is for everyone involved—parents, families, doctors, and counselors.

Not long ago, I asked a Buddhist priest how she felt about abortion. "To tell you the truth," she whispered into the office phone of a California Zen center, "I can't bear the idea of abortion. It makes me sick." Asked if she would still vote prochoice, she answered, "Absolutely. My commitment is to support pregnant women in whatever choice they make."

Among my friends, one consistent difference keeps emerging: non-Buddhists argue, in sweeping socioeconomic and historic terms, for prochoice as the touchstone of women's lives. But when it comes to whether or not the fetus qualifies as life, convincing dialectics often collapse into sighs and hesitation. On the other hand, Buddhist practitioners seem to accept that abortion at any stage, unequivocally, means the taking of life.

In the past year, the American Buddhist women I spoke with (from all different lineages) agreed that abortion may sometimes be necessary but is never desirable, and should never be performed without the deepest consideration of all aspects of the situation. This came from women who said that they themselves would, under no circumstances, ever have an abortion, from women who could imagine circumstances under which they would consider abortion, and from women, like myself, who have experienced abortion. All of us are currently committed to a prochoice ballot.

For women in the vicinity of my own age (forty-eight), a prochoice vote combined with a gut negativity toward abortion has been approached via miscalculated trials and errors—ending with both abortions and babies. At the time of my own abortion in 1960, the outlaw status of abortion defined it as another target ripe for rebellion, along with sexual mores, academic and religious institutions, lipstick, and drugs. Abortion was the precarious safety net waiting to catch the fallout from experimental forays into what we willfully called "sexual liberation." It was our ally, ignorantly touted as a form of birth control and valued as an extension of forbidden pleasures. Abortion was no necessary evil. Many of us were for abortion.

It wasn't until my own pregnancy that I first learned from my Jewish liberal parents of the gray possibilities for abortion, that is to say, what was available in New York City south of black Harlem if you were white and not wealthy. Several alternatives were presented to me before and after my parents made sure to mention that the decision to have a baby or not was mine and that they would support my choice. My twenty-year-old boyfriend had some romantic ideas about us raising kids, but he was a charming dreamer who had yet to display any interest in supporting himself, let alone a family.

I don't know now whether it was fear or reason which brought me to an abortionist's office, but on the Monday before Thanksgiving my older sister accompanied me to a sandstone townhouse on Lexington Avenue near 34th Street. By doctor's orders, men were banned from the premises, and the presence of mothers discouraged. He recommended women escorts similar in age and instructed us not to loiter around the building before entering. My father came with us as far as the bank, where he handed my sister three hundred dollars in cash.

Through the haze of partial anesthesia, I remember only the invasive touch of cold metal and the muted sounds of heavy furniture being pulled across a bare floor. That, and the end of it, when the doctor, a somewhat squat and balding man, bent over the operating table to present a flaccid, shadowed cheek for a kiss of gratitude.

To grieve openly, that is, to have acknowledged, even to myself, a sense of grief, would have been admitting to a death over which to grieve. Not to mention grieving for my own involvement, or grieving for the lost possibility, or for that part of me forever gone. That it was a death, the taking of life, was not clear. Or rather, obscured and convoluted, it was all too clear. But we were different from our working class Catholic neighbors. In my nonreligious and well meaning family, there was a silent collective contract to pretend that we all understood without doubt that abortion at an early stage was not the taking of life. If the first mistake in judgment was getting pregnant at all, then the second was to participate in this denial. Apparently, this was not much comfort to other family members either: years later I would learn of my father telling my sister not long after the fact, "If I have anything to say about it there will never be another abortion in this family."

Somewhere around 1967 or 1968 between the race riots and the anti-war protests, and the proabortion rallies that preceded Roe v. Wade, I vowed never to have another abortion, never to recommend one, and to stop petitioning the government to legalize abortion at home while protesting American killing in Vietnam. Though many friends told me at the time they were completely at peace with their abortions, that the experiences had left no emotional scars or moral qualms, to this day, I wonder if that's true.

Prochoice and the First Precept

When I began reading Buddhist texts I adopted a very literal interpretation of the first precept to fortify my somewhat isolated stand against legalizing abortion. I also became a strict vegetarian. In theory I supported individual choice even then. But I also had some Confucian-influenced idea that for the sake of cultivating a civilized society the government should not sanction killing, and that the moral obligations of society had to supersede individual needs. Therefore, to me prochoice meant keeping abortion illegal, with all the pernicious discrepancies, between rich and poor and white and people of color—not a conclusion that I allowed myself to state at the time, but that's what it amounted to. I could not clearly distinguish prochoice from proabortion. The more literally I could apply the first precept, the more righteous I felt. In retrospect, I was more influenced by a modern sensibility in which life and death were perceived as independent forces—the Creator and the Destroyer not one, not unified, not interdependent, not divine, but secularized, the very perception of separation.

My first studies in Buddhism took place at a Tibetan center where I spent time in the kitchen cooking up big pots of fatty-lined roasts for the most respected lamas. Slowly, I let up on the vegetarian diet but not on abortion. Roe v. Wade had just made history, but a few of the same women who had fought for it in the name of liberation were alongside me in the kitchens of Buddhist centers. Still, I was beginning to discover that it was easier to maintain literal interpretations of the precepts if one studied texts in isolation than if one spent time in the company of teachers. I learned of herders in the isolated Tibetan plateaus whose daily sustenance depended on a cup of blood extracted from the jugular of a yak; and of yaks who "committed suicide" when their breath expired with the help of ropes lassoed around their protruding muzzles; and learned, too, about a great living lama in Nepal who spent each morning at the market buying up buckets of live fish in order to return them to the river.

A vegetarian diet may express the first precept—but only in those cultures where agriculture flourishes. For Zen monks in China and Japan, tending the gardens became an integral part of Buddhist monastic training. But in the Tibetan tradition monks are protected from even cutting down plant foods. What's more, throughout Asia, Muslims work as animal killers and leather workers, allowing Buddhists to enjoy the benefits of dead animals while not having to kill for them. Whatever our circumstances, we are sustained by other forms of life, but while dharma discourses abound on how to show compassion for cows and carrots or fleas and lice, in Buddhist cultures abortion is not openly addressed.

Then about seven or eight years ago a friend gave me a copy of John Irving's *The Cider House Rules.* This Dickensian novel revolves around an orphanage which doubles as an illegal abortion clinic headed by a complicated and conscientious doctor. There, abortion was an unavoidable fact of life—not to be judged but reckoned with. In Irving's terms, illegal abortion attests to the barbaric and humiliating treatment of women. Condemned to kitchen table abortions by an inhumane sense of justice, Irving's women have their lives jeopardized by a society that glorifies the heroics of men at war but shames women at their most vulnerable. There was no way to justify an antiabortion position in the name of civilized morality.

For the first time, I became unequivocally prochoice. And antiabortion. Buddhist studies did not encourage prochoice, but they did expand those perspectives on death most familiar to Westerners. In my own case, I could not find resolution in the black-and-white moral systems of my own culture. Buddhism allowed for an acceptance of that killing which is necessary to life, and of the death and the dying that inform the dimensions of a conscious life. Prochoice can be seen as manifesting "big mind" of Buddhism, not because it promotes or condones abortion, but because it contains all possibilities, and reflects the interdependence of life and death.

It must be admitted however that there is little that relates to abortion in traditional Buddhist societies that is useful to Americans. Information regarding abortion attitudes and practices in Asia is scant. In most Asian countries, patterns of sexism are still too entrenched for women's issues to appear on the political agenda. And nowhere has the male priesthood felt obliged to investigate interpretations of the first precept on behalf of women and the abortion issue. Abortion remains very much a women's problem and a private matter. Women rarely discuss sex, not even with other women, and never with men. What little we know comes from doctors, hospital administrators, and representatives of world health organizations. Vietnamese women, for example, share with many women in other Asian cultures a belief that the unnamed has no consciousness. While Vietnamese priests go on record as being antiabortion, some Buddhist women in the Vietnamese community in Boston explained to me that during the first couple of months of pregnancy, the fetus has no consciousness, no spirit and therefore, first trimester abortion is not the taking of life. This discrepancy may indicate the actual and official Buddhist versions of abortion, or it may be another instance of men attempting to regulate the lives of women.

On the other hand, in the United States an increasing number of American priests, men and women, are being called on to provide rituals or services for aborted fetuses, as well as for those that miscarried. According to women who have participated in these services, much of their value lies in the opportunity to acknowledge abortion in terms of "the great matter."

One American Zen teacher who has been performing services for aborted and miscarried babies is Robert Aitken of the Diamond Sangha in Hawaii. In his collection of essays on ethics, *The Mind of Clover*, Aitken Roshi discusses the Japanese Buddhist funeral for the *mizuko* or "water baby," the poetical term for fetus: "Like any other human being that passes into the One, it is given a posthumous Buddhist name, and is thus identified as an individual, however incomplete, to whom we can say farewell. With this ceremony, the woman is in touch with life and death as they pass through her existence, and she finds that such basic changes are relative waves on the great ocean of true nature, which is not born and does not pass away. Bodhidharma said, 'Self-nature is subtle and mysterious. In the realm of everlasting Dharma, not giving rise to concepts of killing is called the Precept of Not Killing.'"

In the case of Buddhist-inspired programs for homelessness, AIDS patients, or prisoners, we see the Western heritage of social responsibility merging with those Buddhist teachings that urge experiential understanding of the essential unity of the provider and the receiver. In this integration, one tradition enhances another without conflict or contradiction. When it comes to abortion, however, dharma teachings can be used to validate either prochoice or antiabortion politics. For this very reason, abortion places American Buddhists at the crossroads of Western and Eastern perceptions of the individual, society, and what liberation is all about. Anyone considering abortion from Buddhist teachings—and not from political peer pressure—is driven back again and again on interpretation and view, on self-analysis and ambiguity. This, in itself, is Buddhism at its most instructive, demanding an authentic confrontation with oneself.

What Is

Indra's Net, as described in the Avatamsaka Sutra, suggests every particular manifestation of life is necessary to the whole fabric. Every phenomenon has the capacity to illuminate, contain, and reflect the entirety. *Nothing* exists outside this Net of Indra. Nothing can be left out because of personal preference or moral judgement. And the texts are very precise on the all-inclusive nature of this view, as difficult as it is to come to terms with, for it includes babies and bunny rabbits, lovers and teacups, radios and parents, as well as nuclear bombs, abortions and Hitler. To experience all phenomena without judgement, with neither aversion or attraction, is what some Buddhist masters speak of as "what is." This points to a view of "self" which has always been, and will always be, formless, not contained by skin, not structured by bone. The emphasis on Buddhist practice is to apprehend this reality through meditation, and therefore know it internally. But we struggle not just to realize ourselves as impermanent manifestations of the unborn and undying in an impartial universe. We take vows to be where the suffering is. In terms of abortion, this means staying open to the suffering of a woman faced with an unwanted pregnancy, to her lover who may or may not want the child, to the suffering of an aborted fetus, to the suffering of an unwanted baby.

In Buddhism we say there is no birth, no death, no dying, no cessation of dying. Zen master Dogen tells us that wood is wood and ash is ash and wood does not turn into ash. So life is life and death is death and life does not turn into death. All forms manifest what is; gross distinctions between life and death are labels of convenience—useful perhaps, but with no basis in reality. Writing on the Ten Grave Precepts, Robert Aitken opens a discussion on the first precept with "There is fundamentally no birth and no death as we die and are born. When we kill the spirit that may realize this fact, we are violating this precept."

If the essential nature of all phenomena is emptiness, who dies? Who kills? Who is killed and who is reborn? These are the great questions of Buddhist dharma and address the absolute nature of reality. Introducing the absolute dimension to the abortion issue doesn't easily translate into a political agenda. But neither does it serve us well to hold the absolute at bay for fear of misinterpretation. What happens to the question of abortion when, even intellectually, we apprehend that everything is the enlightened way, realized or not, aborted or not? What happens in the big view?

"Life is life recycling itself all the time," says Sylvia Boorstein. A grandmother of four, Boorstein feels fortunate that she herself has never had to face the decision whether or not to abort. As a vipassana teacher, however, she is often called upon to comfort women who come into retreat following an abortion. "What counts," explains Boorstein, "is procarefulness. Procontraception. Proattention, prothoughtfulness. Prothoughtfulness with regard to sex is an expression of a sexuality that is non-exploitative, not compulsive. There is a way to have a compassionate abortion that involves the recognition that this is not the right time for this plant to flourish. But also, life is nothing but continual change and flux, with no beginning and no ending and, from the big view, it really doesn't matter where life appears to stop and where life appears to start."

When asked about abortion at a conference some six or seven years ago, His Holiness the Dalai Lama spoke of it as a violation of the first precept. But he added, sometimes circumstances are such that abortion can result from a compassionate decision.

Many years ago an American couple, unmarried and young, consulted their Tibetan lama when the woman became pregnant. For them, abortion was one option. But, said the lama, "How can you consider taking a life when you have taken the bodhisattva vow to save all sentient beings?" The lama then told them that if, for any reason, they found themselves unable to care for the child once it came into the world, he himself would raise it.

According to Buddhist teachings, the chances of being exposed to true dharma are less likely than the chances of a sea turtle placing its head through the one and only yoke floating in all the ocean waters of the world; any dharma student who has an abortion automatically denies this extraordinarily rare and precious opportunity. Just to attain a human birth at all is considered a cause for celebration, for only in this life form can a sentient being realize its own true nature—which is to say, become enlightened. At the same time, Buddhist teachers also speak of the capacity of those who have passed from this sphere of existence to choose their next set of parents, and therefore participate in addressing their own karmic needs. Presumably this includes choosing wombs that carry to term and those that do not.

Speaking of reality the Zen texts tell us no snowflake falls in an inappropriate place. No exceptions, including wanted and unwanted, healthy, sick and aborted babies. But Zen gardens do not tolerate weeds. Do weeds have a right to live? Or unwanted fetuses? That human beings have this "right" assumes another human—or anthropocentric—argument. It has nothing to do with reality, that is, with snowflake reality. Humans have no more inherent right to live than they have the right to decide that garden weeds or livestock are born to die. This belief in the "right" to life reflects the Western impulse to control and shape reality, to project onto life values that embrace human, as well as individual, supremacy. As Joseph Scheidler, Executive Director of the Pro-Life League put it: "For those who say I can't impose my morality on others, I say just watch me." How difficult it is to consider that life itself may not care whether we live it or not; or take notice of our desires to be special when we are not.

Buddhist teachings emphasize that all form is essentially empty of description. Therefore, the responsibility for description falls to us. Buddhism in the West introduces the possibility that a nonanthropocentric reality can inspire universal respon-

sibility, and that compassion can be cultivated as a way of being, and not as an attitude conditioned by personal judgment.

This has nothing to do with voting for or against abortion. It has everything to do
with how any individual relates to sex, deals with pregnancy, decides whether to
have an abortion or a baby. Yet, unfortunately the abortion debate reflects only a
Western obsession with control, not consciousness.

Recently I spoke with a young man whose girlfriend had become pregnant. He was
a Buddhist practitioner and she wasn't: he wanted to have the baby and she didn't.
She went off to an abortion clinic with a girlfriend and he went to visit his Buddhist
master and burst into tears. He was given a practice to alleviate his anxiety, his longing, and his guilt. I asked if his experience would change the way he might vote on
the abortion issue. After remaining quiet for a few minutes, he said, "I'm not interested in listening to politicians talk for or against life or for or against abortion. I
would vote for anyone who got out there and asked "What is life?"

Building Bridges:
Know One Another

"We . . . have made you nations and tribes that you may know one another."

Qur'an Surah 49:13

The final part focuses on the need to deal with internal struggles within the religious left, and to go beyond those struggles to forge cooperative links. The idea of building bridges requires that we not only work with those who are close to us, but also that we learn to make community with those who are different. The concept of a rainbow coalition is a powerful one. Today the religious left finds itself more fragmented than ever. Groups work across religious lines on single issues, or within their own denominations on the same issue. But the religious left has not come to terms with living with one another in this age of pluralism. These essays suggest some of the work that needs to be done before the religious left could unify itself.

Diana Eck describes the complicated face of religion in America as we look towards the twenty-first century. She suggests that only through religious, ethnic, and racial cooperation will we be able to survive in the future. Ron Young writes from the perspective of the American effort to get Muslims, Jews, and Christians into dialogue about the Middle East so that their conversations can lead to a unified peace-seeking approach in that region. Young was responsible for the development of an interfaith coalition organized by the Society of Friends of Jews, Muslims, and Christians that traveled to the Middle East to promote peace efforts.

Carl Evans writes about working within Christian churches to change attitudes towards Jews. Evans calls for Christians to accept Judaism not as a precursor to Christianity but as a religion in its own right, to rethink the culpability of the Jews in the death of Jesus and to accept the culpability of Christendom in the persecution of Jews. This change in Christian thinking, which has already begun to take place, is a paradigm for reconciliation among all religions.

Wi Jo Kang looks at Christian mission in the light of the Columbus quincentenary, focusing his essay on the need for Christianity to come to terms with its role in the missionizing of the Western hemisphere and the destruction of native populations here. Kang takes a critical look at Christian texts that support these claims.

Ranck's essay is an example of the intergroup cooperation that the religious left is trying to foster. His description of a four-language, multi-ethnic and -racial church in Southern California may be the model of the future and point the way to openings for the religious left to solve its own internal problems.

Diana Eck

---

32   Difference Is No Excuse for Hatred

America today has a greater range of cultural and religious diversity than any other nation on earth. With the democratic traditions of the United States, this might truly allow us to become a model of what a working, multi-religious society might be like. We don't have many models for that kind of society in the world, and perhaps, only perhaps, if we can begin to overcome the fear and the anger and to work seriously to develop a really operative interfaith infrastructure, that might happen.

I'm not going to begin by laying out the litany of violence that has brought us here. We do need, however, to bear clearly in our minds how much in recent years this violence has been fueled with the energy of racial, cultural, ethnic and religious difference.

On a world scale Tamils and Singhalese in Sri Lanka; Muslims and Hindu nationalists in India; Muslims and Christians in Bosnia, Croatia and Serbia; a new spate of anti-Semitism in Europe; the massacre of Muslim worshippers in Hebron; and in America as well. Whatever the sources of violence—economic, educational, etc.—the ways in which violence has increasingly been construed and the lines along which it is increasingly cast, however simplistically this may be the case, are racial, ethnic and even religious. This in an issue we need to face squarely. African-Americans, Korean Americans, Hispanic-Americans, Blacks and Jews, Arabs and Jews, Christians and Muslims. These have too often become the symbolic and rhetorical fault lines for absolutely devastating conflict.

New Model of Bridge Building

The opportunity to provide a new model of bridge-building across the lines of race and ethnicity and religion that our world and that our country so desperately needs

Originally published in *Christian Social Action* (May 1994), 7:32–33. Reprinted with permission from *Christian Social Action* magazine, May 1994; copyright 1994 by the General Board of Church and Society of the United Methodist Church.

is a distinctively American opportunity today—an opportunity that is yours in virtually every city. It is possible and, indeed, incumbent as a witness to a model of communication and community building across the lines of race and religion and culture that is significant if there is to be an interfaith impact in American cities today. If we are to bear witness against violence, against the symbolic dimensions of racial and ethnic and religious violence, then people of faith must make an active effort to demonstrate that difference is no excuse for hatred and that people in every religious tradition—even those with whom we differ most sharply—can work together and can even love one another. So my first point is really to recognize the dimensions of this new multi-religious reality.

The second point I would make is to recognize that fear and the violence it perpetrates and generates is not new. For those of you who are Native Americans or African Americans, one does not need to rehearse very long one's own history to recognize how this is so. But I want to turn again to the new reality that many of us do not know so much about: Our multi-religious history did not begin in 1965 with the change in immigration laws. Our Islamic history, for example, goes back to the slave trade where scholars estimate that 10 percent of the Africans brought to the United States as slaves were Muslims. Our Buddhist history goes back at least to the 1850s with the arrival of thousands of Chinese who came for the Gold Rush, for the mining industry, and for building the transcontinental railroads.

In the first census taken in Montana, when it was still a territory in 1870, 10 percent of the population counted on the frontier in Montana was Chinese. There were Chinese Buddhist temples in Helena and Butte and Chinese graveyards. So what happened to the Chinese Buddhists who were so much a part of the 19th century frontier?

In 1882 the first Chinese Exclusion Act was passed. As that legislation was debated the governor of California insisted, "No Chinaman would ever be able to understand that he should vote intelligently or honestly." A senator from Massachusetts blustered, "This bill does not prohibit the Chinese laborer; it only says if he comes he'll go to the penitentiary." One of his colleagues in the U.S. Senate added, "They do not wear our kind of clothes, and when they die their bones are taken back to their native country."

Chinese were hanged and beaten and driven, almost without a trace, from Montana, Wyoming, Idaho. The racism that was generated with anti-Chinese legislation gradually expanded to include Japanese, Koreans and other Asiatics, as they were called. And at the time of the World's Parliament of Religion in 1893, there were anti-Japanese signs all the way up and down the west coast, to the point that one of the Buddhist representatives of the tradition from Japan said, "If such be the Christian ethics, well, we're perfectly satisfied to remain heathen." He went on to comment that as Japanese Buddhists, they weren't so concerned about which religion you belonged to but whether you actually had an ethic that conformed with the norms of that tradition—which he did not see to be the case in California.

Interfaith Cooperation/Interfaith Violence

In 1893 at the close of the World Parliament of Religion one of the organizers proclaimed, "Henceforth the religions of the world will make war not on each other but on the giant evils that afflict mankind." We can't help but hear those words with a little bit of irony and sadness 100 years later.

It's true that interfaith cooperation has gotten a good start but interfaith violence has kept pace. The world's religious traditions still manage to provide fuel and symbolic weaponry for the world's strife. The giant evils that afflict humankind have grown as rapidly as our dreams. The chasms between the cultural, racial, and religious families of humankind have opened as quickly as the bridges we have built to span them. And still suspicions and fears crystallize and take their public shape around issues of difference: religious difference, ethnic difference, racial difference.

Even with the vibrant burst of interfaith activity, nationally and internationally and locally, there is still not a viable interfaith infrastructure capable of bearing the complexity of our interreligious relations now in the late 20th century—not in the world is there such an interfaith infrastructure, not in any nation and certainly not at the local level. All of these instruments of interfaith cooperation are fairly fragile. Not surprisingly I would conclude with the insistence, then, that there is a lot of work to be done, and that the role of religious communities—especially interreligious communities—could be a powerful witness to a world of cooperation that we so desperately need.

Even within our religious traditions, however, there is tension and polarization and fingerpointing and demonizing as if the world didn't present enough problems—the violence, the division, the hate mongering, within the Christian community. The energy of our religious traditions has become enervated by the internal politics and controversies of our denominations, expending millions and millions of human hours on questions like, "What is the gender of the person you love?" or, "What is the gender of the language you use for the God you love?" A new spate of heresy hunting is occurring in the United Methodist Church. Do we use the word Sophia, which is, after all, in the Bible in a context of Christian worship? And worse: the unconscionable use of Scripture, tearing verses out of context to use them as clubs to brutalize our neighbors and our co-religionists or people of other faiths.

Our religious traditions, our Christian families of faith have much to account for. How quickly we take offense in the discourse between and among our religious, racial and ethnic groups. How quickly we take offense, we escalate offense, we magnify offense, we return offense.

Criticism is difficult, however, if people don't have the on-going responsibility and opportunity for relationship and for reparation that makes criticism a form of growth and not a form of violence. If interreligious dialogue is to move beyond occasional meetings and roundtables, it must become "a culture of dialogue." It must create a whole context of on-going relatedness and trust in which self-criticism and mutual criticism are an acceptable and valuable part of the interreligious exchange and in which criticism and genuine difference are not avoided, but encountered.

That is part of what I would call an interfaith infrastructure, in which genuine difference does not provide the occasion for walking out or walking away from the table, an unacceptable climate in which I will not talk to you because you have said something that offends me. There is no way ahead with this kind of escalation of rhetoric and offense.

Mutual criticism and self criticism also involve apology and reparation, what Jews call "the mendings of the world." To apologize, to accept apology, to move forward rather than over and over the same tracks of pain. If religious communities cannot learn to do this with one another, what hope do we have for a larger secular society torn by violence and suspicion and anger?

Ronald J. Young

33   A Case Study: American Christians, Jews, and Muslims Working Together for Middle East Peace

Shalom, salaam, peace! In all three traditions—Jewish, Christian, and Islamic—the pursuit of peace is fundamental to doing God's will. Yet when it comes to work for peace between the Arab states, Israel, and the Palestinians, interfaith cooperation has been practically nonexistent. Nonetheless, since 1987 several hundred American Jewish, Christian, and Muslim leaders have been working together in the U.S. Interreligious Committee for Peace in the Middle East.

Why is cooperation so difficult? What makes interfaith work for Middle East peace more possible and urgent today? What has been accomplished and what are the challenges? Is peace really possible?

Obstacles and New Hopes

In the decades since the founding of modern-day Israel and the first Arab-Israeli war in 1948, work for peace in the Middle East has confronted multiple obstacles.

First, based on the bitter history of the conflict and what for years were mutually exclusive goals of the two sides, i.e., security for Israel versus the liberation of all of Palestine, most people have felt a profound sense of pessimism about prospects for peace. Such pessimism tended to produce cynical detachment rather than interest and engagement with the issues.

Originally published in *Church and Society* (September/October 1992), 83:70–79. Reprinted by permission of the author.

A second obstacle is the complexity of the conflict. Partisan loyalty to a particular side or the common tendency to simplify issues sometimes leads people to characterize the conflict in terms of right versus wrong. In fact, both sides present compelling moral and historical claims. Most people inclined toward social action prefer more simplified issues.

A third obstacle, especially challenging to interfaith work for peace, is the way in which dealing with the Middle East causes all of us—Jews, Christians, and Muslims—to confront some of our deepest fears and most persistent prejudices.

Developments in the last fifteen years—including the historic Camp David peace treaty between Egypt and Israel (1979), the War in Lebanon (1982), the Palestinian uprising (1987) and subsequent acceptance of a "two-state solution" by the Palestine Liberation Organization (1988), the Gulf War (1990–91), the U.S.-Russia-sponsored Middle East peace process begun in Madrid a year ago and, most recently, the elections in Israel—have had the effect of focusing our attention on issues in the Arab-Israeli-Palestinian conflict and tempering our pessimism with increased hopes for peace.

Furthermore, while for years interreligious dialog in the United States avoided addressing the Middle East, in part out of fear that this would destroy the dialog, now increasing numbers of Christians, Jews, and Muslims are accepting the challenge. Indeed, many are coming to the conclusion that frank and sensitive discussion of the Middle East is essential to the integrity of Jewish-Christian-Muslim dialog.

Coming Together for Peace Efforts

In June 1987, after two years of unpublicized consultations, fifty prominent American Jewish, Christian, and Muslim leaders met to form the U.S. Interreligious Committee for Peace in the Middle East. The committee's founding statement, "A Time for Peace," calls for an active United States role in helping to achieve peace based on:

- Israel's right to secure borders and peace with her neighbors
- the Palestinian people's right of self-determination
- negotiations between the Arab states, Israel, and the Palestinians based on U.N. Resolution 242
- an international conference to provide the framework, process, and guarantees for peace.

In January 1988 the U.S. Committee was announced publicly in Washington with endorsements by more than five hundred American Jewish, Christian, and Muslim leaders. Today there are more than 1,500 endorsers, and related local interreligious committees are active in several U.S. cities.

Obstacles to Cooperation

Why is it so difficult for American Jews, Christians, and Muslims to cooperate for peace in the Middle East? What are the issues in the Christian community and in other communities about which we need to be sensitive as we seek to work together?

Issues for American Jews

An American rabbi and his seven-year-old son were watching television news showing Israeli soldiers in Gaza chase and beat Palestinian youths who had thrown stones at an Israeli patrol. The rabbi's son asked his father, "Why are the soldiers beating those Jewish children?" When his father told him that the youths were Arabs and it was the soldiers who were Jewish, the boy exclaimed, "That couldn't be!"

For Jews, who have experienced centuries of persecution to the extent that being the victim is embedded in the psyche almost as a matter of self-definition, it is extremely hard to accept that, like all peoples who have gained power, Israelis have become victimizers as well as victims.

While opinion polls consistently indicate that most American Jews support the right of self-determination for Palestinians and the idea of Israel exchanging occupied territories for secure peace, many Jews still are reluctant to criticize Israel outside of the Jewish community. This reflects deep fear among Jews, arising from their unique history, that such criticism can easily erode non-Jewish support for Israel and eventually endanger its survival.

In working with Palestinians and listening to their personal histories, Jews are forced to confront the other side of the incredible story of Israel's creation out of the ashes of the Holocaust, that is, the dispersal and suffering of the Palestinians. While ultimately, addressing this moral ambiguity may be liberating, it also is very painful.

For Jews, working with non-Jews for peace means accepting that Israel's fate depends in no small measure on the support of the United States and a world community most of which, only fifty years ago, acquiesced in the abandonment of the Jewish people. Not surprisingly, Jews relate to this reality of interdependence with particular wariness when it comes to issues affecting the survival of Israel.

Issues for Arab-American Christians and Muslim Americans

A basic issue for many Arab-American Christians and even more so for Muslim Americans is that, despite some recent progress, they are still largely invisible minorities in America. It should not be surprising that, as they emerge and their communities gain public recognition, they are wary of getting involved in an issue as controversial as the Arab-Israeli-Palestinian conflict.

Arab-American Christians and Muslim Americans are painfully aware of how much ignorance and prejudice exist in our society toward Arabs and Muslims. As recently as during the Gulf War, Arab Americans and Muslim Americans were targeted by the FBI for intimidating investigations; many experienced incidents of verbal and, in some cases, physical abuse from other Americans. Muslims are very conscious of the contrast between western response to Iraq's invasion of Kuwait, where access to oil was at stake, and to the tragic conflicts in former Yugoslavia and Somalia, where thousands of Muslims have died.

For Christian and Muslim Americans of Middle Eastern origin, discussion of the Middle East involves confronting their own history of suffering during the Crusades and the Inquisition, under the Ottoman Empire, under European colonial rule and, since 1948, in a series of humiliating wars with Israel. Haunted by the memory of their Golden Age less than a millennium ago, when Arab-Muslim societies were the source of some of the greatest achievements of civilization, it is still hard for Arabs to understand what happened to Arab greatness. It is even harder for Arab Americans to share their pain and puzzlement publicly when they feel most Americans have little appreciation for Arab history and culture.

Furthermore, while most Arab Americans acknowledge that Arab suffering in recent decades has resulted in part from a tragic failure in Arab leadership, they fear that any self-critical views they express outside of their community will simply reinforce existing negative prejudices against Arabs.

For Palestinian Americans, working for peace with Jewish Americans involves listening to the history and pain of Jewish suffering and the fears Jews have of Palestinians and other Arabs, based on decades of Arab hostility to Israel. For many Palestinian Americans who have their own history of pain, their own fears and, in many cases, close family members currently suffering under Israeli occupation, it is very hard to be actively sympathetic to the sufferings and fears of Jews.

Issues for Other American Christians

A basic challenge for non-Arab-American Christians is to resist the temptation of thinking that they come to this conflict with clean hands. Perhaps a good reminder of the problem is found in the story of a U.S. Ambassador in the 1950s who is reported to have blurted out, in a moment of frustration, "If only these Arabs and Jews would learn to solve their conflict like good Christians." It is essential that Christians acknowledge their history with the Jewish people and with Arabs and Muslims, much of which is a history of domination and persecution. It is equally essential that Christians acknowledge and challenge the persistent, underlying prejudices that still exist today toward Jews and toward Arabs and Muslims.

Most Christians prefer to think of Jews as just another religious group or, as one person put it, "Unitarians who happen to speak Hebrew." Many reject or still do not understand the concept of Jewish peoplehood, which is the fundamental source of moral legitimacy for Jewish nationalism, i.e., Zionism. This helps explain why for the most part American Christians were silent about the United Nations resolution, only recently repudiated, equating Zionism with racism.

Many American Christians tend to ignore the rich diversity and strong differences of opinion among Israelis. Some Christians react defensively and label any criticism of Israel as anti-Jewish. Others use criticism of Israeli policies to express hostility toward Israel, often thinly disguising deeper resentment against Jews.

On the other side, examples of ignorance and prejudice toward Arabs and Muslims are no less frequent or harmful. Many American Christians still accept very negative stereotypes of Arabs and Muslims. Specifically, in relation to the Middle East conflict, for years most American Christians equated the Palestine Liberation Organization with terrorism, thus denying the PLO's legitimacy, even though for Palestinians this has meant denial of the primary symbol and organizational expression of Palestinian nationalism. Just as Jews feel hurt and angry when Zionism is viewed as inherently negative, so Arabs feel when the PLO or Palestinians are equated with terrorism.

Many American Christians tend to be ignorant about Arab Christians and even more uninformed about Muslims. Most have little knowledge of the teachings in the Qur'an. While there has been progress in development of Christian theology toward the Jewish people, there are only the barest beginnings of a constructive Christian theology toward Islam.

Even a particular concern that motivated their interest in the Middle East may blind American Christians to other dimensions of the conflict. For years Christians who focused on Christian responsibility for anti-Semitism and the Holocaust tended to ignore the suffering of the Palestinians. Christians primarily interested in holy sites or in viewing events as fulfillment of prophesies tend to ignore the real peoples of the Middle East. Many Christians who have become active in sympathy with the 1987 Palestinian uprising tend to overlook Palestinian attacks on Israel and the threats from surrounding Arab states.

There also is a question of what ethic guides American Christians in their approach to the Middle Eastern conflict. Based on experience with other conflicts, many Christians are guided by an ethic of solidarity that teaches them to take sides with the victims. When both Jews and Arabs have been victims, an ethic of reconciliation, with its emphasis on resolving the conflict rather than taking sides, provides better guidance than an ethic of solidarity.

Accomplishments of the U.S. Interreligious Committee

There is no way to avoid dealing with these concerns if we are serious about interreligious cooperation for peace. Despite the daunting nature of the issues, it is possible for Jews, Christians, and Muslims to work together. The story of the accomplishments of the U.S. Interreligious Committee for Peace in the Middle East provides some indicators of approaches that are positive:

• 1987–88—The Committee arranges interreligious tours to the Middle East, the participants playing key roles in organizing the interreligious committee when they return home.

- March 1989—A National Convocation for Peace in the Middle East is held in Washington, D.C., bringing together seven hundred American Jews, Christians, and Muslims from thirty-eight states to hear Arab and Israeli advocates for peace and to visit a hundred key members of Congress. These activities are based on the Committee statement, "A Time for Peace."
- 1989–90—Local Interreligious Convocations for Peace, with prominent Israeli and Palestinian speakers, are sponsored in a dozen cities across the United States.
- 1990–91—In response to the threat of war with Iraq, the Committee issues "Prayers for Peace" by a Jew, a Christian, and a Muslim and encourages interreligious services in hundreds of communities across the country.
- December 1991—In support of the U.S.-Russia-sponsored peace process, the Committee organizes an Interfaith Service of Prayer for Peace at the Washington National Cathedral, attended by four hundred persons, including Secretary of State James A. Baker III.
- January 1992—The Committee issues "An Open Letter to Candidates" by American Jewish, Christian, and Muslim leaders, appealing for sensitivity and support of the peace process.
- February 1992—A delegation of twelve national Jewish, Christian, and Muslim leaders representing the U.S. Interreligious Committee meets with Assistant Secretary of State Edward Djerejian and with Arab and Israeli delegations to the peace negotiations, with a report of these meetings circulated widely by the Committee.
- 1992–93—For the period following U.S. elections, the Interreligious Committee has been developing plans for a second National Convocation for Peace to be held in Washington, D.C., and for events across the country to encourage broad public support for a sustained, active, and creative U.S. role to help the Middle East peace process succeed.

An Approach to Working Together

There are many challenging issues Jews, Christians, and Muslims face in working together for Middle East peace. At the same time, the experience of the U.S. Interreligious Committee demonstrates that working together is possible and that the benefits of cooperation are rich. Working together involves making a commitment that— whether persons begin with a strong loyalty to a particular side or to an idea of what a fair solution would be—they will sensitively seek to understand and work with all sides for a genuinely reconciliatory peace. The commitment to an interreligious approach requires work by all to accept the historical and moral complexities of the Arab-Israeli-Palestinian conflict. All need to feel the fears and pain of others involved in the conflict. Each group needs to be prepared to challenge its own deepest prejudices as well as those prejudices directed against it, something that may not happen in interreligious work on less sensitive issues. If all participants are open and honest, they all are likely to learn something about the difference between God's righteousness and human self-righteousness. Even if it is not possible to agree on all the specifics of what peace requires, participants can at least point the way to peace.

There is growing awareness on all sides of the Arab-Israeli-Palestinian conflict that a negotiated settlement may be possible. By working together, American Christians, Jews, and Muslims can create an effective interreligious climate to support an active, sustained U.S. policy for a secure and fair peace in the Middle East. From a broader perspective, the central role of religion in many of today's ethnic and national conflicts and in struggles for justice and democracy makes interreligious cooperation more urgent than ever. Our experience working together for peace in the Middle East can develop sensitivities and build relationships that are essential for addressing other important issues.

Talking Points on Prospects for Peace, the Peace Process, and the U.S. Role

U.S. Interreligious Committee for Peace in the Middle East

This was prepared following late February meetings of a Christian, Jewish, and Muslim delegation from the U.S. Interreligious Committee for Peace in the Middle East with Assistant Secretary of State Edward P. Djerejian and Deputy Assistant Secretary of State Daniel C. Kurtzer and with the Arab and Israeli delegations to the peace talks on the Middle East.

• We were impressed by the Administration's resolve to pursue peace in the negotiations and the pressures of an election year. We support this commitment by the United States, and we encourage all candidates to support it.

• We support the U.S. insistence on the need for positive gestures by the Arab states, Israel, and the Palestinians to help "build constituencies for peace" among all the parties, in part because progress in formal negotiations may not be apparent until agreement is nearly complete.

Trust-building measures can be unilateral or conditional; they can be large steps or small; and they can be done at an official level or by private initiatives as long as they have real impact. Examples of trust-building measures include:

• Arab states suspending the boycott of Israel
• Israel freezing settlements in the occupied territories
• Syria relaxing emigration restrictions on Syrian Jews
• Israel easing living conditions for Palestinians in the occupied territories
• Palestinian leaders calling for an end to violence related to the Intifada.

• The fact that Israel and the Palestinians have both presented proposals for interim self-rule in the West Bank and Gaza represents a major breakthrough in this conflict. Months of tough negotiations, including an active U.S. mediatory role, will be needed to reconcile the two plans. We believe agreement on interim self-rule is possible with-out compromising the basic rights of either side.

• All of the parties deserve support and encouragement for the serious commitment they have made to the peace process and for their determination to "stay at it" despite violent incidents and the lack of substantive progress so far.

• There is danger if the negotiations do not move forward that violent incidents will escalate, leading eventually to another Arab-Israeli war. Indeed, lack of apparent progress is feeding distrust and fueling extremist elements on both sides who want the talks to fail. We believe the United States needs to become more active in the peace process, both in terms of offering ideas to resolve substantive issues in the negotia-tions and helping to create a more positive atmosphere for progress toward peace.

March 1992 Delegation

• Cherif Sedkey, Member, Arab-American Council on the Middle East
• Rabbi Eugene Lipman, former President, Central Conference of American Rabbis
• Dale L. Bishop, Director, Middle East Office of the National Council of Churches
• Richard D. Schwartz, Chair, American Coalition for Middle East Dialog
• Khalil Jahshan, Executive Director, National Association of Arab-Americans
• Fr. Raymond Helmick, S.J., Professor, Boston College
• Dr. Dawud Assad, President, Council of Mosques, U.S.A.
• Rabbi Mordecai Liebling, Executive Director, Federation of Reconstructionist Syna-gogues
• James F. Sams, former President, National Association of Arab-Americans
• Ronald J. Young, Executive Director, U.S. Interreligious Committee for Peace in the Middle East

Shalom. Salaam. Peace.

Wi Jo Kang

34   Reconsidering Christopher Columbus and the Recovery of a Biblical Theology of Mission

I had my first encounter with Columbus through a Japanese language textbook when I was a fifth grader in Korea under the educational system of the Japanese colonial rule. It was in the midst of the Second World War when Japan was engaged in military conflict in the Pacific against the allied forces. At that time, we were prohibited from playing baseball, basketball, or any sports that originated in the West or North America. In addition, any stories that dealt with Europe or North America were deleted from the textbooks. Strangely enough, however, even in this strong anti-western atmosphere, the story of Columbus remained a part of the Japanese language textbook and was admired by the other fifth graders.

The story of Columbus taught in that textbook went like this. After "the discovery of America," friends of Columbus celebrated his achievement and held a party. In the party there was a contest to see who could get an egg to stand on the table. Of course, nobody was successful in keeping the egg from rolling over. Then Columbus took the egg, pounded the bottom, and placed the egg so that it would stand. Everybody in the party applauded and praised his ingenuity.

This story has bothered me ever since my fifth grade days. It seemed to me that the attitude of Columbus had been arrogant and he had cheated to make the egg stand. His friends had wanted to make an egg stand on the table naturally, but Columbus only succeeded by damaging the egg. Another greater question that bothered me was why the Japanese government allowed the students to learn about Columbus while any other stories dealing with Europe and North America were censored.

Today, as I ponder on the sailing of Columbus to America and reconsider him in the year of his quincentenary, I clearly understand why the Japanese colonial government allowed the students to learn about him and glorify his life. The answer is

Originally published in *Word and World* (Spring 1992), 12:116–122. © *Word and World*. Reprinted with permission. All rights reserved.

simple: the war of Japanese imperialism in Asia and the sailing of Columbus to the "new world" had exactly the same purpose. Both sought to conquer, enslave, and plunder innocent people in order to glorify and increase the wealth and power of another—in the first case the Japanese imperial army, and in the second, the Spanish Conquistadors. The Japanese discovered the political justification in the story of Columbus' brutal subjugation of the Native American people to legitimize their own acts of imperialism and oppression of the people of Asia.

The Japanese empire after the Meiji restoration in 1868 was constantly engaging in wars of imperialism. Japan fought against China in 1894–95 and took over the island of Formosa or Taiwan. In 1904–05 Japan fought against Russia and colonized Korea. Japan further escalated its imperialistic ambition and military actions in China, established the puppet state of Manchukuo in 1932, and engaged in all-out war against China in 1937. In the late 1930s and early 1940s, Japanese armed forces invaded French Indo-China and in 1941 attacked Pearl Harbor. The leaders of the Japanese empire found all these acts of military aggression and territorial expansion congenial with the spirit of Columbus—a criminal spirit of greed, denial of human rights, and unspeakable violence against hundreds of thousands of helpless people.

I. Rethinking Columbus—Rethinking Mission

The *New Catholic Encyclopedia* describes Columbus as "seaman, chartmaker, navigator, discoverer of America." Throughout his life, "Columbus attempted to emulate St. Christopher, 'the Christ bearer.' Ardent in religious devotion, he desired to spread the Christian faith more than he wished for personal glory, wealth and distinction."[1] Without a doubt, Columbus was eager to Christianize the natives. However, Columbus did not want to spread the Christian faith to enrich the life of people by making a new relationship with God through faith in Christ, but rather to enslave the Native Americans to serve Christian nations of Europe. He clearly stated this purpose in a letter to Luis De Santangel, Comptroller of the Treasury of the King and Queen:

> I presented them [the Indians] with a variety of things, in order to secure their affection, and that they may become Christians, and enter into the service of their Highnesses and the Castilian nation, and also aid us in procuring such things as they possess, and we stand in need of.[2]

Columbus also wrote in his diary (dated November 19, 1492), urging the Spanish royalty to convert the "Indians" to Christianity:

> They very quickly learn such prayers as we repeat to them, and also make the sign of the cross. Your Highness should therefore adopt the resolution of converting them to Christianity, in which enterprise I am of opinion that a very short space of time would suffice to gain to our holy faith multitude of people.[3]

Columbus quickly added his real purpose for the "discovery of new world," which was to gain great riches and "vast quantities of gold." Again on December 23, 1492, he wrote: "Our Lord in his mercy directs me to where I may find the gold mine as I have many here who profess to be acquainted with it."[4]

Columbus failed to find gold or gold mines, yet he often lied about this in his letters and diaries. On December 29, 1492, he wrote: "There is so much gold and in so many places, and in this island of Espanola.[5] Columbus and his men ordered the natives to bring quotas of gold; when they failed to bring the gold, their hands were chopped off and they bled to death.[6] When Columbus and his men were unable to acquire the gold, they resorted to becoming slave traders in order to justify the expenses for their trip. From the first voyage on, Columbus ordered the brutal seizure of the native islanders of the West Indies and transported them to Spain for sale as slaves. In 1495 Columbus and his men rounded up 1,500 native men, women, and children to fill up the ships. The ships did not have enough room for 1,500 people, so 500 of the strongest bodies were selected. Yet, even the healthiest and strongest could not survive, due to the inhuman conditions on the ships and the trauma of enslavement. Two hundred of them died in passage as a result of malnutrition, disease, and physical abuse.

Columbus and his men committed indescribable crimes against the very people who had welcomed and aided them. Columbus himself wrote about the kindness, hospitality, and innocence of the native people:

> No request of anything from them is ever refused, but they rather invite acceptance of what they possess, and manifest such a generosity that they would give away their own hearts. Let the articles be of great or small value, they offer it readily, and receive anything which is tendered in return with perfect content.[7]

The culture of the Native Americans had highly-developed values of communal sharing and peaceful resolution of conflicts. Again Columbus wrote:

> They do not possess iron, steel, or weapons and seem to have no inclination for the latter, being timorous to the last degree. They have an instrument consisting of a cane, taken while in seed, and headed with a sharp stick, but they never venture to use it.[8]

In spite of the gentleness of the native people, Columbus enslaved them in the name of "Christianity" and "the Trinity." The question arises, was it Columbus's understanding of Christianity and Trinity that led him to such Christian ways of life? The answer is no. Columbus was a son of his time. Ultimately, the church bears the responsibility for producing such a criminal man and supporting such inhuman acts.

A year after Columbus's "discovery of America" the office of the papacy in Rome issued a bull called *Inter caetera*. In this bull, Pope Alexander VI legitimates the sending of missionaries to the "New World" by the Portuguese and Spanish powers using revenues from the "discovered territories" for the purpose. The same pope issued another bull in 1501, *Examinae devotionis*, which more fully specified the collecting of tithes in the colonies and the use of the money for the "Christianization" of the people. In such ecclesiastical decisions, the church justified the colonization and domination of the native people in other parts of the world by the European powers. Such theology was based on the notion of Christendom, the idea of a temporal kingdom under the spiritual authority of the Christian church, which developed in the medieval period. This theology taught that, outside of Christendom, there was no religion and therefore no culture, only darkness and death. Since the natives did not have "religion," they were destined to die, and often the murdering of the natives was justified. When a people in the so-called new world resisted the orders from the Christian kings and queens who claimed responsibility for extending the glory of the pope, whom they saw as the Vicar of Christ on earth, they were brutally murdered to the point of genocide.

Columbus and his men were not originators of the crimes of stealing, killing and enslavement of the people. During the time of the crusades, from the eleventh to the fourteenth centuries, such crimes were already in practice by Christian soldiers, as a recent article shows:

> Even their hard-bitten contemporaries were shocked by the terrible massacre that followed as the maddened crusaders rampaged through the city [Jerusalem] in a bloody catharsis.[9]

The church should have been the one to stand against such crimes. However, it was the church and church leaders who waged such cruelty. For example:

> During the siege of Caesarea in the spring of 1101, two envoys of the beleaguered Muslim town reproached the patriarch of Jerusalem and the papal legate for having called on the crusaders to slay the Saracens and take their land, thereby contravening the Christian injunctions against murder and robbery. So reports the Genoese chronicler Caffaro, an eyewitness to that siege, who also relates that the patriarch brushed aside this criticism by telling the envoys that Caesarea, the city of Peter, belongs to the Christians by right, and those who impugn God's law ought to be slain.[10]

Four hundred years later, in the time of Columbus, the teachings and attitudes of the church had substantially changed. The exploitation, colonization, conquest, and enslavement of people in other lands were more effectively carried out, using scientific knowledge and the wealth of Spain—money which had been confiscated from the properties of the Jews who were expelled by the Spanish inquisition. Columbus only added his own greed for gold and fame, and the situation in the "new world" became worse. The rich God-given islands of paradise in the West Indies became a place of poverty and suffering inflicted by the "Christian" invaders. Yet the church and church leaders did not change their attitudes, then or now. In the time of Columbus, Bartolome de las Casas, who wrote that "Spain deserved punishment for the destruction we have brought to the Indies,"[11] said about Columbus:

> Many is the time I have wished that God would again inspire me and that I had Cicero's gift of eloquence to extol the indescribable service to God and to the world which Christopher Columbus rendered at the cost of such pain and dangers, such skill and expertise, when he so courageously discovered the New World.[12]

Today, many in the Roman Catholic Church still regard Columbus as the one who emulated Christopher, the Christ bearer. Amid such attitudes, it is no wonder that many young people criticize and leave the church. Manuel Ocampo, a Philippino painter who has been working in Los Angeles since 1986 and is considered one of the most prominent contemporary young artists, recently called Catholicism "one of the major oppressors of Third World cultures." [13]

And what about the Protestant churches? In the eighteenth and nineteenth centuries, the Protestant countries of Northern Europe, Great Britain, and the new nation of the United States of America began to send missionaries abroad. Unfortunately, however, they too repeated the pattern of the earlier Roman Catholic mission. The mission activities of the Protestant churches were also closely identified with the exploration of newly acquired lands and the colonial interests of the European and North American countries. This is apparent in the Indian subcontinent colonized by England, Namibia colonized by Germany, Indonesia colonized by Holland, and the Philippines colonized by the United States.

The nineteenth century saw an increase in Protestant mission work, especially by the churches of the United States. During that time, Protestant theology and practice of mission were not much different than the Roman Catholic mission methods of previous centuries. Like the motives of their Roman Catholic counterparts, the motives of the Protestant missionaries were problematic. Often, the young men and women who went into the lands of the Native Americans, or to the Hawaiian Islands, or to other more distant parts of the world, came into the missionary vocation to demonstrate their spirit of patriotism. Those who responded to the "divine call" were often filled with a superiority complex and tended to perceive different ethnic, national, and cultural traditions as inferior or contrary to Christianity; they were to be subverted and destroyed. Many churches and missionaries identified their Christian mission with the "special destiny" of the United States. Such mission was often identified as the worldwide mission of "moral reform," which was dictated by American Protestant standards. As a result, American cultural expansion and commercial imperialism became closely identified with the mission movement of North American churches.

The first U.S. foreign missionary agency, organized in 1810, admonished its members with these words:

> How can we better testify our appreciation of her free institutions than by laboring to plant them in other lands? For where the gospel goes in its purity and power, there will follow in its train the blessings of civilization, liberty, and good government.[14]

Such identification of national interest and Christian mission produced strong paternalistic attitudes that were unsympathetic to the cultures and customs of the people to whom they were sent, and instead served as a justification for exploitation. The American missionaries maintained a strong American identity with extra-territorial rights. Just as Columbus and his men had arrogant attitudes toward the natives, the American missionaries even ignored the sovereignty of national governments. An instruction received by Dr. Peter Parker, a pioneering medical missionary in China, was a typical example:

> The Christian missionary is not, therefore, to expect, and he is not to seek, the sanctions of heathen governments to his efforts to extend the gospel, but he is to go, with its heavenly message, directly to the people, wherever he can find them; and he is to proclaim its

requirements and sanctions to them as individuals having souls for the salvation or loss of which they are themselves responsible.[15]

Just as the European Christians in the fifteenth and sixteenth centuries, the American missionaries in the nineteenth and twentieth centuries believed that their culture was superior to all other cultures. Becoming Christian thus often required converts to sever relationships with their native cultures. Thus, Jóse Míguel Bonino, Argentinian theologian, rightly pointed out:

> The missionary enterprise of the past 150 years is interwoven with the expansion of economic, political, and cultural influence of the Anglo-Saxon world, whether Catholic or Protestant. We from the Third World call this neo-colonialism or imperialism.[16]

II. Proposals for the Churches

Now in the quincentennial anniversary of Columbus, the real purpose of this paper is not only to criticize Columbus and the past mistakes of the churches but to recover the biblical meaning of Christian mission on the basis of Christian ecclesiology. The Christian church is meant to be an assembly of people, inclusive of different nationalities, languages, cultures, and classes. It is the church's purpose to exist in the world to welcome all kinds of people who "will come from east and west and sit at the table with Abraham, Isaac, and Jacob in the kingdom of heaven" (Matt. 8:11). The ministry of Jesus Christ and his apostles was to cross boundaries and to go out to meet people. In this encounter, all people were received with kindness and grace. Christians were to be gentle and peaceful people to witness to the oneness of creation!

The cruel treatment of other people due to ethnic, class, and cultural differences is a violation of the doctrine of the church and a sin against God. In the church we are all children of God and heirs with Christ (Romans 8). We are to live together, share community, and serve one another. We are not strangers and sojourners but fellow citizens with the saints and members of God's household. In the community of faith, there should be no division by nation, race, or creed, and certainly no violent treatment of other people because of cultural differences. When the first church was founded in Jerusalem on the day of Pentecost, the people came from "every nation under heaven" (Acts 2:5). To recover this true nature of the church's mission to the world in this year of the 500th anniversary of Columbus sailing to the "new world," I have three proposals.

First, let the churches and people confess the crimes and sins committed against our neighbors and environment. Let the people in the Christian community reflect not only upon American history—the genocide of Native Americans, the enslavement of Africans, the mistreatment of Asian railroad workers, and the discrimination against Chicanos—but also upon present violations against oppressed people and the destruction of the environment. Is there not room in the mainline Christian churches for real penitence and rebirth?

The second proposal is to let the United States honor its treaties with the Native Americans. It is scandalous that not a single treaty with the Native Americans has been kept or honored by the United States. However, there are still many important treaties to respect, involving fishing rights and territorial rights of Native Americans. By honoring existing treaties, the United States will do a tremendous service and make a contribution to saving Native Americans from poverty, depression, alcoholism, and environmental degradation. President George Bush said in his 1989 inaugural address: "Great nations like great men must keep their word. When America says something, America means it, whether a treaty or an agreement, or a vow made on marble steps." We have read his lips, now we demand that he keep his word.

The third and final proposal is that the churches in North America open themselves to their new neighbors from other countries and to ethnic groups within their own countries. Let them share their wealth and repay those neighbors who have been forced into hunger, homelessness, and drug addiction. Let the churches pay more attention to being "leaven" at home than to sending missionaries to other parts of the world. In this age of the global village, the world is not in need of a Columbus celebration, but rather a celebration of the true Christian values of peace, justice, and love.

Notes

1. J. B. Heffernan, "Columbus, Christopher," *New Catholic Encyclopedia,* vol. 3 (New York: McGraw Hill, 1967) 1037.

2. Christopher Columbus, *Journal of First Voyage to America with an Introduction by Van Wyck Brock.* (New York: Boni, 1924) 226.

3. Ibid., 27.

4. Ibid., 138.

5. Ibid., 152.

6. Howard Zinn, *A People's History of the United States* (New York: Harper Perennial, 1980) 3–6.

7. Ibid., 226.

8. Ibid., 225.

9. Tim Severin, "Retracing the First Crusade," *National Geographic* 176/3 (September, 1989) 361.

10. Benjamin Z. Kedar, *Crusade and Mission* (Princeton, N.J.: Princeton University, 1984) 97.

11. Bartolome de las Casas, *History of the Indies,* tr. and ed. by Andree Collard (New York: Harper Torchbooks, 1971) x.

12. Ibid., 34–35.

13. *Time* (November 18, 1991) 74.

14. Clifton J. Phillips, *Protestant America and the Pagan World* (Cambridge: Harvard, 1968) 243.

15. Ibid, 183.

16. *Time* (December 27, 1982).

Carl D. Evans

35 The Church's False Witness against Jews

Paul M. Van Buren's offering in The Christian Century's "How My Mind Has Changed" series (June 17–24, 1981) is eloquent testimony to a new awakening occurring in academic circles. Christian theologians, biblical scholars and church historians are becoming increasingly aware of the necessity to rethink what they do in light of Jewish theology, history and exegesis. Van Buren's admission that much of Christian theology has been "wrong about Israel, the people of God, and therefore . . . to that extent wrong about the God of Israel" echoes similar assessments by other scholars.

One obvious sign of this new consciousness is the development of courses in Jewish studies at theological schools around the country. At Harvard Divinity School, for example, the appointment of a Jewish Ph.D. to the faculty has added several important courses in Jewish studies to the standard Christian theological curriculum. Krister Stendahl, professor of divinity and former dean there, has stated the importance of such study in the context of Christian theological education:

> The Ninth Commandment actually says it all: Thou shalt not bear false witness against thy neighbor. For our culture in general and for the ministers, pastors and priests in particular, it is important that we do not picture "the other," the other person's faith, in a manner that they do not recognize as true. Yet much of religious thinking has been shaped by the thoughtless and even unintentional distortions *of* other persons' faith, thoughts, intentions and history. (*Harvard Divinity Bulletin*, November–December 1980)

In Stendahl's terms, the new awakening is the growing recognition that much of Christianity's witness, insofar as it says or implies something about Jews and Judaism, has been a violation of the ninth commandment. This false witness is not confined, of course, to theological systems and seminary curricula. After eight years of

Originally published in *Christian Century* (May 5, 1982), 530–533. Copyright 1982 Christian Century Foundation. Reprinted by permission from the May 5, 1982, issue of the *Christian Century*.

undergraduate teaching at the University of South Carolina, where students in my biblical courses are "products" of Christian churches, I am convinced that false witness against our Jewish neighbors is commonplace, even habitual, in the routine life of the church—in its study, worship and witness. If this were not so, students entering my classes would not hold so many erroneous ideas about Jews and their religion.

It is commonly believed that Judaism is a biblical religion, the religion of what Christians call the "Old Testament." Here one fundamental error already has been made, and a second is bound to follow. The first is the failure to recognize that post-biblical developments dramatically transformed the character of Jewish religion. There emerged, roughly contemporaneous with the rise of early Christianity, what is known as rabbinic Judaism. In many significant ways rabbinic Judaism goes beyond or modifies the religion of the Hebrew Scriptures. The Mishnah and the Talmud, not the Bible itself, embody the spirit and the character of rabbinic Judaism. It is from these rabbinic materials, about which most Christians know so little, that Judaism today draws its inspiration and instruction for faith and practice.

The second mistake that usually follows the first is that Christians tend to interpret the Old Testament religion from the perspective of the New Testament, which for the most part is presented as a fulfillment of the Old. The religion of the Old Testament, by implication, is inadequate, incomplete or unfulfilled. Consequently, not only do Christians consult the wrong sources for their understanding of Judaism, but to make matters worse, the sources used are put at a disadvantage by Christian principles of interpretation. Is it any wonder that Judaism is misrepresented by so much of what we say about it?

Given the common misunderstanding of the sources of Judaism, a number of other fallacies usually succeed it. It is believed by many that Judaism at the time of Jesus was stagnant, rigid and spiritually empty. To the extent that this view is represented in our preaching and our teaching, in our liturgy and our curriculum, we are bearing false witness. Any knowledgeable Jew (or non-Jew, for that matter) can readily identify the evidence of spiritual vitality in first-century Judaism. There were the sectarian groups, of which the Pharisees, Sadducees, Essenes and Zealots were the most prominent. There was temple Judaism and synagogue Judaism, worship by priestly sacrifice and worship by communal prayer. There was Jewish apocalypticism and Jewish gnosticism. There was Hellenistic Judaism and Palestinian Judaism. There were liberals, moderates and conservatives. By any standard, the Judaism of the first century was vibrant, exciting, diversified and spiritually alive. Had this not been the case, the Jewish sect later known as Christianity would not have emerged. Indeed, much of that which is cherished in Christianity today is a by-product of the rich spirituality that gave birth to rabbinic Judaism.

Let me be more specific. It is commonplace to hear Christian sermons that reprove the Pharisees for being self-righteous, sanctimonious, hypocritical and obnoxious. Nothing could be further from the truth, despite the attempts of several New Testament writers to portray them in this way. The Pharisees as a group were quite the opposite. In the words of the historian Ellis Rivkin, they held a firm and unwavering belief in an alluring Triad: (1) God the just and caring Father so loved each and every individual that (2) he revealed to Israel his twofold Law—Written and Oral—which, when *internalized* and faithfully obeyed, (3) promises to the Law-abiding individual eternal life for his soul and resurrection for his body. (*A Hidden Revolution* [Abingdon, 1978])

Within this twofold Law, especially the Oral Law, is an understanding of divine grace, mercy and compassion which rivals anything that can be found in Christianity. For the Pharisees, all of this had to be internalized so that it transformed the character of one's being. Just as for Jesus and Paul, the ultimate was within, not without.

Christian misrepresentation of the Pharisees is not surprising, given what the New Testament says about them. For example, Matthew 23 repeatedly excoriates them for hypocritical actions, and the parable of the Pharisee and the tax collector (Luke 18) portrays the Pharisee as conceited and self-righteous. Herein lies much of the problem. The Christian Scriptures—diligently read, believed and followed by the faithful—present a one-sided perspective on the rivalry that eventually drove a permanent wedge between Christianity and Judaism.

This rivalry, born of strong convictions on both sides, stirred deep emotions and prompted outbursts of careless rhetoric and unrestrained diatribes. The resulting distortions, as reflected in the New Testament, make us see the worst in Judaism rather than the best. The exaggeration in the portrayal of the Pharisees is especially pronounced because it was Pharisaic and rabbinic Judaism, the mainline Jewish religion after the destruction of the Temple in 70 A.D., that engaged early Christianity in the interreligious rivalry.

Further, it is often said that Judaism is a religion of law, whereas Christianity is a religion of grace. Again, to the extent that we propagate this view in our preaching and our teaching, we are guilty of bearing false witness. Rabbinic Judaism does not fit our legalistic stereotypes at all.

Consider, for example, this rabbinic exposition of the verse in the Torah which reads, "I will be gracious to whom I will be gracious" (Exod. 33:19):

In that hour God showed Moses all the treasuries of the rewards which are prepared for the righteous. Moses said, "For whom is *this* treasury?" And God said, "For him who fulfills the commandments." "And for whom is *that* treasury?" "For him who brings up orphans." And so God told him about each treasury. Finally, Moses spied a big treasury and said, "For whom is that?" And God said, "To him who has nothing I give this treasury," as it is said, "I will be gracious to whom I will be gracious and I will show mercy on whom I will show mercy." (*Exod. R.,* Ki Tassa, XLV 6)

Or consider this rabbinic version of the parable of the prodigal son:

A king had a son who had gone astray from his father a journey of a hundred days; his friends said to him, "Return to your father"; he said, "I cannot." Then his father sent to say, "Return as far as you can, and I will come to you the rest of the way." So God says, "Return to me, and I will return to you." (*Pes. R.* 184b–185a)

The rabbinic materials leave no doubt that grace is fundamentally important to Judaism. "To an earthly king, a man goes full, and returns empty; to God, he goes empty and returns full" (*Pes. R; 185a*). From the Gospels one gets the impression that Judaism has no heart, no compassion beyond a devotion to the Law. Meticulous observance of the Law, down to each jot and tittle, is more important to the Jew than relationships with human beings, so we are led to believe. Here is an example of what the rabbinic sources say on the subject:

> A heathen came to Shammai, and said to him, "Accept me as a proselyte on the condition that you teach me the whole Law while I stand on one foot." Then Shammai drove him away with the measuring rod he held in his hand. Then he went to Hillel, who received him as a proselyte and said to him, "What is hateful to you do not to your fellow: that is the whole Law; all the rest is its explanation; go and learn." (*Sab.* 31a)

This is the Golden Rule, at least in negative form—espoused by Hillel *before* the time of Jesus. The school of Hillel, the liberal wing of Pharisaism, was the dominant influence in rabbinic Judaism; therefore, the importance of relationships and deeds of lovingkindness is repeatedly emphasized in the rabbinic sources.

Thus we can see that the common Christian perception of Judaism is distorted as well as inaccurate. We have been guilty of bearing false witness against our Jewish neighbors. What is needed to correct our image is a massive effort to re-examine what we say about Jews and Judaism in sermons, lessons, liturgy and life. The ninth commandment offers a special challenge as we make this effort.

Anyone familiar with church history should feel the urgency of this challenge. From New Testament times to the present, it is difficult to find a single period when the church has not acted shamefully toward the Jews. I'm convinced that anti-Semitism has been such a powerful and persistent nemesis largely because of the church's false witness against the Jews.

The negative concept of Jews and Judaism begun in the New Testament, and developed further in the writings of the church fathers, created an entire *adversos Judaeos* tradition. The titles of the tracts by themselves often indicate the nature of the writings: *An Answer to the Jews* (Tertullian), *Expository Treatise Against the Jews* (Hippolytus), *Three Books of Testimonies Against the Jews* (Cyprian), *Eight Orations Against the Jews* (John Chrysostom), *Tract Against the Jews* (Augustine), and many more.

The sermons of the great orator John Chrysostom offer perhaps the most offensive examples of these patristic diatribes. A single passage from his preaching is all that is needed to make the point:

> I know that many people hold a high regard for the Jews and consider their way of life worthy of respect at the present time. This is why I am hurrying to pull up this fatal notion by the roots. . . . A place where a whore stands on display is a whorehouse. What is more, the synagogue is not only a whorehouse and a theater; it is also a den of thieves and a haunt of wild animals . . . not a cave of wild animal merely, but of an unclean wild animal. . . . The Jews have no conception of [spiritual] things at all, but living for the lower nature, all agog for the here and now, no better disposed than pigs or goats, they live by

the rule of debauchery and inordinate gluttony. Only one thing they understand: to gorge themselves and to get drunk. (*Eight Orations Against the Jews* 1, 3, 4)

The widespread polemics against the Jews in the theological foundations of early Christianity led to serious social consequences for the Jews during the Middle Ages. In an excellent study of the problem, Rosemary Radford Ruether argues that "the negative myth of the Jew, developed in the patristic *adversos Judaeos* tradition, was incorporated into the status of the Jew in Christendom" (*Faith and Fratricide* [Seabury, 1974]). This myth led to a loss of civil rights, to ghettoization, punishment by Inquisition and public executions, expulsion from countries like England, Spain and Portugal, brutal attacks by the Crusaders, pogroms and so on. The medieval treatment of the Jews, buttressed by continuing theological justification, is the legacy that we have inherited in the modern period.

Consider another description of the treatment of Jews and Judaism in the Middle Ages. Jewish author Samuel Sandmel writes:

> Judaism was normally described not as a religion but as either a superstition or a vomit. Jews were barred from the ordinary personal liberties. They were in due course forced to wear "the Jewish badge." They were alleged to use for the Passover Seder not wine but the blood of Christian children whom they kidnapped and killed for that purpose. They were alleged to sneak into churches and stab the holy wafer ("the host"), from which flowed the "real blood" of Jesus. In the Black Plague they were accused of poisoning the wells of the Christians. It was declared that they could be distinguished by their own "Jewish" smell. The Jews of the Rhineland were massacred in the First Crusade in 906, for the Crusaders saw no reason to wait until they reached the Holy Land to show their might to the infidels. The art and folk tales of the age before the invention of printing paved the way for later printed art and picture books showing villainous Jews doing dreadful things to Christians. The Jewish rabbinic writings were recurrently either censored or confiscated and burned. (*Anti-Semitism in the New Testament?* [Fortress, 1978])

To anyone who knows this tragic history, it comes as no great surprise that the Holocaust could and did take place in the heart of Christendom. The Nazis' "final solution" cannot be divorced from the attempts to get rid of the Jews throughout church history—first by forced conversion, then by expulsion, then by extermination.

If all of us knew this tragic history better, I'm convinced that we would feel the urgency to cease our false witness against Jews and Judaism.

How do we begin to correct the problem? For starters, we need to observe the ninth commandment. What we say about our neighbors, including their religion, should be that which they recognize as true. We should consult the sources from which they draw their own religious understanding, or, if this cannot be done, we need to read informed authorities on those sources.

But more than that is required. The dismantling of erroneous views and the construction of new ones take time and effort. Indeed, for many it is a never ending task. Let me suggest how this reconceptualization might take place.

Obviously, the pastor is the key person in any congregation. He or she has the opportunity to correct misconceptions or reinforce appropriate conceptions, whichever the case may be. Here are some things that can be done:

1. Scriptural texts read for public worship should be studied carefully with these questions in mind: How are Jews and Judaism portrayed in these texts? Is this portrayal accurate or is it a distortion? Where distortions are found, the sermon should include information to project a more accurate picture of matters. In lectionary readings for the Lenten season, for example, the responsibility for the crucifixion is often shifted from the Romans to the Jews. The pastor can readily explain the shift, and the resulting historical distortions, by making reference to the apologetic motives that prompted the New Testament writers to avoid statements that would have aroused Roman antagonism against the early Christians.

2. Prayers, litanies and other elements of worship should avoid the thoughtless rhetoric that can subconsciously prejudice people. An order of worship for Good Friday evening in my own United Methodist tradition, for example, includes a prayer of intercession which states:

> O merciful God, who has made all men, and hatest nothing that thou has made, and willest not the death of a sinner, but rather that he should be converted and live: Have mercy upon all who do not know thee, or who deny the faith of Christ crucified. Take thou from them all ignorance, hardness of heart, and contempt of thy Word; and so bring them home, blessed Lord, to thy fold, that we may be made one flock under one shepherd, Jesus Christ our Lord.

It seems to me that such a prayer, uttered by Christian worshipers on Good Friday evening, is bound to suggest that those "who deny the faith of Christ crucified" are none other than "the Jews." The language used to characterize those who "should be converted"—their "ignorance, hardness of heart, and contempt of thy Word"—echoes the negative descriptions of Jews in Scripture and the *adversos Judaeos* tradition. The prejudicial implications of such language can be avoided if the worshiper is led to claim the identity of the sinner.

3. Church school teachers should be sensitized to the problem through workshops and courses of study. We cannot assume that lay teachers will become aware of the anti-Judaism in the Christian tradition unless they are confronted with the wrongness of our stereotypes. A study course in Judaism, preferably taught by a rabbi, would be enormously valuable.

4. Literature and audiovisual aids used in the church school should be carefully selected. Occasionally, even in the literature of the mainline denominations, one will find culpable statements. Even so, use of approved denominational curriculum materials would substantially reduce the problem.

5. Most mainline denominations have adopted official statements with respect to anti-Semitism and other forms of prejudice. These should be presented to our congregants—preferably studied by them—at least once a year.

In essence, I am inviting pastors and congregations to join in the new awakening which is already occurring in many circles. Lest the obvious be overlooked, let me add that wherever possible Christian-Jewish dialogue groups, for both laity and clergy, should be established. We must cease our false witness for the sake of the church's integrity and in fairness to our Jewish neighbors.

Lee Ranck

36   Arena for Interaction

> *We must work to build a city where every child has a good education, where everybody*
> *has access to a job market which guarantees a realistic living income. There must be quality*
> *health care for all, with the cost borne by us all. There must be housing which provides a*
> *healthy living environment. There must also be a police system and a legal system which*
> *safeguards every Angelino equally.*
>
> —Pastor Alan Jones

The flames consuming blocks of South Central L.A. formed a frightening backdrop for the church tower looming in the foreground—of a photograph on the front page of Section T, *Los Angeles Times,* May 14, 1992. However, persons who know about the ministry of Wilshire United Methodist Church may have seen a symbolism in that picture unknown to the creative photographer.

The people of the congregation that worship in and work out of Wilshire Church reflect the multicultural, multiracial population of South Central L.A., Koreatown, Pico Union and the other areas caught up in the devastating late-April devastation stirred by the anger and frustration over the controversial Rodney King verdict. The church's letterhead indicates its unique four-language ministry.

Wilshire United Methodist Church, Iglesia Methodista Unida De Wilshire, Nagkaisang Iglesiya Methodista Sa Wilshire, and 윌서연합감리교회 English Ministry, Ministerio Hispano, Filipino Ministry, and 한 인 목 회. Pastors—Alan Jones, Chang Soon Lee, Janet Gaston-Petty, David Marcelo, Lydia S. Martinez, Seung Hong Cho, Thomas Lopez.

Actually, persons from 35 national backgrounds make up Wilshire's approximately 1,300 membership (though the official statistical report to the California-Pacific Annual Conference lists 1,082 members—Korean ministry, 342; Hispanic ministry, 103; Filipino ministry, 70; and English ministry, about 60 percent black, 567).

Originally published in *Christian Social Action* (December 1992), 5:12–16, 25. Reprinted with permission from *Christian Social Action* magazine, December 1992; copyright 1992 by the General Board of Church and Society of the United Methodist Church.

"The actual committed 'membership' for the Filipino ministry is probably around 180," Pastor Alan Jones explains, "and the Korean ministry should also be higher." Wilshire Church, Jones points out, has received the conference Church Growth Award four times—in 1984, 1985, 1987 and 1991—since the award's creation in 1984.

A Pentecost Sunday visit shows a bustling, youthful vitality in this four-language congregation. Should any person with multi-lingual talents speak Korean, Spanish, Tagalog, and English, he or she could attend the 8:00 A.M. Korean worship in Wilshire's Ritter Chapel, move to the sanctuary for the Filipino worship at 8:30, skip between the English and Hispanic worship services at 10:00 and close the full morning with another Korean worship at noon. In addition, Sunday School classes, prayer groups, choirs and other groups meet during the morning. Frequently one of the ministries closes out the Sunday morning with a meal, and receptions follow the various services.

One Congregation: Four Language Ministries

Obviously the complexities of four language ministries living and worshipping together in one church building (shared ministries instead of shared facilities), as one operation with a mutual operating budget, call for careful work and skilled leadership. The pastors stress that Wilshire is one congregation with four language ministries, not four separate congregations meeting in the same building, or a majority-white congregation providing facilities for the non-English-speaking groups. It is, in essence, an arena for interaction.

Noting the tensions that cultural differences can and do produce and the fact that Koreans "tend to keep to themselves," associate pastor Chang Soon Lee quietly suggests that "the gospel can overcome cultural differences."

In the past Wilshire United Methodist Church did serve a predominantly white congregation whose members came from the surrounding well-to-do neighborhoods. (A walk through the residential area across much-noted Wilshire Boulevard quickly reveals the Los Angeles/Hollywood affluence only a short distance from the starkness of the ghetto that has become a U.S. landmark of festering inner city frustration and potential violence.) The roots of the present congregation sink back to 1887 with the founding of the Simpson Methodist Episcopal Church, which 11 years later became Westlake Methodist Episcopal, which merged in 1927 with Wilshire Methodist Episcopal. That church in 1931 bought and moved into the present facility at the corner of Wilshire and Plymouth.

The Wilshire congregation added the children's educational annex in 1951, which includes church offices and Ritter Chapel. In 1973 the church again merged, this time with Trinity United Methodist Church. Also in that year, it was named a "city monument" by the Cultural Heritage Board of Los Angeles.

From All-White to Racially-Mixed

In the mid-70s the congregation began to become racially mixed, and in 1978 the Rev. Romeo del Rosario became the first racial/ethnic pastor. A year later the Rev. Chang Soon Lee came to Wilshire to begin a Korean ministry. During this period, the senior pastor, the Rev. Irwin Trotter, emphasized the importance of building Korean ministry in partnership with the existing English language congregation.

Then the Hispanic ministry began as a Sunday morning Bible study group in 1985 and evolved into a worship service. Finally, in 1990 the Filipino ministry also began as a Bible study group that grew into a worship service.

Of course, strong leaders have guided the evolution of the four-language congregation. Today each of the seven members of the pastoral staff brings a unique background and varied experiences to his or her responsibilities.

Alan H. Jones, pastor, with a Doctor of Ministry degree from the School of Theology at Claremont, was a member of the British Methodist Church before coming to the United Methodist Church in California. Prior to coming to Wilshire in 1989, he served inner-city pastorates in Britain; as a missionary, with the General Board of Global Ministries, in Sierra Leone; as associate minister of Holman United Methodist Church, well-known black Los Angeles congregation; and as pastor of West Los Angeles United Methodist Church, neighborhood Japanese-American congregation with both Japanese and English language sections.

Chang Soon Lee, associate pastor for Korean ministry, with a Doctor of Ministry degree from the School of Theology at Claremont, was born in North Korea and completed his high school education in South Korea. A graduate of Methodist Theological Seminary in Seoul, Korea, he was ordained in the Korean Methodist Church in 1966 and transferred into The United Methodist Church in 1980.

Janet Gaston-Petty, associate pastor, graduate of Gammon Theological Seminary, has served a congregation in Westland, Michigan, and another in the heart of Detroit, where she was born. In the latter church she had to overcome resistance to having a woman pastor, but after two years received a plaque for her outstanding service to the congregation. "It's important," she has noted, "that the congregation sees me as a whole being, not just as a black or as a woman. As a minister my job is to help people move from where they are to where they need to be."

David Marcelo, associate pastor for Filipino ministry, born and raised in Manila, the Philippines, has served in various ministerial capacities such as youth minister, associate minister and senior minister both in the Philippines and in the United States. The host of a Tagalog radio program on the air each Saturday and Sunday, he is presently studying at the School of Theology at Claremont to fulfill ordination requirements of The United Methodist Church.

Lydia Salazar Martinez, associate pastor for Hispanic ministry, served congregations in the Rio Grande Conference and as the vice president of the General Board of

Church and Society. Throughout her ministry, she has worked actively on Hispanic issues, women's concerns, and other justice issues.

Seung Hong Cho, associate pastor for Korean ministry, with degrees from the Methodist Theological Seminary in Seoul, Korea and the Graduate School of Korea University there, was ordained in the Korean Methodist Church in 1987 and transferred into The United Methodist Church in 1992. He has served as education director and pastor in several Korean Methodist churches.

Tomas Lopez, pastor, Pico-Union Hispanic Ministry and Wilshire youth ministry director, a native of El Salvador, came to Los Angeles in May 1981, where he worked with different youth/young adult groups. In 1988 he began work as a local pastor in the Pico-Union area of Los Angeles; in 1990 he was appointed pastor of the Pico-Union Hispanic ministry, associated with Wilshire Church.

Another unofficial member of the Wilshire pastoral team, one of those "full-time volunteers" providing the creativity and energy for many United Methodist programs, is Linda Pickens-Jones, also a United Methodist minister. A program associate in the Urban Ministries unit of the School of Theology at Claremont, she is well-known as an activist and speaker on women's issues and other justice concerns.

A Focus on the Devastated City

Since the Spring flames erupted in the community served by Wilshire church, that congregation's justice concerns have focused on its city, its community, and its own members, a number of whom were severely affected by the violence. Fourteen members of the Wilshire Korean ministry, for instance, lost their businesses in the conflagration.

"We know that some Korean store owners did not show kindness to the customers," Associate Pastor Chang Soon Lee wrote in a May 29 special supplement to the California-Pacific Conference edition of the *United Methodist Reporter.* "We admit that we did not learn the cultural differences and failed to let them know that we are good people. . . . We do not deny that we need to learn how to live with other racial peoples in this country. But [were our actions] so bad that they set the fires and destroyed over 2,000 businesses, markets, stores and buildings?

"The whole Korean-American community cried," he continued. "[Then] we stopped crying and blaming. We are encouraging one another to start rebuilding."

Wilshire Associate Pastor Lydia Martinez, in the same publication, noted that the Pico Union area, which was on of the hardest hit, and Koreatown "is mostly Latino— yes, most of the residents in Koreatown are Latino, ABC News reported that 40 percent of the businesses lost were Latino-owned. This complicates the issues of poverty, joblessness and so forth. [They are] not only Latino, but mostly from Central America, and are an easy target for victimization by their already marginalized economic status."

"We are reaping what we sowed in the 1980s" Martinez wrote. "We are also reaping what the church hasn't done. Hispanic ministry has not been given the money to reach out to the Hispanic community." However, she also noted in a brief interview, "God's giving us another chance, so we need to be like the leaven, the yeast that makes the bread rise."

On Pentecost Sunday Pastor Jones spoke to the English ministry congregation about the power of the Pentecost spirit and the potential power in their multicultural, multiracial church community. He urged that they be part of an effort to find a way to bring healing to the city.

To Bring Healing to the City

"The Pentecostal fires that burned in our streets a few weeks ago," he said, "remind us that we can transform ourselves into a cadre of committed people who can bring about necessary change. Our church has to be an engaging community, an active participant in building bridges of relationships to each other."

After the days of violent destruction, the members of the Wilshire congregation did come to their church to share experiences, gain support, worship and pray together, and initiate efforts, like other churches and community groups, to provide urgently needed relief. At its Pico-Union Center, Wilshire Church fed some 90 families each day; it gathered and distributed other necessities for survival and daily living; it provided housing for some of the families that had no shelter.

Later, when an ecumenical delegation came to town and held a "listening post" in Wilshire Church, congregation representatives highlighted their concern that plans for renewal of the devastated areas are not based on the expressed needs of the people in the community.

"The response of the church must be to listen and respond to the lessons of the uprising," Pastor Jones noted in a brief piece he wrote for the *Reporter* supplement. "It is not enough to 'sit in judgment.' Yes, we must help with 'disaster relief' for those who have lost much, and those who have lost their livelihoods. But we must do more.

"We must work to build a city where every child has a good education, where everybody has access to a job market which guarantees a realistic living income. There must be quality health care for all, with the cost borne by us all. There must be housing which provides a healthy living environment. There must also be a police system and a legal system which safeguards every Angelino equally."

He concluded: "The community of faith must be activist in this situation. Our 'window of opportunity' has arrived, and we must pass through it, to build that 'beloved community' which is our gospel mandate."

Wilshire Church, perhaps itself a kernel of that "beloved community," with its people of many cultures and many races, seems like the ideal setting for that kind of building to begin.

About the Contributors

MUMIA ABU-JAMAL is an activist and journalist who is on death row in Pennsylvania.

LAILA AL-MARAYATI is president of the Muslim Women's League.

REBECCA T. ALPERT is assistant professor of Religion and Women's Studies at Temple University.

DANIEL BERRIGAN is a Jesuit priest, poet, author, and activist.

RITA NAKASHIMA BROCK is the director of the Mary Ingraham Bunting Institute of Radcliffe College.

LAWRENCE BUSH is editor of *Reconstructionism Today* and the Shefa Fund's *Wealth and Covenant.*

JEFFREY DEKRO is the director of the Shefa Fund.

DIANA ECK is professor of comparative religion and Indian studies at Harvard University.

CARL D. EVANS is associate professor of religious studies at the University of South Carolina in Columbia.

JAMES H. EVANS is president of Colgate Rochester Divinity School.

DAVID FREDRICKSON teaches at Luther Northwestern Theological Seminary.

GUSTAVO GUTIERREZ is chair of theology at the Pontifical Catholic University of Peru and chaplain of the National Catholic Student Union of Peru.

VINCENT HARDING is professor of religion and social transformation at Iliff School of Theology.

BARBARA HOLMES is an attorney, an evangelist in the Apostolic Holiness Church, and a doctoral candidate in ethics, religion, and society at Vanderbilt University.

MARY E. HUNT is codirector of the Women's Alliance for Theology, Ethics and Ritual.

WI JO KANG teaches at the Wartburg Theological Seminary.

FRANCES KISSLING is president of Catholics for a Free Choice.

KENNETH KRAFT is chair of the Department of Religion Studies, Lehigh University.

ANDREW LINZEY holds the world's first post in theology and animal welfare, the IFAW Senior Research Fellowship, Mansfield College.

RICHARD P. MCBRIEN is the Crowley O'Brien-Walter Professor of Theology at the University of Notre Dame.

RICHARD A. MCCORMICK, S.J., is the John A. O'Brien Professor Emeritus of Christian Ethics at the University of Notre Dame.

JOHN J. MCNEILL is a former Jesuit priest who currently practices psychotherapy.

THOMAS J. PAPROCKI is chancellor of the Archives and Records Center, Archdiocese of Chicago.

RON D. PASQUARIELLO writes for the *Christian Century.*

MARY PELLAUER is an independent scholar.

HELEN PREJEAN is a Sister of St. Joseph and director of Pilgrimage for Life, Louisiana Citizens for Abolition of the Death Penalty.

LEE RANCK is past editor of *Christian Social Action.*

ROSEMARY RADFORD RUETHER is Georgia Harkness Professor of Applied Theology at Garrett-Evangelical Theological Seminary.

TODD SALZMAN is assistant professor of Christian ethics at Creighton University.

GEORGE TINKER is professor of cross-cultural ministries at Iliff School of Theology.

HELEN TWORKOV is the editor-in-chief of *Tricycle: The Buddhist Review.*

ELIEZER VALENTÍN-CASTAÑÓN is a program director in the Ministry of God's Human Community, General Board of Church and Society.

JIM WALLIS is editor of *Sojourners.*

ROBERT ALLAN WARRIOR teaches American Indian literature at the English department of Stanford University.

ARTHUR WASKOW is director of the Shalom Center.

DELORES S. WILLIAMS is Paul Tillich Professor of Theology and Culture, Union Theological Seminary.

RONALD T. YOUNG is founder and director of the U.S. Interreligious Committee for Peace in the Middle East.